REPORT

OF THE

Minister of Public Works

FOR THE

PROVINCE OF ONTARIO

FOR THE

TWELVE MONTHS ENDING 31st OCTOBER

1913

PRINTED BY ORDER OF

THE LEGISLATIVE ASSEMBLY OF ONTARIO

TORONTO:

Printed and Published by L. K. CAMERON, Printer to the King's Most Excellent Majesty

1914

Printed By
WILLIAM BRIGGS
29-37 Richmond St. W
TORONTO

CONTENTS.

[3]

To His Honour, SIR JOHN MORISON GIBSON, K.C.M.G., a Colonel in the Militia of Canada, etc., etc., etc., Lieutenant-Governor of the Province of Ontario.

SIR,—I have the honour to submit to you, as required by Statute, the Annual Report on the works under the control of the Public Works Department, comprising the Reports of the Deputy Minister, the Architect, the Engineer, the Superintendent and the Accountant of the Colonization Roads Branch, the Chief Inspector of Boilers, and the Accountant and Law Clerk, for the twelve months ending the 31st of October, 1913.

I have the honour to be, Sir,

` Your obedient servant,

J. O. REAUME,

Minister of Public Works.

Department of Public Works, Ontario.
March 11, 1914.

REPORT

OF THE

Deputy Minister of Public Works

Toronto, March 6th, 1914.

HONOURABLE J. O. REAUME, *Minister of Public Works, Ontario.*

SIR,—I have the honour to transmit the reports of the Provincial Architect, Provincial Engineer, Chief Inspector of the Steam Boiler Branch, Superintendent and Accountant of the Colonization Roads Branch and the Accountant and Law Clerk of the Department of Public Works for the fiscal year ending October 31st, 1913.

The principal building under construction during the year was the residence for the Lieutenant-Governor, in Chorley Park, Rosedale. Good progress has been made with the work, the exterior of the residence is completed, the design and execution reflecting credit upon the Architect and proving his ability to design with the skill of an artist and to direct the building operations to obtain first class workmanship and the best possible results for the money expended. The interior work is proceeding satisfactorily; heating and ventilating, the electric wiring, fireproof floors and partitions are completed ready to proceed with the other trades.

The following important buildings have also been under construction during the year:—The Veterinary College at the corner of University Avenue and Anderson Street, Toronto, is five stories in height, has an area of 10,000 sq. ft., and is of fireproof construction throughout. There was expended to the close of the fiscal year about $121,000.00. It is expected the building will be ready for opening in September next. The total estimated cost including equipment is $300,000. The new buildings at the Ontario Agricultural College, Guelph, include a dining hall to accommodate five hundred students, new Dairy Stables, a Field Husbandry Building and a new poultry Building. Towards the expenditure on the last two buildings there has been allotted from the Federal grant for Agriculture the sum of $80,000, which materially aided in making the equipment of the College more adequate for the important work being done by these Departments. At the Schools for the Education of the Deaf and Dumb, Belleville, and the Blind at Brantford, new dormitory buildings have been under construction. The dormitories for girl pupils commenced during the previous year are nearing completion; the dormitories for boy pupils have made satisfactory progress at both schools. In the new Judicial District of Temiskaming, convenient temporary offices were secured in a business block in Haileybury from Mr. M. P. Wright at a rental of $2,500 per annum, until the new Government Buildings are ready for occupation. Contracts were let early in the year for a new Court House and Registry Office at Haileybury, and satisfactory progress has been made with the work. A new Court House is under construction at Fort Frances for Rainy River District, similar to that at Haileybury.

[7]

As in the previous year the expenditures for the construction, repairs and upkeep of the hospitals for insane were largely attended to by the Inspectors of the Provincial Secretary's Department, the plans and professional advice being supplied by the Architects and Engineers of this Department.

The Steam Boiler Inspection Branch was established during the year to administer the new Steam Boiler Act, which came into force on the 1st of July, 1913. Mr. D. M. Medcalf, who for eight years had been Inspector of Steam Boilers and Machinery for the Ontario Government, was appointed Chief Inspector. He has been most faithful and untiring in his efforts to make the work of the Branch successful. His report shows that during four months that the Act has been in operation 148 designs of steam boilers and 382 designs of boiler accessories have been approved and registered and that the construction of new boilers has been carefully inspected through the whole process; that boilers entering the Province and boilers sold or exchanged in the Province as far as they could be ascertained, were carefully inspected by a small staff of well qualified inspectors. It was expected that the enacting of the Steam Boiler Act and passing of regulations by Ontario in conformity with the regulations of the Western Provinces, would enable the manufacturers of Ontario to have the inspection of the Ontario Branch accepted by the Western Provinces, thus allowing a higher working pressure on their boilers. The Western Provinces have not yet accepted the Ontario inspection, but it is hoped that a conference of representatives from every Province in Canada will shortly be arranged and that uniform regulations will be adopted and the inspection of any Province be accepted by all the others.

The Public Works constructed during the year under the Provincial Engineer comprised eighteen permanent steel bridges, varying in cost from $1,000 to $19,-000; the largest structure being over the Sturgeon River at Sturgeon Falls. Of the others, eight were in New Ontario and ten in Older Ontario. Ten reinforced concerete structures were built, seven in New Ontario and three in Old Ontario, and twenty-one timber bridges, fourteen in New Ontario and seven in Old Ontario. A large combination dam and bridge was built at the outlet of Muskoka Lake. It is a permanent structure composed of masonry piers and steel superstructure. The construction of this dam has given an increased discharging capacity from Muskoka Lake, lessening danger of damage through spring freshets. Pickerel River in Parry Sound and Gananoque River in Leeds County were improved for navigation purposes. The navigation of the Muskoka Lakes, the Magnetawan River and the Huntsville chain of lakes was also improved. Drainage schemes were carried out in Rainy River, Algoma, Nipissing, Manitoulin, Sturgeon Falls, Sudbury and Temiskaming Districts in New Ontario and in Parry Sound, Simcoe County and North Ontario County in Older Ontario. Ten municipal drainage schemes in Older Ontario carried out under the provisions of the Municipal Drainage Act were inspected by the engineers of the Department, and upon their reports payments of grants made to the several municipalities initiating the drainage schemes. In addition to the above about $30,000 was expended in the repair and maintenance of locks, dams and bridges throughout the portion of the Province without County organization and in dredging and removing of obstructions from the lakes and rivers mentioned above.

The season was a most favourable one for the building of roads, the weather being fine throughout the summer months and continuing fine until late in the fall. The report of the Colonization Roads Branch shows by a tabulated statement which gives full details of the work done on each road, that twenty-three miles of the Sudbury-Sault Ste. Marie trunk road were built or improved at a cost of $29,184.16, this, however, does not represent the total expenditure on this trunk road as some expenditure was made on the section west of Blind River by the Northern Development Branch of the Lands, Forests and Mines Department. Ten other trunk roads aggregating 57.43 miles were repaired or constructed at a cost of $35,161.61. Six hundred and fifty-eight roads aggregating 844.07 miles were repaired or constructed at a cost of $242,042.25, the whole cost being paid by the Province. One hundred and one Municipalities constructed 49.67 miles of new roads and improved 692.69 miles of old roads at a cost of $144,868.32 of which the Province paid to the Municipalities under the provisions of the Colonization Roads Act $71,030.51. The total length of roads built and improved during the fiscal year 1912-13 under the Colonization Roads Branch was 1,666.95 miles at a cost of $451,259.34 of which the Province paid $377,411.53. The Province also paid $28,929.99 to the Municipalities for work done in the previous year making the total expenditure by the Province during the fiscal year 1912-13 the sum of $406,341.52 as shown in the statement of the Accountant of the Colonization Roads Branch.

The statements of the Accountant and Law Clerk gives the capital expenditure on Public Buildings, Public Works, Roads, Aid to Railways, etc., and of contracts entered into in connection therewith, during the twelve months ending the 31st of October, 1913, also valuable classified statements of expenditure from the 1st of July, 1867.

I have the honour to be,

Sir,

Your obedient servant,

R. P. FAIRBAIRN,

Deputy Minister of Public Works.

REPORT OF ARCHITECT.

HON. J. O. REAUME, *Minister of Public Works, Ontario.*

SIR,—I have the honour to submit my report of the work done during the past year by the Architect's Branch of the Department of Public Works.

GOVERNMENT HOUSE.

The work in connection with the residence and grounds of the new Government House has been continued throughout the year. The building has been roofed in and all exterior work is about completed. The heating and ventilation apparatus is far enough advanced to permit of heat being put on and when required temporary heating will be supplied to permit of the other trades being carried on during the winter months. Most of the conduit for electric wiring for power and light has been laid. As soon as this is done the concrete fill will be laid over the floors.

Good progress has been made with the work on the grounds; the whole of the levelling and grading with the exception of the north end of the property is about completed. This work will be continued throughout the season ·as the weather permits.

Some slight repairs have been made to the temporary Gubernatorial Residence on St. George and College Street, and the grounds to same have been kept in good order by the Government gardener and staff.

PARLIAMENT BUILDINGS.

All of the work in connection with the reconstruction of the west wing and the library addition to the north side of the building were completed early in the year. Furnishings and fittings to the numerous offices throughout the buildings have been supplied when found to be necessary. A number of the offices have been painted and the buildings kept in good repair generally, including the usual amount of repairs to the slating and copper work on roofs to the older portion of the buildings.

The installation of the electric apparatus by Kilmer, Pullen and Burnham was completed and the change from the City of Toronto Electric Company's service to the Hydro-Electric service was made early in the year.

In December last a proposal was received for the H. W. Johns-Manville Co. to correct the acoustics of the Legislative Chamber by covering the whole of the ceiling and a portion of the walls with heavy felt. Acting under· your instructions your Architect inspected several buildings in the City of New York the auditoriums of which had been corrected by this Company and satisfied himself that this system could be successfully applied to the Legislative Chamber. On his recommendation a contract was awarded to them for the work, this necessitated the redecorating of the Chamber. The contract included this work and was awarded on the condition that the whole should be entirely completed within six weeks from the date of the award. I am pleased to report the work was completed on time and that the recommendation of your Architect has been fully justified, inasmuch that the acoustics of the room are now as near perfection as can be possible. The decorative work was carried out by the Thornton Smith Co., of Toronto, the colour scheme being executed in an artistic manner.

The grounds surrounding the buildings have received the usual good attention of the head gardener and staff. Concrete walks have been laid from the east entrance to the intersections of the roadways to the north-east. A concrete walk has been laid from this to the main entrance of the library addition being continued westerly to the walk on the west side of the west wing. The work was done under contract by the Queen City Concrete Company. A gravel road has also been laid to the main entrance of the library wing, and the road to the north of this building put in good order. The work was done by the City Roads Department—the Government to pay a proportion of the cost of same.

PROVINCIAL BOARD OF HEALTH AND DEPARTMENT OF MINES' LABORATORIES.

No. 5 Queen's Park. Some slight repairs have been made to the building, and proper attention paid to the equipment including the heating, lighting and plumbing. The grounds have been kept in good order.

OSGOODE HALL.

Repairs were made to the older portions of the building as were required from time to time. The corridors of the north wing completed last year were painted. Repairs were made to the caretaker's cottage and a new hot air furnace installed. Renewals of furniture have been made when necessary.

HOSPITALS FOR THE INSANE.

Tenders were called for in the public press for the superstructure of the Reception Hospital and Nurses' Home in connection with the Hospital for Insane, Brockville, the foundation of which was built last year. The contract for general trades was awarded to Mr. W. P. Driscoll, contractor, of Brockville, his being the lowest offer. Good progress has been made with the building, the brick work being nearly completed and ready to receive the roof. The work is being carried on under the supervision of your Department with Mr. T. G. Rieves as Clerk of Works.

Plans and specifications were prepared early in the year for a cottage to accommodate 150 patients to be erected on the grounds of the Hospital for Feeble-Minded at Orillia. The work is being done under the supervision of the Superintendent of the Institution and the officials of this Department. Excavations were made and the concrete foundation walls built to the ground level. This work has been done by the patients under the direction of the mason of the Institution. The barn destroyed by fire last April has been rebuilt. Plans and specifications were made for an Amusement Hall to be built on the grounds of the Hospital for Insane in London, to take the place of the Amusement Hall destroyed by fire last January.

The residence for the Medical Superintendent at the Hospital for Epileptics in Woodstock is about completed.

Work on the Sewage Plant in connection with the Hospital for Insane, Kingston, which had been delayed on account of a change in the system made by the Provincial Board of Health necessitating new plans and specifications, is now proceeding satisfactorily, patients' labour being utilized as far as possible under the supervision of the mason of the Institution and Mr. E. M. Allen of this Department.

SCHOOL FOR THE DEAF, BELLEVILLE.

The work in connection with the Girls' Dormitory, the contract for which was awarded last year is sufficiently advanced to indicate that it will be completed early in the coming year. Considerable delay has occurred in connection with the erection of this building chiefly owing to the contractor being unable to procure materials in sufficient quantities to carry on the work satisfactorily, and to his inability to procure a sufficient number of men.

Plans and specifications were prepared for alterations to the boiler house and enlargement of laundry and reconstruction of, and addition to the boiler plant in connection with the heating apparatus. Tenders were advertised for, the contract for the former being awarded to S. F. Whitham, and the latter to Purdy Mansell Ltd. Good progress has been made with the building, which is about completed. The two new boilers have been installed and the steam connections made with the main building and girls' dormitory. The boiler house has been entirely re-arranged and enlarged, an addition having been built to the north side to give space for two additional 100 horse-power boilers. A circular chimney 100 feet in height has been erected of concrete reinforced with metal. The work was done under contract by the Weber Chimney Co., theirs being the lowest price for the chimney. The two old boilers which were found to be in good condition were placed alongside of the new boilers. Murphy Automatic Stokers have been installed in connection with these boilers and are giving good satisfaction. A tubular ash conveyor is being constructed by The Walker Co., of Belleville, under the front of the boilers, and will be operated by the electric motor operating the stokers. An overhead coal conveyor is also being constructed by this Company to convey the coal from the coal vaults to the stokers. This equipment when finished will be one of the most complete and up-to-date plants in the Province.

Plans and specifications were made and tenders advertised for a dormitory for boys of the same size and similar to the cottage for girls which is fully described in my report for last year. The contract for general trades was awarded to Mr. Thomas Manly, contractor of Belleville, the heating and plumbing to Purdy Mansell Co., and electric wiring to Greenleaf and Sons, Belleville. Good progress has been made with the work.

New supply mains for electric lighting to the main building and cottages have been laid, the work being done by men employed by this Department under our electrician, Mr. F. Stroud.

A large amount of grading has been done round the girls' dormitory and a skating rink formed in the grounds to the south of same. Concrete walks have been laid to the front and sides of the building. The walks to the rear portion will be completed next year.

Preliminary sketches are being prepared for alterations to the main building converting the space occupied by present dormitories into class rooms and remodelling the interior of the building. Repairs to building generally have been properly attended to.

SCHOOL FOR THE BLIND, BRANTFORD.

The dormitory building for girls is nearing completion, and will be ready for occupancy by the first of the year. Furniture has been purchased for same and old furniture used as found to be suitable. The following contracts were awarded in addition to the contract for general trades. For heating, ventilating and plumbing, The Drake Avery Co., of Hamilton, and for electric wiring and fixtures, The Lyons Electric Co., Guelph.

Plans and specifications were made for a dormitory for boys on the same general plan and dimensions as the dormitory for girls. Tenders were called for and the contract for general trades awarded to J. Bartle, of Brantford, heating and ventilation, The Drake Avery Co., of Hamilton, electric wiring and fixtures, The Lyons Electric Co., of Brantford. The work is progressing satisfactorily.

Plans and specifications were made for alterations to boiler plant and boiler house, to give accommodation for additional boilers and apparatus required for heating the two new cottages. Tenders were called for and the contract for general trades awarded to Messrs. Secord and Sons, of Brantford; for alterations and additions to boiler plant to the Drake Avery Co., of Hamilton; and for concrete chimney 100 feet in height to the Weber Chimney Co. These works are about completed. Plans for remodelling the boiler plant were prepared by the Canadian Domestic Engineering Co., who also supervised the work. All of the buildings in connection with the Institution, with the exception of the Superintendent's and Bursar's residence, will be heated from this plant. Repairs to buildings generally have been attended to.

New Veterinary College.

Most of the structural work in connection with this building has been completed. The roof is now being put on. Delays have occurred from time to time in consequence of the scarcity of materials. Work will be continued throughout the coming winter and the building will be completed and equipped in time for the fall session of the College.

Plans and specifications were prepared by Messrs. Griggs & Holbrook for a complete steam heating, and ventilating system. Tenders were called for and the contract awarded to Purdy Mansell, Limited, of Toronto. Tenders were also called for plumbing and electric wiring and the contract for the former awarded to Purdy Mansell, and for the latter to The Bennett & Wright Co., of Toronto. Good progress has been made with these trades.

Ontario Agricultural College.

The new dairy barn, the contract for which was awarded last year, was completed and a portion of the old dairy barn moved to and added on to same. The mason work was done under contract by Contractor R. Rogers, of Guelph, the carpentering and other work by men employed by the Department under the supervision of the chief carpenter of the College.

Satisfactory progress has been made with the erection of the Field Husbandry Building the cost of which is being paid out of the Federal grant. The building will be completed, equipped and ready to be occupied by the end of the year. Other contracts in addition to the contract for the general trades awarded last year include steam heating and plumbing which was awarded to Stevenson & Malcolm, Limited, of Guelph—the electric fixtures being purchased by this Department.

Plans and specifications were made for a new dining hall, including kitchen, serving pantries, scullery and stores, etc., etc. Tenders were called for and the contract awarded for general trades to Messrs. Secord & Sons, of Brantford, for heating and plumbing to Messrs. Stevenson & Malcolm, and for electric wiring to The G. E. B. Grinyer Co., both of Guelph. The structural work on this building is being carried on in an expeditious manner, reflecting credit on the general contractors, and will be continued throughout the winter, provision being made for temporary heat. The building will be completed by the latter part of next summer.

The outside walls of the building are being built entirely of Credit Valley Stone, and when completed will be a good example of this class of work. The interior of walls are being built of brick and terra cotta. The trusses of roof of the front or main portion of building are of steel, the roof covered with slate, the rear portion being covered with felt and gravel.

The building has a frontage of 104 feet exclusive of the large projecting bays at each end, and a depth of 125 feet exclusive of a 21 foot extension of the centre front at entrances, is two storeys in height including the basement. It has been most suitably located to the west of and in line with the main building of the College, a distance of 250 feet from same and about 75 feet from the main roadway to the west.

The main or students' entrance is from the front entering into a spacious vestibule with a staircase leading down to the toilets in the basement and up to the tea room over the vestibule. The front portion is entirely occupied by the dining room which is 59 feet in width, 100 feet in length exclusive of large circular bays at each end, and 27 feet in height and will give accommodation for five hundred students.

The rear or wing building is divided on the first floor into kitchen 35 ft. by 41 ft. with service room, maids' dining room, service pantry, dish washing and machine room adjoining. The first floor of the wing building is on a level with the dining hall, advantage having been taken of the slope of the ground to make a basement under this part of the building a full storey in height, the entrance in the rear being on the ground level. It is divided into receiving room, office, butcher shop, bakery, cold storage rooms, cleaning rooms, and lavatories for employees. The basement under the dining hall is divided into rooms for refrigerating machinery, cold storage, large general store and lavatories for students. The heating will be by steam from the main central heating plant, the ventilation by electrically controlled fans. Up to date sanitary appliances will be installed throughout.

Plans and specifications were made and tenders called for a poultry building, and the contracts awarded to W. J. Taylor for general trades, Messrs. Stevenson & Malcolm for heating and plumbing, and The G. E. B. Grinyer Co., for electric wiring, all of Guelph.

This building is three storeys in height, the foundations being built of concrete and the walls of the superstructure of brick. The basement contains office, students' laboratory, killing room, store rooms, and boiler room. The first floor with two entrances from the front to corridors with two staircases leading to the upper floor contains a class room, offices, egg room, shipping room and museum. The second floor contains a large class room, judging room, reading room and short term class rooms and laboratory. The heating will be done by steam, the steam heating plant being located in the basement. A mechanical system of ventilation is being installed and ample provision is made for lavatories and sanitary appliances.

The progress of the work in connection with this building has been most satisfactory. The roof is on and temporary heat is being provided. Plastering has been commenced and the building will be completed in time for the opening in January next.

JORDAN HARBOUR FRUIT STATION.

The fruit packing house has been completed. Repairs to the buildings have been attended to by the Director of the Station.

EXPERIMENTAL FRUIT FARM, MONTEITH.

Tenders were called for the Farm Director's residence, the plans of which were prepared last year, and the contract awarded to Mr. W. H. Turney, of Haileybury. The work is finished and the building ready to be occupied.

DISTRICTS.

The Registry Office at Kenora was completed early in the season and has been occupied for some months—all of the work was done by day labour, with the exception of the heating and plumbing and electric wiring, which was done under contract by Messrs. Fraser & Magell. Fittings from vault and furniture from the Old Registry Office adjoining the Gaol, which has been disposed of to the Town in exchange for land near the Court House, were moved to the new building and new fittings and furniture supplied as found to be necessary. The ground surrounding the building has been properly graded and sodded and concrete walks laid.

The addition to Registry Office in Bracebridge has been completed.

Plans and specifications were made for a Court House Building and for a Registry and Land Titles Office in Haileybury. Tenders were called for and contracts awarded as follows:—

For general trades of both buildings, Messrs. Secord & Sons, of Brantford; for heating and plumbing and electric work of Registry Office, Mr. F. R. Gibson, of Haileybury. The foundation walls of Court House are completed and the first floor joists laid. The work will be stopped for the winter, proper precautions having been made to protect the foundations from the weather. Satisfactory progress has been made with the work on Registry Office. The building has been roofed and will be completed by February.

Plans and specifications were made for a Court House to be erected in Fort Frances. Tenders were called for and the contract for general trades was awarded to Messrs. Seaman & Penniman, of Fort William, the work being carried on under the superintendence of Mr. A. F. Scott, of Fort Frances. Satisfactory progress has been made. The work will be carried on during the winter months as the weather may permit, and the building completed by about July next.

Repairs have been made to the Provincial Court Houses, Registry and Land Titles Offices, Gaols and Lock Ups throughout the Districts and the equipment thereof.

BOILER INSPECTION.

The boilers in the Government Institutions which were formerly inspected by the Provincial Boiler Inspector, Mr. D. M. Medcalf, who has been put in charge of The Ontario Boiler Inspection Branch of this Department, are now inspected by the Inspectors of that Branch who also inspect all new boilers and repairs to old boilers and apparatus and see that the rules set forth in the Boiler Inspection Act are carried out by the manufacturers and the contractors.

All of which is respectfully submitted.

I have the honour to remain, Sir,

Your obedient servant,

F. R. HEAKES,

Architect.

TORONTO, Jan. 2nd, 1914.

HONOURABLE J. O. REAUME,
   Minister of Public Works,
      Parliament Bldgs., Toronto.

SIR,—I have the honour to submit my first report on the work done in the Steam Boiler Branch of the Public Works Department in the financial year ending October 31st, 1913.

The Act respecting Steam Boilers, 3 George V., chap. 61, came into force and took effect on July 1st, 1913, and during the four months tenure we have surveyed and approved of 148 designs of steam boilers, including the Water Tube, Horizontal Tubular, Vertical Fire Tube, and Locomotive types of boilers. We have also surveyed, approved, and registered 332 designs of boiler mountings and accessories.

Designs of boilers and fittings manufactured in England and United States have been surveyed, approved and registered, and we have made inspections in Philadelphia, New York City, Chicago, Keewanee, Ill., Niagara Falls, N.Y., Dunkirk, N.Y., and Rochester, N.Y. The object in examining boilers outside this Province was to ascertain and fix the maximum working pressure allowable, calculated from the formulæ contained in the Rules and Regulations, before the owners would ship the boilers into Ontario.

The Regulations for the Construction and Inspection of Steam Boilers were drafted from the Regulations in the Western Provinces, with the object of ultimately establishing uniform regulations throughout the Dominion, whereby a boiler built according to these regulations, and inspected during construction by an inspector appointed by any one of the different provinces, would be accepted without further inspection. I regret, however, to say that up to the present time the Ontario inspection will not be accepted in the Western Provinces, although Ontario will accept the inspection made by the inspectors of the different provinces of the West.

Manufacturers in nearly every instance have been willing to co-operate with this branch of the Department, and have frequently expressed their appreciation of the manner in which their designs submitted for approval were handled.

In many cases it was found necessary to make corrections and alterations on designs, and return them to the manufacturers to have the corrections made on the tracings and new prints submitted showing that the corrections had been made, and in some cases, owing to the extent of the work involved, we found it necessary to charge an additional fee for revision. With the exception of one case only, we were able to convince the manufacturers that our calculations and requirements were good practice and according to the regulations, and all changes and corrections were willingly made by them.

The authority of the Act of the Legislature controlling the construction of boilers establishes the following procedure:

The manufacturer is required to submit prints and specifications in triplicate, showing the different dimensions and materials used in the construction. The designs are then surveyed, and the strength of the boiler ascertained, and if found to be drafted in accordance with the formulæ contained in the Rules and Regulations, they are stamped with the allowable working pressure, and registration number. One certified drawing and specification is returned to the manufacturer, from which he may construct an unlimited number of boilers, and the two remaining specifications and drawings are filed in this office. When the boiler is being constructed one of our Inspectors visits the boiler shop and examines the work under construction, and compares this with the approval plans and specifications, and if the workmanship and material is found to be good, and the boiler built according to the approved designs, a final hydraulic test of one and a half times the working pressure is applied, and if found to be satisfactory, the Inspector stamps the boiler, collects the fee, and fills in a shop inspection report sheet, from which the official certificate is issued in duplicate and forwarded to the manufacturer, who retains one certificate and forwards one to the purchaser of the boiler.

The certificates referred to state when and by whom the boiler was constructed, and under what design and record number same was built, also the test pressure and maximum working pressure allowed.

The stamping impressed on the boiler shell by our Inspector shows the tensile strength of the plate, the maker's name, the registration number for Ontario, the name of the boiler plate manufacturers, the date of inspection, and the Inspector's initials. From this stamping and our records on file, it will now be possible to trace a boiler from the manufacturer until it is put on the retired list and condemned from further use.

Boiler fittings are dealt with in a similar manner, with the exception of the inspection of work under construction, and the issue of certificates.

In inspecting boilers that required extensive repairs, we were compelled to condemn five. The plates had deteriorated to such an extent that satisfactory repairs could not be made.

Although steam boilers in service, or built prior to July 1st, 1913, are exempt from inspection by inspectors appointed under the Act (unless same have been extensively repaired), I regret to report that during the past four months the following boiler explosions have been reported to this branch of the department, and upon examination we found that in each case the boilers were very old, and totally inadequate to withstand the pressure carried, and should have been consigned to the scrap pile years ago.

On September 12th one boiler exploded in the City Gas Plant, Oshawa, killing two men and injuring three, and completely wrecking the building.

On September 24th a traction boiler exploded and killed one man and seriously injured three.

On October 21st one boiler exploded in Midland, killing two and injuring four men, and completely wrecking the building in which the boilers were installed.

During the month of September a cast iron heating boiler exploded in Toronto, injuring one man and doing considerable damage to the building.

The requirements of the Steam Boilers Act, relating to the construction and inspection of steam boilers, deal with new boilers built in, or entering this Province, and boilers subject to extensive repairs. We have no jurisdiction over boilers installed prior to July 1st, 1913, although we are aware that many of these are used which are in an unsound condition and a menace to public safety.

We have had considerable trouble in the classification of portable boilers of 25 horse power and under, which are exempt from inspection, and I would respectfully ask you to consider the advisability of amending the Act to provide for the inclusion of this type of boiler. When one considers the illusage the portable boiler frequently receives, and the crowded thoroughfares in which this boiler is very often used, it is marvellous that more serious accidents have not occurred.

We have had many requests from steam users to inspect the boilers in their works, who, after we had explained to them that owing to their boilers having been constructed before the first of July, 1913, we had no jurisdiction over them, waived the exemption and paid the travelling expenses and fee for inspection in order to receive the official certificate from this office.

The exemption from Government inspection of boilers used for agricultural purposes was also disregarded by The Sawyer-Massey Company of Hamilton, who desired to have their designs surveyed and registered. Although they were quite cognizant of the fact that the type of boilers manufactured by them was exempt from inspection, they submitted their designs in the regular manner, paid the fees and received registration numbers for this Province. We found that in every design submitted by this company the construction of boilers shown on their designs was in conformity with our regulations, and suitable for the allowable steam pressure required and designed for by the manufacturer.

In concluding my report I desire to acknowledge the support given by the Deputy Minister of Public Works, and to express my appreciation for the efficient services rendered by my staff in surveying designs, making inspections, and in the general work in this branch of the Department of Public Works, and I trust that my efforts have been in accordance with the policy of the department.

I have the honour to be,

Sir,

Your obedient servant,
D. M. MEDCALF,

Chief Inspector.

REPORT OF THE ENGINEER.

HON. J. O. REAUME,
Minister of Public Works, Ontario.

SIR,—I have the honour to report on the public works constructed by the Engineers' Branch of the Public Works Department during the year ending Oct. 31st, 1913.

A number of different works built of concrete which were under construction on October 31st, 1912, were continued during mild weather, until lower temperatures rendered such work inadvisable. During the winter months various timber bridges were economically completed. Throughout the year all work has been done by day labor under the direction of capable foremen, and the results have been very satisfactory.

The erection of the shorter span steel bridges, which has previously been done by the contractor for the same, was undertaken by this Department in order to shorten the time during which traffic is inconvenienced by temporary crossings of the rivers over which the bridges are being built, and also to allow the laying of a concrete floor and the completion of the entire work before cold weather set in.

A number of steel beam bridges with reinforced concrete floors were carried rapidly to completion. This type of structure is a splendid example of permanent and economical construction.

Reinforced concrete was used extensively in the foundations of and the approaches to a number of bridges, and a box culvert 10 feet wide, 6 feet high and 90 feet long was built of that material.

The usual maintenance of bridges has been thoroughly attended to, and all structures have been kept in a safe condition for public travel. Due to the high price and comparatively short life of timber, it is now advisable, wherever practicable, to construct repairs to piers and abutments of timber bridges, by substituting permanent native rock masonry construction with cement mortar.

The efficient drainage of roads in the Rainy River District was carried out under the direct supervision of a man experienced in that class of work. In the other districts requiring road drainage, capable supervision was given and the expenditure carried out by the local inspectors of colonization roads.

All other work of the Department, such as the examination of bridges, the inspection of drainage works and the preparation of various plans has been promptly attended to.

Algoma District Bridges.

Birch Creek Bridge on Birch Lake Road.—As soon as the cold weather had gone, the concrete floor was laid on the steel bridge and the approaches graded and properly rounded up to give good drainage to the roadway.

Campement D'Ours Island Bridge.—During November and December, 1912, the rock fill between St. Joseph's Island and Campement D'Ours Island was finally completed and put in a safe condition for travel. A winter road was cut out across Campement D'Ours Island from the end of the causeway to a point opposite Kensington Point, on the main land. There is now by this road between St. Joseph's Island and the mainland only 2,100 feet of the St. Mary's River to cross, and during the winter a splendid ice road is maintained.

Leeburn Bridge, Aberdeen.— Over the Thessalon River, on Lot 10, in the First Concession of Aberdeen Township, a sixty foot steel bridge with a roadway 14 feet in clear width was built. The bridge is supported on reinforced concrete piles, and at either end the approaches also of reinforced concrete, extend 45 feet towards the banks of the river. These approaches are composed of two spans of 20 feet clear each, all supported on bents of reinforced concrete piles driven deep into the bed of the river. On the steel span which was erected late in the fall a temporary plank floor has been laid, while six inches of good gravel cover the reinforced floor on the approach spans. The bridge is being used for crossing the river, but some work on the approaches and the providing of a concrete floor for the steel span yet remains to be finished.

Little Rapids Bridge, Little Thessalon.—This substantial structure, ninety-five feet long over all and supported on four bents of reinforced concrete piles is composed of three reinforced concrete beam spans, each of thirty feet clear opening. The roadway, which is fourteen feet clear between wheelguards, is of reinforced concrete, covered with a wearing surface of six inches of good gravel. Reinforced concrete posts, three feet six inches high, support the three lines of one and one half-inch galvanized pipe handrail.

Suddaby's Bridge, Johnson Township.—A reinforced concrete trestle, seventy feet long over all and fourteen feet high above the solid rock foundation, was built here at a total cost of $1,795.49. It is composed of three heavily reinforced concrete beam spans, each of twenty-two feet clear opening, which rest on two curtain wall abutments and two bents of reinforced concrete posts. The roadway is fourteen feet clear between wheelguards and is composed of a wearing surface of six inches of gravel resting on the six inch reinforced concrete floor. The handrail, which is composed of three lines of one and one-half inch galvanized iron pipe, is supported by reinforced concrete posts.

Two Tree Bridge, St. Joseph Island.—At the site of this bridge the mud bottom of the river did not promise an unyielding surface to the weight of concrete abutments, and resort was made to laying a timber grillage across the river, below the bed. Upon the top of the timbers the concrete abutments were built, and a substantial structure safe against the dangers of heavy and unequal settlement built. A steel beam span twenty-six feet long over all, and with a fourteen foot clear reinforced concrete roadway rests on the abutments. On each side of the bridge a strong pipe handrail is securely fastened to the outside beams.

White River Bridge, Bellingham.—The approaches to this bridge were finally completed and the grade down to and over the bridge is now very easily covered by teams drawing heavy loads. .

West's Bridge, Thessalon River.—Due to the late erection of this bridge, during the fall of 1912, the concrete floor was not laid, but immediately this spring, when all danger of frost was passed, the reinforced concrete floor was laid and the bridge put in the best of condition for travel.

KENORA DISTRICT BRIDGES.

Minnitake Bridge.—During the winter of 1912-13 the construction of this bridge was carried out. The structure is composed of five bents of piles, each bent being 14 ft. centre to centre, and the floor 6 ft. above the water level. All timber used was of the best pine and tamarac to be obtained in that locality. The bridge is located on the south side of the Canadian Pacific Railway, and east of Minnitake Station.

Gold Rock Bridges.—On the main trunk road between Gold Rock and Dinorwic three new bridges were placed. The first one, over Two Mile Creek, is a pile trestle 65 ft. long and 14 ft. wide. A good tamarac floor was laid and well spiked down to the stringers, forming a strong, steady bridge for any loads which may come on it. About four miles from Gold Rock and over Pebble Creek a trestle 42 ft. long and 14 ft. wide of cedar was built. Further along the road and at a distance of eight miles from Gold Rock a bridge 130 ft. long and 14 ft. wide was built over Tobacco Creek. The foundations are constructed of stone-filled cribs, all stringers are of tamarac and the floor is of jack pine and tamarac.

West Channel Bridge Floor, Kenora.—The timber floor on the steel bridge over the west branch of the Winnipeg River had decayed, and was considered to be in such condition as to require immediate renewal. British Columbia fir was secured, and new stringers, floor, guard rail, and hand rail built.

Sakoose River.—In the township of Melgund and over the Little Wabigoon River, at a distance of about five miles from Dyment Station, considerable repairs were made to a timber bridge. The old parts of the piers were removed and new squared timbers built in, after which all cribs were filled with stone up to the stringers. All new stringers, corbels, caps and flooring were provided, and the bridge is considered now to be one of the best on the road. A second bridge on the same road and three miles from Dyment was built over a small creek. It is 40 ft. long, 14 ft. wide, and is constructed entirely of round timber. On a new road, and at a distance of four miles from Dyment, a timber bridge, 50 ft. long, 14 ft. wide and 8 ft. high was constructed of tamarac.

Aubrey and Ignace Bridges —On the trunk road south from Oxdrift two bridges were built over Beaver Creek. The first is 60 ft. long, 14 ft. wide, and is constructed of cedar and tamarac, with three cribs and two abutments. Good flatted cedar stringers and floor and a well braced railing is provided. The second bridge is on the same road, and is 45 ft. long, 14 ft. wide and 6 ft. high. It is built entirely of cedar and tamarac and is a very serviceable structure. A bridge 24 ft. long, 14 ft. wide and 6 ft. high, was built of good pine and tamarac. Two small bridges were done away with by placing 18 inch galvanized culverts and constructing a roadway of gravel and cinders.

Norman Dam.—Some small repairs were made to the stoplogs and turntable.

Lawrence Creek Bridge, Goulds Road.—An ingot iron culvert 40 ft. long and 2 ft. in diameter was placed under the old bridge and the entire opening filled in. This type of construction is carried out at a very reasonable cost and is permanent work. The fill is 75 ft. long, 16 ft. wide on top, and 10 ft. high. To obtain sufficient material the grade at the west end of the road was cut down and a very easy approach constructed.

Anderson Branch Road Bridges.—About five miles north of Kenora the road crosses an arm of the Winnipeg River, and a bridge 225 ft. long, 14 ft. wide, and 10 ft. above the water was constructed. Owing to the very low water in the river the bridge was built on mudsills and the bents framed up from them. All timber used was tamarac and jack pine. so that a comparatively long life is to be expected of this structure. The second bridge is half a mile beyond the one just described. It is 125 ft. long, 14 ft. wide, and 8 ft. high, and is constructed of jack pine and tamarac.

Swansons Creek Bridge.—An appropriation of $400 was made to pay for a 6 foot corrugated pipe and to carry out a small amount of grading required to put the bridge in a safe condition with reference to the approaches at each end. This work was finished and the bridge is now open for public travel.

THUNDER BAY DISTRICT BRIDGES.

Corbett Creek Bridge, Oliver.—A worn out timber trestle was removed at this site and a reinforced concrete beam span of 20 feet clear opening built. This opening allows ample waterway for the creek and the type of structure is such that good service and a long life with no maintenance charges is to be expected. A gravel roadway fourteen feet in clear width is provided with the roadway leading to either end of the bridge eighteen feet in length.

Kaministikwia River Bridge, Paipoonge Township.—The erection of the steel superstructure of this bridge, consisting of three steel Pratt truss spans of 100 feet each, was completed during the autumn of 1912, but cold weather prevented the laying of the concrete floor.

Our foreman on the work, Mr. Alfred Jackson, a capable and energetic man, was engaged during the late fall of 1912 and January, 1913, in completing the grading of the long approach to the east end of the bridge. After severe weather compelled the abandonment of all work he was accidentally shot on January 24th, 1913, and died within a few hours. By his death the Department has lost a very valuable, conscientious official.

Early in the spring of 1913 the concrete floor was laid, the grading of the approaches completed and the bridge opened for travel.

Six Mile Bridge, Shuniah.—A steel beam bridge 32 feet long over all and with a roadway fourteen feet wide was erected on this site. The abutments are of concrete, and due to the soft, sandy bottom are supported by heavy timber grillage placed well below the low water line. Due to the lateness of the season when this work was completed, a temporary plank floor has been laid on the steel beams to carry the traffic until a reinforced concrete floor can be laid in the spring.

RAINY RIVER DISTRICT BRIDGES.

Graces Creek Bridge, Crozier Township.—On the Rainy River road, in Lot 12, of the river range of lots in Crozier township a timber trestle 173 feet long and 18 feet high over Graces Creek was entirely removed and an earth embankment with a road 18 feet wide was constructed. To provide opening for the small creek a corrugated iron culvert, seventy feet long and four feet in inside diameter was laid with proper slope. Heavy concrete collars built to protect the upstream and downstream ends of the culvert and also to prevent the washing away of the earth at the foot of the embankment were placed.

McKelvery Creek Bridge.—A timber trestle 295 feet long and 35 feet high in the centre which was located on the Rainy River Road over McKelvery Creek, on Lot 7 in the River Range of Crozier Township was reconstructed. The overall length of the trestle was reduced to 128 feet by filling in 80 feet at the north end and 87 feet at the south end of the old structure. At each end the grade down to the trestle was lengthened so that the floor level of the new bridge is nine feet below that of the old one.

Pine River Bridge.—The work on this bridge was carried on during 1912 until cold weather stopped all activity. An appropriation was granted to complete the work, and this year the approach at the east end of the bridge was graded down to a five per cent. slope, which is a grade easily negotiated by a team with a loaded wagon.

La Vallee River Bridge.—The erection of the steel sixty foot span of this bridge was completed during the winter of 1912-13 and a timber floor 14 feet in width laid. Upon the opening up in the spring the work of filling in the approaches was vigorously gone ahead with, and the entire undertaking was finished during the early part of the summer.

SAULT STE. MARIE DISTRICT BRIDGES.

Garden River Bridge.—The original steel bridge built over Garden River a number of years ago was considered too light for the heavy traffic of the Sudbury-Soo Trunk Road and is being replaced by a 140 feet steel span through Pratt truss, resting on strongly designed concrete abutments.

The roadway is sixteen feet in clear width. A broad base was excavated for the abutments and stout piles of pine, tamarac and spruce were driven deep to form a permanent foundation. At the end of October the concrete work in the abutments was nearly completed and it was expected that the steel span would be erected before January, 1914.

Magpie River Bridge.—Extensive repairs were carried out on the Magpie Bridge. All timber chords of the trusses were either renewed or strongly reinforced with heavy planks. An entirely new floor was laid for the full width of 14 feet and over the entire length of the structure. All danger of washout was avoided by carefully placing a riprap of rock in front of the abutments to break the scouring action of the water. The entire bridge was painted to protect it from the wet and prolong the life of the timbers.

TEMISKAMING DISTRICT BRIDGES.

Otter Creek Bridge.—A timber structure over Otter Creek on line between Concessions 1 and 2, Lot 1, Brethour Township, was completed during the late autumn of 1912 and opened for traffic. The centre span is 45 feet with a trestle approach 48 feet long at each end, the whole structure being supported by piles.

Dack Sunday Creek Bridge.—On line of Concession 4 and at Lot 8 in Dack Township a wooden bridge resting on timber piles was constructed. The main structure is a king post truss, having a span of 28 feet, and with approaches to it from either end of 32 feet each. At the close of the year the work on the structure was not completed, but was being continued and a few weeks would finish everything satisfactorily.

Sunday Creek Bridge, Robillard.—The location of this bridge is over Sunday Creek on line between Lots 2 and 3, Concession 1, Robillard Township. At the end of October some material had been purchased, but due to no labor being available the work had not been started. It was expected that early in November sufficient local men would be at liberty and several weeks' work would complete the entire structure.

Armstrong Township Bridge.—A wooden bridge over a ravine on Lot 7, Con. 4, was destroyed by fire. Operations were at once commenced to renew it, and a pile structure 24 feet long was quickly placed at a small expenditure and furnished a strong, safe bridge for travel.

Hilliard Township Bridge and Culvert.—Fire destroyed a long bridge and culvert on a road crossing a wide ravine. In replacing the structures culverts were considered to be the best type of construction, and a cedar box 56 feet long, 6 feet wide and 3 feet high was placed at one crossing, while a second one 35 feet long, 5 feet wide and 3 feet high gave vent to the water at the second crossing. At either side of the ravine the hills were cut down and the material used to construct the roadway.

Kearns and Armstrong Townline Bridges.—Two structures, one 125 feet long · and one 24 feet long, carrying a highway over Armstrong Creek, were burned out. The longer bridge was shortened by 20 feet, and the balance filled in with earth, while the shorter one was renewed to its original length. Both structures are supported on posts sunk 8 feet in the ground in holes excavated with a post-hole augur.

Jean Baptiste Creek Bridge, Armstrong Township.—After the erection of the steel superstructure of this bridge, during the winter of 1912-13, a small amount of work was required to make the bridge complete and safe for travel. As soon as possible this spring the work was finished and the bridge is now giving good service.

Judge Bridge.—Work on this structure was commenced in 1912 by the Farrelly Construction Company. A proposal to make a combined electric railway and highway bridge was considered, as the extension of the Nipissing Central Railway was being urged, but after due consideration it was decided to make separate structures. Early in the spring the framing of the wooden piers was commenced and the approaches constructed. A contract for the steel superstructure was entered into and the fabricated material delivered. It is expected that the bridge will be opened for traffic about March 16, 1914.

HALIBURTON COUNTY BRIDGES.

Mountain Lake Bridge, Minden.—A steel beam bridge with two spans of 30 and 32 feet respectively, resting on two concrete abutments and one pier, was built at the above site. The old bridge was 175 feet long over all, and a deep fill was required to carry the roadway. All work was completed and a reinforced concrete floor laid on the spans, before the close of the summer.

STURGEON FALLS DISTRICT BRIDGES.

Sturgeon Falls Bridge.—The bridge over the Sturgeon River, on the west road out of Sturgeon Falls was in a shaky condition and it was decided to replace it. A new steel span 210 feet long, centre to centre of bearings, and with a roadway sixteen feet in clear width was contracted for.

On the north side of the bridge a sidewalk six feet in clear width is provided. The substantial concrete abutments are all ready for the superstructure and it is expected that the bridge will be completed and opened for traffic by the spring of 1914.

Warren Bridge, Veuve River.—The steel superstructure for this bridge was completed during the winter of 1912-13, but a considerable amount of work, grading the approaches and laying the floor, was left to be done. All work was completed and the bridge opened for traffic early in the summer.

NIPISSING DISTRICT BRIDGES.

Barbette Creek Bridge, Clara Township.—Between Range A and B, in Clara Township, a reinforced concrete beam bridge of 20 feet clear span was successfully carried to completion. The bottom of the river was of coarse gravel and a little preparation of the foundations was required to furnish the unyielding support which reinforced concrete calls for. The roadway is 14 feet in clear width and is heavily gravelled, the same surfacing of the approaches at either end being carried straight across the bridge.

Papineau Township Bridges.—A steel beam bridge of 24 feet clear span and 14 feet clear roadway was constructed over Boom Creek on Lot 9, in the 10th Concession of the Township of Papineau. The foundation was found to be soft, so that a timber grillage was placed below the bed of the river, and on that the rubble stone and cement mortar abutments were built. A reinforced concrete floor was provided on the steel span and an 18 foot roadway well rounded up furnishes a good approach to each end of the structure.

Between Lots 10 and 11, in the 11th Concession of Papineau Township, a steel beam bridge over Boom Creek, the exact duplicate of the bridge built over that creek on Lot 9, in the 10th Concession of Papineau Township, was completed.

Sampson's Bridge.—Over Kabuska Creek, near Bonfield, Sampson's Bridge, a steel beam bridge with two spans each of 30 feet clear opening, was constructed. The two abutments built of concrete are stoutly designed to carry safely all stresses to which they may be subjected. A centre pier, also of concrete, is provided, and a steel angle protects its upstream nose from the pounding to which the frequent log drives down this creek subject all objects in their path. This bridge was completed late in the fall and a plank floor was placed to carry the traffic until a concrete floor can be laid in the spring.

Sparks Creek Bridge.—A steel beam bridge of 25 feet clear span was completed over Sparks Creek, near Rutherglen, in Bonfield Township. The roadway of reinforced concrete is 14 feet in clear width and the solid abutments are founded on rock. At each end the approach to the bridge was thoroughly prepared and the entire work is a splendid example of permanent construction.

Widdifield Township Bridges: Four Mile Creek Bridge.—On Lot 8, Concession A, of Widdifield Township, a reinforced concrete beam bridge of 24 feet clear span and with a roadway 14 feet in clear width was constructed on a solid rock foundation. The height of the abutments is seven feet and the waterway provided affords ample space for all flood water.

Hogan's Creek Culvert.—A reinforced concrete arch culvert was constructed to afford a crossing for the highway over Hogan's Creek, on Lot 9, Concession B, Widdifield Township. The opening is four feet wide and six feet high. The roadway, 18 feet wide, was continued across the culvert upon its completion.

PARRY SOUND DISTRICT BRIDGES.

Boyne River Bridge, Lot 134, Con. B, Foley Township.—The bottom of the river at the site of the bridge proved to be soft and long timbers were laid from side to side upon which strong rubble stone abutments were founded. All timbers are placed well down in the bed of the stream and form a permanent grillage which safely carries the weight of the masonry. The distance between the abutments is 25 feet, and the roadway of a width of 14 feet is carried over that span by a steel beam bridge, 27 feet long over all. A reinforced concrete floor six inches in thickness forms the roadway of the bridge. At either approach to the bridge substantial handrails provide for the safety of traffic.

Boyne River Bridge, Lot 140, Con. A, Foley Township.—On the main road between Parry Sound and James Bay Junction, and only a short distance west of the latter village, the Boyne is crossed. The foundations were constructed similar to those provided for Boyne River Bridge, on Lot 134, Concession B, of Foley Township, and the substantial rubble stone abutments were of a similar design. The bridge consists of a steel beam span 22 feet long over all, with roadway 14 feet in clear width, and is provided with a reinforced concrete floor six inches in thickness.

Bear Lake Creek Bridge, Lot 9, Con. 11, Monteith Township.—Solid rock was found at this site a few feet below the water level, and a reinforced concrete beam bridge 25 feet in clear span and with a roadway 14 feet in clear width was built. This type of structure is particularly adapted to an unyielding foundation such as solid rock, and when completed is a permanent work, requiring practically no maintenance.

Magnetawan River Bridge, Burks Falls.—An appropriation to complete this structure was granted to provide for the final payment on the superstructure.

Pickerel River Improvement.—To improve the river for navigation the outlet of Wilson's Lake was enlarged and a channel 45 feet wide opened for a sufficient depth to allow the safe passage of boats. At the Wilson dam, which was removed, the channel was made 50 feet wide and the boulders and rock cleared away. Preparations were being made to commence work at Dollar's dam in order to tighten and strengthen it to safely hold the increased height of water. Upon completion of the work a wagon road six miles in length from the Canadian Northern Railway and a boat trip of fifteen miles will land a traveller at Loring, which is now forty miles by road from the Grand Trunk Railway.

Sand Lake Road Bridge.—A design was prepared and work begun on a reinforced concrete beam bridge over the Magnetawan River, between Lots 8 and 9, in the First Concession of Proudfoot Township. Reinforced concrete piles were first driven for the foundation, and a three span bridge with centre opening 32 feet clear and end openings each of 25 feet clear span was commenced. It is now proposed to improve the Magnetawan River at this point so as to allow navigation, and until this question is definitely settled the completion of the bridge is being held in abeyance.

SUDBURY DISTRICT BRIDGES.

Fourth Concession Bridge, Hagar.—During February and March a timber trestle with a centre span composed of a 30 foot king post truss was constructed across the Veuve River, a short distance North of Markstay. The overall length of the structure is 136 feet, and the approaches at either end are composed of three pile bents, each 16 feet centre to centre. A plank floor 14 feet wide is laid and the entire structure provides a strong and safe crossing of the river.

MUSKOKA DISTRICT WORKS.

Big East River Bridge, Chaffey.—The steel superstructure of the bridge was completed just as cold weather set in in the fall of 1912. It was then considered to be not advisable to lay the concrete floor and complete the work. As early as was possible this spring, work was again commenced and the filling in back of the abutments was quickly finished. The road surface, 18 feet wide, was graded and a stout handrail provided at each side and the concrete floor carefully laid. The bridge was opened for traffic during the month of May.

South Channel Bridge and Dam, Bala.—The dam at the south outlet from Bala Bay and Lake Muskoka was in such an advanced state of decay that it was decided to replace it. A short distance downstream from the dam the wooden highway bridge, built a number of years ago, was also in a bad state of repair, and a design for a combined dam and bridge was prepared. The new highway bridge consists of five steel beam spans, each of 20 feet clear opening, between the different piers of the dam. A reinforced concrete floor six inches in thickness is provided, and on each side of the bridge a lattice handrail of good appearance is placed. At either end of the structure strong fences painted white are placed to safely guide the traffic to and from the bridge. Three of the piers which carry the bridge were extended up-stream a sufficient distance to support the 12 feet wide floor of the dam and provide space for the necessary chaces and stoplogs. There are three stoplog openings provided, the sill of the west opening being at an elevation of zero on Bala Gauge, and the two openings to the east of that having their sills at an elevation of one foot on the gauge. As the navigation level of the Muskoka Lake is now 8 feet 6 inches on Bala Gauge, these three openings give splendid discharging capacity, and along with the stoplog openings in the dam at the north outlet, ample space is provided to properly regulate the level of the water in the Muskoka Lake. A new set of Georgia pine stoplogs was purchased, and a pair of easily operated hand-winches enable the logs to be placed or removed very rapidly. The two openings at the west end of the dam are provided with spillways each 20 feet wide, the top of the spillway being at an elevation of 8 feet 6 inches on the gauge. All piers and abutments of the dam are constructed of masonry, being built of the native rock which was blasted out of the bed of the river on the site of the dam, and after being carefully pointed up was placed in the piers and bonded with a cement mortar composed of one part cement to four parts of sand. A strong and lasting structure of splendid appearance was the result and is giving good satisfaction to all concerned.

SIMCOE COUNTY BRIDGES.

North River Bridge.—Owing to the late erection of the steel superstructure, in the fall of 1912 a plank floor was laid to permit traffic across the bridge during the winter. This spring, as soon as the weather permitted safe concrete work, the reinforced floor was laid, the handrails completed, and after a thorough regrading of the approaches the bridge was opened for traffic.

Orillia Township Bridge.—On Lot 2, Concession 2, where the North River crosses the concession line, a reinforced concrete box culvert ten feet wide and six feet high in inside dimensions and ninety feet long was constructed. The floor of the culvert is 15 inches thick and is reinforced with 5⁄8 inch square twisted bars, spaced 9 inches centre to centre, and with longitude rods 1⁄2 in. square, 22 inches centre to centre, to strengthen the culvert in the direction of its length.

The sides are reinforced with vertical 5⁄8 inch square twisted bars one foot centre to centre. A flat slab top two feet thick and heavily reinforced with 3⁄4 inch square twisted rods 5 inches centre to centre, safely carries the heavy clay fill which is 15 feet high over the top of the culvert. The ravine was filled in and a roadway 18 feet wide now provides a splendid crossing of the river.

ADDINGTON COUNTY BRIDGES.

Clare River Bridge.—A steel beam bridge of 42 feet clear span was built over Clare River on Lot 18, between Concessions 3 and 4 of Sheffield Township. The existing rock-filled cedar cribs which supported the old bridge were used as a foundation, and upon them the reinforced concrete abutments were built. A reinforced concrete floor 14 feet in clear width is placed on the bridge, and the entire structure is of very substantial construction.

Denbigh Bridge, Hydes Creek.—The crossing of Hydes Creek on Lot 21, Concession 8, of Denbigh Township was reconstructed. A fill 190 feet long was made with a roadway 22 feet wide. An opening 14 feet wide and 15 feet high was left for the creek, and a strong railing provided on either side of the fill for the full length.

LANARK COUNTY BRIDGE.

A grant of $1,225.00 was made to the County of Lanark in aid of the repairs required on country road No. 7, opposite Lots 22 and 24, in the Ninth Concession of Ramsay Township, which had been damaged by a heavy flood.

RENFREW DISTRICT BRIDGES.

Admanston Bridge.—Over the Bonnechere River, between Lots 24 and 25, in the South Bonnechere Range of Admanston Township, a steel bridge of sixty feet span resting on reinforced concrete piles and with reinforced concrete approaches was built. The roadway is 14 feet in clear width. The approaches at either end consist of a two-span reinforced concrete beam of 22 feet clear opening each, all supported by bents of reinforced concrete piles. With careful construction this type of structure is one of the most economical for rivers up to 150 feet wide.

Griffiths Bridge Repairs.—An old timber bridge across the Madawaska River, on the Batson Road, between Denbigh and Renfrew, Lot 9, Concession 3, of Griffith Township, was reconstructed. An entirely new truss sixty feet long was provided and rests on stone-filled piers. At each shore a glance wall was provided to protect the cribs from the ice and driftwood.

Helferty Bridge, Raglan.—A long cedar bridge over a gully on Lot 32 in the 12th Concession of Raglan Township, was shortened to 40 feet, and the approaches of 100 feet at the west end and sixty feet at the east end were filled in, this giving a smaller bridge to maintain and completing quite an amount of permanent work.

Wilno-Rockingham Bridges.—A new bridge was built on the Wilno-Rockingham Road, over Brennan's Creek, length 40 ft., 14 ft. roadway. The east approach is filled for a length of one hundred feet, average height 5 ft. The west approach is built up for a length of 120 ft., with an average height of 3 ft. Roadway on fill is 18 ft. wide.

Another old bridge on same road and creek was shortened up from 60 ft. to a 20 foot span. New stringers were put on and the approaches properly graded.

Seven cedar culverts were also re-built on this road. The whole amount of the appropriation was spent on this work.

LEEDS COUNTY.

Gananoque River Improvement.—From Lyndhurst south a number of small rapids on the Gananoque River, in the Township of Lansdowne, were opened up to provide navigation for small launches. The following rapids were deepened and cleared out:

Latimer's Rapids.
Jim Day Rapids.
Black Rapids.
Second Beaver Rock Rapids.
Third Beaver Rock Rapids.

A splendid channel is now available, so that settlers and tourists are able to avail themselves of the water route to and from Lyndhurst.

HALIBURTON COUNTY.

Ingoldsby Bridge.—In the Township of Minden and over the Burnt River a timber bridge 111 ft. long was constructed. The floor is supported by framed bents resting on mud sills, and sufficient width and height was given under the bridge to allow the passage of launches. At either end of the structure an approach fill was required for a short distance.

Tory Hill Bridge.—Over Otter Creek, on Lot 24, in the 11th Concession of Monmouth Township, a new timber bridge known as Tory Hill bridge was built. The clear span between the rock-filled cribs is 25 ft., and the height of the floor above the bottom of the river is 9 ft. The entire bed of the river was solid rock, so that a splendid foundation was secured for the cribs. A king post truss composed of 8 by 10 inch square timbers supports the centre needle beam upon which rests the stringers. All flooring consists of three-inch plank for the full width of the bridge, which is twelve feet. This work is a good substantial job which should give good satisfaction for a number of years.

VICTORIA COUNTY BRIDGE.

Tiers Bridge, Hawkers Creek.—A concrete arch with a clear span of 15 ft. was built over Hawkers Creek, in the Township of Verulam. An appropriation of $200 was made toward the construction of the work.

MAINTENANCE LOCKS, DAMS AND BRIDGES.

During the past year the following work was carried on under the direct supervision of the Superintendent of Public Works:—

The breakwater pier immediately below Mary's and Fairy Lakes Lock was decayed in many places, and upon commencing work it was decided to completely renew it. This was done, and a strong, substantial piece of work completed.

At the Ryerson swing bridge an early examination was made in the spring. All parts requiring attention and renewal were put in order, and the bridge carefully adjusted.

A short distance south of Huntsville the high bridge over the river between Mary's and Fairy Lakes was provided with a new tamarac flooring to replace the old deck, which was full of holes.

The dredge which during 1912 was employed improving the channels for navigation near Huntsville was dismantled and the machinery moved to Gravenhurst, where it was installed in the hull kept on the Muskoka Lakes. All summer the dredge was employed by the Dominion Department of Public Works in removing shoals and widening channels in Lake Muskoka.

On the opening of navigation on the Muskoka Lakes all buoys required for safe navigation were carefully posted, and the various works on the lakes brightened up with new paint; the Port Carling bridges, office shelter and lock gates and Port Sandfield swing bridge being so treated. Small repairs needed at Port Sandfield swing bridge and the Port Carling docks were attended to and everything put in order for the busy navigation season.

All obstructions to navigation in the Indian River were searched for and at once removed, and to maintain the navigation level of water in Lake Rosseau required the careful tightening of the Port Carling dam.

The Government dredge was operated in the Muskoka waters during the early part of the season at an expense of $3,466. In the latter part of the season the dredge was taken over by the Dominion Public Works to complete some work on which that Department was engaged.

At Port Carling $1,025 was expended on repairs to the locks and in putting a new floor on part of the dock.

At Port Sandfield the bridge was painted and minor repairs made at an expense of $201.

A new boom was placed at Bala Dam, and general repairs made at an expense of $360.

Extensive repairs were made to the locks at Huntsville, and a glance boom placed at the Huntsville swing bridge. This work cost $1,251.

The swing bridge at Magnetawan was painted and general repairs made at a cost of $218.

Algoma District.—In the district of Algoma the following bridges were repaired and renewed: In the Township of Bright on the line between Concessions 5 and 6, on Lots 1 and 2, three bridges were rebuilt at an expense of $543. The bridges are 18, 29 and 35 feet long, built of cedar with the approaches properly graded.

In the Sylvan Valley, in the Township of McDonald, three bridges were renewed at an expense $468. The bridges are 18, 20 and 27 feet long.

In the Township of Wells, Harris bridge, situate on Lot 7, Con. 4, was renewed. The bridge is 100 feet long, with five spans of 20 feet each, on pile bents. The bridge is 13 feet above water. Flatted cedar was used for stringers and hemlock plank used for flooring. The approaches are log fill, well covered with clay.

The Beaver Creek bridge, on Lot 10, Con. 1, Wells, was also renewed. This bridge is 36 feet long and has two spans of 18 feet. The floor consists of hemlock plank on cedar stringers supported by pile bents. The end bents are double rows of piles. The approaches are timber filled and covered with clay.

Manitoulin Island.—During the heavy storm of March, 1913, the ice pounded the timber approach to the Indian Point swing bridge to pieces. It was decided to make permanent repairs. The remains of the old cribs were removed and a solid stone fill built from the shore line to the bridge, a distance of about 100 feet. The fill is from 4 to 18 feet in height, and is 18 feet wide on top. The cost of the work was $1,036.

Sudbury District.—In the Sudbury district the dams at the outlet of Opickinimica Lake, in the Shining Tree section, were repaired at a cost of $653.69.

A bridge at the Stobie Mine on the Blezard Valley road was renewed in steel and concrete at an expense of $839.

Sturgeon Falls District.—Deer Creek bridge, in the Sturgeon Falls District, was repaired at a cost of $275.

Temiskaming District.—Two bridges were renewed on the Savard-Chamberlain Townline at a cost of $447.

In the Township of Armstrong $403 was spent in renewing two bridges destroyed by fire.

In the Pocupine district a new bridge was built over the Adie Creek at a cost of $226.

During the log-driving season watchmen were stationed at the bridges over La Blanche River in the Temiskaming district. Men were stationed at Short's, Marter, Tomstown, Hilliardton, Pearsons and Judge bridges. The cost of retaining these watchmen during the driving season was $1,388.

Renfrew County.—In Renfrew County the Latchford bridge floor was repaired at a cost of $48.

The Carson Lake Road bridge was rebuilt at a cost of $240.

Seventy-six dollars were expended on the Jewellville bridge.

The pile abutments of the Calabogie bridge were repaired at a cost of $80.

Two bridges on the Ferguson Lake road were renewed at a cost of $224.

Hastings County.—In the County of Hastings the McGeary Creek bridge was renewed at a cost of $236, and the Malcolm Creek bridge was rebuilt at a cost of $207.

Victoria County.—In the County of Victoria a new concrete floor was placed on the Kinmount bridge at a cost of $168.

Britton's bridge, in Verulam, was rebuilt at a cost of $200.

Muskoka District.—In the Muskoka district a new timber floor was placed on the High Bridge at the Huntsville Lock and the timber approaches overhauled and repaired. The total cost of work and material was $425.

The Water Mill bridge on the Muskoka road was repaired at a cost of $100.

Nipissing District.—The La Vause Creek bridge, in the Township of Chisholm, Nipissing District, was rebuilt at a cost of $116.

PAINTING STEEL BRIDGES.

During the late spring and summer months, from April 24th until September 30th, a small gang of men in charge of an experienced painter was engaged in carefully cleaning and painting the following steel bridges which were constructed by the Department:

Spanish River bridge at Webbwood.
Spanish River bridge at Espanola.
Spanish River bridge at Nairn.
Spanish River bridge at Massey.
Iron bridge over the Mississauga River.
Mississauga River bridge at Dean Lake.
Thessalon River bridge at Thessalon.
Goulais River bridge.
Dausey bridge at Blind River.
Larchwood bridge over Vermillion River.
Veuve River bridge at Verner.
Hoodstown bridge over Big East River.
Housey's Rapids bridge, Ryde Township.

At each of the above bridges the programme followed was to first carefully go over the entire structure with a steel brush and scrapers to remove, as far as possible, all old paint and rust. The bare steel was then given two coats of specially prepared paint, which was well brushed in. Attention was given to weather conditions, and painting was only done on dry days when the coat was exposed to the most favorable conditions for good drying.

MUSKOKA LAKES LEVELS.

The precise levelling party of the Georgian Bay Ship Canal Survey located a Bench Mark Number DCC XII on the rock at Dyments Wharf, a few hundred feet north-west from the end of the Grand Trunk Railway, Muskoka Wharf. The adjusted elevation of the Bench Mark is 746.32 feet above the mean sea level established at New York by the United States Coast and Geodetic Survey, and using that elevation of the Bench Mark careful watel level transfers were made to Bench Marks located by this Department at Bala Park, Bala, Rockliffe Point and Port Carling. Careful levels were also run from Georgian Bay Precise Bench Mark number DCC IV at Bracebridge, to a Bench Mark at Bracebridge Wharf. A gauge-reading sea level datum was placed on the Canadian Pacific Railway dock at Bala, and during the winter other gauges reading the same datum will be placed at Gravenhurst, Bracebridge and Port Carling. The readings of the various gauges will then give an accurate determination of the relation of the water levels at the different points.

LOCKMASTERS' RETURNS.

The following are the lockmasters' returns of lockages during the year 1913:—
Port Carling lock: 4,687 steamers, 588 small boats, 454 scows, 67 rafts or cribs of timber.
Magnetawan lock: 800 steamers, 87 small boats, 292 scows, 67 rafts.
Mary's and Fairy Lakes lock: 555 steamers, 507 small boats, 133 scows, 38 rafts.

LONDON HOSPITAL FOR INSANE—SEWAGE PUMP.

The operation of the London Hospital sewage disposal farm is maintained by pumping all sewage from a large intercepting tank located at the Buildings out to the trenches situated 1,530 ft. west of the pump. When the plant was installed a
3 P.W.

number of years ago, a steam driven centrifugal pump was provided, and that set worked satisfactorily, with minor repairs, until a short time ago when, due to excessive wear, the pump was frequently out of commission. A small four inch motor driven Turbine pump with an enclosed type of impeller had been installed, but had never properly handled the liquid in the large volumes required during a very short space of time. Trouble was also experienced with the small openings in the pump becoming obstructed. It was decided to instal a six inch motor driven centrifugal pump with an open type of impeller, and after a careful examination of existing types specifications were prepared by this office. Upon calling for tenders and considering same, the contract was let to the Canada Foundry Company for a six inch motor driven Northey Centrifugal Pump, with a heavy bronze open type impeller. The shaft was equipped with a pulley having a face of 12 inches and a diameter of 10 inches to provide means of operating the pump by steam thrashing engine in case of interruption of electric energy. No outboard bearing was provided on the pump, as such extension of the shaft in the old pump had been found to be a serious defect leading to delayed operation, due to foreign material clogging around the shaft. A heavy collar and thrust bearings were provided to take up the unbalanced running conditions. During December, 1912, the pump was put in commission and at once performed its work so well that great satisfaction was expressed in having such an efficient machine to do the work. During the operation to date no delays have been occasioned due to any obstruction in the pump or to mechanical defects, and each and every time the power has been turned on the pump has never failed to discharge its rated capacity of 700 Imperial gallons per minute.

Mimico Hospital for Insane—Additional Fire Protection.

A new brick pumphouse 20 ft. long and 17 ft. 8 in. wide in inside dimensions, and located immediately south-east of the steam pumphouse at the lake shore, was constructed to house all electrical pumping equipment for fire and domestic water supply at the Mimico Hospital.

On May 5th, 1913, the fire pump was put in operation, and adjustments made. Three days later a test of the service was made, and three splendid fire streams having 95 lbs. pressure per sq. in. at the open hydrants were provided through three nozzles of one inch, one and one-eighth inch and one and one-quarter inch diameter respectively.

The pumping equipment is composed of a direct connected motor driven Mather and Platt No. 4, two stage Turbine pump, capable of discharging 800 Imperial gallons per minute against a pressure of 130 lbs. per sq. in. Power is supplied by a 100 horse-power motor taking 2,200 volt current from the supply line of the Hydro-Electric Power Commission.

A new 8 inch cast iron pipe fire main was laid from the pump to a point a short distance south-west of Cottage 5, where a 6 inch main is connected and forms a loop around the various buildings comprising the Institution. Toward the Superintendent's residence a 4. inch pipe was laid to a hydrant within a short distance of the house, and a 6 inch pipe was placed and connected to hydrants east and west of the Amusement Hall for the better protection of that building. To adequately protect the barn and the other buildings which it is proposed to erect near by, a 6 inch main was run and hydrants provided.

The 6 inch main which was laid around the central portion of the institution has hydrants placed close to the sidewalk at convenient intervals, so that 100 feet of hose will be all that is required to each nozzle at any fire.

Into each of the Cottages, the Administration Building, the Amusement Hall, and the Kitchen wing, a four inch cast iron pipe is run from the fire main, and one or more two inch valves and lengths of fire hose provided on each floor of the buildings.

All work on the installation was carried out in a creditable manner by the staff at the Institution following plans prepared by this office.

During the year a contract for the supply of light and power to the Mimico Institution was entered into with the Hydro-Electric Power Commission. Plans for the switchboards, location of transformers, etc., were prepared, and tenders called for by the Commission, the final approval of such being obtained from the Department.

EXTENSION OF RAILWAYS.

During the year 1913, 748.82 miles of railway were completed and opened to traffic in the Province of Ontario, bringing the mileage of railway in operation in the Province up to a total of 10,788.04. There is now under construction and rapidly nearing completion 190.78 miles of main line.

Algoma Eastern Railway.—During the year this line was completed from mileage 66 at Whitefish to Little Current, a distance of 19.50 miles, making a total mileage of 85½.

Canadian Pacific Railway.—The new line from Glen Tay to Agincourt by the Lake Shore route consisting of 182.6 miles of main line was completed during the year, but will not be opened to traffic before mid-summer.

Canadian Northern Railway.—On the Ottawa-Toronto line 36 miles of track were laid between Ottawa and Sydenham. On the Ottawa-Sudbury line 145 miles of track were laid, and on the Sudbury-Port Arthur line 403 miles of track were laid.

Temiskaming and Northern Ontario Railway.—Seven and one-quarter miles of track were laid between Porcupine Junction and Iroquois Falls. This system now embraces 323 miles of main and branch lines.

REVISED STATEMENT OF RAILWAY MILEAGE IN ONTARIO TO DECEMBER 31ST, 1918.

No.	Name of Railway	Terminal Points		Completed prior to Confederation.	Completed since Confederation.	At present under construction.	Total length completed of each railway or system of railways in miles.
		From	To	Length in miles.	Length in miles.	Length in miles.	Length in miles.
1	**Grand Trunk Railway, Main Line**	East Prov. Bound	Point Edward	457			
2	do Buffalo and Lake Huron Branch	Fort Erie	Goderich	158			
3	do London Branch	St. Mary's	London	23			
4	do Galt and Doon Branch	Galt	Berlin	7			
5	do Waterloo Junction Railway	Waterloo	Elmira		4.5		
6	do Toronto and Nipissing Branch	Toronto	Coboconk		10.25		
7	do Midland Railway, Main Line	Port Hope	Midland	65	88		
8	do Peterboro' Branch	Millbrook	Lakefield	13	54.53		
9	do Lake Simcoe Junction	Stouffville	Jackson's Point		9		
10	do Whitby, Port Perry and Lindsay	Whitby	Lindsay		26.5		
11	do Victoria Railway	Lindsay	Haliburton		46		
12	do Grand Junction Railway	Belleville	Peterborough		55.81		
13	do Belleville and North Hastings	Madoc Junction	Eldorado		64.65		
14	do Toronto and Ottawa	Madoc	Bridgewater		22		
15	do Manilla Link	Wick	Manilla		9		
16	do Omemee Link	Omemee	Peterborough		6.5		
17	do Port Dover and Lake Huron	Port Dover	Tavistock		14		
18	do South Norfolk Railway	Simcoe	Port Rowan		55.68		
19	do Chemong Branch	Peterborough	Chemong Lake		17		
20	do Stratford and Huron	Stratford Junction	Wiarton		9		
21	do Owen Sound Extension	Parkhead Junction	Owen Sound		106.27		
22	do Georgian Bay and Wellington	Palmerston	Durham		12.40		
23	do Northern Railway, Collingwod Line	Toronto	Meaford	94	26		
24	do Muskoka Branch	Barrie	Gravenhurst		21		
25	do Hamilton and Northern, Main Line	Port Dover	Allandale		53		
26	do do Collingwood	Clarksville	Collingwood		135.3		
27	do North Simcoe Junction	Colwell	Penetanguishene		40		
28	do Midland Branch	Wyevale	Tiffin		33.34		
29	do Birch-Tay Branch	Birch	Tay		8.9		
30	do Northern and Pacific Junction Rlwy	Gravenhurst	Nipissing Junction		111.5		
31	do Magnetawan River Railway	Burk's Falls Station	Burk's Falls Wharf		1.01		
32	do Toronto Belt Line Rly., East Section	Don Station, G.T.R	Junc. Northern Ry		8.50		
33	do Western Section	W. Toronto, on G.T.R	Swansea		4.33		

REVISED STATEMENT.—Continued.

No.	Name of Railway.	Terminal Points. From	Terminal Points. To	Completed prior to Confederation. Length in miles.	Completed since Confederation. Length in miles.	At present under construction. Length in miles.	Total length completed of each railway or system of railways in miles.
34	Grand Trunk Railway	East Prov. Bound	Ottawa		68.08		
35	do Ottawa, Arnprior & Parry So'nd Ry.	Ottawa	...		212.60		
36	do Parry Sound Colonization Ry	Scotia Junction	...		51.20		
37	do Central Counties Railway	Glen Robertson	Mury		21		
38	do do	South Indian	Rockland		17		
39	do Railway { Great Western Div. Main Line	Niagara Falls	Windsor	229			
40	do Toronto and Hamilton Branch	Toronto	Hamilton	39.5	145		
41	do Loop Line Division	Glencoe	Gale		20.6		
42	do Kingscourt and Glencoe Link	Kingscourt Junction	Gale	51			
43	do Sarnia Branch	Komoka	Sarnia	7			
44	do Petroles Branch	Wyoming	Pas	8			
45	do Brantford Branch	Harrisburg	Brantford		35.88		
46	do Brantford and	Brantford	Mg		4.12		
47	do Ingen to Brantford	Lynden	Sn	27	82		
48	do Wellington, Grey and Bruce	Harrisburg	Hale		68		
49	do do S. Extension	Wie Park Junction.	Wn		69.75		
50	do G. W. Div., London, Huron & Bruce.	Port Colborne	Port Dalhousie.	25	1,150		3,079.7
51	do Welland Railway	Gwa	Wt Kr old	57	66.40		
52	Canadian Pacific Railway Main Line	Gsa	East Prov. Bound		180.25		
53	do do		alit Ste. Mrie				
54	do gna Branch	Sudbury	Wn Bce	46			
55	do Brockville and Gwa Railway	nlkville					
56	do St. Lawrence and Ottawa Railway	Prescott	Ottawa	59.5	281.25		
57	do and dire Branch	Wt Toronto	St Prov. Bound	12	5		
58	do Onlario and Ilo Railway	Leaside Junction	Wto		119.13		
59	do Don raRch	Toronto			2.60		
60	do Edit aMoy Railway, Main Line	Islington	Mo		61		
61	do Mimico Branch	Streetsville Junction	Wn &		15		
62	do Mo l aRh	Campbellville	Gbe		122		
63	do Guelph Branch	Toronto	Sh		72		
64	do rBnto Grey & Bruce, Main Line.	Orangeville	Wn Snd		4.75		
65	do Teeswater Branch do Toronto Grey & Br ce, Wingham Branch	Glen Annan	Wingham				

REVISED STATEMENT—Continued.

No.	Name of Railway.	Terminal Points. From	Terminal Points. To	Completed prior to Confederation. Length in miles.	Completed since Confederation. Length in miles.	At present under construction. Length in miles.	Total length completed of each railway or system in miles.
66	C.P.R. West Ontario Pacific Railway	Woodstock	London		26		
67	do Detroit Extension	Lodon	Mor		112.50		
68	do Atlantic and North-West Railway	Renfrew	Rgle		19.25		
69	do Lindsay, Bobcaygeon and Pontypool Ry	Burketon	Bobcaygeon		38.79		
70	do Sudbury and Kleinburg Branch	Bolton	Romford Junction		226.20		
71	do South Ontario Pacific Railway	I ah u rán	Hamilton		16.3		
72	do Guelph and Goderich Railway	Guelph	Goderich		88		
73	do Lisel Branch	Lisel	Listowel		16.10		
74	do Walkerton, Hw Railway	Sul Sion	Walkerton		37.70		
75	do Hg, Lake Erie & Pacific	Saugeen Sion	Embro		46.11		
76	do St. Mary's & Wrn Ontario Ry.	Port Burwell	St Mary's		15.90		
77	do Georgian Bay & Seaboard Railway	Embro Ml	Bethany		90.86		
78	do Campbellford, Lake Ontario and Western Rway	Port					
79	Mhigan Ce tral Railway, formerly Canada Southern, Main Line	Glen Tay Jnction	Asurt		182.60		3,170.19
80	Michigan Caral Railway, St. Clair B wch	Mor Sion	Niagara Falls		226.80		
81	do r Marg Branch	St. Clair	Courtright		62.2		
82	do Oil Springs Branch	Amherstburg rán	Essex Centre		15.7		
83	do Petrolea Branch	Oil City u rán	Eddy's		5.2		
84	do Inn & St. Clair Branch	Petrolea Junction	Petrolea		4.9		
85	do Port Erie Branch	Comber	Leamington		15.9		
86	do aghrs Branch	Welland Sion	Port Erie		17.4		
87	Cobourg, Peterboro' & M'mors Ry., M'mors Line	Port Erie	Niagara	30			378.10
88	Kingston & Pembroke Railway	Oorg	Harwood	14.5	103		14.50
89	Lake Erie and Detroit River Railway	Kingston	Renfrew		126.85		103
90	do Erie and Huron Railway	Walkerville	St. Tmas		70.47		
91	Lodon & Port Stanley Railway	Rondeau	Snia				222.32
92	Lodon Northern Railway, formerly Port, Amur, Ihth and Wrn Railway and Ontario & Rainy River Railway, Main Line	London	Port Stanley	25	287		
93	do Ihth Extension	Port Arthur	West Prov. Bound		66.54		
94	do James Bay Railway	Stanley Junction	Gun Flint Lake		3.7		
95	do Toronto & Sudbury Line	Canada Atlantic Ry.	Parry Harbor		265		
96		Toronto	uh.				

REVISED STATEMENT—Concluded.

No.	Name of Railway.	Terminal Points. From	Terminal Points. To	Completed prior to Confederation. Length in miles.	Completed since Confederation. Length in miles.	At present under construction. Length in miles.	Total length completed of each railway or system in miles.
96	Canadian Northern Ontario Key Branch	Key Junction	Key Harbor		6.2		
97	do Hinton Branch	Sudbury Junction	Sellwood Junction		27.8		
98	do Garson Branch	Garson Junction	Garson Mine		3.7		
99	do Orillia Branch	Orillia J'nction	Atherly Junction		7.4		
100	do Ottawa, Hawkesbury	Ottawa	Hawkesbury		58		
101	do Ottawa-Capreol	Ottawa	Capreol		185.75	118.94	
102	do Port Arthur, Sudbury	Ruel	Port Arthur		545.00		
103	do Toronto-Ottawa	Toronto	Ottawa		219.61		
104	do Central Ontario Railway	Trenton, on G.T.R.	Maynooth		110.00	20.00	
105	do Bay of Quinte Railway	Deseronto	Bannockburn		78.46		
106	do do	Yarker	Sydenham		11.37		
107	do do	Deseronto	Grand Trunk Ry.		3.50		
108	do Irondale, Bancroft and Ottawa Ry	Kinmount	Bancroft		45.00		2,011.03
109	Brockville, Westport and Sault Ste. Marie	Brockville	Westport		45.00		
110	do Prince Edard City Railway	Pton	Trenton and G.T.R.		32.44		
111	do Ontario & Belmont & Northern Ry	Central Ontario Ry.	Belmont Me		9.57		
112	Toronto, Hamilton and Buffalo Railway	Waterford	Brantford		18		
113	do do	Brantford	Welland		62.5		80.50
114	Ottawa and New York Railway	Cars	Cornwall		55.00		55
115	Pembroke Southern Railway	Pembroke	Golden Lake		21.50		21.50
116	Algoma Central and Hudson Bay Railway	alt Ste. Marie	Hearst		245.01	50.22	
117	do Moolen Branch	Michipicoten Harbor	Min Line		22.10	0.62	267.11
118	do Edsrn Railway	Sudbury	Little Current		85.50		85.50
119	dis Mes and lda Railway	Bruce Mines	Rock Lak.		17		17
120	Temiskaming and Northern Ontario Railway	North Bay	Cochrane		252		
121	do do Branch Lines				71.29		323.29
122	Huntsville and Lake of Bays Railway	Peninsula Lake	Lake of Bays		1.5		1.5
123	National Transcontinental Railway	East Prov. Bound	West Pro'v. Bound		758		758
124	Grand Trunk Pacific Ry., Lake Superior Branch	Fort William	Lake Superior Junc.		188.77		188.77
125	Thessalon, Northern Ontario Railway	Thessalon Junction	Thessalon		1.93		1.93
126	Essex Terminal Railway	Walkerville	M.C. Yard		9.10	1.00	9.10
				1,447.5	9,340.54	190.78	10,781.04

STATEMENT OF ELECTRIC RAILWAY MILEAGE IN ONTARIO

Number.	Name of Company.	Length of line.		Number of power houses.		Remarks.
		Completed.	Under construction.	Steam power.	Water power.	
1	Berlin and Waterloo...........8.02	......	......	1	......	Power purchased from Berlin Central Heating Co.
	Leased Line, Berlin and Bridgeport..................2.50	5.52				
2	Brantford Street....................	8.95	......	1	......	Power supplied by the Cataract Power Co.
3	Brantford and Hamilton Electric Ry.	23.00	......	......	......	" "
4	Chatham, Wallaceburg and Lake Erie	40.0	......	......	......	Power, Chatham Gas Co.
5	Cornwall Street....................	6.5	......	1	1	
6	Grand Valley	20.76	......	1	......	Power purchased from Cataract Power Co., Decew Falls.
7	Guelph Radial	6.	......	1	......	
8	Galt, Preston and Hespeler.....15.67 Leased Line, Preston to Berlin 10.75	26.42	......	1	......	Hydro-Electric Power.
9	Hamilton Street....................	22.0	10.	......	......	Power, Cataract Power Co.
10	Hamilton and Dundas	7.00	......	......	......	Power, Cataract Power Co.
11	Hamilton Radial	22.00	......	1	......	" "
12	Hamilton, Grimsby and Beamsville..	23.00	......	1	......	" "
13	International Transit Co............	3.3	......	......	......	Sault Ste. Marie rent h. p. from Lake Superior.
14	Kingston, Portsmouth and Cataraqui.	8.	......	1	......	
15	London and Lake Erie Railway and Transportation Co.................	29.	......	......	......	Hydro-Electric Power.
16	London Street	34.97	......	1	......	Hydro and Steam.
17	Mount McKay and Kakabeka Falls..	4.0	......	......	......	
18	Niagara Falls Park and River......	11.85	..	......	1	Subject to the control of Niagara Falls Park Commissioners.
19	Niagara, St. Catharines and Toronto.	82.78	7.	......	......	
20	Niagara Falls, Wesley Park & Clifton	4.5	......	......	......	
21	Nipissing Central	11.0	......	......	......	The Northern Ontario Power Co.
22	Ottawa City Passenger	24.67	......	......	1	
23	Oshawa Railway......	8.3	......	......	......	
24	Port Arthur and Fort William	28.0	......	......	1	Power, Kaministikwia Power Co.
25	Peterboro Radial	6.10	......	......	2	Peterborough Light and Power Co.
26	Port Dalhousie, St. Catharines and Thorold	8.17	......	......	......	
27	Sarnia Street......................	9.25	......	......	......	Sarnia Gas and Electric Light Co.
28	Sandwich, Windsor and Amherstburg	29.27	......	1	......	Canadian Salt Co.
29	St. Thomas Street	7.5	......	......	......	Hydro-Electric Power,
30	Toronto and York Radial, Toronto, Metropolitan Branch	59.44	......	2	......	
	Toronto and Mimico.................	11.11	......	......	......	Power hired.
	Toronto and Scarborough	11.45	......	......	......	Power hired.
31	Toronto Civic Car Lines............	8.42	......	......	......	Hydro-Electric Power
32	Toronto Suburban	9.81	......	1.	......	Power hired.
33	Toronto Street.....................	132.62	......	......	......	The Toronto Power Co. Mileage includes turn-outs and terminals.

STATEMENT OF ELECTRIC RAILWAY MILEAGE IN ONTARIO—Continued.

Number.	Name of Company.	Length of line.		Number of power houses		Remarks.
		Completed.	Under construction.	Steam power.	Water power.	
34	Windsor and Tecumseh Electric Ry.	10.	......	......	......	Operated by the Sandwich, Windsor and Amherstburg Ry.
35	West Shore Electric..................	....	30.	......	......	Huron and Bruce Counties.
36	Woodstock, Thames Val. and Ingersoll	11.5	......	1	......	Power, Cataract Power Co., Decew Falls.
37	Windsor, Essex and Lake Shore Ry..	40.0	......	1	......	
	Total mileage.	761.16	47.00	......	......	

DRAINAGE WORKS.

ALGOMA DISTRICT DRAINAGE.

McDonald Township Drain, Sections 20 and 21.—In order to properly drain a portion of the main road, a ditch 2,178 feet long was opened up to Echo Bay.

The outlet is constructed eight feet wide and one and one-half feet deep. Along the side of the road for 720 feet, a side ditch four feet wide and one and one-half feet deep was excavated. All sections of the drain are working satisfactorily and giving relief from the former flooded condition of the road.

Carter Creek, Johnson Township.—Carter Creek which flows across lots 3 and 4 in the 3rd and 4th concessions of Johnson Township was cleaned out, deepened, straightened, widened and all obstructions to the rapid flow of the water removed. The channel so constructed now provides a splendid outlet for a large volume of water, which runs off an extensive area where it has heretofore been standing and damaging the roads.

The work covers a distance of 1½ miles and now gives a clear run for the water, from the 4th concession to the large pond known as, Suddaby's Mill Pond. All bush one rod on each side of the centre line of the creek was cleared away to enable the work to proceed.

Clearing Black Creek, Matchedash Township.—A rocky chute on lot 6, in Concession 7 was holding the water back upon low lying land and drowning out the side road between lots 6 and 7 during certain seasons of the year. Due to the dry weather this summer the work of blasting and clearing away the rock for a depth of three feet and also the excavating and opening up of the old channel of the creek was performed at great advantage, there being practically no water to contend with. The entire creek for a distance of about three-quarters of a mile was cleaned out, widened and deepened and left in such shape that it will carry all the water flowing to it.

NIPISSING DISTRICT DRAINAGE.

In the District of Nipissing the following drains were opened up by local foremen acting under the direction of J. A. Depencier, the District Road Inspector:

136 rods of ditching on a creek on Lots 24 and 25, Concession 10, Ferris.
135   "   "   "   "   "   16 and 17, Concession 8, Ferris.
 44   "   "   "   "   "   13 and 14, Concession 2, Ferris.
 61   "   "   "   "   "   21, Concession 4, Ferris.
 66   "   "   "   "   "   23, Concession 10, Ferris.
190   "   "   "   "   "   11, 12 and 13, Concession 11. Ferris.
165 feet rock cut at the Wassa Dam in Chisholm.

The full amount of the appropriation of $1,500 was expended on this work.

PARRY SOUND DISTRICT DRAINAGE.

In the Parry Sound District a number of rock cuts were made to relieve flooded roads and lands. The works are located as follows:

A rock-cut 34 ft. long on Lot 34, 13th Con. of Machar.

A rock-cut 36 ft. long on Lot 11, Con. 7, Shawanaga.

A tile drain 362 ft. long and 42 rods of open drain was constructed on Lot 15, Con. 9, McMurrich.

An open drain 34 rods long, from two to four feet deep, and six feet wide was constructed at Lots 1 and 2, in Burton Township.

STURGEON FALLS DRAINAGE.

In the 5th Concession of McPherson a rock-cut 80 ft. long, 4 ft. deep and 4 ft. wide was blasted out, and 400 rods of creek opened up with a mean width of 8 ft. and a depth of 4 ft. $600 was expended on this work.

In the 6th Concession of McPherson 400 rods of creek was opened up to a mean width of 4 ft., with a depth of 3 ft. $400 was expended on the work.

These works were done under the supervision of J. C. Leblanc, District Road Inspector, by local foremen.

MANITOULIN DRAINAGE.

Three hundred dollars were expended by Thomas Fawcett in opening up a drain along the Campbell-Carnarvon Townline and across the 16th Concession of Campbell.

$116.33 was expended by Wilfred Brown in opening up a drain 125 rods long on Lot 9 in the 10th Con. of Sandfield.

$100 was expended by F. Lowrie in opening up a drain on Lots 9 and 10 in the 7th and 8th Concession of Mills.

TEMISKAMING DRAINAGE.

$2,500 was expended in the Temiskaming District continuing drains started in 1912 in the Townships of Brethour, Evanturel, Harley and Hilliard.

In Brethour 225 rods of ditch 6 ft. wide and 3 ft. deep were opened up and the right of way cleared for a further distance of 80 rods.

In Evanturel 351 rods of a flat creek bed were opened.

In Harley 240 rods of ditch 6 ft. wide and 3 ft. deep were opened up.

In Hilliard 400 rods of ditch 9 ft. wide and 3 ft. deep were dug, also 158 rods 4 ft. wide and 2½ ft. deep were opened up and a road culvert constructed.

SUDBURY DRAINAGE.

$450 was expended by Overseer Daniel Forget in opening up a drain from the west side of Lot 11, Con. 3, Capreol, across Lots 11, 10 and 9, to a creek on Lot 9, Concession 3.

$149 was expended by Louis Giroux opening up a drain on Lots 8-9-10 in the 3rd Concession of Balfour.

$841 was expended by Overseer A. Campeau in opening up a drain through Lots 4, 5, 6 and 7 in the 3rd Concession, and thence to Garson Creek in the 2nd Concession of Capreol.

MARA TOWNSHIP, ONTARIO COUNTY DRAINAGE.

Corrigan Drain.—The work commenced on Lot 15 in the 10th Concession of Mara Township and crosses Lots 16 and 17, emptying into a municipal drain on Lot 18. A general depth of from three to four feet was maintained over the entire length of the work, with a bottom width of two and one-half to three feet; and side slopes to one and one-quarter to one. Good fall was obtained over the entire distance of three-quarters of a mile, and the ditch is capable of handling a very large volume of water. For the great part of the distance the excavating consisted of hard-pan, boulders and heavy clay, which in several instances required the use of dynamite. The completion of the drain has been of great benefit to the roads in the locality, as the lowering of the water in the side ditches has been followed by the hardening of the road surface.

Edwards Drain.—On the north half of Lot 16 in the 8th Concession of Mara Township this work begins and continues across Lot 17 to the 8th Concession Line which it follows to the Canadian Pacific Railway ditch. This year the upper end of the work, for a distance of half a mile on Lots 16 and 17, was completed to a general depth of from one and one-half to four feet, and with well battered side slopes. Although the work is through a naturally flat section of country a sufficient grade was obtained to give velocity to the water and carry it away from the roads.

Mahoney Drain.—Work was commenced on south half of Lot 27 in the 11th Concession of Mara Township and continues across the corner of Lot 26 and thence to Lot 25, where it turns north into the 12th Concession. On the site of this drain the original ditch had become gradually filled up so that a deeper, wider and straighter channel was required. The new drain is of an average depth of from two and one-half to five feet, with side slopes of about one horizontal to one vertical, and the general width of the bottom is about three feet. A good outlet has been furnished for all the water and any flooding of roads, etc., is now avoided.

McGrath's Drain.—This drain starts on Lot 19 in the 12th Concession of Mara Township, and runs across Lot 20 to 21 where it enters an old channel and continues a short distance to Sucker Creek. The general depth of the drain is two feet and the bottom width is two and one-half feet. Upon the completion of the work a splendid outlet for the water which formerly flooded lands and roads was obtained.

DRAINAGE AID.

Big Marsh Drainage, Pelee Island.—This drainage scheme, the ditches and pumps of which were completed and installed some thirty years ago, had through time become gradually clogged and obstructed with sediment, drift and muck. In many places the channels were almost choked with vegetation, so that the drainage pumps were unable to draw the water from the well freely. The pumps themselves were obsolete, and were incapable of starting quickly in an emergency.

It was decided to have a complete examination and report on the whole drainage scheme made, and upon presentation the report was embodied in By-law No. 199 of the Township of Pelee. That By-law was finally passed and adopted

June 27th, 1908. It called for an expenditure of $41,954.00; but on reference the drainage referee reduced the work and the new estimate of $25,271.00, as embodied in By-law No. 214, was adopted. A supplementary By-law, No. 215, provided a further sum of $1,681, bringing the total estimated cost to $26,952.00.

All work was carried out under By-law No. 214, which specified 24,535 lineal feet of dredge work, 8,781 lineal feet of team excavating work, amounts to cover repairs and additions to buildings and machinery at the east and west pumphouses, repairs and additions to highway and from bridge also other expenses incidental to the improvement. The total area affected by the work is 7,030 acres.

The entire work was examined by me during August, 1913, and was found to be completed in a very satisfactory manner. On the recommendation of the Department the Legislative grant of $2,000 in aid of Big Marsh Drainage, Pelee Island, was paid to the Treasurer of the Township of Pelee.

Moira Lake Drainage, Huntingdon.—On Lot Number 3 in the 14th Concession of Hungerford Township, Conley's Dam, originally constructed for power purposes, raised the water level in Moira River and Lake approximately five feet, and as a result 1,300 acres of low lying land bordering on the above lake and river were flooded and rendered useless for cultivation.

The Township of Huntingdon on May 13th, 1912, provisionally adopted a By-law No. 32 D. which proposed by an estimated expenditure of $4,259.75 to remove Conley's Dam and also to clear the channel for a width of 50 to 100 feet of all boulders and rocky outcrops.

In addition to the above estimate of $4,259.75 to be borne by the Township of Huntingdon the initiating municipality, the Township of Rawdon was assessed for $169.45 and the Township of Hungerford for $223.10.

During September I examined the work and found it to be completed in a satisfactory manner. On the recommendation of the Department the grant of $1,000 voted at the last Session of the Legislature was paid to the Township of Huntingdon, the initiating municipality.

McDonald Robertson Drain, Lochiel.—This work, in the First and Second Concessions of Lochiel Township, was undertaken with a view to draining and thus improving for cultivation 3,364½ acres in the Township of Lochiel, and 562½ acres in the Township of Lancaster, at an estimated cost of $9,984.82, of which $902.21 was assessed against lands in the Township of Lancaster and $9,082.61 against lands in Lochiel Township.

The system is divided into three parts, namely, the main drain, the A. D. McDonald Branch and the J. J. McDonald Branch.

The main drain commences on the line between the south halves of Lots 6 and 7 in the First Concession of Lochiel, and runs north-westerly 27,400 feet to the boundary between the Gore of Lochiel and the Township of East Hawkesbury.

The J. J. McDonald Branch begins at the boundary road between the Township of Lancaster and Lochiel, about the centre of the west half of Lot 5 in the first concession of Lochiel, and runs easterly and northerly 2,992 feet to join the main drain.

The A. D. McDonald Branch starts about the line between the east and west halves of Lot No. 6 in the First Concession of Lochiel and runs easterly and southerly to a junction with the main drain about on line of the east and west halves of Lot 5 in the First Concession of Lochiel.

A petition for a drain in the Second Concession of Lochiel was combined with the above mentioned three drains. It is known as the Glen Robertson Branch, and begins at the west side of road between Lots 7 and 8 in the First Concession. From that point the course is easterly and northerly 13,975 feet to where it joins the main drain on Lot 1 of the Second Concession gore, Lochiel.

All of the above scheme was embodied in by-law No. 78 of the Township of Lochiel.

This work was examined by me during September, 1913, and was found to be completed in a satisfactory manner. On the recommendation of the Department the grant of $1,500 voted at last Session of the Legislature was paid to the Treasurer of the Township of Lochiel, the initiating municipality.

WHITEBREAD PUMPING SCHEME.

This work, comprises the cutting of drains and building embankments and installing pumping machinery, to reclaim about 1,000 acres of marsh land in the north part of the township of Dover. The estimated cost of the complete scheme was $17,640. The work was examined in September last. The drains and embankment were complete, the pumping machinery installed, but had not up to that time been operated.

The grant of $1,000 made in aid of this work was paid to the Township of Dover.

PULSE CREEK DRAIN.

The Pulse Creek drain in the Township of Sarnia consists of a dredge cut following Pulse Creek from Lot 5 at the London Road north-east to Perche Creek, near the Grand Trunk Railway, a distance of about four miles. The work was examined in September, 1913, and being found completed in a workmanlike manner, the grant of $1,500 made in aid of this work was paid to the Township of Sarnia.

I have the Honor to be, Sir,

Your obedient servant,

A. J. HALFORD,

· *Engineer Public Works.*

To the Honourable the Minister of Public Works.

SIR,—I have the honour to submit a report of the work of building and improving Colonization Roads throughout the Province, as carried on by your direction under the supervision of the Colonization Roads Branch, Department of Public Works, in the year 1913.

In this report the usual classification of roads has been maintained, that is to say:—

(1) Sudbury-Soo Trunk Road.
(2) New Trunk Roads.
(3) Colonization Roads (ordinary).
(4) Colonization Roads (Municipal By-law).

And the territory over which the operations extend is subdivided into "North," "West," "East" and "Temiskaming" Divisions, and the details of work and cost thereof in each case are set forth in the tabulated schedule attached hereto.

In again referring to the work of the construction of Colonization Roads, I am pleased to say that much of the improvement anticipated in our report of 1912 has been realized, all works which were undertaken have been concluded and the accounts therefor closed out well within the fiscal year. In this respect the past season has been perhaps one of the most successful in the history of the Department.

The weather was good for outdoor work, there were little or no interruptions or delays in this respect, and no difficulty was experienced in securing plenty of labor with which to carry on the works.

An analysis of the details of the work performed during the season, as shown on the accompanying schedule, will disclose the fact that the cost per mile was exceptionally reasonable, and that while the maximum of $415.00 per mile was reached in the Northern Divisions it was apportionately overbalanced by a minimum cost of $252.00 per mile in the eastern and western divisions.

The higher cost of work in the Northern and newer areas of the Province is accounted for by the fact that on a greater percentage of the work in that Section large expenditures have to be made to provide maintenance, road machinery, tools, etc., whereas in the older settled parts these are, to a great extent, supplied free of cost by the local municipalities or individual residents, hence the overhead cost of the work is reduced accordingly.

Wages for labor, as well, are considerably higher in the northern areas than in the eastern or western, and the work in the former being chiefly the opening up of new roads while that in the latter is more the improving of old, existing roads; so that the mileage or extent of work done in the north for the expenditure per mile, necessarily appears less than in the older settlements.

1. *Sudbury-Soo Trunk Road.*

Our operations on this main highway during the year were localized to the eastern portion and consisted of the construction of the section from Nairn Centre to Victoria Mines, nearly all of which was new road. Repairs were also made to various other sections extending over a distance of about 13 miles. Two road camps were established and maintained on this job throughout the season and the work done by each was quite satisfactory.

Altogether there were ten miles of new road built, and thirteen miles of old road re-constructed at a cost of $29,184.16.

2. *Trunk Roads.*

This classification of roads includes many main and leading highways which are being built or extended to connect numerous isolated settlements with their nearest commercial centres, as well as to open a line for traffic from one town or village to another, with results that are highly beneficial to the residents. These Trunk Roads, however, being mostly new roads and having to bear traffic which concentrates from the sidelines and running, as they do, through sections from which little or no local resources in the form of road funds are yet available, will require in the near future a generous provision for further improvement and maintenance.

The mileage of Trunk Roads constructed during the season was 13¾ new road and 43¾ miles of old road graded, re-surfaced and otherwise well improved and the total expenditure was $35,164.61.

3. *Colonization Roads (Ordinary).*

In this class are included a great number of new short roads and sidelines in Northern Ontario, as well as the improvements of the roads which have already been built there in recent years, and the re-construction of many miles of old road in the sparsely settled sections of older Ontario. On account of the great variety of roads under this classification it is difficult here to do more than briefly allude to the work done in general terms as being very satisfactory. We have endeavored to introduce and maintain, in every instance, the most modern principles of road organization and the best style of improvement suitable to the local conditions so as to secure work of as permanent a character as possible.

Under the classification of "Ordinary Colonization Roads" there were 148 miles of new road built and 614 miles of old road repaired, and the expenditure thereon was $239,042.25.

The following is a summary of the new and old roads (in miles) which has been built or improved and the cost thereof in the order of the foregoing classification.

—	New Roads.	Old Roads.	Cost.
Sudbury-Soo Trunk Road	10	13	$29,184 16
Trunk Roads	13¾	43¾	35,164 61
North Division	79½	211	102,344 96
West Division	15	77¾	25,835 51
East Division	19¾	273¼	71,196 01
Temiskaming Division	34	51¼	42,665 77
	172	670	$306,391 02

4. *Municipal By-law Roads.*

The By-law system of contributing Government aid towards the construction and improvement of roads has continued to produce good results. The Act has been operative for four years, and its adoption invariably receives the unanimous endorsation of the Municipal Councils who take advantage of it, as well as the favorable support of the many representative men who have become familiar with the administration.

Moreover the introduction of this co-operative system has also, to a great degree, stimulated local interest in the work of road improvement; it also fosters a disposition of self-reliance and encourages the establishing by Township Councils of a more business-like organization for the purpose of carrying on the important work of road-building; and I may say that in nearly every Township in which the system has been tried a great improvement in the road situation has taken place.

The number of Municipalities to which this system has been applied has increased from 35 in 1909 to 115 in 1913, and the indications are that this number will be further increased in 1914.

The following is a summary showing the number of miles of new road and old road built or improved and the expenditure made thereon under the By-law system in 1913.

—	Miles of New Road Built.	Miles of Old Road Improved.	Total Expenditure.	Government Grant.
North Division	20½	185½	$59,607 49	$45,506 10
West Division		77⅞	15,722 57	11,522 07
East Division	3½	341¾	52,512 98	32,044 61
Temiskaming Division	25	8	17,025 28	10,877 72
	49	682⅔	$144,868 82	$99,950 50*

*Includes the sum of $28,929.99 unpaid balances 1912.

In closing I desire to make especial reference to the excellent and exhaustive work performed by Mr. M. P. Doherty, the Accountant of this Branch, to whose efforts are largely due the satisfaction which has been given by the prompt settlement of the great number and variety of road accounts which annually pass through his hands.

A statement in detail of the expenditure made during the year 1913 accompanies this report.

All of which is respectfully submitted.

I have the Honour to be,

Sir,

Your obedient servant,

GEO. W. BENNETT,

Superintendent Colonization Roads.

COLONIZATION ROADS BRANCH

DEPARTMENT OF PUBLIC WORKS
ONTARIO, 1913

TABULATED STATEMENT

SHOWING:

1. Details of work on the Sudbury-Soo Trunk Road.
2. Details of work on the New Trunk Roads.
3. Details of work on the Colonization Roads (Straight grants.)
4. Details of work on the By-laws (Proportionate grants.)
5. Recapitulation of above.

Schedule showing amount of Road Construction under the Colonization

Number.	NAME AND LOCATION OF WORK	NEW ROAD.													
		Cut out and Cleared.		Stumped and Grubbed.		Graded and Shaped.		Surfacing.			Outlet Ditches.			Corduroy	
		Length rods.	Width feet.	Length rods.	Width feet.	Length rods.	Width feet.	Material.	Length rods.	Width feet.	Length rods.	Width feet.	Depth feet.	Length rods.	Width feet.
1	2	3	4	5	6	7	8	9	10	11	12	13	14	15	16
	SUDBURY-SOO TRUNK ROAD														
1	Mileage, 5 to 13 Section														
2	Garden River and Echo Bay Section														
3	Webbwood Espanola Section (repairs)														
4	Nairn-Victoria Mines Section...	320	66	320	66	320	24				330	2	1		
	Total Sudbury-Soo Trunk Rd	320		320		320					330				
	TRUNK ROADS.														
1	Bridgeland Trunk Road: Lot 11, Houghton, to Lot 9, Con. 3, Bridgeland	1,280	40	1,280	24										
2	Lots 2 and 1, Galbraith, and Lot 12, Houghton	640	66	640	40			earth	12	16					
3	Dryden-Richan Trunk Road...													175	16
4	Firstbrook and Barr Trunk Rd	880	60	880	30	880	22	stone	100	16	240	5½	1½	71	16
5	Golden City Trunk Road (balance, 1912)														
6	Kenora and Reddit Trunk Rd. (balance, 1912)														
7	Lee-Valley and Espanola Trunk Road	1,220	45	1,220	45	1,220	24	earth	1,220	24	1,220	2	1	155	16
8	LeRoy Lake and Nicol Trunk Road													12	16
9	Little Current and Manitowaning Trunk Road: Sheguiandah Township, 20th Sideroad, Cons. 2 and 12														
10	Howland and Bidwell Townships	175	50	175	25	200	24	gravel	200	6	25	4	3		
11	Howland, Con. 11, Lots 1 to 11														
12	Mellick and Rice Lake Trunk Road													37	16
13	Night Hawk Lake Trunk Road (balance, 1912)														
14	Sioux-Lookout Trunk Road	175	50	175	18	175	18							56	12
15	South Lorraine Trunk Road...	37	66	37	66									50	16
16	Sudbury-Coniston Trunk Road.													62	16
	Total Trunk Roads ...	4,407		4,407		2,475			1,532		1,465			648	

Roads Branch, Department of Public Works, Ontario, in 1913.

OLD ROAD.

Cleared		Graded and Shaped.		Surfacing.			Outlet Ditches.			Bridges over 16 feet.					Culverts.		Total Miles of Road Built and Improved.	Total Cost of Work.	Number.
													Material.						
Length rods.	Width feet.	Length rods.	Width feet.	Material.	Length rods.	Width feet.	Length rods.	Width feet.	Depth feet.	Number.	Length feet.	Sub-structure	Super-structure.	Number.	Material.				
17	18	19	20	21	22	23	24	25	26	27	28	29	30	31	32	33	34	35
																	$ c.	
......	....	800	24	earth	640	24	1,600	3	2	......	....			1	wood	8.00	....	1
......	....	......	....	gravel	1,120	24	......	..	..	......	....			......	....	3.50	....	2
......	....	400	16	gravel	80	16	......	..	..	4	side	railing	s	......	....	3.00	....	3
2,880	66	2,730	24	gravel	820	16	2,740	2	1½	......	....			1	re-Con.	9.50	29,184 16	4
2,880	....	3,920	....	......	2,160	....	4,340	....	....	4	....			2	....	23.00	$29,184 16	
640	66	40	20	clay	320	9	......	..	..	..	....			2	wood	9.50	2,001 11	1
......	....	......	....	......	......	..	......	..	..	..	....			......	....	2.00	500 68	2
380	20	4,480	18	gravel	4,480	9	4,480	2	1	3 R	....	wood	wd.	12	wood	14.00	5,006 69	3
......	....	......	....	......	......	..	......	..	..	1	23	wood	wd.	15	woo	2.75	2,946 27	4
......	....	......	....	......	......	..	......	..	..	..	....			......	....	....	94 13	5
......	....	......	....	......	......	..	......	..	..	..	....			......	....	....	88 23	6
......	....	......	....	......	......	..	......	..	..	..	....			5	iron	3.81	3,993 06	7
1,920	20	155	24	gravel	834	8	285	3	2	1	50	wood	wd.	8	wood	6.00	6,210 50	8
800	50	275	22	gravel	800	5	......	..	..	2 1	16	wood	wd.	1	stone	2.50	1,006 59	9
1,000	45	510	24	gravel	715	5	45	3	2	1 2	16	stone	wd.	3	wood	5.00	3,454 29	10
......	....	25	28	gravel	275	5	......	..	..	2	....	railings		3	stone	87	499 60	11
50	85	480	18	gravel	860	6	41	3	2	..	....			9	wood	1.50	500 00	12
......	....	......	....	......	......	..	......	..	..	..	....			......	....	....	185 34	13
610	18	350	16	gravel	886	6	350	8	1½	2	28	wood	wd.	8	wood	2.50	1,005 13	14
......	....	1,280	24	earth	90	12	900	2	1	1	....			3	wood	4.00	900 00	15
......	....	372	66	earth	372	24	744	3	2	..	....							16
......	....	......	....	stone	40	24	......	..	..	1	20	concrete	ste'l	}		3.00	8,886 07	
....	....	......	....	H.cut	90	24	......	..	..	1	16	rock	cd'r					
5,350	....	7,947	....	......	8,762	....	6,845	....	....	14	....			74	....	57.43	$85,164 61	

Schedule showing amount of Road Construction under the Colonization

NEW ROAD.

Number	Name and Location of Work	Cut out and Cleared. Length rods	Width feet	Stumped and Grubbed. Length rods	Width feet	Graded and Shaped. Length rods	Width feet	Surfacing. Material	Length rods	Width feet	Outlet Ditches. Length rods	Width feet	Depth feet	Corduroy Length rods	Width feet
1	2	3	4	5	6	7	8	9	10	11	12	13	14	15	16
	NORTH DIVISION.														
1	Aberdeen Road and Bridge. Lot 1, Con. 5					10	20								
2	Aberdeen Road and Bridge, Lots 3-4, Con. 3	20	66	20	80	20	18								
3	Aberdeen Additional Road, West from East Boundary														
4	Allen, 10th Sideroad, Cons. 6 and 8														
5	Assiginack, John Lane's to Ingrams					250	20	earth	50	5					
6	Assiginack, 13th Sideroad to Squirrel Town							gravel	125	5					
7	Assiginack, 5th Con.							gravel							
8	Assiginack and Tehkummah Township Roads	80	28					gravel	80	5					
9	Aubrey Township Roads	160	50	160	25	90	18	gravel	45	18	150	2	1		
10	Balfour, Cons. 5 and 6, and Boundary of Dowling and Balfour:														
	Poulin Section	480	55	480	55	480	20				640	2	1		
	Trotter Section	180	60	180	50	240	20				160	2	1		
11	Balfour and Morgan Road:														
	Belanger Section	80	50	80	50	80	20	earth	16	6				16	16
	Mainville Section														
	Gruolx Section	240	50	240	50	240	30				640	2	1		
12	Balfour, Lots 5 and 7, across Cons. 5-6	320	50	320	20	320	16				70	2	.5		
13	Baldwin Township Roads:														
	Belch Section	50	30	50	30	50	20								
	Oiche Section					60	18	earth	70	5					
14	Barr River and Sylvan Valley Road														
15	Barris Island Road	90	40	40	22			stone	20	6					
16	Bass Lake Road, between Lots 11 and 12, Plummer Township, Con. 4	240	40	240	30	80	18	gravel	10	6					
17	Bidwell, 10th Sideroad, Cons. 4 and 6														
18	Bidwell, Con. 10, Lots 18 to 23					100	12	gravel	175	5					
19	Bidwell, 5th Sideroad, Cons. 2 and 3														
20	Billings, 20th Sideroad, 8th and 10th Cons.														
21	Billings, Con. 12, to Spears														
22	Billings, Con. 12, across Lots 2 and 3														
23	Billings, 25th Sideroad (Lemon Road)	25	30			200	16								
24	Billings and Carnarvon Townline														
25	Birch Lake Road, east end														
26	Billings from Smith's Store West														
27	Bright Road, Con. 5, Lots 4, 5 and 6														
28	Bright Road and Bridge, Lot 3, Con. 6														
29	Broder Township Roads:														
	Lots 11 and 12, Con. 4														
	Lot 6, Con. 3, to Lot 7, Con. 8	160	35	30	35	35	12				24	3	1½		
	Between Lots 6 and 7, Cons. 4, 5 and 6									40	3	1½			
	Dill and Broder Boundary	80	40	80	40	80	16								
	Long Lake Road to Trembly's	320	45	160	45	320	16				640	2	1		
30	Burnt Land Road, Salter, Lots 4 to 7							stone	10	4½					
31	Broken Front, Salter, Lots 4 to 7							gravel	250	4½					
32	Burpee Blind Line, Lot 22, westward					50	20	gravel	100	4½					

Roads Branch, Department of Public Works, Ontario, in 1913.

OLD ROAD.

Cleared		Graded and Shaped.		Surfacing.			Outlet Ditches.			Bridges over 10 feet.		Material.		Culverts.		Total Miles of Road Built and Improved.	Total Cost of Work.	Number.
												Sub-structure.	Super-structure.					
Length rods.	Width feet.	Length rods.	Width feet.	Material.	Length rods.	Width feet.	Length rods.	Width feet.	Depth feet.	Number.	Length feet.			Number.	Material.			
17	18	19	20	21	22	23	24	25	26	27	28	29	30	31	32	33	34	35
																	$ c.	
										1	60	wood	w'd			.82	400.00	1
										1	80	wood	w'd			.25	400 00	2
240	30	120	24	gravel	720	5								4	cedar	.75	400 00	3
		100	20	earth	110	5								2	wood	.34	126 76	4
														1	wood	.79	148 25	5
																.86	200 00	6
150	20			earth	275	5								1	wood	.40	100 00	7
																.25	100 00	8
100	25	480	1	y	480	18								{5 / 2}	wood / iron	2.59	710 54	9
										1	16	wood	w'	3	wood	1.50	1,500 40	10
														1	wood	.75	1,014 50	
																.25	450 00	11
														1	wood	.94	500 29	
240	50	300	16											1	wood	1.50	900 00	
		240	20															
														6	wood	1.00	450 05	12
		20	22	earth	100	5								2	wood	.48	200 00	13
														1	wood	.23	99 21	
				gravel	820	5										1.00	299 89	14
				gravel	125	5										.40	150 83	15
														3	cedar	.75	300 82	16
				gravel	175	5								1	wood	.54	150 00	17
														2	wood	.55	200 34	18
				gravel	175	5										.54	145 60	19
		175	26	gravel	75	5										.55	149 97	20
		50	22	earth	50	16										.16	76 00	21
		80	22	earth	100	5										.31	98 79	22
														2	stone	.63	100 40	23
		175	24	gravel	75	5										.55	151 14	24
		24	27	earth	24	27										.08	350 00	25
		20	23	stone	75	5										.26	100 14	26
		400	22											5	wood	1.25	301 30	27
		560	24							2 {	78 / 62	wood / wood	w'd / w'd			1.75	899 26	28
240	18	160	16				160	2	1½					3 / 3	cedar / wood	.75 / .50	200 00 / 150 00	29
		960	16											1	cedar	3.00	250 40	
														1	cedar	.25	100 00	
														1	cedar	1.00	498 81	
		320	28	gravel	320	7								4	cedar	2.00	275 00	30
																.31	200 00	31
														1	wood	.31	199 35	32

Schedule showing amount of Road Construction under the Colonization

Number	NAME AND LOCATION OF WORK	Cut out and Cleared		Stumped and Grubbed		Graded and Shaped		Surfacing			Outlet Ditches			Corduroy	
1	2	Length rods 3	Width feet 4	Length rods 5	Width feet 6	Length rods 7	Width feet 8	Material 9	Length rods 10	Width feet 11	Length rods 12	Width feet 13	Depth feet 14	Length rods 15	Width feet 16
33	Burpee, 20th Sideroad	00	50	75	22	......		{ stone	30	4½	}			12	10
34	Bellevue Road, Vankoughnet..	80	20			80	24	earth	12	6					
35	Campbell Township Roads:							gravel	80	5	40	2½	1½		
	20th Sideroad, across Cons. 8 and 9	......		......		......		{ stone	10	8	}				
	Lots 19 and 20, Con. 12...	......		......		......		{ gravel	60	5	}				
	Lots 21 and 22, Con. 10...	......		......		......									
	10th Sideroad, Cons. 6 and 8	......		......		......									
36	Capreol Township Roads:														
	Lots 9 and 10, Con. 4......	320	25	320	25	320	12	......							
	Lots 4 and 5, Con. 2	134	24	134	24	......		earth	16	24	8	4	3		
	Cons. 3 and 4, Lots 5 to 9.	......		......		......									
37	Carnarvon Township Roads:														
	Billings and Carnarvon Bdy.	......		......		......									
	10th Sideroad, Con. 8 ...	......		......		......									
38	Carnarvon, 20th Sideroad ...	......		......		55	20	earth	20	6	100	2½	2		
39	Carnarvon, Lots 19 and 20, Con. 2	}		......		......		{ gravel	100	6	}				
40	Carter's Road Deviation, Jocelyn	......		......		......		stone	30	6					
41	Centre Line Road, Hincks	......		......		50	30	earth	25	20					
42	Chapleau Township Roads.....	20	50	......		......		gravel	54	5					
43	Cobden Township Roads......	120	66	120	30	120	22	gravel	30	5	35	5	2		
44	Cockburn Island Roads......	......		......		......									
45	Columbus Hill Road, Howland	......		......		......								}	
46	Conmee Township Roads:														
	East end, Lots A and 1, Con. 3	444	40	444	24	140	18	earth	140	18	......				
47	West end, Lots 4 and 5, Con. 3	320	40	320	24	......					......			40	16
	Cook's Road, Lot 3, Con. 4. Aberdeen	......		......		......									
48	Cuthbertson Location, Con. 7..	......		......		......									
49	Cuthbertson Road, north from Con. 6	320	45	......		28	24	gravel	15	6	15	2	2		
50	Day Township, Cons. 1 and 2..	240	66	240	22	320	18								
51	Diamond Lake Road	......		......		......									
52	Dill Township Roads:														
	Dill and Broder Boundary Lot 12	80	40	80	40	80	16								
	Lots 9, 10, 11, Con. 5, Dill.	320	50	320	50	320	18								
53	Dowling Township Roads, Lots 7 to 11, Con. 1	80	18	80	50	80	16								
54	Dorion Township Roads:														
	Lots 8 to 10, Con. 3.......	......		......		......									
	Lots 4 and 5, Cons. 6 and 7.	160	40	160	24	......									
	Lot 5, Con. 7	......		......		......									
	Lots 8 and 9, Con. 6	240	40	240	24	......								8	12
	Lots 11 and 14, Con. 5.....	108	40	108	24	115	18	earth	108	18					
	Cons. 2 and 3, Lots 13 and 14	108	40	80	18	......					80	2	1		
	Lots 7 and 8, Cons. 3 to 6.	......		......		......									
	Lots 12 and 13, Cons. 3 and 4	......		......		......									
	Lots 13 and 14, Cons. 5 and 6	160	40	160	24	......									
	Lots 9 and 11, Con. 4......	......		......		......									
	Lots 11 and 12, Cons. 2 and 3	68	40	32	34	......									
	Lots 4 to 8, Cons. 3 and 4..	......		......		......									
	Lot 5, Cons. 3 and 4......	......		......		......									
	Lots 1 and 2, Cons. 4 and 5.	160	40	160	24	......									
55	Dorion, Lots 8 and 9, Con. 3.	......		......		......									
56	Elizabeth Bay Road, 10th Con. and 5th Sideroad, Burpee..	......		......		......									
57	Eton Township Roads	160	50	160	25	160	18	clay	160	18	320	4	2	50	15
58	Fairbank Township:														
	Dowling and Fairbank Bdy	320	16	64	18	320	16	......			160	2½	1½		
	Sec. 2, Dowling and Fairbank Boundary	......		......		......									
59	Falconbridge Township Roads	......		......		......									
	Lot 10, Con. 1	......		......		......									
60	Fenwick Sideroad	......		......		......		gravel	190	5					
61	Fenwick, Secs. 11 and 12....	......		56	30	190	24				120	2½	2	66	12
						56	20								

Roads Branch, Department of Public Works, Ontario, in 1913.

OLD ROAD.

Cleared		Graded and Shaped		Surfacing			Outlet Ditches			Bridges over 10 feet		Material		Culverts		Total Miles of Road Built and Improved	Total Cost of Work	Number
Length rods	Width feet	Length rods	Width feet	Material	Length rods	Width feet	Length rods	Width feet	Depth feet	Number	Length feet	Sub-structure	Super-structure	Number	Material			
17	18	19	20	21	22	23	24	25	26	27	28	29	30	31	32	33	34	35
																—	$ c.	
														1	wood	.31	150 00	33
										1	30 R	wood	w'd	2	wood	.25	296 87	34
																.22	75 50	35
																.22	126 25	
50	45	60	20	gravel	75	5	20	2	1					2	wood	.63	100 45	
		80	22	gravel	175	5	20	2	1½					1	wood	.63	200 00	
				gravel	200	4½												
														2	cedar	1.00	250 00	36
														3	cedar	.50	450 00	
320	6	320	16				640	3½	1½					2	cedar	1.00	1,001 50	
		100	24		75	5										.31	149 86	37
		40	24	gravel	160	5								1	wood	.50	146 70	
														2	wood	.24	100 48	38
																.31	200 00	39
																.63	200 75	40
														2	wood	.50	317 10	41
				stone	10	15								6	wood	.09	529 41	42
																.63	500 00	43
75	55	100	20	earth	5	6	50	3	1½					2	wood	.63	251 03	44
		200	20	earth	50	5								1	stone	.75	399 95	45
				stone	30	8								1	wood			
										4	14	wood	w'd	11	wood	1.39	797 50	46
														7	cedar	1.00	395 50	
		320	24	gravel	320	7										1.00	303.75	47
		80	30	gravel	135	5	206	8	3					1	concr'te	.81	397 57	48
																1.00	299 75	49
														3	wood	1.00	391 75	50
80	30	40	24	gravel	80	6								2	cedar	.50	300 41	51
														2	cedar	.45	100 85	52
320	50	480	20				400	3	1	2	21	wood	w'd	8	cedar	1.50	497 83	
		400	16				60	3	1		16	wood	w'd	2	cedar	1.75	505 29	53
		480	18	earth	480	18								1	cedar	1.50		
				gravel	32	7										.50		
														1	cedar	.10		
														3	wood	.75		
																.45		
																.34		
40	40	80	18	earth / gravel	80 / 160	18 / 7										.50		
		240	18	earth	240	18								1	tamarac	.75		
														1	tamarac	.50		
		160	18	earth	160	18				1	18	plank	w'd			.50		
		80	18	earth	80	18										1.20		
60	24	160	18	earth	160	18								6	cedar	.50		
				earth	60	24								3	spruce	.10		
														2	poplar	.50	2,800 12	54
				gravel	15	16								2	cedar	.06	100 00	55
250	22	250	22	gravel	175	5								2	wood	.80	196 15	56
420	25	640	18	c ay	640	18	500	6	4	3	16	wood	w'd	4	wood	3.00	997 00	57
														5	cedar	1.00	300 50	58
		700	18				640	2	1					2	wood	2.50	300 29	
																3.00	202 90	59
480	24	160	15													.66	498 96	60
																.50	500 54	61

Schedule showing amount of Road Construction under the Colonization

Number.	NAME AND LOCATION OF WORK	Cut out and Cleared.		Stumped and Grubbed.		Graded and Shaped.		Surfacing.			Outlet Ditches.			Corduroy	
		Length rods.	Width feet.	Length rods.	Width feet.	Length rods.	Width feet.	Material.	Length rods.	Width feet.	Length rods.	Width feet.	Depth feet.	Length rods.	Width feet.
1	2	3	4	5	6	7	8	9	10	11	12	13	14	15	16
62	Fraser-Leeburn Road, Lots 8 to 10, Con. 8														
63	Galbraith and Aberdeen Townline														
64	Galbraith, Lots 5 and 6, Con. 5														
65	Galbraith Road, Cons. 1 and 2.														
66	Garden Bay Road														
67	Gillies Township Roads:														
	Lots 7 and 8, Con. 3	160	50	160	40	78	18	earth	76	18					
	Lots 4 and 5, Cons. 5 and 6.	160	40	160	30	120	30	earth	120	30					
	Lots 6 and 7, Con. 4														
	Lots 7 and 8, Con. 4	160	50	160	30										
	Con. 3 hill														
	Lot 7, Cons. 2 and 3														
	Lots 5 and 6, Cons. 4 and 5														
68	Gold Rock Road														
69	Gordon and Allan Township Roads:														
	Allan, Con. 6, Lots 28 and 29					10	18	gravel	25	5					
	Allan, Lots 25 and 26, Con. 9														
	Gordon, Lot 5, Cons. 6 and 8														
	Gordon, Lot 10, Con. 7							gravel							
	Allan, Lots 24 and 25, Con. 10							gravel	50	5					
70	Gore Bay to Hope's Hill														
71	Gore Bay to Barrie Island					10	20	stone	170	5					
72	Gorham, between Lots 12 and 13, Cons. 2, 3 and 4	300	40	300	24	292	18	earth	292	18				16	18
73	Gorham, Lots 8 and 9, Cons. 1, 2, 3 and 4	280	40	224	24	224	18	earth	224	18					
74	Gorham, between Cons. 3 and 4, Lots 13-16	184	40	184	24	160	18	earth	160	18				56	16
75	Gorham, between Cons. 4 and 5, Lots 13-16	288	40	284	24	284	18	earth	284	18					
76	Gorham, Cons. 5 and 6, Lots 17 and 18	244	40	244	24	200	18	gravel	200	18					
77	Gorham, Cons. 5 and 6, Lots 15 and 16	172	40	172	24	160	18	earth	160	18					
78	Gorham, Cons. 4 and 5, Lots 17 and 18	100	40	160	24	160	18	earth	160	18					
79	Gorham and Ware Boundary	244	40	232	24	240	18	earth	240	18				100	18
80	Goulais Bay Settlement Road			66	30	140	24	gravel	140	6					
81	Goulais Bay Government Road														
82	Goulais Bay and Bellevue Road	75	36	75	36	164	20	gravel	160	5	36	3	2	18	12
83	Hagar Township Roads	640	50												
84	Hallam, Spencer Road					320	24	earth	12	16					
85	Hallam and May, Con. 4			320	30	320	16								
86	Hallam Road, Con. 3 to Con. 1														
87	Hallam, Con. 1, Lot 9														
88	Hanmer Township Roads:														
	Lots 1 to 8, Con. 4														
	Lots 10 and 11, Con. 3	160	30	160	30	30	16	earth	16	16					
	Lots 4 to 7, Con. 2														
	Lots 10 and 11, Con. 2														
	Lots 7 and 8, Con. 5														
89	Hartman Township Road	1,120	30	1,120	18	175	16	gravel	180	16	300	2	1	30	16
90	Havilah and Dunn's Valley Rd.														
91	Hinck's Location, Con. 6														
92	Howland, 9th Con., Taylor's to L. C.														
93	Howland and Bidwell Townline.														
94	Ignace Township Roads	480	50	480	20						68	3	2	48	16
95	Iron Bridge and Paton Road														
96	Johnson and Plummer Additional Boundary	120	66	120	40			gravel	74	5					
97	Johnson, Torrance Road	160	66	160	24	160	22								
98	Kagawong to Gore Bay														
99	Kagawong to Pervale Shore Rd.	300	30	300	15	200	16	earth	15	5					
100	Kagawong to Providence Bay					200	24	stone	50	5					
101	Kars Township, Goulais Bay Road Extension	960	18	640	24	400	28				109	3	2		
102	Kayes Road	960	40	240	36										

Roads Branch, Department of Public Works, Ontario. in 1913.

OLD ROAD.

Cleared		Graded and Shaped.		Surfacing.			Outlet Ditches.			Bridges over 10 feet.		Material.		Culverts.		Total Miles of Road Built and Improved.	Total Cost of Work.	Number.
Length rods.	Width feet.	Length rods.	Width feet.	Material.	Length rods.	Width feet.	Length rods.	Width feet.	Depth feet.	Number.	Length feet.	Sub-structure.	Super-structure.	Number.	Material.			
17	18	19	20	21	22	23	24	25	26	27	28	29	30	31	32	33	34	35
																	$ c.	
....	....	480	20	gravel	400	5	....							5	wood	1.50	299 82	62
....	....	....	....	gravel	160	5	....									.50	249 95	63
....	....	160	18	gravel	20	5	....							6	wood	.50	400 40	64
....	....	120	20	gravel	40	6	....									.50	301 47	65
5	20	77	18	gravel	74	5	....									.50	306 90	66
....	....	....	....				....							2	plank	.50	....	
....	....	....	....				....							5	plank	.50	....	
....	....	320	18	earth	320	18	....									1.00	....	
....	....	20	18				....							2	wood	.50	....	
....	....	160	18				....									.06	....	
160	30	160	18	earth	320	18	....									.50	....	
80	24	320	18	earth	320	18	....							8	timber	1.00	799.15	67
400	18	1,380	16	gravel	590	14	648	d	2	1	30	wood	w'd	5	wood	7.00	597.21	68
....	....	....	....				....							1	wood	.22	78.82	69
....	....	....	....	gravel	125	5	....									.89	97.50	
....	....	....	....	gravel	120	5	....									.88	100.00	
....	....	....	....	earth	65	5	....									.20	50.00	
....	....	....	....				....							1	stone	.15	75.00	
....	....	100	22	earth	75	5	....									.31	100.08	70
....	....	....	....				....							8	wood	.53	150.00	71
....	....	....	....				....							6	cedar	.93	696.42	72
....	....	....	....				....							4	spruce	.88	696.04	73
....	....	....	....				....							2	spruce	.57	710.47	74
....	....	40	18				....							5	tamarac	1.02	697.82	75
....	....	....	....				....							1	tamarac	.78	500.00	76
....	....	....	....				....							2	j'k p'ne	.54	500.00	77
....	....	80	18	earth	80	18	....							3	j'k p'ne	.75	700.73	78
....	....	160	18	earth	160	18	....							5	wood	1.96	999.81	79
....	....	....	....				....									.44	600.00	80
960	12	60	24	gravel	400	5	....									6.00	799.75	81
....	....	....	....				....									.51	495.55	82
....	....	1,120	20				2,400	3	1					15	stone	5.50	1,502.58	83
....	....	....	....				....									1.00	800.00	84
....	....	560	22	earth	21	16	....							9	wood	1.00	848.75	85
320	22	....	....	earth	80	16	80	4	3	1	12	wood	w'			1.75	350.15	86
....	....	....	....				....									.25	99.75	87
640	40	640	18				....									2.00	200 00	88
....	....	....	....				....									.50	200 00	
160	50	160	18				160	3	2					1	cedar	.50	502 54	
80	66	320	20				480	5	3					4	cedar	1.00	502 04	
....	....	320	16				300	3	1½							1.00	300 00	
....	....	....	....				....							16	wood	3.50	506 97	89
....	....	160	18	gravel	480	7	....									1.50	306.55	90
....	....	....	....	gravel	45	5	....									1.25	300 00	91
....	....	....	....				....									.55	200 00	92
....	....	175	20	gravel	75	5	....							1	stone	.85	125 20	93
....	....	110	24	gravel	90	5	....							4	wood	2.05	502 62	94
....	....	175	18	c'nds	175	18	27	3	2					8	cedar	.75	295 90	95
240	66	160	22	gravel	25	7	....									.75	300 05	96
....	....	....	....				....							2	cedar	1.00	350 32	97
....	....	....	....				....							2	wood	1.55	499 97	98
....	....	....	....	gravel	500	5	....									.94	99 14	99
....	....	....	....				....							2	stone	.63	151 08	100
....	....	....	....				....									3.00	450 00	101
....	....	....	....				....									3.00	450 42	102

Schedule showing amount of Road Construction under the Colonization

		NEW ROAD.													
		Cut out and Cleared.		Stumped and Grubbed.		Graded and Shaped.		Surfacing.			Outlet Ditches.			Corduroy	
Number.	NAME AND LOCATION OF WORK	Length rods.	Width feet.	Length rods.	Width feet.	Length rods.	Width feet.	Material.	Length rods.	Width feet.	Length rods.	Width feet.	Depth feet.	Length rods.	Width feet.
1	2	3	4	5	6	7	8	9	10	11	12	13	14	15	16
103	Kelley Lake Road:														
	Broder, Lots 8 to 10, Con. 6.			240	50	240	18								
	Broder, Lots 10,11, Con. 6.														
104	Killarney to Collin's Inlet. . . .	100	20			200	18	earth	100	5					
105	Lake Manitou Road														
106	Lees Road, Walford														
107	Long Bay to Hope's Hill														
108	Lorne and Nairn Township Roads:														
	Lots 11 and 12, Con. 4, Lorne														
	Lots 10 and 11, Con. 6, Nairn														
109	Lumsden Township Roads:														
	Lumsden and Rayside Bdy. .														
	Lumsden, Cons. 1 and 2, Lot 5			26	80	80	16								
	Lumsden and Hanmer Bdy. . .	320	66	160	66	240	20								
110	Lybster Township Roads:														
	Lots 4 and 5, Con. 6.	160	40	160	24	160	16	earth	160	16					
	Lots 3 and 4, Con. 5.														
	Lots 2 and 3, Con. 6.	160	40	160	24	40	16	earth	40	16					
	Lots 8 and 9, Cons. 5 and 6.														
	Lot 8, Con. 6														
111	Main Road, Lots 26-28, Con. 4, Tehkummah														
112	Marks Township Roads:														
	Lots 2 to 9, Con. 2.														
	Lots 2 to 7, Con. 6.	320	40	320	24										
	Lots 2 and 3, Cons. 1-3. . . .	160	40	16	24										
	Lots 6 and 7, Cons. 2 and 3.	80	40	80	24										
	Lots 4 and 5, Con. 1.														
113	Martin Road, Lots 24 and 25, Tehkummah	100	45	50	20										
114	May, Cons. 3 and 4, Lots 9 & 10	160	66	160	30	160	20	gravel	50	7	100	2	1		
115	May, Con. 5, Lots 9 and 10. . .	320	66	320	30	240	20	gravel	50	7	100	2	1		
116	May and Salter Boundary.														
117	Meldrum Bay, towards Lighthouse														
118	Melgund Township Roads.	240	20	240	20						208	2	1		
119	Mellick and Jaffray Tp. Roads.	480	40	480	18						7	8	2		
120	Merritt Township Roads:														
	Lots 10 and 11, Con. 3. . . .	25	33	25	33	100	20	gravel	10	5					
	Lot 3, Con. 4.	100	33	100	33	90	18	gravel	10	5					
121	Michipicoten Mining Roads:														
	Grace Mine Road														
	WaWa Road														
	Steep Hill Falls Road. . . .													115	9
	Michipicoten Falls Road. . . .	700	16					gravel	480	16					
122	Mills Township Roads:														
	Lot 10, Cons. 6 and 8.	15	30					gravel	60	6					
	Lots 19 and 20, Con. 6.							stone	30	12					
123	Mutrie Township Roads.	250	40	250	18	60	18	gravel	40	16	160	2	1	40	16
124	McGregor Township Roads. North Branch			240	20	200	16	earth	200	12					
125	McIntyre and Gorham Boundary, Secs. 4 and 3	316	40	316	24	280	18	earth	280	18				20	12
126	McIntyre, across Centre Line, Sec. 5	160	40	160	24	132	18	earth	132	18					
127	McIntyre, Secs. 21 and 22, etc.														
128	McIntyre, Secs. 4 and 5														
129	Nexterville Road West														
130	O'Connor Township Roads:														
	Con. 5, Lots 4 and 5.														
	Con. 5, Lots 8 and 9.														
	Con. 7, Lots 9 to 11.														
	Con. 5, Lot 1	48	40	48	24										
	Con. 5, Lot 4	60	40												
	Marks and O'Connor Bdy. . .														
	Between Lots 7 and 8, Cons. 2 and 3													36	12
	Lot 5, Con. 4														

Roads Branch, Department of Public Works, Ontario, in 1913.

OLD ROAD.

Cleared		Graded and Shaped.		Surfacing.			Outlet Ditches.			Bridges over 10 feet.				Culverts.		Total Miles of Road Built and Improved.	Total Cost of Work.	Number.
Length rods.	Width feet.	Length rods.	Width feet.	Material.	Length rods.	Width feet.	Length rods.	Width feet.	Depth feet.	Number.	Length feet.	Sub-structure.	Super-structure.	Number.	Material.			
17	18	19	20	21	22	23	24	25	26	27	28	29	30	31	32	33	34	35
																	$ c.	
160	50	160	18							1	16	cedar	c'dr	4	cedar	1.25	250 05	103
160	40	640	20				160	2½	1					4	cedar	3.00	249 00	104
														2	wood	.73	248 75	
350	40	160	22	gravel	400	5										1.56	250 20	105
				gravel	120	6										.50	298 81	106
10	20	10	18	gravel	275	5										.88	199 60	107
				earth	25													
		100	20	stone	15	6								1	wood	.31	150 00	108
		125	22 {	gravel	30	5										.89	149 95	
				stone	8	5	}											
26	30	320	16				640	4	3					1	wood	1.00	198 54	109
																.25	302 80	
																1.00	999 50	
														3	spruce	.50		
160	18									1 R	20	wood	wd			.50		
																.50		
480	24	480	18	earth	480	18								6	cedar	1.50		
80	24	80	18	earth	80	18								2	spruce	.25	799 87	110
				gravel	150	5	25	3	1					1	wood	.47	149 97	111
		200	18	earth	200	18										.63		
		46	18	earth	46	18								1	p ank	1.15		
		48	18											1	p ank	.65		
		40	18	earth	40	18				1 R	24	wood	wd			.37		
				earth	40	16										.12	797 18	112
										1	20	wood	wd			.81	102 25	113
																.50	300 43	114
																1.00	296 65	115
		960	24	gravel	600	9	960	3	2							6.00	501 00	116
		160	20	gravel	50	5								9	wood	.51	149 65	117
400	30	1,800	20	gravel	950	18	403	2	1						wood	5.75	799 02	118
480	18	720	18	gravel	280	16	650	2	1	1	18	wood	wd	11	wood	7.00	1,001 37	119
														4	wood	.81	150 00	120
														1	wood	.82	145 00	
				gravel	20	16				1	20	wood	w'd	1	wood	.06		
300	10			gravel	20	16				1 R	20	wood	w'd			6.00		
		115	10													1.25		
																5.50	1,400 00	121
														1	wood	.19	150 40	
		100	20	gravel	100	5								1	wood	.34	149 89	122
470	25	480	18	gravel	305	16	500	4	2					5	wood	3.23	798 80	123
														4	spruce	.75	906 85	124
														3	wood	1.00	700 48	125
														1	stone	.50	299 99	126
		276	18	earth	276	18								1	tamarac	.88	685 86	127
		343	18	earth	343	18										1.07	697 46	128
		80	22	gravel	35	6								1	cedar	.29	300 00	129
20	24	32	18	earth	32	18										.15		
20	24			earth	20	16								2	cedar	.06		
		240	24	earth	240	24								1	cedar	.75		
				earth	12	24										.15		
100	30	160	30											3	cedar	.04	552 55	
																.69		
55	24			earth	86	12	8	2	1					2	cedar	.17		
60	24			earth	16	16								2	cedar	.19	503 86	130

Schedule showing amount of Road Construction under the Colonization

Number	Name and Location of Work	Cut out and Cleared (Length rods)	(Width feet)	Stumped and Grubbed (Length rods)	(Width feet)	Graded and Shaped (Length rods)	(Width feet)	Surfacing (Material)	(Length rods)	(Width feet)	Outlet Ditches (Length rods)	(Width feet)	(Depth feet)	Corduroy (Length rods)	(Width feet)
1	2	3	4	5	6	7	8	9	10	11	12	13	14	15	16
131	Oliver Township Roads	100	40	100	24	100	24	earth	100	24					
132	"P" Line Hill, St. Joseph ...														
133	"P" Line to Wharf St. Joseph..	320	66	320	30	240	18				20	3	2	20	16
134	Paipoonge Township Roads....														
135	Pearson Township Roads:														
	Lots 9 and 10, Cons. 3 and 2	160	40	160	24	160	18	earth	160	18					
	Lot 9, across Cons. 4 and 5..	160	40	160	24	160	18	earth	100	18					
	Con. 5, Lots 13 and 14.....	160	40	160	24	18	18	earth	18	18					
136	Plummer Additional Road....	480	66	320	30	320	22								
137	Plummer Road, Cons. 3 and 4..	80	66	80	30	40	20	earth	15	16					
138	Poplar to Gore Bay														
139	Prince, Second Line														
140	Prince, Secs. 25 and 26.....					80	16	gravel	200	16	120	2	1		
141	Providence Bay to New House..														
142	Road at east end of Basswood Lake														
143	Road Secs. 5 and 8, Laird...														
144	Road and Bridge, north of Spanish					160	16								
145	Rockville Road, Con. 2, Bidwell to Carnarvon					150	24	gravel	75	5					
146	Robinson, north of Con. 12...														
147	Robinson, Cons. 9 and 10....	90	30	90	12	25	18	gravel	120	5					
148	Rydal Bank, north of Humphrey's							earth fill							
149	Rydal Bank Road, north (washout)							clay fill	8	60					
150	Rydal Bank Bridge Approaches							fill	14	24					
151	Richard's Landing to Humbug Point			30	16			gravel	160	6					
152	Salter Road, Secs. 25 and 30..														
153	Salter, Sec. 35														
154	Sandfield, Cons. 7 and 9, Lots 26-28														
155	Sandfield, Con. 10, Lot 9...														
156	Sandfield, Con. 9, Lots 18 and 19														
157	Sandfield Mills to McCullough's.	100	35	100	15	100	15	gravel	125	5					
158	Sandfield, Con. 2 and 5th Sideroad to Mills	15	35			15	20	gravel	125	5					
159	Sandford Township Roads.....														
160	Scoble Township Roads:														
	Lots 10 and 11, Cons. 1 and 2	100	40	160	24	12	18	earth	12	18					
	Lots 1, 2, 3, Con. 5.....														
	Lot 12, Cons. 3 and 4.....	240	40	240	24	240	18	earth	240	18					
161	Shakespeare, Centre Line....							c'y fill	40	24	480	4	2		
162	Shaw Line Road, Thessalon..					240	24								
163	Sheguindah, Lots 19 and 20, Con. 10					65	20	earth	50	7					
164	Silverwater to Dawson Townline	640	22			320	16	gravel	640	5					
165	Slash Road, 5th Sideroad, 16th Con.					175	20	gravel	100	5					
166	South Bay Mouth Road ...	80	35			15	22	{ earth stone }	40	6					
167	Southworth Township Roads..														
168	Spanish-Walford Road ...													10	16
169	St. Joseph's, Lots 15 and 16. Harten's Road														
170	Steinburg Road														
171	Stobie Road			400	24	400	24				15	2	1		
172	Strange Township Roads:														
	Lots 1 to 6, Cons. 2 and 3..													4	16
	Lots 2 and 3, Cons. 3 and 4..														
173	Sylvan Valley and Echo Bay Rd.														
174	Stobie and Blessard Road Right-of-way														

Roads Branch, Department of Public Works, Ontario, in 1913.

OLD ROAD.

Cleared		Graded and Shaped		Surfacing			Outlet Ditches			Bridges over 10 feet				Culverts		Total Miles of Road Built and Improved	Total Cost of Work	Number
												Material						
Length rods	Width feet	Length rods	Width feet	Material	Length rods	Width feet	Length rods	Width feet	Depth feet	Number	Length feet	Sub-structure	Super-structure	Number	Material			
17	18	19	20	21	22	23	24	25	26	27	28	29	30	31	32	33	34	35
		300	24	earth	300	24	300	2	2					2, 1	iron, wood	1.25	$ c. 899 32	131
		80	24													.25	295 00	132
														1	wood	1.00	500 00	133
180	30	400	20	earth	400	24	100	2	1					3, 1	iron, wood	1.25	906 07	134
		320	18	earth	320	18								1	spruce	1.50		
		1,120	18	earth	1,120	18								5	stone	3.50		
														1	spruce	.50		
														1	spruce	.50	789 40	135
														3	wood	1.5	499 73	136
														1	wood	.87	300 85	137
		75	22	gravel	100	5								1	wood	.31	253 31	138
							15	2	1						12″ tile	.06	300 04	139
																.63	200 00	140
				gravel	225	5								1	wood	.73	200 70	141
																4.00	397 50	142
800	30	960	20													1.00	299 75	143
		20	21	gravel	20	5	185	4	8	1	40	wood	w'd			.50	348 41	144
														1	wood	.55	200 36	145
				gravel	140	5										.14	99 35	146
														1	cedar	.47	208 42	147
		320	20	gravel	80	6								4	woo	1.00	490 90	148
				gravel	8	20								1	concrete	.03	351 02	149
		60	24	gravel	24	6								1	wood	.80	302 45	150
										1	20	wood	w'd	4	wood	.50	299 31	151
		480	26	gravel	480	7										1.50	500 10	152
80	66	320	24	fill		25								1	wood	1.00	300 88	153
				gravel	175	5								1	wood	.54	150 00	154
				stone	40	5										.12	101 13	155
				gravel	65	5								1	wood	.20	50 00	156
														1	stone	.39	200 00	157
																.22	150 70	158
160	25	480	25	{ clay g'vl }	480	20	500	3	2					6	wood	2.50	500 17	159
														2	wood	.50		
160	24	480	18	earth	400	18								9	wood	1.50	807 20	160
														7	wood	.75	325 00	161
																.75	334 00	162
																.20	99 08	163
														4	wood	3.00	650 12	164
																.63	200 00	165
																.12	99 98	166
850	30	480	18	gravel	480	7	500	3	2	1R	80	wood	w'd	8	wood	4.00	489 73	167
		330	24													1.00	200 08	168
		100	24	gravel,	320	5										1.00	299 40	169
										2	16	cedar	c'd	4	cedar	1.25	299 25	170
		240	24											6	wood	.75	300 57	171
														2	J'kpine	3.00		
160	24	160	16	earth	160	16				2R	50	wood	w'd	3	cedar	.50	400 00	172
		80	18	earth	88	18										.09	208 06	173
				earth	30	66											356 50	174

Schedule showing amount of Road Construction under the Colonization

		NEW ROAD.													
		Cut out and Cleared.		Stumped and Grubbed.		Graded and Shaped.		Surfacing.			Outlet Ditches.			Corduroy	
Number.	NAME AND LOCATION OF WORK	Length rods.	Width feet.	Length rods.	Width feet.	Length rods.	Width feet.	Material.	Length rods.	Width feet.	Length rods.	Width feet.	Depth feet.	Length rods.	Width feet.
1	2	3	4	5	6	7	8	9	10	11	12	13	14	15	16
175	Tarbutt, Con. 6, Kensington Rd		40												
176	Tehkummah, 10th Sideroad, Lot 11, Cons. 6 and 7	75	40					earth	100	6					
177	Tehkummah, 15th Sideroad, Lot 16, Cons. 4 and 5	800	40	200	22										
178	Tehkummah, 10th Sideroad, south end	100	30			25	22	gravel	86	5					
179	Temple Township Roads	320	50	320	18						8	3	2	50	16
180	Thessalon and Day Townline														
181	Tossll Hill to Tehkummah														
182	Townline, North Shedden and Victoria														
183	Tunnell Bridge Road	240	66	240	30	400	18								
184	Van Horne Township Roads	480	50	480	18			clay	45	18				45	12
185	Vankoughnet Road					170	24	earth	30	16					
186	Vankoughnet Road through Sec. 17	303	40	283	40	283	22	gravel	30	18	55	3	2	8	18
187	Victoria Road, Secs. 29 and 30	1,440	50	650	18						18	4	2	175	18
188	Wabigoon Township Roads														
189	Wainwright Township Roads	170	50	170	14									45	16
190	Walford, Victoria Road														
191	Ware, between Cons. 2 and 3, across Lots 1 to 6	240	40	240	24	200	18	earth	200	18					
192	Ware, between Cons. 4 and 5, Lots 1 to 4	200	40	192	24	172	18	earth	172	18					
193	Ware, across Cons. 1 to 4, from Dawson Road, northerly	144	40	116	24	116	18	earth	116	18				90	16
194	Ware, Dog Lake Road	84	50	84	30	64	24	earth	64	24				18	16
195	Wells Township Roads														
196	West Bay to Honora														
197	West Bay to McAnsh's														
198	White-Pennell Road			160	30			earth	160	30	330	2	1		
199	Wilson Road							loam	150	8	44	2½	1½		
200	Zealand Township Roads	15	50	15	30	15	26	gravel	15	24	15	2	1	22	16
201	Inspection, 1913, balances, 1912, and works in progress end of 1912														
	Total, North Division	25,439		20,064		15,591			9,815		5,225			2,160	
	WEST DIVISION.														
1	Armour, Lot 11, Con. 5, to Lot 12, Con. 7														
2	Armour, Lot 21, Con. 11, west to 15th Sideroad														
3	Armour 10th Sideroad, Cons. 12 and 13			125	20	50	20								
4	Ahmic Harbour Road, Croft Township, Lots 4 and 5, Con. 8														
5	Bala and Sahanatien Road	60	40	60	40	60	18	stone	60	18					
6	Bethune, Lot 8, Con. 8, east to Lot 10														
7	Bethune, Lot 2, between Cons. 2 and 3														
8	Broadbent Road, between Broadbent and Hemlock														
9	Carling New Road from Lot 47. Con. 12, to Lot 8, Con. 1	240	20	240	20	240	20	earth	240	20	340	2	1		
10	Carling New Road, from Lot 7, Con. 1, west to Lot 16, Con. 1			160	20	160	20	earth	160	20	160	2	1		
11	Carling Blind Line between Cons. 11 and 12, from Lot 28, to Snug Harbour	103	20	103	20	103	20	earth	103	20	103	2	·1		
12	Carling and Shawanaga Road, from Shebeshekong to Shawanaga Station	160	20	160	20	160	20								

Roads Branch, Department of Public Works, Ontario, in 1913.

OLD ROAD.

Cleared Length rods (17)	Cleared Width feet (18)	Graded Length rods (19)	Graded Width feet (20)	Surfacing Material (21)	Surfacing Length rods (22)	Surfacing Width feet (23)	Outlet Length rods (24)	Outlet Width feet (25)	Outlet Depth feet (26)	Bridges Number (27)	Bridges Length feet (28)	Sub-structure (29)	Super-structure (30)	Culverts Number (31)	Culverts Material (32)	Total Miles (33)	Total Cost of Work (34) \$ c.	Number (35)
		648	24	gravel	120	5	85	2	1½					2	wood	1.08	305 00	175
																.81	200 00	176
																.94	99 98	177
														1	wood	.24	100 00	178
400	25	400	25	gravel	400	18	640	2	1	1	25	wood	w'd	7	wood	4.00	999 52	179
		160	18	gravel	10	5										1.00	297 50	180
				gravel	300	5								2	wood	.94	196 00	181
		320	18											8	cedar	1.00	200 60	182
														12	wood	1.25	406 25	183
														7	wood	6.50	942 46	184
400	20	1.300	18	gravel	500	16	1.500	3	2					1	cedar	.53	400 00	185
														1	cedar	.90	500 11	186
																1.00	300 05	187
145	18	320	22	gravel	14	18								12	wood	5.44	900 00	188
		145	16	clay	145	15	160	3	2	1R		wood	w'd	5	iron	5.58	950 00	189
675	18	800	18	gravel	775	5	520	4	2					8	wood	1.50	299 10	190
		480	24											1	wood	.75	1,000 37	191
														4	stone			
														2	cedar	.62	997 78	192
														1	stone			
														1	wood			
														3	cedar	.45	875 10	193
														3	J'kpine	.26	779 90	194
										1	50	wood	w'd	8	wood	4.50	628 78	195
1.440	16	1.440	18				200	4	2							.47	149 78	196
80	40		50	26	gravel	150	5									.24	349 95	197
				gravel	50	6										.50	300 00	198
										2	24	wood	w'd	1	plank	.47	100 00	199
														17	wood	6.05	999 96	200
1.920	20	560	26	gravel	450	24	850	3	2									
																	11,845 09	201
16,685		37 419			24,354		15,692			34				533		292.61	102,844 96	
		79	20	gravel	79	20	79	2	1							.25	200 00	1
240	30	240	18													.75	200 00	2
														1	stone	.50	200 50	3
		76	20	gravel	400	20	400	2	1					3	stone	1.25	301 54	4
		160	18	earth	100	18								2	wood	.75	406 07	5
		80	20	earth	80	20				1r		wood	w'd	8	stone	1.00	200 75	6
50	20	160	20				80	2	1					5	cedar	.50	200 00	7
		480	20	earth	480	20	480	2	1							1.50	176 12	8
														3	tile	.75	500 00	9
160	20	160	20	earth	160	20	160	2	1					2	stone	1.50	1,009 85	10
														16	wood			
														2	wood	.81	199 90	11
																.50	201 15	12

Schedule showing amount of Road Construction under the Colonization

		NEW ROAD.													
		Cut out and Cleared.		Stumped and Grubbed.		Graded and Shaped.		Surfacing.			Outlet Ditches.			Corduroy	
Number.	NAME AND LOCATION OF WORK	Length rods.	Width feet.	Length rods.	Width feet.	Length rods.	Width feet.	Material.	Length rods.	Width feet.	Length rods.	Width feet.	Depth feet.	Length rods.	Width feet.
1	2	3	4	5	6	7	8	9	10	11	12	13	14	15	16
13	Chapman, 10th Sideroad, northward														
14	Chapman and Strong Boundary north from Distress Road...	160	20			160	20				160	2	1	20	12
15	Chapman and Ryerson Boundary, from Lots 2 to 16, Con. 14, Ryerson														
16	Chapman and Lount Boundary, Lots 20 and 21	160	40	160	18	160	18								
17	Croft, 25th Sideline, Con. 11	160	20	160	20	160	20				160	2	1	20	12
18	Christie Road, Con. 8, Lots 23.33														
19	C.P.R. Station to Byng Inlet														
20	Draper River Road, Lots 18 to 7, Con. 7														
21	Draper and McCauley Boundary, Lot 9, Con. 13														
22	Eagle Lake Road and Nipissing Road (10th Sideroad)	160	20			80	20				160	2	1		
23	Eagle Lake Road, Machar, Lots 13-22, Con. 5														
24	Franklin, Lot 16, Con. 5, to Lot 24, Con. 3	344	20	344	16	244	12								
25	Glen Robert Road from Schoolhouse	160	20	160	20	160	20	earth	160	20	160	2	1		
26	Gravenhurst Station to Sanatarium														
27	Great North Road and Golden Valley Road														
28	Great North Road, between Wabaumic and McKellar														
29	Gurd, 20th Sideroad, Cons. 6 and 7	160	20	160	20	160	20								
30	Gurd and Himsworth Boundary, Con. 6														
31	Hardy and McConkey Boundary, north of Loring														
32	Himsworth North, Cons. 24 and 25	400	20			220	20	earth	400	20	400	2	1		
33	Himsworth North, 5th Sideroad, Cons. 2, 3, 4	160	20	40	20	26	20				26	3	2		
34	Himsworth North, Con. 26, from Lake Nipissing	400	20												
35	Himsworth North, extension of 5th Sideroad	160	20	160	20	107	20	earth	160	20	160	2	1		
36	Himsworth North Road to Callender and North Bay														
37	Himsworth South, between Cons. 2 and 3, Lots 13 to 17														
38	Himsworth South, Con. 12, 5th and 10th Sideroads														
39	Himsworth and Chisholm Boundary, Cons. 13.14	240	20	240	20	240	20	gravel	8?	6	240	2	1		
40	Himsworth and Nipissing, Lot 25, Cons. 18 and 19														
41	Himsworth and Nipissing, Lots 20.25, Cons. 18-19					160	20				160	2	1		
42	Joly, across Lots 7 to 10, Cons. 8 and 9														
43	Lake Joseph Road, between Ferndale Sideline and the Foreman Road														
44	Lorimer Lake Settlement Road to Waubaumic through Lock Erne														
45	Loring and Restoule Road, Lots 14 to 21, Con. 3														
46	Loring and Salines Road														
47	Machar, between Cons. 12 and 13 to Nipissing Road	160	20	160	20	160	20				160	2	1		
48	McCauley, Moors Hill, Cons. 6 and 7														
49	McCauley, Baysville Road														
50	McDougall Schoolhouse Road, Con. 2			160	20	160	20	earth	160	20	160	2	1		

Roads Branch, Department of Public Works, Ontario, in 1913.

OLD ROAD.

Cleared		Graded and Shaped		Surfacing			Outlet Ditches			Bridges over 10 feet		Material		Culverts		Total Miles of Road Built and Improved	Total Cost of Work	
Length rods	Width feet	Length rods	Width feet	Material	Length rods	Width feet	Length rods	Width feet	Depth feet	Number	Length feet	Sub-structure	Super-structure	Number	Material			Number
17	18	19	20	21	22	23	24	25	26	27	28	29	30	31	32	33	34	35
		160	20	gravel	45	8	160	2	1							.50	150 10	13
																.50	239 67	14
		480	20				480	2	1							1.50	201 00	15
																.50	199 61	16
																.50	199 76	17
800	20	800	20											3	cedar	2.50	400 14	18
		160	24	stone	95	18	160	2	1							.50	175 00	19
500	30			earth	40	16								1	wood	2.50	300 00	20
60	20	60	20	gravel	60	14								1	wood	.25	300 06	21
														2	cedar	.50	200 73	22
		106	20													.50	200 09	23
														3	wood	1.25	249 95	24
														2	stone	.50	299 95	25
80	35	480	18	gravel	400	7								1	wood	1.50	300 00	26
		160	20	earth	160	20	160	2	1					6	stone	1.50	299 87	27
720	20	720	20	gravel	150	6	720	2	1							2.50	699 45	28
																.50	175 00	29
		480	20	gravel	75	20	480	3	2					3	stone	1.50	249 98	30
240	20	240	20	earth	240	20	240	3	2	2	14	wood	w'd	3	wood	.75	401 77	31
														3	cedar	1.25	203 26	32
																.50	200 38	33
																1.25	203 09	34
														3	cedar	.50	200 02	35
		560	20	earth	560	20	560	2	1					2	wood	1.75	299 99	36
		240	20	gravel	64	8	240	2	1							.75	205 90	37
400	20	480	20	gravel	420	20	420	2	1							1.31	200 09	38
																.75	300 45	39
		160	20				160	2	1							.50	199 86	40
														1	cedar	.50	200 15	41
		78	20				78	2	1					2	wood	.25	148 27	42
80	20	80	18	gravel	80	5	100	3	1					1	wood	.25	199 80	43
		640	20	earth	640	20	640	2	1	1	1R	32	cedar	cd'r	3	cedar	2.00	375 00	44
400	20	206	20					206	3	2	1R	wood	w'd	4	cedar	1.25	394 97	45
1,440	40						1,440	2	1	3	wood	w'd	3	cedar	4.50	1,003 90	46
														3	wood	.50	199 94	47
40	20	40	20	gravel	40	6								1	stone	.25	303 80	48
480	30			gravel	480	5				1	28	wood	w'd	3	plank	1.50	499 93	49
														2	stone	.50	201 35	50

Schedule showing amount of Road Construction under the Colonization

Number	NAME AND LOCATION OF WORK	NEW ROAD.													
		Cut out and Cleared.		Stumped and Grubbed.		Graded and Shaped.		Surfacing.			Outlet Ditches.			Corduroy	
		Length rods	Width feet	Length rods	Width feet	Length rods	Width feet	Material.	Length rods	Width feet	Length rods	Width feet	Depth feet	Length rods	Width feet
1	2	3	4	5	6	7	8	9	10	11	12	13	14	15	16
51	McDougall, McCoy Hill Deviation of McDougall Road														
52	McMurrich, 5th Sideline across Cons. 10 and 11..........	160	20	160	20	80	20	earth	80	20	80	2	1		
53	Medonte, Con. 12, Lots 10 & 11			121	30	53	22	earth	68	16	68	4	2½		
54	Medonte Sideroad, Lots 20 and 21, Con. 14														
55	Morrison, between Lots 25 and 26, across Cons. 7 and 8....														
56	Matchedash, between Lots 6 and 7, Con. 8														
57	Nipissing Road in Gurd, Lots 175-180, Cons. A and B....					63	20				160	2	1		
58	Nipissing Road through Commanda														
59	Nipissing Road, between Rye and Mount Creek Road....														
60	Nipissing, across Lots 4 and 5, Con. 2														
61	Nipissing, 30th Sideroad, north of Alsace														
62	Nipissing, 10th Sideroad, Cons. 6-8														
63	Nipissing Road, Lot 13, Con. 10, etc.														
64	North Cardwell Road, Lot 35, Con. 12														
65	North Muskoka Road from Huntsville to Novar														
66	Old Muskoka Road to Katrine, Lot 8. Con. 2														
67	Orillia Road on Con. 6														
68	Orillia, Con. 2, from Foxmead, north														
69	Orillia, Con. 3, Lots 15 and 16	120	45	120	22	105	22	gravel	120	8					
70	Orillia, Con. 7, Lots 10 to 16..														
71	Orillia, Dalton Road from Muskoka Road to Boundary of N. Ontario														
72	Orillia. Con. 2 Deviation														
73	Perry and Chaffey Boundary Lots 26-31														
74	Pringle, between Cons. 8 and 9, across Lot 3														
75	Proudfoot and Armour Road..														
76	Parry Sound and Rose Point Road														
77	Ryde, 5th and 6th Sideroad south from Con. 10														
78	Sequin Falls and Orrville Road from Nipissing Road to Lot 35														
79	Spence, Nipissing Road, Lots 22-26														
80	Strong, 20th Sideroad, Cons. 11-12														
81	Strong, 10th Sideroad across Cons. 7 and 8	160	20	160	20	160	20	earth	70	20	100	2	1		
82	Strong, Con. 11, Pinkerton's Hill	160	20	160	20	80	20	rock cut							
83	Sundridge Road, Cons. 8-9														
84	Smith's Creek Bridge between Trout Creek and Loring....														
85	Trout Lake Road. from North Road to Trout Lake	800	20	800	20										
86	Utterson Station to Port Sydney														
87	Westphalia Road from South River Bridge to Colter's Hill														
88	Wood Lake Road from Townline Draper to Lot 5, Con. 8, Oakley														
89	Inspection, 1913, balances, 1912														
	Total, West Division...	4,787		4,113		3,511			1,788		2,857			40	

Roads Branch, Department of Public Works, Ontario, in 1913

OLD ROAD.

Cleared		Graded and Shaped.		Surfacing.			Outlet Ditches.			Bridges over 10 feet.		Material.		Culverts.		Total Miles of Road Built and Improved.	Total Cost of Work.	
Length rods.	Width feet.	Length rods.	Width feet.	Material.	Length rods.	Width feet.	Length rods.	Width feet.	Depth feet.	Number.	Length feet.	Sub-structure	Super-structure.	Number.	Material.			Number.
17	18	19	20	21	22	23	24	25	26	27	28	29	30	31	32	33	34	35
																	$ c.	
......	....	160	24	......	......	....	160	2	1	....	......	......	......	......	......	.50	395 62	51
......	....	......	...	......	......	....	......	..	..	....	......	......	......	1	stone	.50	151 97	52
......	....	......	...	......	......	....	......	..	..	....	......	......	......	2	cement	.89	300 00	53
......	....	52	22	gravel	36	8	......	..	..	....	......	......	......	......	......	.30	198 08	54
......	....	400	20	gravel	400	6	......	..	..	....	......	......	......	{ 1	wood	} 1.50	299 50	55
														2	concr'te			
......	....	......	...	bk.sn.	191	10	......	..	..	1	16 R	wood	w'd	1	stone	.75	203 45	56
......	....	......	...	......	......	....	......	..	..	1	....	stone	cd'r	......	......	.50	300 10	57
......	....	200	16	......	......	....	......	..	..	1 R	66	plank	pl'k	......	......	.75	191 74	58
......	....	640	20	......	......	....	......	..	..	....	......	......	......	......	......	2.00	199 96	59
......	....	60	20	gravel	60	20	60	2	1	1	15	wood	w'.	......	......	.19	200 37	60
......	....	90	20	......	......	....	90	8	2	....	......	......	......	......	......	.50	200 50	61
......	....	150	20	......	......	....	150	2	1	....	......	......	......	2	wood	.47	154 40	62
......	....	......	...	rock cut	......	....	160	2	1	....	......	......	......	......	......	.50	200 10	63
200	30	100	18	earth	100	18	......	..	..	....	......	......	......	3	wood	.75	200 00	64
......	....	330	18	gravel	330	....	......	..	..	....	......	......	......	1	wood	1.00	299 97	65
......	....	84	20	stone	84	20	......	..	..	....	......	......	......	......	......	.10	199 75	66
......	....	......	...	gravel	210	8	......	..	..	....	......	......	......	......	......	.64	199 96	67
137	24	91	20	gravel	150	10	......	..	..	....	......	......	......	1	stone	2.00	401 41	68
......	....	330	16	......	......	....	......	..	..	....	......	......	......	1	stone	1.50	296 69	69
125	10	190	24	stone	150	30	......	..	..	....	......	......	......	......	......	.75	206 34	70
......	....	45	22	gravel	91	8	......	..	..	....	......	......	......	......	......	1.50	275 00	71
......	....	......	...	......	......	....	......	..	..	....	......	......	......	......	......	......	950 00	72
......	....	300	20	earth	300	14	160	2	1	....	......	......	......	2	log	1.00	199 99	73
......	....	476	20	rock cut	......	....	476	2	1	....	......	......	......	{ 2	wood	} .25	150 20	74
														2	stone			
......	....	160	16	......	......	....	......	..	..	....	......	......	......	......	......	.50	200 16	75
......	....	240	20	gravel	240	20	240	2	1	....	......	......	......	......	......	.75	178 75	76
960	30	......	...	earth	300	6	......	..	..	....	......	......	......	......	......	3.00	300 75	77
560	40	313	18	......	......	....	320	3	1	....	......	......	......	......	......	1.75	224 93	78
320	40	320	18	gravel	160	28	320	2	1	....	......	......	......	......	......	1.00	215 19	79
480	20	480	20	gravel	105	20	480	2	1	....	......	......	......	......	......	1.50	250 00	80
......	....	......	...	......	......	....	......	..	..	....	......	......	......	1	stone	.50	248 86	81
......	....	......	...	......	......	....	......	..	..	....	......	......	......	......	......	.50	199 89	82
......	....	36	20	gravel	36	8	......	..	..	1	26	stone	w'd	1	stone	1.25	200 00	83
......	....	......	...	stone	20	8	20	2	1	....	......	......	......	1	stone	.06	198 20	84
......	....	300	18	gravel	400	6	......	..	..	....	......	......	......	3	wood	2.50	203 87	85
......	....	......	...	......	......	....	......	..	..	....	......	......	......	2	iron	2.50	501 17	86
720	20	720	20	earth	720	20	720	2	1	....	......	......	......	{ 3	stone	2.75	404 26	87
														2	wood			
......	....	1,800	18	gravel	107	6	......	..	..	....	......	......	......	2	wood	6.00	400 07	88
......	....	......	...	......	......	....	......	..	..	....	......	......	......	......	......	......	1.251 63	89
9,202	....	15,707	...	......	8,985	....	11,479	..	..	14	......	......	......	140	......	92.77	25,835 51	

Schedule showing amount of Road Construction under the Colonization

		Out out and Cleared.		Stumped and Grubbed.		Graded and Shaped.		Surfacing.			Outlet Ditches.			Corduroy	
Number.	NAME AND LOCATION OF WORK	Length rods.	Width feet.	Length rods.	Width feet.	Length rods.	Width feet.	Material.	Length rods.	Width feet.	Length rods.	Width feet.	Depth feet.	Length rods.	Width feet.
1	2	3	4	5	6	7	8	9	10	11	12	13	14	15	16
	EAST DIVISION.														
1	Addington, Kaladar Station to Northbrook														
2	Admaston Township Roads: Opeongo Line														
3	Mount St. Patrick Road														
4	Ashdad Road														
	Airy Township Roads:														
5	Bridge on Hay Creek														
6	Bridge on Con. 2, Lot 9														
7	15th Sideline, Con. 2													287	16
8	Old Perley Road from Lot 9	144	24	190	20	144	16								
	Alice Township Roads:														
9	Lot 19, Con. 6														
10	Lots 18 and 19, Con. 8 Bridge														
11	Lot 6, Con. 9, Bridge														
12	Anson and Hinden Township Roads														
13	Alice and Wilberforce Townline														
14	Anstruther Township Roads														
15	Appleton and Almonte Road (Re-vote 1912)														
16	Arden and Harlowe Road	80	85	80	35	80	30	gravel	8	4	8	2	1		
	Bagot and Blythfield Township Roads:														
17	Calabogie and Ashdad Road														
18	Byers Settlement Road														
19	Renfrew and Calabogie Road														
20	Balsover and Dalrymple Road														
21	Bancroft and Herman Road														
22	Bangor Township Roads														
23	Barrie Road from Lot 28, Con. 7 to Boundary													12	50
24	Bay Lake Road, Faraday														
25	Bedford Mills Road														
	Belmont Township Roads:														
26	Oak Lake Road														
27	Stoney Lake Road														
28	Bancroft to Coe Hill														
29	Bigwood Township Roads	960	50	960	50										
30	Lot 4, Con. 10														
31	Boundary Road from Con. 11, north	80	60	80	25	160	14				80	2	1	6	16
32	15th Sideline from Con. 8	40	66	80	24	120	14								
33	20th Sideline to Con. 6	320	30	180	20	10	16								
34	Boundary Road from Con. 2	100	44	180	24	180	10								
35	Con. 6, Lot 5														
36	Lot 30, Con. 3														
37	Bondfield Hill														
	Boulter Township Roads:														
38	Lot 10, Con. 14														
39	Bonfield and Powassan Road														
40	Bromley Township Roads														
	Brougham Township Roads:														
41	D'Acre Road														
42	Mt. St. Patrick and D'Acre														
43	Ferguson Lake Road														
	Buckhorn Road:														
44	Freeborn Section														
45	Irwin Section														
46	Guthrie Section														
47	Windover Section														
48	Burleigh Township Road														
49	Burwash Township Roads			92	50	185	30								
	Brudenell and Lyndoch Township Roads:														
50	Maley Road														

Roads Branch, Department of Public Works, Ontario, in 1913.

OLD ROAD.

Cleared		Graded and Shaped.		Surfacing.			Outlet Ditches.			Bridges over 10 feet.				Culverts.		Total Miles of Road Built and Improved.	Total Cost of Work.	Number.
												Material.						
Length rods.	Width feet.	Length rods.	Width feet.	Material.	Length rods.	Width feet.	Length rods.	Width feet.	Depth feet.	Number.	Length feet.	Sub-structure.	Super structure.	Number.	Material.			
17	18	19	20	21	22	23	24	25	26	27	28	29	30	31	32	33	34	35
																	$ c.	
.....	.....	400	16	earth	640	12	.....	.....	.....	.....	.....	{ 18 cedar	10 stone }			4 50	804 49	1
.....	.....	160	16	loam	160	16	.....	.....	.....	.....	.....	3	cedar			.50	200 33	2
.....	.....	320	16	loam	320	16	.....	.....	.....	.....	.....	2	cedar			1.00	200 02	3
.....	.....	320	16	loam	320	16	.....	.....	.....	.....	.....	3	cedar			1.00	201 06	4
.....	.....	22	16	.....	.....	.....	97	6	2	1	20	wood	v'd			.75	205 80	5
.....	.....	20	14	earth	40	8	.....	.....	.....	1	17	wood	w'd			.50	198 00	6
.....	.....	20	12	.....	.....	.....	.....	.....	.....	.....	.....			4	wood	2.50	300 00	7
.....	.....	.....	.....	.....	.....	.....	.....	.....	.....	.....	.....			9	wood	.50	299 40	8
.....	.....	80	18	stone	80	18	.....	.....	.....	1	20	cedar	:'dr			.25	218 91	9
.....	.....	.....	.....	.....	.....	.....	.....	.....	.....	1	60	cedar	cd'r			.01	300 06	10
.....	.....	.....	.....	.....	.....	.....	.....	.....	.....	1	51	cedar	iron			.01	301 30	11
.....	.....	100	14	gravel	100	18	.....	.....	.....	.....	.....					.63	157 75	12
.....	.....	160	16	gravel	80	16	.....	.....	.....	.....	.....					.50	202 75	13
.....	.....	218	12	gravel		6	.....	.....	.....	1	26	stone	c'dr	1	cedar	.87	204 70	14
.....	.....	.....	.....	.....	54	.....	.....	.....	.....	.....	.....					.50	500 50	15
.....	.....	160	24	blk.st.	160	12	.....	.....	.....	.....	.....			4	stone	1.75	300 00	16
480	14	.....	.....	gravel	480	6	.....	.....	.....	.....	.....			{ 4	cedar }			
.....	.....	320	16	loam	320	16	.....	.....	.....	.....	.....	1	cedar			1.00	211 96	17
.....	.....	80	24	loam	80	12	.....	.....	.....	.....	.....					.25	46 50	18
.....	.....	320	16	loam	320	16	.....	.....	.....	.....	.....					1.00	188 75	19
.....	.....	160	14	gravel	150	7	.....	.....	.....	.....	.....					.50	99 62	20
80	20	80	14	gravel	40	7	.....	.....	.....	.....	.....	4	stone			.25	203 19	21
83	20	80	14	.....	.....	.....	.....	.....	.....	.....	.....	3	cedar			.25	202 10	22
.....	.....	.....	.....	.....	.....	.....	.....	.....	.....	.....	.....					.04	200 27	23
12	40	12	40	gravel	12	12	.....	.....	.....	.....	.....	2	cedar			.38	102 44	24
120	15	120	12	.....	.....	.....	.....	.....	.....	.....	.....	1	tile			.19	101 00	25
.....	.....	60	20	stone	80	11	60	2	1	.....	.....					.24	100 00	26
.....	.....	.....	.....	C.st'n	73	5	.....	.....	.....	.....	.....					.40	200 12	27
.....	.....	69	18	B.st'n	60	5	.....	.....	.....	.....	.....					.50	201 18	28
180	20	160	14	.....	.....	.....	.....	.....	.....	.....	.....	2	cedar			3.00	399 66	29
.....	.....	.....	.....	.....	.....	.....	.....	.....	.....	.....	.....					.50	209 75	30
.....	.....	20	18	gravel	20	10	.....	.....	.....	.....	.....	3	wood			.25	200 88	31
.....	.....	.....	.....	.....	.....	.....	.....	.....	.....	.....	.....			3	wood	.50	200 00	32
.....	.....	.....	.....	.....	.....	.....	.....	.....	.....	.....	.....	2	wood			1.25	199 35	33
.....	.....	.....	.....	.....	.....	.....	.....	.....	.....	.....	.....	2	wood			.50	322 17	34
640	24	.....	.....	earth	160	8	.....	.....	.....	.....	.....	3	wood			2.00	200 25	35
108	20	.....	.....	.....	.....	.....	96	4	2½	.....	.....					.36	153 14	36
.....	.....	.....	.....	rk.cut	4	30	.....	.....	.....	.....	.....					.02	199 10	37
.....	.....	640	16	.....	.....	.....	.....	.....	.....	.....	.....	3	wood			2.00	305 25	38
.....	.....	160	16	gravel	120	5	.....	.....	.....	1	16	wood	w'd			2.00	301 55	39
.....	.....	320	16	B.st'n	320	16	.....	.....	.....	.....	.....					1.00	306 77	40
.....	.....	240	16	loam	240	16	.....	.....	.....	.....	.....	1	cedar			.75	100 10	41
.....	.....	120	16	gravel	120	16	.....	.....	.....	.....	.....	4	cedar			.38	100 55	42
.....	.....	160	18	gravel	160	18	.....	.....	.....	1	13	cedar	ced.	3	cedar	.50	146 65	43
.....	.....	.....	.....	B.st'n	76	6	.....	.....	.....	.....	.....					.24	198 66	44
.....	.....	.....	.....	gravel	23	6	.....	.....	.....	.....	.....					.08	100 05	45
.....	.....	.....	.....	B.st'n	32	6	.....	.....	.....	.....	.....			1	wood	.10	99 50	46
.....	.....	.....	.....	.....	.....	.....	.....	.....	.....	1	180	cd.crossing				.04	100 00	47
.....	.....	272	6	stone	272	6	.....	.....	.....	.....	.....	4	wood			.86	600 13	48
.....	.....	.....	.....	.....	.....	.....	.....	.....	.....	.....	.....					.57	297 83	49
.....	.....	320	16	loam	320	16	.....	.....	.....	.....	.....	2	cedar			1.00	200 24	50

Schedule showing amount of Road Construction under the Colonization

		NEW ROAD.													
Number.	NAME AND LOCATION OF WORK	Cut out and Cleared.		Stumped and Grubbed.		Graded and Shaped.		Surfacing.			Outlet Ditches.			Corduroy	
		Length rods	Width feet	Length rods	Width feet	Length rods	Width feet	Material.	Length rods	Width feet	Length rods	Width feet	Depth feet	Length rods	Width feet
1	2	3	4	5	6	7	8	9	10	11	12	13	14	15	16
	Brudenell and Lyndoch.—*Con.*														
51	Branch Road														
52	Quadville Road														
53	Quadville and Rockingham Rd.														
54	Smallpiece Settlement Road.														
54a	Bell's Rapids Bridge														
55	Carden Road, between Carden and Victoria Road														
56	Carden, 4th Quarter Line, Cons. 5-6														
57	Carden, Con. 1, btn. Lots 17-18.														
58	Carden and Mara Boundary, opposite Cons. 3-6														
59	Cardiff Township Roads														
	Cameron Township Roads:														
60	Lot 1, Con. 25	160	60	120	30	120	16								
61	Con. 25 from Lot 6	825	60	20	30	20	14								
62	Lot 24, Range A and B.														
63	Carlow Township Roads														
64	Caldwell Township Roads														
	Calvin Township Roads:														
65	10th Sideline from Con. 6														
66	Con. 2, from Lot 18														
67	20th Sideline, Con. 3					160	14	grave	40	7					
68	Townline of Calvin to Con. 2 Papineau														
69	Lot 26, Con. 6			160	80	160	24				160	2	1		
70	California Road, from Keelerville to Boundary of Leeds														
71	California, Camden and Sheffield														
72	Cavendish Township Roads: White Lake Road														
73	Gooderham Road														
	Chandos Township Roads:														
74	Couch Road														
75	Tanner Road														
76	Post Road														
77	Scott Road East														
78	East Road														
79	Smith's Road														
80	Owenbrook Road														
81	Casimir Township Roads														
82	Clarendon Road, Frontenac to Clarendon	20	30	20	30	20	14								
83	Clarendon and Miller Deviation	200	70	200	20	280	12	sand	280	8	250	2	1		
	Chisholm, Ferris and North Bay Road:														
84	Con. 4, north on 20th Sideline			200	40			earth	166	7				165	16
85	Con. 6, Lot 20													24	12
86	Con. 5, north			80	20	30	12							24	12
	Chisholm Township Roads:														
87	Con. 12, from Lot 14	160	66	160	30			earth	45	10				45	10
88	Con. 16, from 10th Sideroad.														
89	Chisholm and Ferris Boundary, Lot 13														
90	20th Sideline, Con. 6 Deviation	240	40	240	40			gravel	1	12				10	12
91	10th Sideroad to Con. 16	160	66	140	24	15	16								
92	5th Sideroad, Con. 4														
93	5th Sideline, Con. 6	240	60	240	30										
	Cross Lake and Madawaska Rd.:														
94	Lot 14, Con. 3 in Lyell														
95	Lot 12, Con. 4 in Lyell														
	Cosby Township Roads:														
96	Lots 6 and 7 to Con. 3	160	30												
97	Burnt Road														
98	Crosby and Ratter Road to Ratter Station														
99	Crerar Township Roads			80	60	80	30								
100	Clay Bank Road McNabb														
101	Dalton and Rama Boundary														
102	Dalton and Carden Boundary														
103	Dalton, Con. 7, opposite Lot 27.														

Roads Branch, Department of Public Works, Ontario, in 1913.

OLD ROAD.

Cleared		Graded and Shaped.		Surfacing.			Outlet Ditches.			Bridges over 10 feet.				Culverts.		Total Miles of Road Built and Improved.	Total Cost of Work.	
Length rods.	Width feet.	Length rods.	Width feet.	Material.	Length rods.	Width feet.	Length rods.	Width feet.	Depth feet.	Number.	Length feet.	Sub-structure.	Super-structure.	Number.	Material.			Number.
17	18	19	20	21	22	23	24	25	26	27	28	29	30	31	32	33	34	35
																	$ c.	
.....	....	18	16	stone	80	16	.....	.....	.....	.....	.....	.....	.....	2	ceda	.25	99 50	51
.....	....	160	16	loam	160	16	.....	.....	.....	.....	.....	.....	.....	.....	.....	.50	101 16	52
.....	....	240	18	gravel	240	18	.....	.....	.....	.....	.....	.....	.....	.....	.....	.75	151 00	53
.....	....	20	16	gravel	20	16	.....	.....	.....	.....	.....	.....	.....	.....	.....	.06	74 07	54
.....	....	.....	.....	.....	.....	.....	.....	.....	.....	1R	25	cedar	ced.	.....	.....	.....	25 00	54a
										1R		wood	w'd					
.....	....	320	18	gravel	320	18	.....	.....	.....	.....	.....	.....	.....	.....	.....	1.00	198 12	55
.....	....	10	12	stone	160	14	.....	.....	.....	.....	.....	.....	.....	1	cedar	1.75	201 66	56
.....	....	.....	.....	gravel	79	7	.....	.....	.....	.....	.....	.....	.....	.....	.....	.25	99 88	57
150	25	70	20	stone	60	6	80	4	2	.....	.....	.....	.....	.....	.....	1.50	298 88	58
480	30	240	14	.....	.....	.....	.....	.....	.....	.....	.....	.....	.....	.....	.....	1.50	199 99	59
.....	....	.....	.....	.....	.....	.....	.....	.....	.....	.....	.....	.....	.....	.....	.....	.50	250 24	60
.....	....	.....	.....	.....	.....	.....	.....	.....	.....	.....	.....	.....	.....	.....	.....	2.56	251 95	61
40	16	120	16	.....	.....	.....	.....	.....	.....	.....	.....	.....	.....	2	wood	.88	200 00	62
.....	....	160	14	gravel	160	7	80	2	1	.....	.....	.....	.....	5	cedar	.50	199 09	63
.....	....	.....	.....	earth	160	16	.....	.....	.....	1	30	wood	w'd	3	wood	.50	400 50	64
480	40	40	12	earth	40	8	.....	.....	.....	.....	.....	.....	.....	5	wood	1.50	200 90	65
.....	....	120	16	earth	40	8	.....	.....	.....	.....	.....	.....	.....	.....	.....	.50	200 00	66
.....	....	.....	.....	.....	.....	.....	.....	.....	.....	.....	.....	.....	.....	.....	.....	.63	200 25	67
.....	....	80	12	gravel	80	8	.....	.....	.....	.....	.....	.....	.....	.....	.....	.25	200 00	68
.....	....	.....	.....	.....	.....	.....	.....	.....	.....	.....	.....	.....	.....	2	wood	.50	186 89	69
.....	....	400	12	gravel	100	10	200	2	1	.....	.....	.....	.....	14	tile	1.50	801 13	70
.....	....	200	14	gravel	800	10	500	2	1	.....	.....	.....	.....	4	stone	4.00	299 50	71
.....	....	.....	.....	earth	145	18	.....	.....	.....	1	90	wood	w'd	.....	.....	.47	200 25	72
330	20	151	13	.....	.....	.....	.....	.....	.....	.....	.....	.....	.....	.....	.....	1.00	100 00	73
.....	....	.....	.....	earth	29	6	.....	.....	.....	.....	.....	.....	.....	.....	.....	.09	50 00	74
100	40	182	12	earth	.....	.....	16	3	2	1	.....	wood	w'd	.....	.....	.57	100 73	75
.....	....	.....	.....	earth	82	6	.....	.....	.....	1	50	stone	st'n	1	stone	.07	100 25	76
.....	....	.....	.....	earth	132	6	.....	.....	.....	.....	.....	.....	.....	.....	.....	.41	100 00	77
.....	....	.....	.....	earth	13	16	.....	.....	.....	.....	.....	.....	.....	.....	.....	.04	50 00	78
.....	....	.....	.....	earth	125	5	.....	.....	.....	.....	.....	.....	.....	8	cedar	.89	100 00	79
.....	....	60	30	stone	8	18	.....	.....	.....	.....	.....	.....	.....	.....	.....	.19	93 96	80
160	20	180	30	gravel	80	6	.....	.....	.....	.....	.....	.....	.....	5	wood	.50	897 88	81
.....	....	640	16	gravel	10	10	.....	.....	.....	.....	.....	.....	.....	10	wood	7.06	898 76	82
.....	....	.....	.....	.....	.....	.....	.....	.....	.....	.....	.....	.....	.....	1	ceda	.88	102 06	83
.....	....	.....	.....	.....	.....	.....	.....	.....	.....	.....	.....	.....	.....	8	wood	.63	404 47	84
130	24	80	12	.....	.....	.....	.....	.....	.....	.....	.....	.....	.....	1	wood	.88	206 15	85
.....	....	.....	.....	.....	.....	.....	.....	.....	.....	.....	.....	.....	.....	2	wood	.25	200 25	86
20	40	80	16	.....	.....	.....	.....	.....	.....	.....	.....	.....	.....	1	wood	.50	201 55	87
.....	....	.....	.....	.....	.....	.....	.....	.....	.....	.....	.....	.....	.....	2	wood	.88	161 55	88
120	18	120	16	.....	.....	.....	.....	.....	.....	.....	.....	.....	.....	8	wood	.88	151 29	89
.....	....	.....	.....	.....	.....	.....	.....	.....	.....	2	15	wood	w'd	2	wood	.75	197 77	90
.....	....	160	16	.....	.....	.....	.....	.....	.....	.....	.....	.....	.....	3	wood	.50	150 30	91
.....	....	.....	.....	.....	.....	.....	.....	.....	.....	.....	.....	.....	.....	.....	.....	.50	150 60	92
.....	....	.....	.....	.....	.....	.....	.....	.....	.....	.....	.....	.....	.....	.....	.....	.75	200 00	93
.....	....	.....	.....	.....	.....	.....	.....	.....	.....	.....	.....	.....	.....	2	wood	.50	245 80	94
.....	....	160	14	.....	.....	.....	.....	.....	.....	.....	.....	.....	.....	2	wood	.54	252 99	95
.....	....	172	14	.....	.....	.....	.....	.....	.....	.....	.....	.....	.....	.....	.....	.81	232 15	96
.....	....	100	30	.....	.....	.....	15	2	1	.....	.....	.....	.....	4	wood	3.00	199 46	97
.....	....	160	30	earth	800	8	70	2	1	.....	.....	.....	.....	2	wood			
330	14	330	30	earth	330	40	80	2	1	.....	.....	.....	.....	7	wood	2.00	836 67	98
.....	....	.....	.....	.....	.....	.....	.....	.....	.....	1	18	wood	w'd	2	wood	.50	302 02	99
.....	....	160	16	gravel	160	16	.....	.....	.....	.....	.....	.....	.....	.....	.....	.50	202 89	100
.....	....	195	16	gravel	75	7	10	8	2	.....	.....	.....	.....	.....	.....	.64	99 93	101
.....	....	.....	.....	gravel	80	7	.....	.....	.....	.....	.....	.....	.....	.....	.....	.25	100 15	102
.....	....	75	18	gravel	75	18	.....	.....	.....	.....	.....	.....	.....	.....	.....	.24	99 90	108

Schedule showing amount of Road Construction under the Colonization

Number	NAME AND LOCATION OF WORK	NEW ROAD.													
		Cut out and Cleared.		Stumped and Grubbed.		Graded and Shaped.		Surfacing.			Outlet Ditches.			Corduroy	
		Length rods.	Width feet.	Length rods.	Width feet.	Length rods.	Width feet.	Material.	Length rods.	Width feet.	Length rods.	Width feet.	Depth feet.	Length rods.	Width feet.
1	2	3	4	5	6	7	8	9	10	11	12	13	14	15	16
104	Darling, 8th Line														
105	Darling, between Lots 10.11, Cons. 4-6														
106	Dead Creek Road														
107	Delemere Township Roads	320	50	132	35	180	35				70	2	1		
108	Dummer Township Roads, Con. 9														
109	Dungannon Township Roads,														
110	Dungannon and Monteagle Bdy.														
	Donro Township Roads:														
111	Young's Point Road														
112	Telephone Road														
113	Eganville and Germanicus Road														
114	Eldon and Carden Boundary														
115	Eganville Road, between Rankin and Lake Dore														
116	Escott Road														
117	Faraday and Herschel Boundary														
118	Faraday Township Roads														
119	Faulkner and Martland Bdy.			480	50	320	30				160	3	2		
	Ferris Township Roads:														
120	Repairs to North Bay and Bonfield Road														
121	North Bay and Trout Lake.														
122	20th Sideroad, Con. 16														
123	Lot 9, Con. 4														
124	Con. 8, from Lot 5, west														
125	Lot 20, Con. 3, north														
126	Bridge, Con. 2, Lot 6														
127	North Bay and Bonfield, Con. 12														
128	Lot 19, Con. 2, north														
129	Fifth Depot Lake														
130	Fiss School (to complete fill)														
131	Forests Mills Road (cutting hill)														
132	Field, Cons. 4 and 5 (washout)														
	Galway Township Roads:														
133	Gully and Kinmount Road														
134	Jackson and Galway Road														
135	Gannon's Bridge Road														
136	Grant Township Roads														
	Grattan Township Roads:														
137	McGrath Road														
138	D'Acre to Lowery's Hill														
139	Opeongo Line from Davisons														
140	Caldwell Station Road														
141	Graphite Mines Road														
	Griffith and Matchawan Road:														
142	Matawatchan Road														
143	Griffith and D'Acre Road														
144	Leclaire Road														
145	Matawatchan and Miller Road														
	Glamorgan Township Roads:														
146	Monck Road														
147	Buckhorn Road														
	Hagarty, Richards and Burns Township:														
148	Perrigo Road					320	24	loam	320	16					
149	Killaloe and Wilno Road														
150	Brudenell and Killaloe Road														
151	Haliburton to Pine Lake Road.					480	16								
	Harvey Township Roads:														
152	Squaw River Road														
153	Bobcaygeon Road														
154	Lakehurst Road														
155	Deer Bay Road														
156	Hastings and Addington Bdy														
157	Hastings Road, south of Bancroft														
158	Hastings Road, between Ormsby and Lot 80, Limerick														

Roads Branch, Department of Public Works, Ontario, in 1913.

OLD ROAD.

Cleared		Graded and Shaped.		Surfacing.			Outlet Ditches.			Bridges over 10 feet.				Culverts.		Total Miles of Road Built and Improved.	Total Cost of Work.	
Length rods.	Width feet.	Length rods.	Width feet.	Material.	Length rods.	Width feet.	Length rods.	Width feet.	Depth feet.	Number.	Length feet.	Material. Sub-structure	Super-structure	Number.	Material.			Number.
17	18	19	20	21	22	23	24	25	26	27	28	29	30	31	32	33	34	35
																	$ c.	
		240	24	gravel	240	12								1	cedar	.75	111 20	104
80	50	240	24	gravel	240	14								1	tile	.75	121 85	105
		98	15	stone	98	12	160	8	2					1	tile	.80	97 06	106
320	10			gravel	168	5								4	wood	1.00	384 47	107
80	20	40	18	st. fill	10									3	cedar	1.00	200 00	108
160	25	240	16											1	cedar	.32	204 30	109
																.75	304 50	110
		56	18	gravel	56	18								2	concr'te	.17	86 75	111
		15		stone	15	14								1	cedar	.05	99 90	112
		320	16	loam	320	16								2	cedar	1.00	202 32	113
		7	14	gravel	70	6								1	cedar	.22	1.1 85	114
40	40	240	24	loam	240	16								2	cedar	.75	202 50	115
		100	14	earth	65	12	120	2	1					4	tile	.81	100 00	116
130	20	130	18											3	cedar	.88	203 88	117
		120	14	gravel	120	7								1	cedar	.88	200 26	118
														5	wood	2.50	405 88	119
		240	16	gravel	40	7										.25	100 90	120
20	20	100	16	earth	40	12								2	wood	.75	300 00	121
		320	16											2	wood	1.05	200 00	122
		80	16											2	wood	.35	150 67	123
120	16													2	wood	.88	150 15	124
		91	16							2	16	wood	w'd	2	wood	.39	151 55	125
		8	16							1	31	wood	w'd			.06	200 29	126
		220	16											3	wood	1.25	200 00	127
		21	16							1	14	wood	w'd	1	wood	0.13	150 63	128
		250	16	gravel	250	12	250	3	1					4	stone	1.00	197 50	129
		20	20	gravel	20	17								5	cedar	.08	108 25	130
		150	20	stone	15	18								1	stone	.47	343 37	131
		60	30				28	2	1					2	wood	.19	102 22	132
		289	18							1 R	75	plank	pl'k	1	con'te	.87	201 75	133
		282	18													.88	200 00	134
		125	21	gravel	75	5										.89	200 00	135
		240	30	earth	240	80								4	wood	.75	200 10	136
		480	24	gravel	480	12								1	cedar	1.50	150 45	137
		180	16	gravel	180	16								3	cedar	.75	108 30	138
		320	16	loam	320	16								3	cedar	1.00	196 50	139
				stone	30	20										.06	151 61	140
		1,600	18	gravel	1,600	14								6	cedar	5.00	800 08	141
		160	16	loam	160	16				1	12	cedar	c'dr	1	cedar	.50	104 50	142
		320	18	gravel	640	14				1	50	cedar	c'dr	2	cedar	2.00	300 52	143
		160	16	gravel	160	16								2	cedar	.50	100 50	144
		80	16	loam	50	16								4	cedar	.25	125 50	145
				gravel	160	8										.50	263 16	146
				gravel	160	8										.50	250 00	147
160	20	220	18	stone	320	14				2	20	cedar	c'dr			2.00	519 28	148
		400	16	loam	400	16								2	cedar	1.50	208 58	149
		980	16	stone	480	16								2	cedar	1.50	300 75	150
														1	wood	1.50	400 54	151
		22	16	gravel	45	5								3	ceda/	.20	100 12	152
														2	stone			
				gravel	97	6								2	cement	.80	160 44	153
				stone	41	15										.12	149 99	154
				gravel	65	5								1	wood	.21	100 06	155
		160	24											4	cedar	.50	100 00	156
40	20	160	16											5	cedar	.50	201 89	157
320	30	320	14											7	cedar	1.00	307 68	158

Schedule showing amount of Road Construction under the Colonization

		NEW ROAD.													
	NAME AND LOCATION OF WORK	Cut out and Cleared.		Stumped and Grubbed.		Graded and Shaped.		Surfacing.			Outlet Ditches.			Corduroy	
Number.		Length rods.	Width feet.	Length rods.	Width feet.	Length rods.	Width feet.	Material.	Length rods.	Width feet.	Length rods.	Width feet.	Depth feet.	Length rods.	Width feet.
1	2	3	4	5	6	7	8	9	10	11	12	13	14	15	16
	Head, Clara and Maria:														
159	Mattawan and Pembroke, Lot 3, Range A and B, Head..														
160	Mattawan and Pembroke, Lot 65, Range A and B, Maria														
161	Mattawa and Pembrhoke, Lot 16, Range A and B, Clara.														
162	Herschel Township Roads														
163	Herschel, Con. 9, west of Hastings Road	40	40	40	20	80	18	stone fill							
164	Hugel Township Roads			200	50	200	30		10	6					
165	Hugel and Kirpatrick Boundary Road from Warren to Verner.														
166	Jones Falls and Mortons Road..														
167	Jones Falls and Crosby Road..														
168	Kehoe Hill, Lots 25 and 26....														
169	Kingston and Perth Roads.....														
170	Kirkfield and Dalrymple Road..														
171	L'Amable and Fort Stewart Rd.														
172	Lanark and Darling Boundary.														
173	Larocque Road														
	Laxton, Digby and Longford Townships:														
174	Con. 4, Laxton														
175	Monck Road, Lots 26 to 28..														
176	North Quarter-line Laxton, Con. 3														
177	Cameron Road from Norland to Boundary of Bixley....														
178	Lennox and East Hastings Bdy.														
179	Louden and McPherson Bdy...	320	50	320	12									28	16
	Lutterworth Township Roads:														
180	Bobcaygeon Road, Lot 15, Con. A														
181	Cameron Road, Lot 14, Con. 7														
182	Davis Lake Road, Lots 5-10..														
183	Miners Bay Road														
	Lyle Township Roads:														
184	Madawaska and Hastings Rd., Lot 39														
185	Madawaska and Hastings Rd., Lot 50														
186	Madawaska and Hastings Road:														
187	Bridge on Sucker Creek, Lot 11														
	Lot 29, Con. 12, Lyle														
188	Mara, from 7th Con. to Brechin Village														
189	Mara, Cons. 4 and 5, west from Boundary														
190	Marlbank Road in Hungerford..														
191	Marlbank to Forest Mills Col. Rd														
192	Martland and Scollard Boundary	320	50			160	35				21	2	1		
193	Martland Township Roads.....														
194	Mallory's Junction to Vallanchera														
195	Mallory Hill Road in Miller....														
	Mattawa and Pembroke Roads:														
196	Con. 9, from 5th Sideroad..	80	40	80	24	80	16								
197	20th Sideroad from Con. 12.														
198	Con. 10 from Lot 3, east..														
	Mattawan Township Roads:														
199	Les Erables Road, Lot 28...														
200	Lot 35, Con. 9														
201	Con. 8 from Lot 29.......														
202	Lot 21 from Con. 10.......														
203	Con. 3 from Lot 56.......	160	24	160	20			gravel	10	8					
204	Mayo Township Roads														
205	Methuen Township Roads: North end														

Roads Branch, Department of Public Works, Ontario, in 1913.

OLD ROAD.

Cleared Length rods	Width feet	Graded and Shaped Length rods	Width feet	Surfacing Material	Length rods	Width feet	Outlet Ditches Length rods	Width feet	Depth feet	Bridges No.	Length feet	Sub-structure	Super-structure	Culverts No.	Material	Total Miles of Road Built and Improved	Total Cost of Work	No.
17	18	19	20	21	22	23	24	25	26	27	28	29	30	31	32	33	34 ($ c.)	35
		240	16											1	wood	1.50	251 00	159
		140	14											3	wood	2.50	150 08	160
640	16	120	16											5	wood	2.50	300 55	161
80	20	80	16											3	cedar	.25	200 32	162
														3	cedar	.25	200 07	163
																.63	400 09	164
		800	20				66	2		1				18	wood	3.50	499 35	165
		80	16	stone	160	12								2	concre'e	.50	98 12	166
		240	14	gravel	40	12	300	2		1				2	tile	.75	101 85	167
		4	24	stone fill												.01	149 42	168
		125	14	sand	250	12	280	2		1				1	tile	.77	201 21	169
		35	14	gravel	80	7										.36	99 87	170
40	20	240	16											{ 2 steel, 5 cedar }		.75	302 81	171
330	40	330	24	gravel	320	14								1	cedar	1.00	234 80	172
480	30	480	30				6	3	3					3	wood	1.50	375 00	173
		180	20	stone	250	6								1	stone	.82	198 98	174
		118	14	gravel	110	6	7	2	1							.43	207 09	175
80	16	80	18											1	stone	.25	100 58	176
				gravel	600	6										1.87	200 24	177
		115	14	b.stne	115	12	115	3	1½							.86	100 00	178
										1	16	wood	w'd	3	wood	1.00	291 96	179
										2	12	cedar	cd'r			.63	50 00	180
		200	14													2.50	100 00	181
		300	18	rock	cut					1	12	cedar	cd'r			1.00	100 00	182
		320	12							3	12	cedar	cd'r			1.25	99 56	183
		160	16				160	3	2					3	wood	.50	250 00	184
		320	16				200	2	1					3	wood	1.00	264 96	185
		45	12	earth	20	7				1	31	wood	w'd	2	wood	1.25	100 00	186
		640	14	earth	30	14								3	wood	2.50	400 00	187
				stone	140	8										.84	100 13	188
		360	33	gravel	275	6								2	cedar	2.00	300 33	189
		160	14	gravel	320	7	20	3	4					2	stone	1.00	400 55	190
		75	16	stone	75	14	160	2	1					2	wood	1.00	600 40	191
				earth	170	12				1	20	stone	w'd	7	cedar	.52	198 44	192
60	10	480	12	earth	160	7										5.00	300 06	193
		200	34	gravel	200	6										2.00	100 00	194
														1	wood	.25	240 40	195
		160	18											1	wood	.50	149 80	196
40	50	40	16				80	2	1					1	wood	.25	150 00	197
														1	wood			198
		80	20	gravel	40	8								2	wood	.38	150 00	199
		80	18	gravel	90	8								1	wood	.50	152 00	200
		120	10	earth	40	8								2	wood	.62	101 00	201
200	40													3	wood	.50	151 25	202
																.50	150 58	203
80	15	160	11											{ 1 cedar, 4 steel }		.50	*200 37	204
		198	16											1	wood	.62	100 75	205

Schedule showing amount of Road Construction under the Colonization

		NEW ROAD.													
		Cut out and Cleared.		Stumped and Grubbed.		Graded and Shaped.		Surfacing.			Outlet Ditches.			Corduroy	
Number.	NAME AND LOCATION OF WORK	Length rods.	Width feet.	Length rods.	Width feet.	Length rods.	Width feet.	Material.	Length rods.	Width feet.	Length rods.	Width feet.	Depth feet.	Length rods.	Width feet.
1	2	3	4	5	6	7	8	9	10	11	12	13	14	15	16
206	South end, Methuen Tp.														
	Minden Township Roads:														
207	Minden and Carnarvon, from Con. 10														
208	Sideroad between 26 and 27, Cons. 1-2														
209	Bobcaygeon Road from Peterson Road														
210	Minden and Gelert Road..														
211	Monck Road from Rama to Rathburn														
	Monmouth Township Roads:														
212	Con. 1, Lot 12, from Hotspur													8	16
213	Torry Hill Road														
214	Dummitt Road														
215	Montague Road (revote, 1912).														
216	Musclowes Schoolhouse Road, Con. 6														
217	McClure and Wicklow Township Roads ...														
218	McPherson Township Roads...	400	50	400	12										
219	New Boyne Road														
220	North Algona Township Roads.	80	34	90	18	80	16	sand	80	16					
221	Opinicon Road from Boundary of Loboro														
222	Pakenham, 6th Line, between 1 and 6														
	Papineau Township Roads:														
223	Con. 15, from Lot 24..														
224	Con. 15, from Lot 32......	140	40	140	25	140	14								
225	Con. 10, from Lot 27......														
226	5th Sideroad from Mattawa and Pembroke South.....														
227	5th Sideroad, from Mattawa and Pembroke East..														
228	25th Sideroad, from Con. 12														
229	Bridge at Con. 10 and 20th Sideroad														
	Papineau, Con. 10:														
230	Con. 10, from Lot 34, east..														
231	From Con. 10 to Lot 10....														
232	Papineau, 5th Sideline from Con. 12														
	Petawawa Township Roads:														
233	Lake Range, Lots 6 and 7..														
234	Lots 15 and 16, Cons. 1 & 2														
235	Range A, Lots 1 to 5..														
	Pembroke Township Roads:														
236	Con. 1, Lots 5 to 8........														
237	Lot 1, Con. 3														
238	Con. 1, Lots 2 and 8.....														
239	Pembroke and Beanville Road														
240	Peterson Road West from Maynooth														
241	Peterson Road, Maynooth to Combermere														
242	Portland and Loboro Boundary on Con. 4														
243	Potter Settlement Road					320	14	gravel	240	7					
	Radcliffe Township Roads:														
244	Rockingham and Palmer Rapids Road														
245	Combermere and Barrie Bay Road														
246	Combermere and Ft. Stewart Road														
	Raglan Township Roads:														
247	Rosenthal Road														
248	Hardwood Lake Road														
249	10th Con. Road														

Roads Branch, Department of Public Works, Ontario, in 1913.

OLD ROAD.

Cleared		Graded and Shaped		Surfacing			Outlet Ditches			Bridges over 10 feet		Material		Culverts		Total Miles of Road Built and Improved	Total Cost of Work	Number
Length rods	Width feet	Length rods	Width feet	Material	Length rods	Width feet	Length rods	Width feet	Depth feet	Number	Length feet	Sub-structure	Super-structure	Number	Material		$ c.	
17	18	19	20	21	22	23	24	25	26	27	28	29	30	31	32	33	34	35
		232	16													.75	100 45	206
		400	14											2	stone	1.25	99 00	207
		200	14	gravel	80	6										.68	100 00	208
				earth	640	6										2.00	99 75	209
		10	16	gravel	80	6								1	wood	.12	50 00	210
				gravel	48	6										.50	130 00	211
60	20	740	14	earth	30	7				1R		wood	w'd	2	cedar	2.63	199 25	212
960	50	75	14											3	cedar	3.00	100 20	213
		160	16													1.50	50 45	214
		40	24	gravel	80	10								1	con'te	.25	299 73	215
360	20	360	14											8	cedar	1.12	402 41	216
		240	16	E. fill	16	16								3	cedar	.75	199 50	217
										1	16	wood	w'd	7	wood	1.50	897 50	218
				E. fill	80	16										.25	101 92	219
		160	16	loam	160	16										.75	301 29	220
		300	14	gravel	400	8	500	2	1					5	tile	3.00	299 94	221
		320	16	gravel	320	16								2	con'te	1.00	307 05	222
		80	14	gravel	40	8								1	wood	.38	150 00	223
														1	wood	.38	150 11	224
		120	16											1	wood	.38	200 00	225
		240	16	earth	40	8										1.25	200 00	226
		15	24	gravel	120	14										.50	200 00	227
		20	16	earth	140	7								1	wood	.50	200 90	228
		10	20							1	34	stone	w'd	1	stone	.08	101 45	229
		40	16	earth	140	7								2	wood	.50	175 00	230
		240	16				240	2	1					2	wood	.75	300 00	231
		120	18	earth	80	8	200	2	1					3 / 1	wood / stone	1.60	301 25	232
		160	24	clay	180	14								1	cedar	.50	200 00	233
		400	16	loam	400	16								5	wood	1.25	200 39	234
		320	24	gravel	320	14										1.00	416 78	235
20	66	360	18	loam	360	14									1.50	150 00	236
		160	16	gravel	160	16										.50	246 88	237
		800	24	gravel	800	12										2.50	576 76	238
		240	16	shl.rk	240	16								3	cedar	.75	227 67	239
120	10	120	14	gravel	120	7	120	2	1	1	18	cedar	ced.	2	cedar	.38	201 80	240
200	30	400	16				400	2	1					4	cedar	1.25	401 97	241
		35	18	gravel	35	18										.11	153 01	242
														1 / 4	stone / cedar	1.00	199 16	243
		480	16	gravel	480	16								7	cedar	1.50	204 85	244
		160	16	loam	160	16								3	cedar	.50	97 90	245
		240	16	loam	240	16								2	wood	.75	100 49	246
		480	16	loam	480	16								1	cedar	1.50	200 04	247
80	30	120	16	loam	120	16								2	cedar	.38	101 85	248
80	16			gravel	80	10										.25	100 00	249

Schedule showing amount of Road Construction under the Colonization

		NEW ROAD.													
		Cut out and Cleared.		Stumped and Grubbed.		Graded and Shaped.		Surfacing.			Outlet Ditches.			Corduroy	
Number.	NAME AND LOCATION OF WORK	Length rods.	Width feet.	Length rods.	Width feet.	Length rods.	Width feet.	Material.	Length rods.	Width feet.	Length rods.	Width feet.	Depth feet.	Length rods.	Width feet.
1	2	3	4	5	6	7	8	9	10	11	12	13	14	15	16
250	18th Con. Road, Raglan														
251	Little Ireland Road													20	16
252	Rama and Dalton Boundary from Con. 1														
253	Ratter and Dunnett Township Roads	100	40								100	3	2		
254	Rolph Township Roads	160	50												
255	Scollard Township Roads														
256	Sharbot Lake Road	35	22	35	22	35	22	gravel	35	18					
257	Sharbot Lake and Hinchinbrooke Road to Parham	58	30	58	30	58	20	gravel	58	20	58	2	1		
	Sebastopol Township Roads:														
258	Ryan Mountain Road														
259	Foymount Road														
	Sherwood and Jones Township Roads:														
260	Bella Rapids Road			240	14	320	80	gravel	240	16					
261	Wilno and Rockingham Road														
262	Bark Lake Road														
263	Sherebourne Township Roads														
264	Sherbinan Road														
265	Sherebrook Road														
266	Snow Road	122	30	122	20	122	12	sand	12	7	244	2	1		
	Snowden Township Roads:														
267	Bobcaygeon Road														
268	Minden and Gelert Roads														
269	South Algona Township Roads														
270	Stafford Township Roads														
	Stanhope Township Roads:														
271	Maple Lake Road														
272	Grit Road														
273	Peterson Road from Cameron														
	Summerville Township Roads:														
274	Bobcaygeon Road, south of Con. 6														
275	Base Line between Pardue and Baddow														
276	Coboconk Road to Burnt River														
277	Burnt River and Burry's Green Road														
278	Monck Road, Lots 11, 12, 13														
279	Base Line at Lot 17, Con. 1					100	18								
280	Burnt River Road														
281	Trout Lake Road, Addington	68	30	68	22	68	14	sand	10	6	136	2	1		
282	Tyendinaga and Richmond Bdy from C. P. Railway, south to Kingsford														
283	Tyendinaga and Richmond Bdy. from Con. 3, south														
284	Townline of Frontenac & Leeds														
285	Verner and Desaulner Bridge														
286	Victoria Road, north of Uphill													28	12
287	Whalen Settlement Road, Keatley's Swamp														
288	White Lake Road, from Lot 16, Con. 10, to Lot 27, Con. 6.														
289	Westmeath Township Roads														
	Widdifield Township Roads:														
290	Lot 18, Con. D, east														
291	Lot 17, Con. B, north														
292	Gormanville Road from Con. C														
293	Lot 14, Con. B, east														
294	18th Sideroad, Con. B														
295	Con. 5, from 14th Sideroad														
296	Con. 4, from Lot 14, east														
297	Cook Mill Road, from Con. 4														
298	Hunters Hill, Lot 9, Con. 2														
299	18th Sideline, from Con. 2							earth	45	7				15	9
300	Wilberforce, Extension, Mud Lake Road	45	20												
	Wilberforce, Township Roads:														
301	Con. 15, Lots 3 to 6														

Roads Branch, Department of Public Works, Ontario, in 1913.

OLD ROAD.

Cleared		Graded and Shaped.		Surfacing.			Outlet Ditches.			Bridges over 10 feet.		Material.		Culverts.		Total Miles of Road Built and Improved.	Total Cost of Work.	Number.
Length rods.	Width feet.	Length rods.	Width feet.	Material.	Length rods.	Width feet.	Length rods.	Width feet.	Depth feet.	Number.	Length feet.	Sub-structure.	Super-structure.	Number.	Material.			
17	18	19	20	21	22	23	24	25	26	27	28	29	30	31	32	33	34	35
		160	16	loam	160	16										.50	100 00	250
		160	16	loam	160	16								2	cedar	.62	124 65	251
		400	18	gravel	50	7	200	3	1					5	wood	2.00	149 97	252
																.81	400 00	253
640	24	640	24	gravel	240	14				1	12	stone	w'd	4	cedar	2.00	492 00	254
160	28	160	28							2R		cedar	ced.	3	wood	1.00	310 85	255
							65	2	1					2	stone	.11	100 00	256
														4	tile	.18	400 80	257
		320	16	stone	320	16								3	cedar	1.00	304 75	258
		240	16	loam	240	16								1	cedar	.75	104 90	259
														1	cedar	1.00	196 20	260
		400	16	loam	400	16								3	cedar	1.25	300 00	261
		160	16	loam	16	16				1R		cedar	ced.	4	cedar	.50	103 25	262
		400	16	gravel	160	7	200	2	1					5	wood	1.50	399 85	263
		240	14	gravel	240	7	100	2	1					3	steel	.75	201 00	264
		95	18	gravel	95	18								1	cedar	.30	100 00	265
														1	tile			
														7	stone	.89	399 79	266
		160	14	gravel	110	7	20	3	2					1	cedar	.50	50 00	267
		60	16	loam	320	18								2	cedar	.58	150 25	268
		320	18	loam	640	18								5	cedar	1.00	300 21	269
		640	18													2.00	549 51	270
		80	14	gravel	300	6	100	3	2					1	cedar	1.50	113 86	271
		40	16	gravel	12	6				1R	15	cedar	ced.	1	wood	.22	50 50	272
				earth	240	14										.75	49 50	273
		103	16													.32	100 38	274
		20	20	gravel	20	20	20	2	1							.06	102 10	275
		180	14	stone	180	6										.56	199 99	276
																	90 00	277
			b	stone	90	7										.29	106 78	278
														1	stone	.81	99 01	279
																.69	100 00	280
		200	18	earth	18	7								4	stone	.32	197 48	281
		90	15	sand	90	10	180	2	1					1	stone	.29	103 62	282
				gravel	320	7										1.00	175 00	283
		90	14	earth	120	12	200	2	1	1				4	tile	.88	100 20	284
		500	30				100	2	1	1	3	10	wood	w'd	3	wood	6.00	499 68	285
				gravel	100	12										4.00	100 00	286
80	10	160	14	gravel	180	7								1	steel	.50	201 12	287
		700	16	loam	700	16								2	iron	2.50	508 47	288
		320	24	gravel	320	14								1	cedar	1.00	400 44	289
		70	16	gravel	80	8								6	concr'te	2.50	258 70	290
800	5	800	18	gravel	480	8										3.00	450 50	291
		1,200	18											2	wood	3.50	349 71	292
				gravel	200	7								2	wood	.63	101 25	293
				stone	20	9										.06	100 00	294
				gravel	200	7										.63	100 75	295
																.50	149 27	296
27	23	80	14	gravel	130	10										5.00	297 25	297
		400	20	gravel	160	8										.25	150 00	298
		36	16	stone	6	16								2	wood	.13	50 00	299
		160	16	loam	160	16								3	cedar	.86	508 84	300
		160	16	loam	160	16	80	2	1							.50	198 29	301

6 P.W.

Schedule showing amount of Road Construction under the Colonization

		Cut out and Cleared.		Stumped and Grubbed.		Graded and Shaped.		Surfacing.			Outlet Ditches.			Corduroy	
Number.	NAME AND LOCATION OF WORK	Length rods.	Width feet.	Length rods.	Width feet.	Length rods.	Width feet.	Material.	Length rods.	Width feet.	Length rods.	Width feet.	Depth feet.	Length rods.	Width feet.
1	2	3	4	5	6	7	8	9	10	11	12			15	16
302	Con. 20, Lots 10 and 11....														
303	Con. 6, Lots 2 to 4......														
304	Lots 1 to 3, Cons. 21 and 22														
305	Lots 28 to 31, Cons. 19 & 20														
306	Con. 14, Lots 16 to 19......														
307	Con. 22, Lots 31 to 33......														
308	Wolfe Grove Road														
309	Wylie Township Roads......														
310	Balances, 1912, and Inspection, 1913														
	Total, East Division	6,329	....	5,679	r....	4,607	....	......	1,614	....	1,364	....	....	684	....
	TEMISKAMING DIVISION														
	Armstrong Township:														
1	Cons. 4 and 5, Lots 1 to 6..	480	40	480	22	330	12	......	....	....	640	3	1½	....	....
2	Armstrong and Beauchamp Boundary	80	40	80	20	160	24	......	....	....	....	....	....	....	....
3	Lots 4 and 5, Cons. 1 and 2.	300	25	300	15	640	24	earth	540	20	....	....	....	....	....
4	Armstrong, Lots 4 and 5, Con. 3	....	....	330	15	300	24	......	....	....	40	2½	1½	....	....
	Beauchamp Township:														
5	Between Cons. 2 and 3, across Lots 4, 5, 6	280	60	420	30	68	18	......	....	....	....	....	....	....	....
6	Cons. 1, 2, 3, across Lots 2-3	210	30	460	30	543	24	earth	41	16	241	5	2	41	16
	Bryce Township:														
7	Cons. 5 and 6, across Lots 3, 4, 5	330	40	400	30	160	30	......	....	....	....	....	....	66	16
8	Bryce and Beauchamp Boundary, Con. 5	180	40	160	30	180	24	......	....	....	10	2	2	16	16
	Buck Township Roads:														
9	Lots 6 and 7, across Con. 1, Dymond, and Con. 6, Buck	....	....	....	....	....	....	......	....	....	....	....	....	....	....
10	Boundary Line across Lots 2 and 1, Bucke, and 1, 2, 3, 4, Firstbrook	640	60	640	30	....	....	......	....	....	....	....	....	....	....
11	Brethour Township Roads: Pense and Brethour Townline, Lots 1 to 6	....	....	....	....	....	....	......	....	....	....	....	....	....	....
12	Con. 2, Lots 8 and 9.......	....	....	177	20	....	....	earth	160	16	160	3	1½	160	16
13	Brethour & Casey Townline..	....	....	....	....	....	....	......	....	....	....	....	....	....	....
	Cane Township Roads:														
14	Cons. 4 and 5, Lots 1 to 12.	....	....	....	....	....	....	......	....	....	....	....	....	55	16
15	Lots 4 and 5, east on Cons. 2 and 3	185	30	185	30	185	24	earth	100	5	....	....	....	25	16
16	Lots 8 and 9, Cons. 3 and 4 half Lots 5 and 6......	480	60	160	30	....	....	......	....	....	15	3	1	....	....
17	West Boundary across north Lots 6 and 7 to T. N. O. ...	280	60	320	30	220	24	......	....	....	15	3	2	....	....
18		240	60	240	30	240	24	......	....	....	....	....	....	....	....
	Casey Township Roads:														
19	Lots 2 and 3, across Con. 5.	320	40	320	24	250	12	......	....	....	250	6	3	....	....
20	Lots 2 and 3, across Cons. 1, 2, 3	160	50	280	18	280	10	......	....	....	280	6	3	....	....
21	Cons. 2 and 3, across Lots 8-11	80	40	80	30	80	22	gravel	80	20	160	5	3	....	....
22	Con. 5, across Lot 5	....	....	10	30	80	10	earth	30	10	21	6	3	....	....
	Dack Township Roads:														
23	Lots 8 and 9, across Cons. 2 and 1	320	40	160	30	160	24	......	....	....	....	....	....	....	....
24	Lots 8 and 9, across Con. 5..	....	....	160	15	320	24	......	....	....	....	....	....	....	....
25	Cons. 3 and 4, from Lot 9..	320	60	240	30	35	24	earth	85	24	....	....	....	....	....
	Dymond Township Roads:														
26	Between Lots 6 and 7, across Con. 6	120	40	120	40	280	30	......	....	....	....	....	....	....	....
27	West Road from New Liskeard to West Boundary	....	....	....	....	....	....	......	....	....	....	....	....	....	....
28	Con. 3, across Lots 11 and 12	....	....	....	....	....	....	......	....	....	....	....	....	....	....
	Evanturel Township Roads:														
29	Wendigo Road, across Cons. 5 and 6	....	....	....	....	....	....	......	....	....	....	....	....	....	....
30	South Boundary, across Lots 11-12	240	30	240	30	160	24	......	....	....	....	....	....	....	....

Roads Branch, Department of Public Works, Ontario, in 1913.

OLD ROAD.

Cleared		Graded and Shaped.		Surfacing.				Outlet Ditches.			Bridges over 10 feet.		Material.		Culverts.		Total Miles of Road Built and Improved.	Total Cost of Work.	
Length rods.	Width feet.	Length rods.	Width feet.	Material.	Length rods.	Width feet.	Length rods.	Width feet.	Depth feet.	Number.	Length feet.	Sub-structure.	Super-structure.	Number.	Material.			Number.
17	18	19	20	21	22	23	24	25	26	27	28	29	30	31	32	33	34	35
																	$ c.	
.....	....	160	16	loam	160	16	80	3	2					.....		.50	100 00	302
.....	....	320	16	loam	320	16	.....							.....		1.00	206 80	303
.....	....	330	24	gravel	320	14	.....							1	cedar	1.00	199 95	304
.....	....	480	16	loam	460	16	.....							5	cedar	1.50	299 85	305
.....	....	320	16	loam	320	16	.....							.....		1.00	200 21	306
.....	....	250	16	loam	240	16	.....							.....		.75	205 75	307
.....	....	640	16	gravel	640	16	.....							3	concr'te	2.00	494 95	308
160	30	480	18	gravel	480	18	.....							.....		1.50	451 11	309
																	6,462 35	310
11,160	....	49,621	....	....	37,465	....	5,731	....	....	48	....	.....	.....	560	.....	292.97	71,196 01	
.....	....													5	wood	2.50	1,199 69	1
.....	....															.50	261 36	2
160	15	240	24	earth	240	14	240	1	1					4	wood	4.00	300 49	3
.....	....															1.00	299 66	4
.....	....									2	25	wood	w'd	3	wood	1.50	1,000 00	5
.....	....									1	62	wood	w'd	7	wood	2.00	998 13	6
80	40									1	31	wood	w'd	3	wood	1.25	800 02	7
.....	....													3	wood	.50	500 19	8
552	20	552	20	gravel	77	10	.....							.....		3.00	1,008 84	9
.....	....													.....		2.00	1,495 94	10
.....	....	100	24				105	3	1	1	80	wood	w'd {	3	wood }	1.50	1,100 00	11
.....	....													2	iron	.50	200 27	12
.....	....						1,215	3	11					1	wood	1.25	998 89	13
.....	....	300	20	earth	140	10	350	3	1					2	wood	6.00	275 00	14
.....	....	100	24				.....							3	wood	.89	500 00	15
.....	....													1	wood	1.50	750 00	16
.....	....													2	wood	1.50	999 30	17
.....	....													2	wood	.75	599 07	18
.....	....													1	wood	1.06	900 00	19
.....	....													.....		.88	690 47	20
.....	....													.....		.95	500 77	21
.....	....									1	265	wood	w'd	.....		.09	301 95	22
.....	....													3	wood	1.00	499 24	23
.....	....													3	wood	1.00	439 54	24
.....	....													5	wood	1.00	750 22	25
.....	....									1	21	wood	w'd	4	wood	1.00	499 95	26
.....	....				bk.st.	68	9									.22	300 00	27
.....	....				earth	30	24									.25	300 49	28
.....	....	640	24	earth	30	24								9	wood	2.00	400 45	29
.....	....													3	wood	.75	450 00	30

Schedule showing amount of Road Construction under the Colonization

Number.	NAME AND LOCATION OF WORK	Cut out and Cleared.		Stumped and Grubbed.		Graded and Shaped.		Surfacing.			Outlet Ditches.			Corduroy	
		Length rods.	Width feet.	Length rods.	Width feet.	Length rods.	Width feet.	Material.	Length rods.	Width feet.	Length rods.	Width feet.	Depth feet.	Length rods.	Width feet.
1	2	3	4	5	6	7	8	9	10	11	12	13	14	15	16
31	Con. 2, across Lots 11 and 12	75	50	15	22	215	20	earth fill	40	20					
32	Between Cons. 4 and 5, across Lots 5.6			820	30	330	24				20	2	1½		
	Firstbrook Township:														
33	Lots 2 and 3, across Con. 5 and 6	640	66	640	35	40	34	gravel	160	10'				90	10
34	Lot 1, between Cons. 4 and 5													20	16
	Harris Township Roads:														
35	Harris and Casey Boundary, across Lots 2 and 4	160	25	160	15	360	20				244	5	2	84	16
36	Lake Shore Road														
37	Between Lots 4 and 5, across Cons. 5 and 6														
38	Between Lots 2 and 3, across Con. 6	40	30	40	10			earth	40	16	40	5	2		
	Harley Township Roads:														
39	Between Cons. 3 and 4, across Lots 7 and 8	250	60	320	30	250	30	gravel	250	26					
40	Between Cons. 5 and 6, across Lots 5 and 6			240	18	300	24	E. fill	80	24					
41	Between Lots 2 and 5, across Con. 6					160	20	earth	160	20	100	3	2		
42	Between Cons. 2 and 3, across Lots 5 and 6														
	Henwood Township Roads:														
43	Between Cons. 4 and 5, across Lots 1 to 12														
44	Between Lots 10 and 11, across Cons. 3, 4, 5	560	10	480	30	400	24	earth	80	24					
45	Between Cons. 2 and 3, across Lots 5 and 6	240	40	240	30	225	15	earth	20	15				25	15
46	Between Lots 6 and 7, across Con. 4			320	30	560	24	E. fill	15	24	160	3	1		
	Hilliard Township Roads:														
47	Between Lots 2 and 3, across Cons. 1 and 2			250	30	374	26	E. fill	80	15	85	3	1		
48	Con. 5, across Lots 8 and 9	355	40	355	30	40	30								
	Hudson Township Roads:														
49	Between Lots 2 and 3, across Cons. 1, 2, 3	320	40	303	30	633	24	earth	8	16	29	3	2	18	16
50	Dymond and Hudson Boundary, across Con. 5			110	14			E. fill	120	16	10	2	1		
51	Twin Lake Road from Con. 3	480	40	480	15	240	15								
	Ingram Township Roads:														
52	Between Cons. 4 and 5, from Lot 1					266	24	gravel	266	20	500	2	1	38	16
53	Line on Con. 4					160	24	E. fill	20	16	162	3	2	140	12
54	Between Lots 6 and 7, across Cons. 1, 2, 3	966	60	960	33	160	24				160	2	1		
	Pense Township Roads:														
55	Between Lots 2 and 3, across Cons. 1, 2, 3	800	36	800	25	480	25	E. fill	80	16				22	16
56	Between Cons. 1 and 2, across Lots 3.4	320	25	314	25										
	Robillard Township Roads:														
57	Between Lots 2 and 3, across Cons. 2 and 3	640	40	640	30										
58	Inspection, 1913, balances, 1912, and works in progress end of 1912														
	Total Temiskaming Division	11,031		12,949		9,574			2,405		3,142			803	

RECAPITULATION

1	Sudbury-Soo Trunk Road	320		320		320					320				
2	Trunk Roads	4,407		4,407		2,475		2,532			1,485			648	
3	North Division	25,439		30,064		15,891			9,815		5,325			2,190	
4	West Division	4,787		4,113		3,511			1,788		2,857			40	
5	East Division	6,329		5,679		4,607			1,614		1,364			684	
6	Temiskaming	11,031		12,949		9,574			2,405		3,142			803	
	Grand Total	52,313		47,522		36,378			18,154		14,493			4,335	

Roads Branch, Department of Public Works, Ontario, in 1913.

OLD ROAD.

Cleared		Graded and Shaped.		Surfacing.			Outlet Ditches.			Bridges over 10 feet.		Material.		Culverts.		Total Miles of Road Built and Improved.	Total Cost of Work.	Number.
Length rods.	Width feet.	Length rods.	Width feet.	Material.	Length rods.	Width feet.	Length rods.	Width feet.	Depth feet.	Number.	Length feet.	Sub-structure	Super-structure.	Number.	Material.			
17	18	19	20	21	22	23	24	25	26	27	28	29	30	31	32	33	34	35
										1	24	wood	w'd	2	wood	1.25	$ c. 275 00	31
														3	wood	1.00	500 60	32
										1		wood		1	wood	2.00	2,821 18	33
		40	18	bk. st.	51	13								1	wood	.29	270 42	34
																1.00	596 92	35
10	10	560	18	gravel	360	12								9	box	1.75	399 33	36
				earth	160	16	360	3	2							.50	388 75	37
				gravel	175	12										1.05	796 95	38
														2	wood	1.00	502 35	39
														1	wood	.94	511 58	40
										1	95	wood	w'd	1	wood	.50	615.88	41
100	20			earth	100	20	20	2½	1½					2	wood	75	400 50	42
		400	24	earth	185	24	1,600	8	2					19	wood	6.00	299.95	43
														7	wood	1.75	995 75	44
										1	24	wood	w'd	3	wood	2.00	499 99	45
														2	wood	2.00	800 00	46
														2	wood	2.00	1,027 47	47
										1	82	cedar	ced.			1.25	995 88	48
										1	16	wood	w'd	4	wood	3.00	1,202 10	49
										1	16	wood	w'd	1	wood	1.00	200 00	50
																1.62	873 85	51
										1	27	wood	w'd	10	wood	1.00	600 03	52
														4	wood	1.50	800 06	53
																3.00	1,225 29	54
										1 R 1	70 30	wood wood	w'd w'd	5	wood	2.50	1,458 62	55
																1.00	480 65	56
																2.00	992 66	57
																	3,767 18	58
902		2,932			1,716		3,890			16				154		85.29	42,665 77	
2,880		3,920			2,160		4,840			4				2		23.00	29,184 16	1
5,850		7,947			8,762		6,845			14				74		57.43	35,164 61	2
16,685		37,419			34,551		15,692			34				533		292.61	102,344 96	3
9,202		15,707			8,953		11,479			14				140		92.77	25,835 51	4
11,160		49,621			37,465		5,731			48				560		292.97	71,196 01	5
902		2,932			1,716		3,890			16				154		85.29	42,665 77	6
46,179		117,546			83,440		43,977			130				1,463		844.07	306,391 02	

Schedule showing the amount of Work of Road Construction

Number.	Township.	Cleared, cut, stumped and grubbed.		Graded.		Surfaced.			Corduroy.		Ditches.		
		Length in rods.	Width in feet.	Length in rods.	Width in feet.	Material.	Length in rods.	Width in feet.	Length in rods.	Width in feet.	Length & rods.	Width in feet.	Depth in feet.
1	2	3	4	5	6	7	8	9	10	11	12	13	14
	NORTH DIVISION.												
1	Alberton By-law No. B			625	24	gravel	280	8					
2	Assiginack By-law No. 946 ..			625	24	gravel	1,840	8			20	3	3
3	Atwood & Curren By-law No. 82	75	66	199	22								
	Grant to Alberton Township.												
	Grant to Assiginack Township												
	Grant to Atwood and Curren Township												
4	Balfour By-law No. 26			2,000	24						2,000	2	1
5	Blake By-law No. 315	320	40	320	24								
	Grant to Balfour Township.												
6	Carnarvon By-law No. 273	100	35	800	24	{ earth { gravel	50 1,445	16 8	} ..				
7	Chapple By-law No. 150.	2,270	40	1,467	30	gravel	283	6	124	16	251	2	1
8	Cockburn Island By-law No. 35.	110	40	255	24	earth	260	16			30	3	2
9	Conmee By-law No. 1	640	40	388	24	{ earth { gravel	424 82	16 10	} 6	10	232	3	2
10	Crooks By-law No. 314	640	40						4	16			
	Grant to Chapple Township.												
11	Dilke By-law No. 47........	628	40	506	30				51	16	131	2	1
	Grant to Drury, Dennison and Graham												
12	Emo By-law No. 159	420	40	2,752	28	gravel	1,345	8			184	2	1
	Grant to Emo Township												
13	Gordon By-law No. 119......	40	40	155	22	{ earth { gravel	175 1,070	16 20	} ..				
14	Hilton By-law No. 349	193	66	812	22	gravel	685	8					
15	Howland By-law No. 71			200	20	gravel	1,100	5					
	Grant to Howland Township.												
16	Jaffray & Mellick By-law No. 35	960	40	980	18	gravel	705	12	12	16	557	3	2
17	Jocelyn By-law No. 261......	225	40	460	24	gravel	425	6			160	3	2
18	Johnson By-law No. A 34....	10	30	98	22	gravel	353	5					
19	Korah By-law No. 108......	870	30	5,405	24	gravel	2,565	5			195	4	2
	Grant to Korah Township.												
20	Laird By-law No. 96	40	20	555	22	gravel	415	6			297	3	2
21	Lavallee By-law No. 106......	557	16	2,616	24	gravel	443	8	125	16	313	3	2
	Grant to Laird Township.												
22	McIrvine By-law No. 148	207	66	242	28	gravel	398	6					
23	McKim By-law No. 122			3,520	24						800	2	1
24	Morley & Pattulo By-law No. 96	1,145	83	1,384	30	gravel	1,005	6	128	16	590	3	2
	Grant to McIrvine												
	Grant to McKim												
25	Neebing By-law No. 313	400	66	520	30	earth	520	30					
26	Neelon & Garson By-law No. 66			6,980	24						1,600	3	2
	Grant to Neelon and Garson Townships												
27	Oliver By-law No. 147	480	35	240	18	{ earth { gravel	84 60	16 7	} ..		40	3	2
28	Plummer Additional By-law No. 126			1,600	22	gravel	664	6					
29	Prince By-law No. 37	1,286	12	152	24	{ earth { gravel	200 601	16 8	} ..		405	2	1
30	Rayside By-law No. 112......	160	50	1,440	24						800	3	2
	Grant to Rayside												
31	Sandfield By-law No. 188	200	40	65	24	gravel	590	6					
32	St. Joseph By-law No. 398....	320	20	160	24	gravel	2,400	7			800	3	2
33	Shuniah By-law No. 381	80	66	720	24	{ earth { gravel	920 860	16 7	}				
	Grant to Sandfield Township												
34	Tarbutt and Tarbutt Additional Bylaw No. 5			75	22	gravel	566	6					
35	Tarentorus By-law No. 126 ..	438	66	2,282	24	gravel	2,007	7			103	4	2
36	Tehkummah By-law No. 202...	160	40	225	18	gravel	620	5					{
37	Thessalon By-law No. 10......	40	30	120	24	gravel	136	6					
	Grant to Tarbutt and Tarbutt Additional												
	Grant to Tarentorus Township												
	Total, North Division ..	12,814		40,298			25,226		445		9,888		

Colonization Roads Branch under Municipal By-Laws, 1913.

Cut or Fill.		Bridges.			Culverts.		Miles of New Road.	Miles of Old Road.	Municipal Expenditure.	Government Contribution.	Number.
Material	Amount in Cubic yards.	Number.	Span in feet.	Material.	Number.	Material.					
15	16	17	18	19	20	21	22	23	24	25	26
									$ c.	$ c.	
							.88		646 20	222 10	1
					15	wood	5.39		1,424 72	712 37	2
					2	wood	.76		255 10	182 55	3
										1,220 00	
										700 00	
										215 25	
					11	cedar	6.50		1,800 00	800 00	4
earth	200				4	cedar		1.00	836 63	418 32	5
										900 00	
earth	200	4	16	wood	7	wood	1.18	3.94	1,800 00	800 00	6
earth	540	2	23	wood	16	wood	.21	9.72	2,682 45	1,341 73	7
rock	55				2	wood	1.07		417 63	200 00	8
earth	300				15	cedar	2.00	2.07	1,500 00	750 00	9
					5	cedar		2.00	914 20	457 10	10
										1,193 46	
					4	wood		2.27	915 48	457 71	11
										963 07	
					8	wood		11.41	3,000 00	1,500 00	12
										1,975 71	
{ earth	50				9	wood	.34	3.57	1,185 60	592 80	13
{ rock	40										
earth	18				1	stone		3.89	1,500 00	750 00	14
{ earth	25				6	metal		3.45	1,200 00	600 00	15
{ rock	15										
										825 00	
earth	14				16	wood		6.25	1,000 00	500 00	16
{ earth	300				4	wood	.31	2.57	800 00	400 00	17
{ rock	100										
earth	697							1.40	600 00	300 00	18
earth	646	4	23	plank	{ 17	metal }	5.68	11.18	4,000 00	2,000 00	19
					{ 7	cedar }					
							3.31			400 00	20
rock	750								800 00	800 00	
earth	36	2	18	wood	9	wood		9.69	2,644 90	1,322 45	21
										425 25	
					8	iron	.65	1.38	2,874 36	1,425 18	22
					8	cedar		11.00	2,000 00	1,000 00	23
earth	200	2	22	wood	21	wood	1.08	5.50	2,910 00	1,450 00	24
										521 54	
										1,200 00	
earth	1,500	1	33	cedar	6	metal	1.25	1.25	2,000 00	1,000 00	25
					13	cedar		21.50	2,000 00	1,000 00	26
										521 12	
					8	wood		1.72	900 00	450 00	27
					{ 8	stone }		5.78	1,800 00	650 00	28
		1R		wood	{ 5	wood }					
earth	270				6	cedar	1.25	8.06	1,108 11	554 05	29
					9	cedar		5.00	1,200 00	600 00	30
										533 33	
rock	185				{ 8	stone }		1.38	580 00	290 00	31
					{ 8	wood }					
earth	192							12.50	2,000 00	1,000 00	32
earth	70				13	wood	.25	15.06	6,000 00	3,000 00	33
										282 02	
earth	200							2.01	600 00	300 00	34
earth	532	1	28	wood	9	iron	3.75	3.50	2,999 97	1,499 99	35
earth	75				1	stone }		1.87	800 00	400 00	36
rock	145				2	wood }	.50			250 00	37
earth	710				1	iron		.71	501 19		
										150 00	
										1,500 00	
	3,468	17			267		20.53	185.66	59,607 49	45,506 10	

Schedule showing the amount of Work of Road Construction

Number.	Township.	Cleared, cut, stumped and grubbed.		Graded.		Surfaced.			Corduroy.		Ditches.		
		Length in rods.	Width in feet.	Length in rods.	Width in feet.	Material.	Length in rods.	Width in feet.	Length in rods.	Width in feet.	Length in rods.	Width in feet.	Depth in feet.
1	2	3	4	5	6	7	8	9	10	11	12	13	14
	WEST DIVISION												
1	Albemarle By-law No. 495....			599	24	gravel	271	8			70	3	2
2	Amabel, By-law No. 134	90	20			gravel	405	8					
	Grant to Albemarle Township												
3	Chapman By-law No. 7			1,840	24	gravel	1,840	8			730	2	2
4	Eastnor By-law No. 948......	400	33	195	48	gravel	526	8			270	2	1
	Grant to Eastnor Township.												
5	Joly By-law No. 135			144	24	{ earth	90	} 16					
						{ gravel	24						
6	Lindsay, By-law No. 137					gravel	979	8					
	Grant to Lindsay Township.												
7	Medonte, By-law No. 484			46	24	gravel	56	16					
8	Medora & Wood, By-law No. 267	420	20	2,740	16	gravel	310	16	100	16	280	2	1
9	Monck By-law No. 388......			1,740	20	gravel	461	8			60	2	2
10	Muskoka, By-law No. 263....	800	20	5,209	16	gravel	480	8			640	2	2
11	Strong By-law No. 328......			750	20	gravel	420	8			100	2	2
12	St. Edmonds, By-law No. 147..	57	30	210	24	gravel	656	8			41	3	2
	Grant to St. Edmonds Township												
	Grant to South Himsworth Township												
	Total, West Division ...	1,767		13,464			7,088		100		1,681		
	EAST DIVISION.												
1	Bagot and Blythfield, By-law No. 278			1,920	24	{ gravel	1,840	} 16					
						{ earth	960						
2	Bedford, By-law No. 492.....	70	10	1,042	24	earth	1,800	16			1,600	2	2
3	Belmont and Methuen, By-law No. 535	160	10	230	20	stone	132	8					
4	Bexley, By-law No. 428			80	24	stone	340	8					
5	Bromley, By-law No. 204			1,920	24	gravel	1,920	16					
6	Caldwell, By-law No. 164			1,872	30	gravel	1,441	8			199	2	2
7	Casimer, Jennings and Appelby. By-law No. 58			6,060	30	gravel	1,000	8			700	2	2
8	Carlow, By-law No. 48........	80	20	560	20	......			20	14			
	Grant to Carlow Township..												
	Grant to Casimer, Jennings and Appelby												
	Grant to Caldwell Township												
9	Dummer, By-law No. 777.....			276	24	gravel	558	16					
10	Dungannon, By-law No. 67....	280	10	400	18	stone	40	16					
11	Dysart, By-law No. 587	960	50	800	18	{ earth	18,000	} 16					
						{ gravel	2,800						
12	Eldon, By-law No. 397			800	24	gravel	1,525	6					
13	Elzevir and Grimsthorpe, By-law No. 312			480	24	gravel	800	8					
14	Faraday, By-law No. 88	540	20	560	16	gravel	200	10	20	18			
	Grant to Faraday Township.												
15	Galway and Cavendish, By-law No. 242			242	16	{ gravel	145	} 16					
						{ earth	251						
16	Harvey, By-law No. 316			85	16	gravel	85	16					
17	Hinchinbrooke, By-law No. 7.. Hinchinbrooke, By-law No. 2..	} 40	12	1,500	18	{ earth	2,425	} 16			1,925	2	1
						{ gravel	266						
18	Huntingdon, By-law No. 828..			560	24	gravel	480	10					
19	Horton, By-law No. 24.......			124	20	gravel	194	10					
	Grant to Horton Township...												
20	Kennebec, By-law No. 5.....			901	20	{ earth	845	} 16					
						{ gravel	500						
21	Kingston, By-law No. 5			195	20	stone	195	8					
	Grant to Kingston Township.												

Colonization Roads Branch under Municipal By-Laws, 1913.

Cut or Fill.		Bridges.			Culverts.		Miles of New Road.	Miles of Old Road.	Municipal Expenditure.	Government Contribution.	Number.
Material.	Amount in Cubic yards.	Number.	Span in feet.	Material.	Number.	Material.					
15	16	17	18	19	20	21	22	23	24	25	26
									$ c.	$ c.	
earth	31	1	16	st'ne & wood	6	tile		3.02	1,200 00	600 00	1
rock	237				1	wood		2.44	1,603 00	800 00	2
										600 00	
					9	tile		5.75	1,065 40	499 46	3
					8	stone					
		1	18	con. & wood	3	tile		8.78	1,670 52	799 71	4
					2	wood				600 00	
earth	210					wood		.80	200 00	100 00	5
rock	407	1	24	wood	1	wood		3.08	1,600 00	800 00	6
										800 00	
earth	4,300	1	20	con. & wood	1	cement		.20	2,077 60	966 00	7
		2	18	wood	15	wood		12.00	1,500 00	750 00	8
earth	400				2	cement		14.00	1,799 06	899 58	9
rock	100				7	wood		28.00	1,008 00	500 00	10
					1	concrete					
					4	tile		2.34	799 00	399 50	11
					4	cedar		2.20	1,200 00	600 00	12
rock	240									474 67	
										1,333 00	
	5,965	6			64			77.61	16,722 57	11,522 07	
					2	cedar		7.50	1,200 00	600 00	1
					20	tile		31.00	1,999 39	999 95	2
					5	cedar					
								1.25	1,131 65	565 83	3
								1.70	612 45	300 00	4
rock	50	1R		wood	1	cedar		6.00	2,300 00	1,150 00	5
rock	300	1	24	cedar	2	concrete		12.02	2,000 00	1,000 00	6
		5	16	wood	13	wood					
								36.50	1,600 00	800 00	7
					5	cedar		1.63	611 27	300 00	8
										16 67	
										750 00	
										1,000 00	
		1	24	wood	1	stone		1.86	600 00	280 00	9
rock	33				7	cedar		1.25	600 00	300 00	10
		1	20	wood	19	wood	3.00	65.00	4,685 12	1,955 00	11
		1R	20	wood	2	concrete		4.76	2,091 63	999 69	12
		1	12	con.- wood	3	metal		2.50	800 00	400 00	13
					5	cedar		1.75	700 00	350 00	14
					12	cedar	.31			266 00	
					2	wood		2.00	250 00	125 00	15
		2	72	stone- wood	2	metal		.31	700 00	350 00	16
		1	75	stone	4	cedar			1,200 00	600 00	17
					25	tile		58.00	1,000 00	500 00	18
					1	cedar		1.75	600 00	300 00	19
		1	24	conc.-cedar	3	concrete		.61	1,224 93	582 45	
										100 00	
earth	40				93	cedar		22.50	1,500 00	750 00	20
rock	560				2	metal		.61	500 00	250 00	21
										250 00	

Schedule showing the amount of Work of Road Construction

Number.	Township.	Cleared, cut, stumped and grubbed.		Graded.		Surfaced.			Corduroy.		Ditches.		
		Length in rods.	Width in feet.	Length in rods.	Width in feet.	Material.	Length in rods.	Width in feet.	Length in rods.	Width in feet.	Length in rods.	Width in feet.	Depth in feet.
1	2	3	4	5	6	7	8	9	10	11	12	13	14
22	Lakefield, By-law No. 507....			200	18	c. stone	200	10			1,457	6"	tile
23	Limerick, By-law No. 9......	60	20	600	12								
24	Loughboro, By-law No. 52A....			20	20	stone	540	8			40	2	1
	Grant to Loughboro Township												
25	Madoc, Bylaw No. 328			1,215	20	gravel	895	8					
26	Marmora & Lake, By-law No. 460			640	16	gravel	480	16					
27	Martland, By-law No. 64......	549	66	985	20						437	3	2
28	Mayo, By-law No. 250			360	24	gravel	360	12					
29	Monteagle and Herschel, By-law No. 413	420	20	780	20	stone	32	12					
30	McNab, By-law No. 37			720	16	{earth {s'one	160 530	16 16	}				
	Grant to Madoc Township..												
	Grant to Martland Township.												
31	North Monaghan, By-law No. 662												
	Oso, By-law No. 70			715	24	earth	1,015	16			1,180	2	1
	Pittsburg, By-law No. 3.....			120	20								
32	Ratter & Dunnett, By-law No. 36			1,680	30	gravel	640	80			320	3	2
33	Rawdon, By-law No. 323			320	14	gravel	320	8					
36	Ross, By-law No. 302	40	20	1,520	20	gravel	1,600	8					
	Grant to Ratter and Dunnett.												
	Grant to Ramsay												
	Seymour, By-law No. 351			36	18	gravel	654	8					
	Springer, By-law No. 270.....	400	66	3,160	20						2,680	3	2
37	Stafford, By-law No. 630.....			1,265	24	{earth {gravel	200 1,096	} 16	30	18			
38	Smith, By-law No. 710......			243	18	stone	224	5					
	Grant to Springer Township..												
	Grant to Smith Township...												
	Grant to Storrington Township												
41	Tudor and Cashel, By-law No. 13	40	20	120	16								
42	Tyendinaga, By-law No. 615...			120	24	gravel	800	8					
43	Westmeath, By-law No. 86....			1,480	14	gravel	1,480	12					
44	Wollaston, Bylaw No. 8......	200	16	260	14	stone	60	8					
	Total, East Division....	3,839		37,256			49,376		.70		11,221		
	TEMISKAMING DIVISION.												
1	Casey, By-law No. 14	1,885	40	1,622	24	earth	25	16	8	16	947	3	2
	Grant to Casey Township....												
2	Dymond, By-law No. 92	395	48	2,565	24	{earth {gravel	1,535 477	} 16	25	16	850	3	1
	Grant to Dymond Township..												
3	Evanturel, By-law No. 96......	850	48	3,830	24	{earth {gravel	270 60	} 16			845	3	2
4	Hudson, By-law No. 33.......	160	66	7,540	24	{earth {gravel	1,141 289	} 16	5	16	766	3	2
5	Harley, By-law No. 136.......	1,609	40	4,012	24	{earth {gravel	117 842	} 16	64	16	541	3	2
6	Harris, By-law No. 28.......	560	66	3,400	24	gravel	140	16			1,170	3	2
7	Hilliard, By-law No. 29.......	740	66	3,458	24	{earth {gravel	410 60	} 16			1,007	3	2
8	Kerns, By-law No. 96.......	1,185	48	4,160	24	{earth {gravel	170 30	} 16			1,021	3	2
	Total, Temiskaming Division	7,384		28,587			9,176		97		6,647		
	RECAPITULATION.												
1	North Division	12,814		40,298			25,226		445		9,386		
2	West Division	1,767		13,464			7,088		100		1,681		
3	East Division	3,839		37,256			49,376		70		11,221		
4	Temiskaming Division	7,384		28,587			9,176		97		6,647		
	Grand Total	25,804		119,605			90,866		712		28,937		

* This amount includes the sum of $28,929.99, which was unpaid balance at the end of the fiscal year 1912.

Colonization Roads Branch under Municipal By-Laws, 1913.

	Cut or Fill.		Bridges.			Culverts.		Miles of New Road.	Miles of Old Road.	Municipal Expenditure.	Government Contribution.	Number.
Material.	Amount in Cubic Yards.	Number.	Span in feet.	Material.	Number.	Material.						
15	16	17	18	19	20	21		22	23	24	25	26
										$ c.	$ c.	
									.63	1,113 20	400 00	22
rock	800				3	stone			1.89	600 00	300 00	23
					1	stone			6.00	600 00	300 00	24
											225 00	
					8	stone	}		3.78	800 00	400 00	25
rock	40				2	cedar						
					15	metal	}		2.01	1,000 00	500 00	26
rock	100				2	cedar			4.40	1,000 00	500 00	27
earth	167	1R		wood	18	wood			1.13	600 00	300 00	28
		1	25	cedar	1	cedar						
rock	114	1	23	cedar	22	cedar			2.40	1,000 00	500 00	29
					1	cedar			2.86	2,000 00	1,000 00	30
											600 00	
											400 00	
		1	56	conc. arch					.02	738 17	300 00	31
					15	cedar			13.00	751 37	875 69	32
rock	120		16	concte-steel					.88	768 25	334 13	33
									7.50	1,000 00	500 00	34
					1	cedar			1.00	885 45	400 00	35
					2	stone	}		5.00	2,000 00	1,000 00	36
					1	cedar						
											1,000 00	
											833 33	
					8	concrete			2.58	1,666 74	650 98	37
rock	110								13.25	2,000 00	1,000 00	38
									4.10	1,204 96	600 00	39
					2	cement			.72	500 00	250 00	40
											1,000 00	
											250 00	
											100 00	
					1	cedar			.88	600 00	300 00	41
rock	700				1	cement			2.75	897 45	448 73	42
									4.63	2,380 45	1,086 16	43
rock	60				8	cedar			1.12	600 00	300 00	44
	2,983	19			337			3.31	241.88	52,512 98	32,044 61	
earth	243	3R		wood	17	wood		5.80	2.70	1,953 12	339 26	1
											1,676 55	
earth	2,915				9	wood		1.89	9.90	2,963 00	1,481 50	2
rock	462	}									825 82	
earth	681	4	20	wood	9	wood		2.75	10.25	1,594 71	797 36	3
earth	325	1	10	wood	6	wood		3.05	22.64	1,600 00	800 00	4
earth	1,895	1	10	wood	6	wood		6.09	18.85	3,000 00	1,500 00	5
rock	60											
earth	1,259	1	30	steel-concte	12	wood	}	.88	8.31	2,399 62	1,199 81	6
		3R	70	wood								
earth	1,558	2	106	plank	12	wood		2.82	7.12	1,514 83	757 42	7
earth	2,945	1	54	wood	7	wood		2.67	12.77	2,000 00	1,000 00	8
	12,603	15			78			25.90	88.04	17,025 28	10 377 72	
	8,468	17			267			20.58	185.66	59,607 49	45,506 10	1
	5,968	6			64				77.61	15,722 57	11,523 07	2
	2,983	19			337			3.31	241.88	52,512 98	32,044 61	3
	12,603	15			78			25.90	88.04	17,025 28	10,377 72	4
	30,022	57			746			49.79	592.69	$144,868 32	$99,950 50	

STATEMENT OF EXPENDITURE

ON

COLONIZATION ROADS AND BRIDGES

IN THE YEAR 1913

STATEMENT OF EXPENDITURE ON COLONIZATION ROADS AND BRIDGES IN
THE YEAR 1913.

NORTH DIVISION.

Name of Road.	Expenditure.
Aberdeen Road and Bridge, Lot 1, Con. 5	$400 00
Aberdeen Road and Bridge, Lots 3 and 4, Con. 3	400 00
Aberdeen Additional Road, West from East Boundary	400 00
Allen, 10th sideroad, Cons. 6 and 8	126 76
Assiginac, John Lane's to Ingram	149 25
Assiginac, 13th sideroad to Squirrel Town	200 00
Assiginac, 5th Con.	100 00
Assiginac and Tehkummah Township Roads	100 00
Aubrey Township Roads	710 54
Balfour, Cons. 5 and 6 and Boundary of Dowling and Balfour:—	
Poulin Section	1,500 40
Trottier Section	1,014 50
Balfour and Morgan Road:—	
Belanger Section	450 00
Mainville Section	500 29
Groulx Section	900 00
Balfour, Lots 6 and 7 across Cons. 5 and 6	450 05
Baldwin Township Roads:—	
Belch Section	200 00
Piche Section	99 21
Barr River and Sylvan Valley Road	299 89
Barrie Island Roads	150 83
Bass Lake Road	300 82
Bidwell, 10th sideroad, Cons. 4 and 6	150 00
Bidwell, Con. 10; Lots 18 to 23	200 34
Bidwell, 5th sideroad, Cons. 2 and 3, towards the school	145 60
Billings, 20th sideroad, 8th Con. to Foster's	149 97
Billings, Con. 12 to Spear's	76 00
Billings, Con. 12, Kagawong Lake to Tustian	99 79
Billings, 25th sideroad East and West along bye-road	100 00
Billings and Carnarvon Townline	151 14
Birch Lake Road, East End	350 00
Billings, from Smith's store, West	100 14
Bright Road, Con. 5	301 30
Bright Road and Bridge, Lot 3, Con. 6	399 26
Broder Township Roads:—	
Lots 11 and 12, Con. 4	200 00
Lot 6, Con. 3	150 00
Old Long Lake Road	250 40
Dill and Broder Boundary	100 00
Long Lake Road to Tremblay's	498 81
Broken Front, Salter, Lots 4, 5, 6 and 7	275 00
Burnt Land Road, East to Meldrum Bay	200 00
Burpee Blind Line, Lot 22, Westward	199 35
Burpee, 20th sideroad	150 00
Bellevue (short road)	298 87
Campbell Township Roads:—	
Langtry Section	75 50
Gilchrist Section	126 25
Clark Section	100 45
Van Horne Section	200 00
Capreol Township Roads:—	
Lots 9 and 10, Con. 4	250 00
Lots 4 and 5, Con. 2	450 00
Cons. 3 and 4, Lots 5 to 9	1,001 50
Carnarvon Township Roads:—	
Dunlop Section	149 86
Hopkin Section	146 70

Carnarvon, 20th sideroad	100 48
Carnarvon, Vincer's, East	200 00
Carter's Road Deviation, Jocelyn	200 75
Centre Line Road, Hinck's	317 10
Chapleau Township Roads	529 41
Cobden Township Roads	500 00
Cockburn Island Roads	251 03
Columbus Hill Road, Howland	299 95
Conmee Township Roads:—	
East End	797 50
West End	395 50
Cook's Road	303 73
Cuthbertson Location, Con. 7	397 57
Cuthbertson Road, North from Con. 6	299 75
Day Township, Cons. 1 and 2	391 75
Diamond Lake Road	300 41
Dill Township Roads:—	
Demonge Section	100 85
Laforest Section	497 83
Dowling Township Roads	505 29
Dorion Township Roads	2,300 12
Dorion, Lots 8 and 9, Con. 3	100 00
Elizabeth Bay Road, 10th Con. and 5th sideroad, Burpee	196 15
Eton Township Roads	997 00
Fairbank Township, and Dowling and Fairbank Boundary Roads:—	
Sauve Section	300 50
Brosseau Section	300 29
Falconbridge Township Roads	202 90
Fenwick Sideroad	498 97
Fenwick, Sections 11 and 12	500 45
Fraser-Leeburn Road	399 82
Galbraith and Aberdeen Townline	249 95
Galbraith, Lots 5 and 6, Con. 5	400 40
Galbraith Road on Cons. 1 and 2	301 47
Garden Bay Road	206 90
Gillies Township Roads	799 15
Gold Rock Road	597 21
Gordon and Allen Township Roads:—	
Donaldson Section	78 82
McArthur Section	97 50
Batty Section	100 00
Noble Section	50 00
Turner Section	75 00
Gore Bay to Hope's Hill	100 03
Gore Bay to Barrie Island	150 00
Gorham, between Lots 12 and 13, Northerly across Cons. 2, 3 and 4	696 42
Gorham, between Lots 8 and 9, Northerly, Cons. 1, 2, 3 and 4	696 04
Gorham, between Cons. 3 and 4 across Lots 13 to 16	710 47
Gorham, between Cons. 4 and 5 across Lots 13 to 16	697 82
Gorham, between Cons. 5 and 6 across Lots 17 and 18	500 00
Gorham, between Cons. 5 and 6 across Lots 15 and 16	500 00
Gorham, between Cons. 4 and 5 across Lots 17 and 18	700 73
Gorham and Ware Boundary	999 81
Goulais Bay Settlement Road	600 00
Goulais Bay Government Road	799 75
Goulais Bay and Bellevue Road	495 55
Hagar Township Roads	1,502 58
Hallam, Spencer Road	300 00
Hallam and May, Con. 4	348 75
Hallam Road from Con. 3 to Con. 1	350 15
Hallam, Con. 1, Lot 9	99 96

Name of Road.	Expenditure.
Hanmer Township Roads:—	
Lots 1 to 8, Con. 4	200 00
Lots 10 and 11, Con. 3	200 00
Lots 12 to 10, Con. 2	502 54
Lots 10 and 11, Con. 2	502 04
Lots 7 and 8, Con. 5	300 00
Hartman Township Roads	506 97
Havilah and Dunn's Valley Road	306 55
Hinck's Location Road, Con. 6	300 00
Howland, 9th Con. Taylor's to L.C.	200 60
Howland and Bidwell Townline	125 20
Ignace Township Roads	502 62
Iron Bridge and Patton Road	295 90
Johnston and Plummer Additional Boundary	300 05
Johnston Torrance Road	250 92
Kagawong to Gore Bay	499 97
Kagawong to Pervale Shore Road	99 14
Kagawong to Providence Bay	151 03
Kars Township, Goulais Bay Road Extension	450 00
Kaye's Road	450 42
Kelley Lake Road:—	
Winnerstrom Section	250 05
Lake Section	249 00
Killarney to Collin's Inlet	248 75
Lake Manitou Road	250 20
Lee's Road, Walford	298 81
Long Bay to Hope's Hill	199 60
Lorne and Nairn Township Roads:—	
Fenson Section	150 00
Edward's Section	149 95
Lumsden Township, and Lumsden and Hanmer Township Roads:—	
Lumsden and Rayside Boundary	198 54
Cons. 1 and 2	302 80
Hanmer and Lumsden Boundary	999 50
Lybster Township Roads	799 87
Main Road, Lots 26, 27 and 28 on Con. 4, Tehkummah	149 97
Marks Township Roads	797 18
Martin Road, Lots 24 and 25, Range A., Tehkummah	102 25
May, Cons. 3 and 4, Lots 9 and 10	300 42
May, Con. 3, Lots 9 and 10	296 85
May and Salter Boundary	501 00
Meldrum Bay towards lighthouse	149 65
Melgund Township Roads	799 02
Mellick and Jaffrey Township Roads	1,001 37
Merritt Township Roads:—	
Lanthier Section	150 00
Lafrenniere Section	145 00
Michipicoten Mining Roads	1,400 00
Mills Township Roads:—	
Lowrie Section	150 40
Moscrip Section	149 69
Mutrie Township Roads	793 80
McGregor Township Roads, North Branch	908 85
McIntyre and Gorham Boundary, Sections, 4 and 3 and South	700 48
McIntyre across the centre line of Section 5	299 99
McIntyre, Northerly from the Red River Road, between Sections 21 and 22	685 86
McIntyre, Section 4, Westerly on line between Sections 4 and 19	697 46
Nesterville Road	300 00

Name of Road.	Expenditure.
O'Connor Township Roads:—	
North End	532 55
South End	503 86
Oliver Township Roads	899 32
"P" Line Hill, St. Joseph	295 00
"P" Line to Wharf St. Joseph	500 00
Paipoonge Township Roads	900 07
Pearson Township Roads	789 40
Plummer Additional Road	499 73
Pulmmer Road, Cons. 3 and 4	300 85
Poplar to Gore Bay	253 21
Prince, 2nd line	300 04
Prince Township, Roads between Sections 25 and 26	200 00
Providence Bay to New House	200 70
Road at East End of Basswood Lake	397 50
Road, Sections 6 and 8, Laird	299 75
Road and Bridge North of Spanish	348 41
Rockville Road, Con. 2, Bidwell to Carnarvon	200 36
Robinson, North of Con. 12	99 25
Robinson, Cons. 9 and 10	208 42
Rydal Bank Road, North of Humphrey's	490 20
Rydal Bank Road, North, Washout	351 02
Rydal Bank, Bridge Approaches	302 45
Richard's Landing to Humbug Point	200 31
Salter Road, Sections 25 and 30	500 10
Salter, Section 35	300 38
Sandfield, Cons. 7 and 9, Lots 26 to 28	150 00
Sandfield, Con. 10, Lot 9	101 13
Sandfield, Con. 9, Lots 18 and 19	50 00
Sandfield Mills to McCullough's	200 00
Sandfield, Con. 2 and 5th sideroad to Mills	150 70
Sandford Township Roads	500 17
Scoble Township Roads	807 20
Shakespeare Centre Line	325 00
Shaw Line Road, Thessalon	234 00
Sheguiandah, 10th Con., Lots 19 and 20, Myer's Road	99 08
Silverwater to Dawson Townline	650 12
Slash Road, 5th sideroad and 16th Con.	200 00
South Bay-Mouth Road	99 98
Southworth Township Roads	489 73
Spanish Walford Road	200 08
St. Joseph, Lots 15 and 16, Harten's Road	299 40
Steinburg Road	299 25
Stobie Road	300 57
Strange Township Roads	400 00
Sylvan Valley and Echo Bay Road	298 06
Stobie and Blezard Right-of-Way	386 50
Tarbutt, Con. 6, Kensington Road	305 00
Tehkummah, 10th sideroad, Lot 11, Cons. 6 and 7	200 00
Tehkummah, 15th sideroad, Lot 16, Cons. 5 and 6	99 98
Tehkummah, 10th sideroad, South End	100 00
Temple Township Roads	999 52
Thessalon and Day Townline	297 50
Tossil Hill to Tehkummah	196 00
Townline North, Sheddon and Victoria	200 60
Tunnell Bridge Road	406 25
Van Horne Township Roads	942 46
Vankoughnet Road	400 00
Vankoughnet Road, through Section 17	500 11
Victoria Road, Sections 29 and 30	300 05

Name of Road.	Expenditure.
Wabigoon Township Roads	900 00
Wainwright Township Roads	950 00
Walford, Victoria Road	299 10
Ware, between Cons. 2 and 3 across Lots 1 to 6	1,000 37
Ware, between Cons. 4 and 5 across Lots 1 to 4	997 73
Ware, across Cons. 1 to 4 from the Dawson Road Northerly	975 10
Ware, Dog Lake Road	779 90
Wells Township Road	628 78
West Bay to Honora	149 78
West Bay to McAnsh's	249 95
White-Pennell Road	300 00
Wilson Road	100 00
Zealand Township Roads	999 96
"P" Line St. Joseph, 1912 account	100 00
Gibbs Road, balance 1912	49 75
Haines Road, balance 1912	8 76
May and Hallam, balance 1912	23 38
Kelley Lake Road, balance 1912	11 98
Fenwick, Section 7, balance 1912	13 69
Plummer Road, balance 1912	2 50
May and Salter Road, balance 1912	50 22
Red River Road, balance 1912	50 80
Desbarats Road, balance 1912	26 00
Hagar Township Road, balance 1912	1 00
Meigund Road, balance 1912	36 37
Wagg's Corner to West Bay	1 55
Doble and Carpenter, balance 1912	100 94
Doble, 2 and 3, balance 1912	175 33
Gillies Road, balance 1912	49 58
Neelon and Garson, balance 1912	98 58
Shawendowan Road, balance 1912	20 70
"P" line Road, balance 1912	10 00
McIntyre Road, balance 1912	10 55
Louise Township Road, balance 1912	25 35
Doble Road Contract, 1911	171 00
Kars Road Account, 1912	72 75
Gordon and Allen Account, 1912	17 80
James Fraser. Law Costs, Sims & Co. Account	30 55
Sutherland-Sifton Road Account, 1912	48 36
Works in Progress at end of Fiscal Year:—	
Neebing and Scoble Trunk Road	1,792 44
Sudbury and Coniston Trunk Road	436 46
Kenora and Mellick Trunk Road	432 74
Sioux-Lookout Trunk Road	500 73
McIntyre and Gorham Road (Special Warrant)	307 23
Inspection	6,618 45

SUDBURY-SOO TRUNK ROAD.

Services of Engineer	2,030 71
Webbwood Section, Repairs	276 26
Blind River Section, balance 1912	82 89
Garden River Section, balance 1912	194 41
Spanish River Section, balance 1909	19 70
Mile Post 179 to 183, gravelling (Dinsmore Contract)	3,405 74
Webbwood-Espanola Section	695 57
Sudbury and White Fish, Repairs	916 51
Nairn and Victoria Section (Litster's Accounts)	14,594 62
Nairn and Victoria Section (Accounts paid direct)	6,766 14
Garden River Road (Washout)	201 61

NEW TRUNK ROADS.

Name of Road.	Expenditure.
Kenora and Reditt Trunk Road, balance 1912	33 23
Golden City to Lakeview Trunk Road, balance 1912	94 13
Night Hawk Road, balance 1912	125 24
Sudbury-Coniston Trunk Road	8,886 07
Bridgeland Trunk Road:—	
Chisholm Section	2,001 11
Henderson Section	500 68
Dryden-Richan Trunk Road	3,008 69
Mellick and Rice Lake Trunk Road	500 00
Little Current, Gore Bay and Manitowaning Trunk Road:—	
McAnsh Section	3,454 29
Lewis Section	1,006 59
Orr Section	499 60
Sioux-Lookout Trunk Road	1,005 13
LeRoy Lake and Nickel Township Road	6,210 50
Lee Valley and Espanola Trunk Road	3,993 08
Lavallee Road and Sudbury-Coniston Survey	48 05

BY-LAWS.

Alberton, By-law No. B	323 10
Assiginac, By-law No. 346	712 37
Atwood and Curran, By-law No. 82	182 55
Grant to Alberton Township	1,220 00
Grant to Assiginac Township	700 00
Grant to Atwood and Curran Township	818 25
Balfour, By-law No. 26	800 00
Blake, By-law No. 315	418 32
Grant to Balfour Township	900 00
Carnarvon, By-law No. 273	800 00
Chapple By-law, No. 150	1,341 73
Cockburn Island, By-law No. 85	200 00
Conmee, By-law No. 1	750 00
Crooks, By-law No 314	457 10
Grant to Chapple Township	1,192 46
Dilke, By-law No. 47	457 71
Grant to Drury, Dennison and Graham Municipality	963 07
Emo, By-law No. 159	1 500 00
Grant to Emo Township	1,975 71
Gordon By-law No. 119	592 80
Hilton, By-law No 349	750 00
Howland, By-law No. 71	600 00
Grant to Howland Township	625 00
Jaffrey and Mellick, By-law No. 35	500 00
Jocelyn, By-law No. 261	400 00
Johnston, By-law No. A34	300 00
Korah, By-law No. 105	2,000 00
Grant to Korah Township	3,000 00
Laird, By-law No. 96	400 00
Grant to Laird Township	426 25
Lavallee, By-law No. 106	1,322 45
McIrvine, By-law No. 148	1,425 18
McKim, By-law No. 122	1,000 00
Morley and Pattulo, By-law No. 96	1,450 00
Grant to McIrvine Township	321 54
Grant to McKim Township	1,200 00
Neebing, By-law No. 313	1,000 00
Neelon and Gerson, By-law No. 66	1,000 00
Grant to Neelon and Carson Municipality	521 12
Oliver, By-law No. 147	450 00
Plummer Additional, By-law No. 126	650 00
Prince, By-law No. 37	554 05
Rayside, By-law No. 113	600 00

Name of Road.	Expenditure.
Grant to Rayside Township	533 33
Sandfield, By-law No. 188	290 00
Grant to Sandfield Township	282 02
St. Joseph, By-law No. 398	1,000 00
Shuniah, By-law No. 381	3,000 00
Grant to Tarbutt and Tarbutt Additional Township	150 00
Grant to Tarentorus Township	1,500 00
Tarbutt and Tarbutt Additional By-law No. 8	300 00
Tarentorus, By-law No. 126	1,499 99
Tehkummah, By-law No. 126	400 00
Thessalon, By-law No. 10	250 00

WEST DIVISION.

Armour, Lot 11, Con. 5, North to Lot 12, Con. 7	$200 00
Armour, Lot 21, Con. 11, West to the 15th sideroad	200 00
Armour, from the 10th sideroad, Easterly along Cons. 12 and 13.....	200 50
Ahmic Harbor Road, West from line between Lots 4 and 5, 8th Con., Croft	301 54
Bala and Sahanatien Road	406 07
Bethune, Lot 8, Con. 8, Easterly to Lot 10, Con. 8	200 75
Bethune, on Lot 2, between Cons. 2 and 3	200 00
Broadbent Road between Broadbent and Hemlock	176 12
Carling New Road from Lot 47, Con. 12 to Lot 8, Con. 1.............	500 00
Carling New Road from Lot 7, Con. 1, Westerly to Lot 16, Con. 1 ...	1,009 35
Carling, blind line, between Cons. 11 and 12, from Lot 28 to Snug Harbor...	199 90
Carling and Shawanaga Road, from Shebeshekong to Shawanaga Station ..	201 15
Chapman, 10th sideroad Northward	150 10
Chapman and Strong Boundary, North from Distress Road	239 67
Chapman and Ryerson from Lot 2, West to Lot 16, Con. 14, Ryerson ...	201 00
Chapman and Lount Boundary, Lot 20 to connect with Chapman Valley...	199 61
Croft, 25th sideline from Ahmic Harbor North to Magnetawan..........	199 76
Christie Road to the Town of Parry Sound	400 14
C.P.R. Station to Byng Inlet	175 00
Draper, River Road, Lot 18 to Lot 7 in Con. 7......................	300 00
Draper and Macaulay Boundary, Lot 9, Con. 13	300 05
Eagle Lake Road and Nipissing Road (10th sideroad).................	200 72
Eagle Lake Road in Machar from Lot 22 to Lot 13, Con. 5	200 09
Franklin, Lot 16, Con. 5 to Lot 24, Con. 3	249 95
Glen Robert Road from schoolhouse to 5th sideroad, Cons. 10 and 11	299 95
Gravenhurst Station to Sanitarium	300 00
Great North Road and Golden Valley Road, Cons. 8 and 9, Pringle	299 87
Great North Road between Wabaumic and McKellar	699 45
Gurd, 20th sideroad across Cons. 6 and 7	175 00
Gurd and Himsworth Boundary between Lots 9 and 10 from Lot 35, Con. 6	249 98
Hardy and McConkey Boundary North of Loring	401 77
Himsworth North, 24th and 25th Cons.	203 26
Himsworth North, 5th sideroad from 4th to the 2nd and 3rd Cons.	200 38
Himsworth North, 26th Con. from Lake Nipissing, 3 miles	209 09
Himsworth North, extension of the 5th sideroad	200 02
Himsworth North, road to Callander and North Bay	299 99
Himsworth South, between Cons. 2 and 3 across Lots 13 to 17	205 90
Himsworth South, from the 5th to the 10th sideroads in Con. 12.....	200 09
Himsworth and Chisholm Boundary, Cons. 13 and 14	300 45
Himsworth and Nipissing, Lot 25, Cons. 18 and 19..................	199 88
Himsworth and Nipissing across Lots 20 to 25, Cons. 18 and 19	200 15
Joly, across Lots 7 to 10 in Cons. 8 and 9........................	148 27
Lake Joseph Road between Ferndale sideline and Foreman Road	199 80
Lorimer Lake Settlement Road to Waubaumic through Lock Erne	375 00
Loring and Restoule Road, Lot 21, Con. 3, to Lots 14 and 15	394 97
Loring and Salnes Road	1,003 90

Name of Road.	Expenditure.
Machar Concession Line between 12 and 13 in Machar and West	199 94
Macaulay, Moot's Hill, Cons. 6 and 7	303 80
Macaulay, Baysville Road	499 93
McDougall, Schoolhouse Road in Con. 2	201 35
McDougall, McCoy Hill Deviation of McDougall Road	396 62
McMurrich, 5th sideline across Cons. 10 and 11	151 97
Medonte, sideroad, Lots 20 and 21, Con. 14	198 08
Medonte, Con. 12, sideroad, Lots 10 and 11	300 00
Morrison between Lots 25 and 26 across Con. 7 and Con. 8	299 50
Matchedash, between Lots 6 and 7, Con. 6	203 45
Nipissing Road in Gurd, Lots 175 to 180, Cons. A and B	200 10
Nipissing Road through Commanda	191 74
Nipissing Road between Rye and Mount Creek Road	199 95
Nipissing across Lots 4 and 5, Con. 2	200 37
Nipissing, 30th sideroad North of Alsace Road to Rosseau Road	200 50
Nipissing, 10th sideroad from Cons. 6 to 8	154 40
Nipissing Road, Lot 13, Con. 10, and 6 and 7th Cons. in Nipissing	200 10
North Cardwell Road, Lot 35, Con. 12	200 00
North Muskoka Colonization Road, from Huntsville to Novar	299 97
Old Muskoka Road at Katrine, Lot 8, Con. 2, Armour	199 75
Orillia Road on the 6th Con.	199 98
Orillia, Con. 2 from Foxmead Northwards	401 41
Orillia, Con. 3 from sideroad between Lots 15 and 16, Northerly	295 69
Orillia, Con. 7 from Lots 10 to 16	209 34
Orillia, Dalton Road, from Muskoka Road to Boundary of N. Ontario	275 00
Orillia, Con. 2, Deviation	950 00
Perry and Chaffey Boundary from Lots 26 to 31	199 99
Pringle between Cons. 8 and 9 across Lot 3	150 20
Proudfoot and Armour Road from boundary West to Burk's Falls	200 16
Parry Sound and Rose Point Road	178 75
Ryde, 5th and 6th sideroad, South from Con. 10	300 75
Sequin Falls and Orrville Road from Nipissing Road to Lot 35	224 93
Spence, Nipissing Road, Lot 22 to 26	215 19
Strong, 20th sideroad across Cons. 11 and 12	230 00
Strong, 10th sideroad across Cons. 7 and 8	248 86
Strong, Con. 11, Pinkerton's Hill	199 89
Sundridge Road, Cons. 8 and 9 East from the boundary	200 00
Smith's Creek Bridge, between Trout Creek and Loring	198 20
Trout Lake Road, from North Road to Trout Lake	203 87
Utterson Station to Port Sydney	501 17
Westphalia Road, from South River Bridge to Colter's Hill	404 26
Wood Lake Road, from townline Draper Tp. to Lot 5, Con. 8, Oakley	400 07
Nipissing Road, balance 1912	25 56
Sunflower Road, balance 1912	10 57
Booth Road, balance 1912	29 25
Mills Road, balance 1912	7 25
Inspection	1,179 00

BY-LAWS.

Albermarle, By-law No. 495	$600 00
Amabel, By-law No. 134	800 00
Grant to Albermarle Township	600 00
Chapman, By-law No. 7	499 46
Eastnor, By-law No. 943	799 71
Grant to Eastnor Township	600 00

Name of Road.	Expenditure.
Joly, By-law No. 135	100 00
Lindsay, By-law No. 187	860 00
Grant to Lindsay Township	800 00
Medonte, By-law No. 484	966 00
Medora and Wood, By-law No. 267	750 00
Monck, By-law No. 388	899 53
Muskoka, By-law No. 263	500 00
Strong, By-law No. 328	399 50
St. Edmunds, By-law No. 147	600 00
Grant to St. Edmunds Township	474 87
Grant to Himsworth Township	1,333 00

EAST DIVISION.

Addington, Kaladar Station to Northbrooke	$804 49
Admaston Township Roads:—	
Opeongo Line	200 33
Mount St. Patrick Road	200 02
Ashdad Road	201 05
Airy Township Roads:—	
Bridge on Hay Creek	205 80
Bridge on Con. 2, Lot 9	198 00
15th sideline, Con. 2	300 00
O'd Perley Road from Lot 9	299 40
Alice Township Roads:—	
Edward's Section	218 91
Carm'chael Section	300 06
Bandit Section	301 30
Anson and Hindon Township Roads	157 75
Anstruther Township Roads	204 70
Appleton and Almonte Road (Re-vote 1912)	500 50
Arden and Harlowe Road	300 00
Alice and Wilberforce Townline	202 75
Bagot and Blythefield Roads:—	
Calabogie and Ashdad Road	211 96
Byer's Settlement Road	46 50
Renfrew and Calabogie Road	188 75
Bells' Rapids Bridge	25 00
Balsover and Dalrymple Road	99 62
Bancroft and Herman Road	203 19
Bangor Township Roads	202 10
Barrie Road from Lot 28, Con. 7 to Barrie and Clarendon	200 27
Bay Lake Road, Faraday	102 44
Bedford Mills Road	101 00
Belmont Township Roads:—	
Oak Lake Road	100 00
Stoney Lake Road	200 12
Bancroft to Coe Hill	201 18
Bigwood Township Roads	399 66
Bonfield Township Roads:—	
Lot 4, Con. 10	209 75
Boundary Road from Con. 11, North	200 33
15th sideline from Con. 8	200 00
20th sideline through Con. 6	199 35
Boundary Road from Con. 2	322 17
Con. 6, Lot 5	200 25
Lot 30, Con. 3	153 14
Bonfield Hill	199 10
Boulter Township Roads:—	
Lot 10, Con. 14	305 25
Bonfield and Powassan	301 55
Bromley Township Roads	306 77
Brougham Township Roads:—	
D'Acre Road	199 10

Name of Road.	Expenditure.
Mount St. Patrick and D'Acre	100 55
Ferguson Lake Road	146 65
Buckhorn Road:—	
Freeborn Section	198 66
Irwin Section	100 05
Guthrie Section	99 50
Windover Section	100 00
Burleigh Township Roads	600 13
Burwash Township Roads	297 83
Brudenell and Lyndoch Township Roads:—	
Maley Road	200 24
Branch Road	99 50
Quadville Road	101 15
Quadville and Rockingham Road	151 00
Smallpiece Settlement Road	74 07
Carden Road between Uphill and Victoria Road	198 12
Carden, 4th quarter line between Cons. 6 and 5	201 66
Carden, Con. 7 between Lots 17 and 18	99 88
Carden and Mara Boundary opposite Cons. 3 to 6	298 88
Cardiff Township Roads	199 99
Cameron Township Roads:—	
Lot 1, Con. 25	250 24
Con. 25 from Lot 6	251 95
Lot 24, A and B Range	200 00
Carlow Township Roads	199 09
Caldwell Township Roads	400 50
Calvin Township Roads:—	
10th sideline from Con. 6	200 90
Con. 2 from Lot 18	200 00
20th sideline from Con. 4	200 25
Townline of Calvin from Con. 2, Papineau	200 00
Lot 26, Con. 6	186 89
California Road, from Keelerville to boundary of Leeds	301 13
California, Camden and Sheffield	299 50
Cavendish Township Roads:—	
White Lake Road	200 25
Gooderham Road	100 00
Chandos Township Roads:—	
Couch Road	50 00
Tanner Road	100 73
Post Road	100 25
Scott Road, East	100 00
East Road	50 00
Smith's Road	100 00
Owenbrook Road	93 95
Cassimer Roads	297 88
Clarendon Road from Frontenac to Clarendon	398 76
Clarendon and Miller Deviation	102 05
Chisholm Township Road:—	
Con. 12 from Lot 14	201 55
Con. 16 from 10th sideroad	151 55
Chisholm and Ferris Boundary, Lot 13	151 29
20th sideline, Con. 6, Deviation	197 77
10th sideroad from Con. 16	150 30
5th sideroad from Con. 4	150 00
5th sideline from Con. 6	200 00
Chisholm, Ferris and North Bay Road:—	
Con. 4, North on 20th sideline	404 47
Con. 6, Lot 20	206 15
Con. 5, North	200 35
Cross Lake and Madawaska Road:—	
Lot 14, Con. 3 in Lyell	245 80
Lot 12, Con. 4 in Lyell	252 99

Name of Road.	Expenditure.
Cosby Township Roads:—	
Lots 6 & 7 to Con. 3	292 15
Burnt Road	199 46
Cosby & Ratter Road, to Ratter Station	398 67
Crerar Township Roads	302 02
Clay Bank Road, in McNabb	202 89
Dalton & Rama Boundary	99 93
Dalton & Carden Boundary	100 15
Dalton, Con 7. opposite Lot 27	99 90
Darling, 8th line	111 20
Darling, between Lots 10 and 11 from Con. 4 to Con. 6	121 85
Dead Creek Road	97 05
Delamere Township Roads	394 47
Dummer Township Roads (9th line)	200 00
Dungannon Township Roads	204 30
Dungannon and Monteagle Boundary	304 50
Douro Township Roads:—	
Young's Point Road	98 75
Telephone Road	99 90
Eganville and Germanicus Road	202 32
Eldon and Carden Boundary, West of Mud Lake	101 35
Eganville Road, between Rankin and Lake Dore	202 50
Escott Road	100 00
Faraday and Herschell Boundary	203 38
Faraday Township Roads	200 26
Faulkner and Martland Boundary	403 33
Ferris Township Roads:—	
Repairs to North Bay and Bonfield Road from Lot 23	100 00
North Bay and Trout Lake Road	200 00
20th sideroad, con. 16	200 00
Lot 9, Con. 4	150 67
Con. 8 from Lot 5, West	150 13
Lot 20, Con. 3, North	151 55
Bridge Con. 2, Lot 6	200 29
North Bay and Bonfield, Con. 12	300 00
Lot 19, Con. 2, North	150 63
Fifth Depot Lake Road	197 50
Fiss School to Complete a fill	103 25
Forest Mills Road, cutting hill	248 37
Field, Cons. 4 and 5, washout	102 92
Galway Township Roads:—	
Gully and Kinmount Road	201 75
Jackson and Galway Road	200 00
Gannon's Bridge Road	200 00
Grant Township Roads	300 10
Grattan Township Roads:—	
McGrath Road	150 45
D'Acre to Toohy's Hill	108 30
Opeongo Line from Davidson's	198 50
Coldwell Station Road	151 61
Graphite Mines Road	800 03
Griffith and Matawatchan Township Roads:—	
Matawatchan Road	104 50
Griffith and D'Acre Road	300 52
Leclaire Road	100 50
Matawatchan and Miller Road	125 50
Glamorgan Township Roads:—	
Monck Road	253 16
Buckhorn Road	250 00

Name of Road.	Expenditure.
Hagarty, Richards and Burns Township Roads:—	
Perrigo Road	519 23
Killaloe and Wilno Road	208 58
Brudenell and Killaloe Road	300 75
Haliburton to Pine Lake Road, West Guilford (Re-vote)	400 54
Harvey Township Roads:—	
Squaw River Road	100 12
Bobcaygeon Road	150 44
Lakehurst Road	149 99
Deer Bay Road	100 06
Hastings and Addington Boundary	100 00
Hastings Road, South of Bancroft	201 89
Hastings Road, between Ormsby and Lot 80, Limerick	307 68
Head, Clara and Maria Roads:—	
Mattawa and Pembroke, Lot 3, A. and B. Range, Head	251 00
Mattawa and Pembroke, Lot 65, A. and B. Range, Maria	150 05
Mattawa and Pembroke, Lot 16, A. and B. Range, Clara	300 55
Herschell Township Roads	200 32
Herschell, Con. 9, West of Hastings Road	200 07
Hugel Township Roads	400 09
Hugel and Kirkpatrick Boundary from Warren to Verner	499 35
Jones Falls and Morten's Road	98 12
Jones Falls and Crosby Road	101 83
Kehoe Hill, on quarter line between Lots 25 and 26, Dalton	149 42
Kingston and Perth Roads	201 21
Kirkfield and Dalrymple Road	99 87
L'Amable and Fort Stewart Road	302 81
Lanark and Darling Boundary, from Haw's Mills to Cheese Factory	234 50
Larcque Road, Con. 6 to Bastedo	375 00
Laxton, Digby and Longford Township Roads:—	
Con. 4, Laxton	198 93
Monck Road, Lot 26 to 28	207 09
North quarter line of Laxton, 8th Con.	100 58
Cameron Road, from Norland to Boundary of Bexley	200 24
Lennox and Hastings Boundary	100 00
Louden and McPherson Boundary	291 26
Lutterworth Township Roads:—	
Bobcaygeon Road, Lot 15, Con. A.	50 00
Cameron Road, Lot 14, Con. 7	100 00
Davis Lake Road, Lots 5 to 10	100 00
Miners' Bay Road	99 56
Lyell Township Roads:—	
Madawaska and Hastings Road, Lot 39	250 00
Madawaska and Hastings Road, Lot 50	264 96
Madawaska and Hastings Roads:—	
Bridge on Sucker Creek, Lot 11	100 00
Lot 29, Con. 12, Lyell	400 00
Mara, from the 7th Con. to the Village of Brechin	100 13
Mara, Cons. 4 and 5, West from boundary	300 32
Marlbank Road in Hungerford to Sheffield	400 53
Marlbank to Forest Mills Colonization Road	99 62
Martland and Scollard Boundary	300 40
Martland Township Roads	198 44
Mallory's Junction to Vennachar Road	300 08
Mallory Hill Road, in Miller	100 00
Mattawa and Pembroke Road:—	
Con. 8 from 5th sideroad	204 40
20th sideroad from Con. 12	149 80
Con. 10 from Lot 3, East	150 00
Mattawan Township Roads:—	

Name of Road.	Expenditure.
Les Erables Road from Lot 28	150 00
Lot 35, Con. 9	152 00
Con. 8 from Lot 29	101 00
Lot 21 from Con. 10	151 25
Con. 2 from Lot 36	150 53
Mayo Township Roads	200 37
Methuen Township Roads:—	
North End	100 75
South End	100 45
Minden Township Roads:—	
Minden and Carnarvon from Con. 10	99 00
Sideroad between 26 and 27, Cons. 1 and 2	100 00
Bobcaygeon Road from Peterson Road	99 75
Minden and Gelert Road	50 00
Monck Road, from Rama to the Rathburn Road	130 00
Monmouth Township Roads:—	
Con. 1, Lot 10 and road from Hotspur	.199 25
Tory Hill Road	100 20
Dunnett Road	50 45
Montague Road (Re-vote 1912)	299 73
Musclows' Schoolhouse Road, 6th Con. line to the 2nd Con.	402 41
McClure and Wicklow Township Roads	199 50
McPherson Township Roads	397 50
New Boyne Road	101 92
North Algona Township Roads	301 29
Opinicon Road from Boundary of Loboro'	299 94
Pakenham, 6th Line between 1 and 6	307 03
Papineau Township Roads:—	
Con. 15 from Lot 24	150 00
Con. 15 from Lot 32	150 11
Con. 10 from Lot 27	200 00
5th sideroad from Mattawa and Pembroke, South	200 00
5th sideroad from Mattawa and Pembroke, East	200 00
25th sideroad from Con. 12	200 90
Bridge at Con. 10 and 20th sideroad	101 45
Papineau, 10th Con.:—	
Con. 10 from Lot 34, East	175 00
Con. 10 from Lot 10	300 00
5th sideline from Con. 12	301 25
Petawawa Township Roads:—	
Radtke Section	200 00
Priebe Section	200 39
McGregor Section	416 78
Pembroke Township Roads:—	
Fraser Section	150 00
Howison Section	246 88
Cottnam Section	576 76
Pembroke and Eganville Road South from Lot 8, Lake Dore Range	297 67
Peterson Road West of Maynooth	201 80
Peterson Road, Maynooth to Combermere	401 97
Portland and Loboro Boundary on the 4th Con.	152 01
Potter Settlement Road	199 16
Radcliffe Township Roads:—	
Rockingham and Palmer Rapids Road	204 85
Combermere and Barry's Bay Road	97 90
Combermere and Fort Stewart Road	100 49
Raglan Township Roads:—	
Rosenthal Road	200 04
Hardwood Lake Road	101 85
10th Con. Road	100 00
18th Con. Road	100 00
Little Ireland Road	134 65

Name of Road.	Expenditure.
Rama and Dalton Boundary from Con. 1, Rama to Dalton Road	149 97
Ratter and Dunnett Township Roads	400 00
Rolph Township Roads	493 00
Scollard Township Roads	310 85
Sharbot Lake Road	100 00
Sharbot Lake and Hinchinbrooke Road to Parham	400 30
Sebastopol Township Roads:—	
Ryan Mountain Road	304 75
Foymount Road	104 90
Sherwood and Jones Roads:—	
Bells' Rapids Road	198 20
Wilno and Rockingham Road	300 00
Bark Lake Road	103 25
Sherbourne Township Roads	399 85
Sherbinan Road	201 00
Sherbrooke Road	100 00
Snow Road	399 79
Snowdon Township Roads:—	
Bobcaygeon Road	50 00
Minden and Gelert Road	150 25
South Algona Township Roads	300 21
Stafford Township Roads	549 51
Stanhope Township Roads:—	
Maple Lake Road	113 86
Grit Road	50 50
Peterson Road from Cameron	49 50
Summerville Township Roads:—	
Bobcaygeon Road South of 6th Con.	100 38
Base line between Pardue and Baddow	102 10
Coboconk Road to Burnt River	199 99
Burnt River and Bury's Green Road	90 00
Monck Road, Lots 11, 12 and 13	106 78
Base line at Lot 17, Con. 12	99 01
Burnt River Road	100 00
Trout Lake Road, Addington	197 48
Tyendinaga and Richmond Boundary from C.P.R., South	103 62
Tyendinaga and Richmond Boundary	175 00
Townline Frontenac and Leeds	100 20
Verner to Desaulnier Bridge	499 68
Victoria Road, North of Uphill	100 00
Whalen Settlement Road, Keatley's Swamp	201 12
White Lake Road from Lot 16, Con. 10 to Lot 27, Con. 6	508 47
Westmeath Township Roads	400 44
Widdifield Township Roads:—	
Lot 18, Con. D. East	259 70
Lot 17, Con. B. North	450 30
Gormanville Road from Con. C. Lot 20	349 71
Lot 14, Con. B. East	101 25
18th sideroad, Con. B. North	100 00
Con. 5 from 14th sideroad	100 75
Con. 4 from Lot 14, East	149 27
Cook's Mill Road, from Con. 4, Lot 20	297 25
Hunter's Hill, Lot 9, Con. 2	150 00
18th sideline from Con. 2	50 00
Wilberforce Extension, Mud Lake Road	508 34
Wilberforce Township Roads:—	
Leach Section	198 29
Berndt Section	206 86
Butt Section	199 95
Hein Section	299 85

Name of Road.	Expenditure.
Zell Section	100 00
Smith Section	200 21
Raxime Section	205 75
Wolf Grove Road	494 95
Wylie Township Roads	451 11
Buckhorn Road, balance 1912	19 85
Fraser Road, balance 1912	25 55
Seabright Road, balance 1912	10 00
Pigeon Creek Road, balance 1912	24 02
Chisholm Township Road, balance 1912	24 97
Mississippi Road, balance 1912	24 00
Escott Road, balance 1912	10 00
Ramsay Road, balance 1912	39 60
Anson and Hindon, balance 1912	16 83
Blackdonald Road, balance 1912	13 50
Bexley Road, balance 1912	24 56
Monck Road, balance 1912	10 00
Seabright Deviation, balance 1912	10 50
Herschell Road, balance 1912	25 92
Kingston and Perth Road, balance 1912	17 50
Rama and Mara, balance 1912	24 96
Ramsay, 7th Con. Road, balance 1912	10 00
Pigeon Road, balance 1912	3 50
Minden Road, balance 1912	3 50
Richmond Road, balance 1912	23 11
Widdifield Township Roads (washout) balance 1912	64 75
Beaulieu Road, balance 1912	22 95
Oso and Clarendon Road, balance 1912	48 20
Griffith and Matawatchan Road, balance 1912	26 43
Inspection	5,938 15

BY-LAWS.

Bagot and Blythefield, By-law No. 278	600 00
Bedford By-law, No. 492	999 95
Belmont and Methuen, By-law No. 535	565 83
Bexley, By-law No. 428	300 00
Bromley, By-law No. 204	1,150 00
Caldwell, By-law No. 164	1,000 00
Cassimer, Jennings and Appleby, By-law No. 58	800 00
Carlow, By-law No. 48	300 00
Grant to Carlow Township	16 67
Grant to Cassimer, Jennings and Appleby	750 00
Grant to Caldwell Township	1,000 00
Dummer, By-law No. 777	280 00
Dungannon, By-law No. 67	300 00
Dysart, By-law No. 537	1,955 00
Eldon, By-law No. 387	999 69
Elzevir and Grimsthorpe, By-law No. 312	400 00
Faraday, By-law No. 38	350 00
Grant to Faraday Township	266 00
Galway and Cavendish, By-law No. 242	125 00
Harvey, By-law No. 316	350 00
Hinchinbrooke, By-law No. 7	600 00
Hinchinbrooke, By-law No. 2	500 00
Huntingdon, By-law No. 828	300 00
Horton, By-law No. 24	582 45
Grant to Horton Township	100 00
Kennebec, By-law No. 5	750 00
Kingston, By-law No. 5	250 00
Grant to Kingston Township	250 00
Lakefield, By-law No. 507	400 00
Limerick, By-law No. 9	300 00
Loborough, By-law No. 52A	300 00

Name of Road.	Expenditure.
Grant to Loborough Township	225 00
Madoc, By-law No. 328	400 00
Marmora and Lake, By-law No. 460	500 00
Martland, By-law No. 64	500 00
Mayo, By-law No. 250	300 00
Monteagle and Herschell, By-law No. 413	500 00
McNabb, By-law No. 37	1,000 00
Grant to Madoc Township	600 60
Grant to Martland Township	400 00
North Monaghan, By-law No. 662	300 00
Oso, By-law No. 70	375 69
Pittsburg, By-law No. 3	384 13
Ratter and Dunnet, By-law No. 36	500 00
Rawdon, By-law No. 323	400 00
Ross, By-law No. 302	1,000 00
Grant to Ratter and Dunnet Township	1,000 00
Grant to Ramsay Township	833 33
Seymour, By-law No. 851	650 98
Springer, By-law No. 270	1,000 00
Stafford, By-law No. 630	600 00
Smith, By-law No. 710	250 00
Grant to Springer Township	1,000 00
Grant to Smith Township	250 00
Grant to Storrington Township	100 00
Tudor and Cashel, By-law No. 13	300 00
Tyendinaga, By-law No. 615	448 73
Westmeath, By-law No. 86	1,086 16
Wollaston, By-law No. 8	300 00

TEMISKAMING.

Armstrong Township:—	
Cons. 4 and 5, Lots 1 to 6	1,199 69
Armstrong and Beauchamp Boundary, Con. 1	251 36
Lots 4 and 5, Cons. 1 and 2	300 49
Con. 3, between Lots 4 and 5	299 66
Beauchamp Township:—	
Cons. 2 and 3 across Lots 6, 5 and 4	1,000 00
Cons. 1, 2 and 3 across Lots 2 and 3	998 13
Bucke Township:—	
Lots 6 and 7 across Con. 1, Dymond and Con. 6, Bucke	1,003 84
Boundary line across Lots 2 and 1, Bucke and 1, 2, 3 and 4, Firstbrook	1,495 94
Bryce Township:—	
Cons. 5 and 6 across Lots 3 to 5	800 02
Boundary between Beauchamp and Bryce, Con. 5	500 19
Brethour Township:—	
Pense and Brethour Townline, Lots 1 to 6	1,100 00
Con. 2, continuation of 1912 work	200 27
Brethour and Casey Townline across Lots 6 to 1	998 69
Cane Township:—	
Cons. 4 and 5 from Lots 1 to 12	275 00
Lots 4 and 5 across Con. 3 and East on Con. 2	500 00
Lots 8 and 9 across Cons. 4 and 3	750 00
West Boundary across North half Cons. 5 and 6	999 30
Lots 6 and 7 to T. & N. O.	599 07
Casey Township:—	
Lots 2 and 3 across Con. 5 and West on Con. 6	900 00
Lots 2 and 3 across Cons. 1, 2 and 3	690 47
Cons. 2 and 3 across Lots 8 to 11	500 77
Con. 5 across Lot 5	301 95
Dack Township:—	
Lots 8 and 9 across Cons. 2 and 1	499 24
Lots 8 and 9 across Con. 6	499 54
Cons. 3 and 4 from Lot 9	750 22

Name of Road.	Expenditure.
Dymond Township:—	
Between Lots 6 and 7 across Con. 6...............................	499 95
West Road, from Liskeard to West Boundary	300 00
Con. 2 across Lots 11 and 12	306 49
Evanturel Township:—	
Windigo Road across Cons. 5 and 6	400 45
South Boundary across Lots 11 and 12..............................	450 00
Con. 2 across Lots 11 and 12	275 00
Between Cons. 4 and 5 across Lots 5 and 6........................	500 60
Firstbrook Township:—	
Lots 2 and 3 across Cons. 5 and 6.................................	2,321 18
Lot 1 between Cons. 4 and 5	270 42
Harris Township:—	
Townline Harris and Casey across Lots 2 and 4 ·..................	596 92
Lake Shore Road	399 33
Between Lots 4 and 5 across Cons. 5 and 6	388 75
Between Lots 2 and 3 across Con. 6	798 95
Harley Township:—	
Between Cons. 3 and 4 across Lots 8 and 7	503 35
Between Cons. 5 and 6 across Lots 5 and 6	511 38
Between Lots 2 and 3 across Con. 6	615 88
Cons. 2 and 3 across Lots 5 and 6................................	400 80
Henwood Township:—	
Between Cons. 4 and 5 across Lots 1 to 12	299 95
Between Lots 10 and 11 across Cons. 3, 4 and 5	995 75
Between Cons. 3 and 2 across Lots 5 and 6	499 99
Between Lots 6 and 7 across Con. 4	800 00
Hilliard Township:—	
Between Lots 2 and 3 across Cons. 1 and 2.......................	1,027 47
On 6th Con. across Lots 8 and 9 and South	995 88
Hudson Township:—	
Between Lots 2 and 3 across Cons. 1, 2 and 3.....................	1,202 10
Boundary of Dymond and Hudson across Con. 5	200 00
Twin Lake Road from 3rd Con., Lots 11 and 12 and South	873 85
Ingram Township:—	
Between Cons. 4 and 5 from Lot 1, Easterly.......................	600 03
Line on Con. 4	300 06
Between Lots 6 and 7 across Cons. 1, 2 and 3	1,225 29
Pense Township:—	
Between Lots 2 and 3 across Cons. 1, 2 and 3.....................	1,458 62
Between Cons. 1 and 2 across Lots 3 and 4	480 65
Robillard Township:—	
Between Lots 2 and 3 across Cons. 2 and 3:......................	992 66
Chamberlain and Pacaud, balance 1912	97 34
Charlton and Heaslop, balance 1912	34 65
Henwood Road, balance 1912	25 06
Matheson and Munro Road, balance 1912..........................	47 40
Evanturel Road, balance 1912	92 87
Walker Road, balance 1912	67 58
Casey Road, balance 1912	33 99
Truax Road, balance 1912	103 19
Harris and Casey Road, balance 1912.............................	1 92
Brewer Road, balance 1912	117 90
Bryce and Robillard Road, balance 1912	45 37
Clute Road, balance 1912	25 20
Evanturel Township Road, balance 1912	20 35
Hilliard Road, balance 1912	46 77
Pense and Brethour Road, balance 1912	9 00
Marter Road, balance 1912	24 44
Gowganda Road Contract, balance 1908	685 00
South Lorraine Road, from Belle Ellen Mine Trunk Road	900 00
Firstbrook and Barr Trunk Road	2,946 37
Inspection	1,400 70
Road Making Machinery	319 45
Charlton and Long Lake Road (Progress Work).....................	569 50

By-Laws.

Name of Road.	Expenditure.
Casey, By-law No. 14	839 26
Grant to Casey Township	1,676 55
Dymond, By-law No. 92	1,481 50
Grant to Dymond Township	825 82
Evanturel, By-law No. 96	797 36
Hudson, By-law No. 38	800 00
Harley, By-law No. 136	1,500 00
Harris, By-law No. 28	1,199 81
Hilliard, By-law No. 29	757 42
Kerns, By-law No. 96	1,000 00

Recapitulation.

North Division	208.353 56
West Division	37,357 58
East Division	103,240 62
Temiskaming	57,389 76
	$406,341 52

DEPARTMENT OF PUBLIC WORKS, TORONTO,
October 31st, 1913.

M. P. DOHERTY,
Assitsant Colonization Roads.

STATEMENTS

OF THE

ACCOUNTANT

AND

LAW CLERK

Department of Public Works, Ontario.

Toronto, February, 1914.

HON. J. O. REAUME,

Minister of Public Works, Ontario.

SIR,—I have the honour to submit the following statements of capital expenditure on public buildings, works, roads, aid to railways, etc., and of contracts entered into in connection therewith, being: (1) The capital expenditure for public buildings and public works, etc., for 12 months to the 31st of October, 1913; (2) the total capital expenditure on public buildings, public works, colonization and mining roads, aids to railways, etc., from the 1st of July, 1867, to the 31st of October, 1913; (3) a classified statement showing (*a*) the expenditure for thirty-seven years and six months from the 1st of July, 1867, to the 31st of December, 1904; (*b*) the expenditure for eight years and ten months from the 1st of January, 1905, to the 31st of October, 1913; and (*c*) the grand total of expenditure from the 1st of July, 1867, to the 31st of October, 1913, and (*d*) a statement showing the several contracts and bonds entered into with His Majesty during the 12 months ending the 31st of October, 1913, for the carrying out of the sundry works under the control of your Department.

I have the honour to be, Sir,

Your obedient servant,

J. P. EDWARDS,

Accountant, etc.

STATEMENT No 1.

Being Statement of Expenditures on Capital Account, Public Buildings and Public Works, for the year ending October 31st, 1913. (See also Statement No. 2.)

Name of Work.	—	Amount.
	$ c.	$ c.
PUBLIC BUILDINGS:		
New Government House	....	224,396 37
Parliament Buildings, North Wing:		
" " Construction	64,062 85	
" " Furnishings	9,512 77	
" " Library Fittings	11,157 60	
		84,732 72
" " West Wing:		
" " Reconstruction	44,133 64	
" " Insurance	800 00	
		44,933 64
" " Painting, outside and inside.........	1,994 99	
" " Hydro Equipment......................	11,784 48	
" " Legislative Chamber acoustics.......	8,185 00	
" " Repairs and alterations	1,162 04	
" " Renewing elevators	3,175 00	
" " Fire Alarm System	2,316 91	
" " Hydro-underground	985 18	
		29,603 60
Osgoode Hall, Repairs furnishings	25,166 35	
" " Iron fence and gates	1,188 23	
" " Furnishings, New Addition	486 68	
		26,841 26
Hospital for the Insane, Brockville	....	47,972 25
" " Cobourg	....	3,357 67
" " Hamilton	....	27,652 59
" " Kingston	....	24,484 01
" London	46,764 89	
" " Electric wiring (Special Warrant)	3,760 88	
		50,525 77
" Mimico	....	19,604 07
" Penetanguishene	....	20,544 47
" Toronto	2,503 94	
" " Buildings, etc., Whitby...	209,568 46	
		212,072 40
Hospital for the Feeble Minded, Orillia	....	28,918 15
Hospital for Epileptics, Woodstock	....	11,262 64
Central Prison, Toronto	2,041 04	
New Provincial Prison, Guelph	338,975 97	
		341,017 01
Mercer Reformatory, Toronto	....	3,440 10
Normal and Model Schools, Toronto	....	4,784 26
" " " Ottawa	2,466 46	
" " " Ottawa, vacuum cleaner	600 00	
		3,066 46
Normal School, London ....:	395 08	
" " London, vacuum cleaner	575 00	
		970 08
" " Hamilton.............................	2,325 99	
" " Hamilton, vacuum cleaner	575 00	
		2,900 99
" " Peterborough	619 03	
" " Peterborough, tool house..................	1,300 00	
" " Peterborough, vacuum cleaner	575 00	
		2,494 03
" " Stratford	709 68	
" " Stratford, tool house	500 00	
" " Stratford, Interior decoration	1,451 85	
" " Stratford, vacuum cleaner	575 00	
		3,236 53

STATEMENT No. 1.—Continued.

Name of Work.	—	Amount.
	$ c.	$ c.
Normal School, North Bay	374 83	
" " North Bay, vacuum cleaner	600 00	
		974 83
English-French Training School, Sandwich	....	8,834 04
School for the Deaf, Belleville	19,884 26	
" " " New Dormitory for Girls	52,507 19	
" " " New Dormitory for Boys	15,171 22	
		87,562 67
School for the Blind, Brantford	14,878 69	
" " " New Dormitory for Girls	51,917 69	
" " " New Dormitory for Boys	9,112 81	
" " " Fire escapes (Special Warrant)	2,660 00	
		78,564 19
Agricultural College, Guelph	468 74	
" " New dining hall	39,308 02	
" " Dairy stables	6,940 40	
" " Hydro-Electric equipment	2,446 35	
		49,163 51
Horticultural Experiment Station, Jordan Harbour	5,426 38	
(Transferred from Public Works, see Public Accounts)	761 23	
		6,187 61
Ontario Veterinary College, Toronto, new building	....	112,957 68
Immigration Office, Toronto, Front Street	....	2,577 70
Ontario Government Building, London, England (Special Warrant)	....	500 00
Fish and Game Branch, Boat Houses	2,543 34	
Fish and Game Branch, Fish Hatchery Building	290 18	
		2,833 52
Muskoka District:		
Court House, Registry Office, Bracebridge	289 92	
Registry Office, addition to, Bracebridge	1,695 00	
		1,984 92
Parry Sound District:		
Court House, Gaol, Registry Office, etc. Parry Sound	....	778 12
Manitoulin District:		
Court House, Gaol, etc., Gore Bay	204 35	
Lock-up, Manitowaning	22 00	
		226 35
Sudbury District:		
Court House, Gaol, and Registry Office, Sudbury	....	2,202 62
Nipissing District:		
Court House, Gaol and Registry Office, North Bay	....	1,620 80
Algoma District:		
Court House, Gaol and Registry Office, Sault Ste. Marie	119 60	
Industrial Farm, Sault Ste. Marie	63 10	
		182 70
Rainy River District:		
Gaol, etc., Fort Frances	32 95	
Court House, Fort Frances	12,777 95	
		12,810 90
Thunder Bay District:		
Court House, Gaol, etc., Port Arthur	317 18	
Lock-up at White River	499 77	
Industrial Home, Fort William	24,053 70	
		24,870 65

STATEMENT No. 1.—Continued.

Name of Work.	—	Amount.
Kenora District:	$ c.	$ c.
Court House, Gaol, etc., Kenora	1,011 49	
New Registry Office, Kenora	8,075 09	
New Registry Office Furniture and Furnishings	1,454 79	
		10,541 37
Temiskaming District:		
Temporary Court House, Haileybury, Rent	1,875 00	
Temporary furnishings, repairs and alterations	906 31	
New Court House, Haileybury	12,873 51	
New Registry Office, Haileybury	6,200 11	
Gaol, South Porcupine	166 45	
Gaol, heating, South Porcupine (Special Warrant)	395 93	
		22,417 31
Haliburton, Provisional County of:		
Court House and Gaol	....	500 00
PUBLIC WORKS:		
Admaston Bridge, Bonnechere River	....	1,977 97
Aubrey and Ignace Bridges	....	881 02
Barbette Creek Bridge, Clara	....	993 92
Bass Creek Bridge, Tp. of Limerick	....	1,200 00
Big East River Bridge, Chaffey	....	875 00
Birch Creek Bridge, Birch Lake Road	....	1,802 85
Birch Creek Bridge, Birch Lake Road, (Unpaid accounts, 1912)	....	296 70
Black Creek Bridge	....	149 05
Black Creek Bridge, (Unpaid accounts, 1911-1912) Dalton	....	187 40
Blind River Bridge	....	200 00
Boyne Bridges, Foley	....	2,160 98
Burnt River Bridge, Buckhorn Road, (Unpaid accounts, 1911-1912)	....	34 60
Campement D'Ours Island Bridges	....	1,470 09
Cardiff, Monmouth Townline and Maxwell Bridges	....	399 59
Clare River Bridge	....	747 33
Corbett Creek Bridge, Oliver	....	1,598 16
Completing Pumping Plant, Jordan Harbor (Transferred to *Public Buildings* 761 23)		
Denbigh Bridge, Hydes Creek	....	847 25
Dog Lake Dams	....	558 50
Dog Lake Dams (Unpaid accounts. 1912)	....	39 80
Driftwood Bridges, Tp. Walker (Unpaid Accounts, 1911-12)	....	4 50
Echo Bay Bridge	....	313 50
Equipment, Machinery, Instruments, etc.	....	2,470 44
Fourth Concession Bridge, Hagar	....	1,058 51
Gananoque River Improvement	....	366 23
Garden River Bridge, Trunk Road	....	6,482 58
Golden Lake Bridge	....	1,732 56
Gold Rock Bridges	....	501 93
Graces Creek Bridge	....	874 25
Helferty Bridge Raglan	....	380 00
Hoeffler Bridge (Unpaid Accounts, 1911-12)	....	59 85
Ingoldsby Bridge	....	299 94
Jean Baptiste Bridge, Armstrong	....	962 64
Judge Bridge, White River	....	5,228 83
Kabuska Creek Bridge, Bonfield	....	1,762 72
Kaministikwia River Works, (Unpaid Accounts, 1911-12)	....	348 00
Kaministikwia Bridge, Paipoonge	....	8,053 58
Kaministikwia Bridge, (Unpaid Accounts, 1912)	....	355 00
Kashe Bridge, Morrison	....	299 76
Lanark County; allowance for washout	....	1,225 00
Larder Lake Road Bridges	....	196 00
Larder Lake Road Bridges, (Unpaid Accounts 1911-12)	....	41 10
La Vallee River Bridge	....	1,763 22
Lawrence Bridge, Gould Road	....	500 00

STATEMENT No. 1.—Continued.

Name of Work.	—	Amount.
	$ c.	$ c.
Leeburn Bridge, Aberdeen....................	....	2,174 48
Little Rapids Bridge, Little Thessalon	....	2,496 97
Madawaska Village Bridge	....	1,819 00
Magnetawan River Bridge, Burk's Falls	....	8,765 10
Magnetawan River Bridge (Unpaid Accounts, 1911-12)......	....	48 42
Maintenance, Locks, Dams, Bridges, etc....................	....	29,951 49
Maintenance (Unpaid Accounts 1912).............	....	252 69
Magpie River Bridge	....	489 28
McCreights Bridge, Kirkwood	....	776 69
McCreights Bridge (Unpaid Accounts 1911-12)	....	49 00
McKelvery Creek Bridge, Crozier....................	....	1,887 67
Minnitake Bridge	....	552 34
Montreal River Bridge (Unpaid Accounts 1912)	....	24 86
Mountain Lake Bridge, Minden	....	1,845 48
North River Bridge	....	2,086 39
North River Bridge (Unpaid Accounts 1911-12)	....	24 87
Opickinimika River Dams (Unpaid Accounts 1912)	....	34 22
Orillia Township Bridge	....	2,494 15
Otter Creek Bridge, Brethour	....	1,003 52
Papineau Bridges, Boon Creek	....	8,074 28
Pickeral River Improvement	....	1,891 84
Pine River Bridge, to Complete	....	200 00
Purchase of Rubber Boots	....	122 95
Root River Bridge (Unpaid Accounts 1912)	....	11 25
Ryerson Townline Bridge (Unpaid Accounts 1911-12) ...	....	7 25
Sampsons and Sparks Creek Bridge, Bonfield	....	1,444 02
Sakoose Bridges	....	947 68
Sand Lake Road Bridge, Magnetawan River	....	2,882 15
Six Mile Bridge, Shuniah....................	....	1,417 71
South Channel Bridge and Dam, Bala	....	5,182 95
Sturgeon Falls Bridge	....	11,596 08
Sudaby's Bridge, Johnson	....	1,794 79
Sunday Creek Bridge, Robillard	....	88 71
Sunday Creek Bridge, Dack	....	821 11
Surveys, Inspections, etc.	....	8,531 60
Swanson's Creek Bridge, to complete....................	....	862 00
Tiers Bridge, Hawkers' Creek....................	....	200 00
Tory Hill Bridge	....	499 85
Trenough Bridge, Rama	....	1,000 00
Two Tree Bridge, St. Joseph's	....	1,802 95
Unpaid Accounts 1911-12 (See under the several works) .	....	
Veuve River Bridge, Markstay	....	1,110 18
Wages and Expenses, supervising foremen	....	2,022 12
Warren Bridge, Veuve River	....	2,501 14
Walker River Bridge (Unpaid Accounts 1912)	....	877 27
Wahnapitae Log Canal (Miscellaneous)	....	1,000 00
West Channel Bridge floor, Kenora	....	962 84
West's Bridge, Thessalon River....................	....	2,025 88
West's Bridge (Unpaid Accounts 1912).............	....	5 65
White River Bridge, Bellingham approaches	....	200 00
Widdifield Bridges	....	528 16
Wilno and Rockingham Bridges	....	499 84
Wissa-Wassa Bridge (Unpaid Accounts 1911-12)	....	8 00
DRAINAGE WORKS:		
Algoma District Drainage	792 57	
Clearing Black Creek, Matchedash	496 91	
Nipissing District Roads, drainage	1,495 82	
Nottawasaga River, drainage	455 00	
Manitoulin District Roads, drainage	750 54	
Mara Township Roads, drainage	762 17	
Parry Sound District, drainage	1,889 31	
Rainy River Roads, drainage	6,045 54	

STATEMENT No. 1.—Concluded.

Name of Work.	—	Amount.
	$ c.	$ c.
Rainy River Roads (Unpaid Accounts 1912)	6 50	
Rama Township Road, drainage	200 00	
Sturgeon Falls District, drainage	997 93	
Sudbury District, drainage	1,440 00	
Temiskaming District, drainage	2,497 81	
		17,279 60
DRAINAGE AID GRANTS:		
Big Marsh drainage, Pelee Island	2,000 00	
Carp River drainage	1,000 00	
Hardy Creek Drain, Warwick...........................	225 00	
Henry Marentette Drain, Sandwich......................	1,500 00	
Long Marsh Drain, extension, Anderdon	1,500 00	
McDonald Robertson Drain, Lochiel	1,500 00	
Moira Lake drainage, Huntingdon	1,000 00	
Pulse Creek Drain	1,500 00	
Whitebread Bumping Scheme, Dover	1,000 00	
		11,225 00
Total Public Buildings	1,636,597 56	
Total Public Works	179,884 67	
Total Public Buildings and Works	....	1,816,432 23

Department of Public Works, Ontario.
    Toronto, February, 1914.

                                J. P. EDWARDS,
                            Accountant, Public Works.

STATEMENT No. 2.

Being a statement of expenditures on Capital Account for Public Buildings, Public Works, Colonization and Mining Roads, Aid to Railways, etc., as follows:—
(1) The total expenditure from the 1st of July, 1867, to the 31st of October, 1912; (2) The expenditure for the twelve months ending the 31st of October, 1913; and (3) The grand total of expenditure from the 1st of July, 1867, to the 31st October, 1913.

Name of Work.	Expenditure 1st July, 1867, to 31st Oct., 1912.	Expenditure Fiscal Year ending 31st Oct. 1913.	Total Expenditure to 31st Oct., 1913.
	$ c.	$ c.	$ c.
PUBLIC BUILDINGS—			
Old Government House	183,860 86	....	183,860 86
New Government House	451,440 30	224,396 37	675,836 67
Old Parliament and Departmental Buildings	85,285 98	....	85,285 98
New Parliament and Departmental Buildings (Cost of Construction)	1,282,679 04	....	1,282,679 04
Parliament and Departmental Buildings (equipment, furnishings, library fittings, grounds, roads, plant house, alterations, etc., No. 5 Queen's Park included)	243,130 87	6,332 03	249,462 99
Parliament Buildings, Automatic Fire Alarm, East and Centre Buildings	2,917 48	2,316 91	5,234 39
No. 5 Queen's Park, purchase of house, ground rent, insurance, etc.	12,515 44	....	12,515 44
No. 5 Queen's Park, alterations and equipment	14,063 85	....	14,063 85
Hydro underground service	....	985 18	985 18
Hydro equipment	....	11,784 48	11,784 48
Legislative Chamber, correcting accoustics	....	8,185 00	8,185 00
Parliament Buildings, addition of New North Wing, furnishings, equipment, library, etc.	645,402 89	84,732 72	730,135 61
Parliament Buildings, Reconstruction and Fireproofing West Wing	609,114 38	44,933 64	654,048 02
Osgoode Hall, Toronto	260,137 52	26,354 58	286,492 10
Osgoode Hall, Toronto, addition to Centre Building (North Wing and equipment)	143,494 62	486 68	143,981 30
Hospital for Insane, Brockville	650,533 63	47,972 25	698,505 88
" " Cobourg	140,413 34	3,357 67	143,771 01
" " Hamilton	1,108,811 96	27,652 59	1,136,464 55
" " Kingston	644,732 97	24,484 01	669,216 98
" " London	1,207,623 74	50,525 77	1,258,149 51
" " Mimico	763,928 68	19,604 07	783,532 75
" " Penetanguishene	149,247 15	20,544 47	169,791 62
" " Toronto	446,345 93	2,503 94	448,849 87
" " Whitby, additional buildings, land, equipment, etc.	136,489 04	209,568 46	346,057 50
Hospital for Feeble Minded, Orillia	655,441 96	23,913 15	679,355 11
Hospital for Epileptics, Woodstock	248,104 92	11,262 64	259,367 56
Central Prison, Toronto	957,626 26	2,041 04	959,667 30
New Provincial Prison, Guelph	609,415 65	338,975 97	948,391 62
Mercer Reformatory for Females, Toronto	287,512 70	3,440 10	290,952 80
Normal and Model Schools, Toronto	280,712 96	4,784 26	285,497 22
Normal and Model Schools, Ottawa	267,075 46	3,066 46	270,141 92
Normal School, London	121,111 83	970 08	122,081 91
Normal Schools, additional (four)	4,618 33	....	4,618 33
" " Hamilton	87,866 13	2,900 99	90,767 12
" " North Bay	98,941 07	974 83	99,915 90
" " Peterborough	94,176 89	2,494 03	96,670 92
" " Stratford	85,325 87	3,236 53	88,562 40
English-French Training School, Sandwich	8,715 06	3,334 04	12,049 10
Reformatory for Boys, Penetanguishene	191,512 00	....	191,512 00
School for the Deaf, Belleville	381,191 65	87,562 67	468,754 32

STATEMENT No. 2.—Continued.

Name of Work.	Expenditure 1st July, 1867, to 31st Oct., 1912.		Expenditure Fiscal Year ending 31st. Oct 1913.		Total Expenditure to 31st Oct., 1913.	
	$	c.	$	c.	$	c.
PUBLIC BUILDINGS—*Continued.*						
School for the Blind, Brantford..........	329,361	13	78,564	19	407,925	82
Agricultural College, Guelph	860,136	63	49,163	51	909,300	14
Provincial Buildings, Canadian National Exhibition Association, Toronto (Grant).	25,000	00	....		25,000	00
Horticultural Experimental Station, Jordan Harbor	36,084	68	6,187	61	42,272	29
Dairy School, Kingston	23,613	56	....		23,613	56
Dairy School, Strathroy	14,583	71	....		14,583	71
Veterinary College, Toronto	252	23	....		252	23
New Veterinary College, University Avenue, Toronto	30,515	71	112,957	68	143,473	39
School of Mining, Kingston	4,070	00	....		4,070	00
Normal College, Hamilton (equipment Domestic Science Room	854	25	....		854	25
School of Practical Science (College of Technology)	59,100	26	....		59,100	26
School of Practical Science, Queen's Park .	252,535	56	....		252,535	56
School of Practical Science, New Chemistry and Milling and Mining Building	448,213	15	....		448,213	15
Children's Shelter, Toronto	8,864	95	....		8,864	95
Immigration Office, Toronto	6,305	63	2,577	70	8,883	33
Fish and Game, Boat House and Hatchery Building	....		2,833	52	2,833	52
Ontario Government Office Building, London England	44,836	21	500	00	45,336	21
Winter Fair Building, Guelph	25,101	25	....		25,101	25
Hygenic Institution, London	74,297	41	....		74,297	41
Agricultural Hall, Toronto	324	00	....		324	00
Government Farm, Mimico	51,646	84	....		51,646	84
Pioneer Dairy Farm, Algoma	5,178	43	....		5,178	43
Brock's Monument, Queenston Heights	4,605	31	....		4,605	31
Niagara River Fence	8,025	43	....		8,025	43
ALGOMA DISTRICT:						
Court House, Gaol and Registry Office, Sault Ste. Marie	34,531	26	119	60	34,650	86
Registry Office, addition to, Sault Ste. Marie	11,658	02	....		11,658	02
Lock-up, Bruce Mines	3,117	48	....		3,117	48
" Blind River	2,642	87	....		2,642	87
" Chapleau . ..	1,126	49	....		1,126	49
Cutler . . .	864	70	....		864	70
Echo Bay	500	00	....		500	00
Hilton	500	00	....		500	00
Thessalon . . .	2,221	99	....		2,221	99
" Wawa	1,330	16	....		1,330	16
Industrial Farm, Sault Ste. Marie	....		63	10	63	10
KENORA DISTRICT:						
Court House and Gaol, Gaoler's Residence. Registry Office, etc., Kenora	42,433	41	1,011	49	43,444	90
New Registry Office. Kenora	5,871	08	9,529	88	15,400	96
New Court House, Kenora	59,238	52	....		59,238	52
Land Titles Office, Kenora	575	00	....		575	00
Sea Wall, Kenora	3,197	65	....		3,197	65
Grounds and Walks, Kenora	1,148	76	....		1,148	76
Lock-up at Dryden, transferred from Rainy River District	521	00	....		521	00

STATEMENT No. 2.—Continued.

Name of Work.	Expenditure 1st July, 1867, to 31st Oct., 1912.	Expenditure Fiscal Year ending 31st Oct., 1913.	Total Expenditure, to 31st October 1913.
	$ c.	$ c.	$ c.
PUBLIC BUILDINGS—Continued.			
MUSKOKA DISTRICT:			
Court House, Gaol and Registry Office at Bracebridge	34,236 60	1,984 92	36,221 52
Lock-up and Court Room at Huntsville	8,364 85	....	8,364 85
Lock-up and Court Room at Bayside	300 00	....	300 00
Immigration Sheds at Gravenhurst	355 00	....	355 00
MANITOULIN DISTRICT:			
Grand Manitoulin Island, three Lock-ups (Gore Bay, Little Current, and Manitowaning), transferred from Algoma District	22,287 60	....	22,287 60
Lock-up, Killarney, transferred from Algoma District	1,298 97	....	1,298 97
Court House, Gaol, etc., Gore Bay	8,176 41	204 35	8,380 76
Lock-up, Manitowaning	357 74	22 00	379 74
Lock-up, Providence Bay, Grant	500 00	....	500 00
Lock-up, Little Current	58 95	....	58 95
NIPISSING DISTRICT:			
Lockup, Court Room and Registry Office and Gaoler's House, North Bay	49,731 68	1,620 80	51,352 48
Lock-up at Bonfield	694 67	....	694 67
" Cache Bay	500 00	....	500 00
" Markstay	600 00	....	600 00
Mattawa	14,949 19	....	14,949 19
" Sturgeon Falls	2,266 28	....	2,266 28
Warren	600 00	....	600 00
PARRY SOUND DISTRICT:			
Registry Office, Lock-up and Court Room, House for Gaoler, Land Titles Office, etc., Parry Sound	47,758 88	778 12	48,537 00
Lock-up at Magnetawan	645 56	....	645 56
Lock-up and Court Room, Burk's Falls	6,621 96	....	6,621 96
Lock-up at French River	1,198 62	....	1,198 62
" Dunchurch	609 00	....	609 00
" Emsdale	300 00	....	300 00
" Byng Inlet	1,232 35	....	1,232 35
" South River	500 00	....	500 00
Powassan	1,250 00	....	1,250 00
Callender	500 00	....	500 00
" Sundridge	500 00	....	500 00
RAINY RIVER DISTRICT:			
Registry Office, Fort Frances	2,274 33	....	2,274 33
Gaol, etc., Fort Frances	17,780 63	32 95	17,813 58
Court House, Fort Frances	....	12,777 95	12,777 95
Lock-up at Mines Centre	1,205 48	....	1,205 48
" Emo	1,888 94	....	1,888 94
" Atikokan	1,571 31	....	1,571 31
" Beaver Mills	1,840 71	....	1,840 71
SUDBURY DISTRICT:			
Court House and Gaol and Registry Office, Sudbury	79,477 83	2,202 62	81,680 45
Lock-up at Sudbury, transferred from Nipissing District	12,595 48	....	12,595 48

STATEMENT No. 2.—Continued.

Name of Work.	Expenditure 1st July, 1867, to 31st Oct., 1912.	Expenditure Fiscal Year ending 31st Oct. 1913.	Total Expenditure to 31st October, 1913.
PUBLIC BUILDINGS—*Continued.*	$ c.	$ c.	$ c.
SUDBURY DISTRICT: —*Continued.*			
Lock-up at Chelmsford, transferred from Algoma District	511 90	....	511 90
Lock-up at Chelmsford	503 88	....	503 88
Lock-up at Massey, transferred from Algoma District	702 74	....	702 74
Lock-up at Nairn, transferred from Algoma District	300 00	....	300 00
Lock-up at Webbwood, transferred from Algoma District	1,749 15	....	1,749 15
THUNDER BAY DISTRICT:			
Registry Office, Lock-up, Court House, etc., Port Arthur	69,424 95	317 18	69,742 13
Lock-up at Fort William	9,723 90	....	9,723 90
" Silver Islet	2,304 79	....	2,304 79
" Nepigon	1,279 23	....	1,279 23
" Schreiber	700 00	....	700 00
" Superior Junction (Sioux Lookout)	1,159 04	....	1,159 04
" White River	....	499 77	499 77
Industrial Home, Fort William	15,334 66	24,053 70	39,388 36
TEMISKAMING DISTRICT:			
Lock-up, Cobalt, transferred from Nipissing District	5,418 99	....	5,418 99
Lock-up, Cochrane, transferred from Nipissing District	1,000 00	....	1,000 00
Lock-up, Charlton, transferred from Nipissing District	500 00	....	500 00
Lock-up, Englehart, transferred from Nipissing District	975 00	....	975 00
Lock-up, Gowganda, transferred from Nipissing District	3,105 07	....	3,105 07
Lock-up, New Liskeard, transferred from Nipissing District	657 00	....	657 00
Lock-up, North Porcupine, transferred from Nipissing District	2,671 18	....	2,671 18
Lock-up, North Porcupine, transferred from Sudbury District	138 80	....	138 80
Lock-up, South Porcupine, transferred from Sudbury District	5,350 18	562 38	5,912 56
Lock-up, Matheson, transferred from Sudbury District	1,263 86	....	1,263 86
Temporary Court House, Haileybury	....	2,781 31	2,781 31
New Court House, Haileybury	....	12,873 51	12,873 51
New Registry Office, Haileybury	....	6,200 11	6,200 11
COUNTY OF HALIBURTON:			
Registry Office at Minden	5,918 42	....	5,918 42
Gaol and Court House at Minden (grant)	500 00	500 00	1,000 00

STATEMENT No. 2.—Continued.

Name of Work.	Expenditure 1st July 1867, to 31st Oct., 1912.	Expenditure Fiscal Year ending 31st Oct., 1913.	Total Expenditure to 31st October, 1913.
	$ c.	$ c.	$ c.
PUBLIC WORKS:			
Admaston Bridge, Bonnechere River	....	1,977 97	1,977 97
Antoine Creek Bridge, Tp. Mattawan	3,223 36	....	3,223 36
Ardock Bridge, County Frontenac	900 00	....	900 00
Aubrey and Ignace Bridges	....	881 02	881 02
Axe Creek, Housey's Outlet and Kahshee Bridges	1,221 57	....	1,221 57
Balsam and Cameron Lakes Locks	23,959 02	....	23,959 02
Balsam River Works	16,585 11	....	16,585 11
Bar River, Tp. McDonald (removing obstructions) ..	130 55	....	130 55
Barbette Creek Bridge, Clara	....	993 92	993 92
Bass Creek Bridge, Tp. Limerick	....	1,200 00	1,200 00
Base Lake Dam, Tp. Galway, Peterborough	1,000 00	....	1,000 00
Baysville Bridge (McLean and Ridout) ..	2,947 50	....	2,947 50
Bear Creek Dam and Slide	1,617 52	....	1,617 52
Beaudette River (to aid in dredging, etc.)	3,000 00	....	3,000 00
Beaver Creek Bridge, Kenora District	784 68	....	784 68
Beaver Creek Bridge, Monck Tp.	996 77	....	996 77
Beeline Bridge, Alice Tp.	499 63	....	499 63
Bell's Rapids Bridge, County Renfrew	2,494 79	....	2,494 79
Bens River and Black Creek Bridges	2,132 24	....	2,132 24
Berriedale Bridge, Tp. Armour	935 77	....	935 77
Big East and Black Creek Bridges	2,659 61	....	2,659 61
Big East River Bridge	5,596 03	....	5,596 03
Big East River Bridge, Chaffey	....	875 00	875 00
Bigwood Bridges, Nipissing District	7,389 80	....	7,389 80
Birch Creek Bridge, Sudbury, Soo Trunk Road ..	8,157 86	....	8,157 86
Birch Creek Bridge, Birch Lake Road	2,185 72	1,802 85	3,988 57
Birch Creek Bridge (Unpaid Accounts 1912)	....	296 70	296 70
Bissett's Creek Bridge, Nipissing District.	699 57	....	699 57
Black Creek Bridge, Himsworth Tp.	449 33	....	449 33
" " Robertsville ..	....	149 05	149 05
" " Dalton Tp.	4,841 09	....	4,841 09
" " (Unpaid Accounts, 1911-1912) Dalton.	....	187 40	187 40
Black River Works (Lake Simcoe)	3,136 10	....	3,136 10
Black River Bridge, Tp. Draper, Muskoka (to rebuild)	509 48	....	509 48
Black Sturgeon Bridge	1,179 10	....	1,179 10
Black River Bridge, Matheson	3,938 68	....	3,938 68
Black Bridge, Muskoka, Construction of ..	1,500 00	....	1,500 00
Black Creek Bridge, Tp. Palmerston	250 00	....	250 00
Black Duck and Indian River Bridges	869 48	....	869 48
Black Creek, removing obstructions, Tps. Monck and Watt	1,480 76	....	1,480 76
Black Bay Road Bridge, Port Arthur	5,000 00	....	5,000 00
Blanche River Bridge, High Falls	2,882 33	....	2,882 33
Blanche River Bridge, Marter Tp.	3,153 54	....	3,153 54
Blind River Bridge	2,772 34	....	2,772 34
Blind River Bridge, Soo Trunk Road	7,881 21	200 00	8,081 21
Boon Creek Bridge	2,276 72	....	2,276 72
Bonnechere River Bridge, Bromley Tp ...	2,566 38	....	2,566 38
Bonnechere River Bridge, Horton Tp (grant) ..	1,000 00	....	1,000 00
Bonnechere River Works	338 50	....	338 50

STATEMENT No. 2.—Continued.

Name of Work.	Expenditure 1st July, 1867, to 31st Oct., 1912.	Expenditure Fiscal Year ending 31st Oct., 1913.	Total Expenditure to 31st Oct. 1913.
	$ c.	$ c.	$ c.
PUBLIC WORKS—*Continued.*			
Boston Creek Bridge	1,332 95	....	1,332 95
Bottle Lake Dam and Missaissicua Creek Dam	4,068 72	....	4,068 72
Boyne Bridges, Foley	....	2,160 98	2,160 98
Brower Creek Bridge, Tp. Glackmeyer ...	240 00	....	240 00
Brule Creek Bridge	489 85	....	489 85
Bracebridge Bridge	7,000 00	....	7,000 00
Bucklake Bridge (to rebuild)	305 06	....	305 06
Bunting Creek Bridge	586 13	....	586 13
Burk's Falls Bridge, Magnetawan River..	2,606 14	....	2,606 14
Burnt River Bridge, Tp. Snowdon	2,017 11	....	2,017 11
Burnt River Bridge, Tp. Somerville	4,930 61	....	4,930 61
Burnt River Bridge, Buckhorn Road	3,106 18	34 60	3,140 78
Burnt Bridges, Vermilion River, Tp. Capreol, replacing	2,317 87	....	2,317 87
Bushkong Lake Bridge, Paterson Road ...	3,386 92	....	3,386 92
Bushkong Lake Bridge, Tp. Stanhope	3,030 91	....	3,030 91
Cache Creek Bridge, Springer Tp.	344 27	....	344 27
Calabogie Bridge, Tp. Bagot	1,800 00	....	1,800 00
Campement D'Ours Island Bridge	3,500 00	1,470 09	4,970 09
Canard River Bridge	1,000 00	....	1,000 00
Cardiff, Monmouth Townline and Maxwell Bridges	3,323 65	399 59	3,723 24
Cardwell and Baxter Bridges	2,108 64	....	2,108 64
Cashmere Dam, Middlesex	1,144 19	....	1,144 19
Cassimer River, removing obstructions ...	205 56	....	205 56
Chapleau Bridge	2,231 40	....	2,231 40
Chemong Lake Bridge	3,500 00	....	3,500 00
Clare River Bridge	....	747 33	747 33
Clear Creek Bridge, Orford Tp............	500 00	....	500 00
Clearing and Log Houses on free land grants, Settlers' Homestead Fund	16,780 75	....	16,780 75
Commanda Lake Bridge	465 95	....	465 95
Corbett Creek Bridge, Oliver	....	1,598 16	1,598 16
Completing Pumping Plant, Jordan Harbor (transferred to *Public Buildings*), $761.23.			
Cobb's Lake Outlet	1,102 08	....	1,102 08
Concrete Mixing Machine	950 00	....	950 00
Cosby Bridge, Nipissing District	493 85	....	493 85
Couchiching Lake Works	427 82	....	427 82
Crocodile Creek, Nipissing District	780 94	....	780 94
Cull's, Barry Bay and Calabogie Bridges ..	931 48	............;	931 48
Dacre Bridge, Brougham Tp.	395 63	....	395 63
Damage by rising water near Kenora	800 00	....	800 00
Dausey Bridge at Blind River, Algoma.....	4,048 85	....	4,048 85
Dawson Road Bridge	1,480 36	....	1,480 36
Deep Bay Narrows, improvement	248 35	....	248 35
Delta Creek, improvements	99 24	....	99 24
Deer Lake Works, Dam and Slide, Tp. Anstruther	1,420 17	....	1,420 17
Denbigh Bridge, Hydes Creek	....	847 25	847 25
Desbarats Bridge, Algoma	789 52	....	789 52
Des Joachims Rapids Bridge and approaches	9,937 72	....	9,937 72
Detola Branch Road Bridge	200 00	....	200 00
Docks at Southampton. Saugeen River ..	1,739 04	....	1,739 04
Docks on the Rainy River	3,163 44	....	3,163 44
Docks (landing) at Beaudraul's, Wabigoon	777 95	............,..	777 95

STATEMENT No. 2.—Continued.

Name of Work.	Expenditure 1st July, 1867, to 31st Oct., 1912.	Expenditure Fiscal Year ending 31st Oct.,1913.	Total Expenditure to 31st Oct., 1913.
PUBLIC WORKS—*Continued.*	$ c.	$ c.	$ c.
Dog Lake Dams, storage of water	72,760 20	598 30	73,358 50
Dickson Creek Bridge, Bucke Tp.	1,564 01	....	1,564 01
Dorset Bridge, Tp. Dorset	7,621 72	....	7,621 72
Draper Bridge	500 00	....	500 00
Driftwood Bridges, Tp. Walker	2,191 39	4 50	2,195 89
Dryden Bridge	7,420 93	....	7,420 93
Dymond and Harris Townline Bridge	911 28	....	911 28
Eagle Lake Dam, Anstruther Tp.	1,173 84	....	1,173 84
Eau Claire Bridge	5,534 13	....	5,534 13
Echo River Bridge	1,332 11	....	1,332 11
Echo Bay Bridge	7,569 83	313 50	7,853 33
Eels Creek Bridge, Co. Peterboro	1,500 00	....	1,500 00
Emily Creek Bridge	2,389 29	....	2,389 29
Embankment along River, Dover Tp.	500 00	....	500 00
Englehart Bridge and approaches	2,795 89	....	2,795 89
Equipments, instruments, machinery, etc. ..	13,967 33	2,470 44	16,437 77
Espinola Bridge	17,980 23	....	17,980 23
Fawcetts, Stephenson Townline and Kahshee. River Bridges	2,877 66	....	2,877 66
Faulkner Bridge, Monetteville, Lake Nipissing	589 47	....	589 47
Filiatrault Lake Bridge, boundary between Martland and Crosby	1,894 91	....	1,894 91
Forsyth's Creek Bridge, Tp. Christie	519 45	....	519 45
Fourth Cancession Bridge, Hagar	....	1,058 51	1,058 51
Frog Creek Bridge, McIrvine Tp.	497 93	....	497 93
Gananoque River Improvement	....	366 23	366 23
Gannons Narrows Bridge, contribution	1,000 00	....	1,000 00
Garden River Bridge, Trunk Road	1,584 37	6,432 58	8,016 95
Gardner Lake Bridge, Hagerman Tp.	399 72	....	399 72
Georgian Bay Works	7,149 97	....	7,149 97
Glenelg Bridges	1,000 00	....	1,000 00
Golden Lake Bridge	2,913 43	1,782 56	4,645 99
Gooderham and Kinmount Bridges	3,876 79	....	3,876 79
Goulais Bay Road Bridges	1,559 76	....	1,559 76
Goulais River Bridge	7,448 51	....	7,448 51
Gold Rock Portage Bridges	500 00	501 93	1,001 93
Grassy River Bridge, McCrosson Tp.	1,325 32	....	1,325 32
Graces Creek Bridge	....	874 25	874 25
Gratuity to Arthur Brown, injured at Tomstown Bridge	140 00	....	140 00
Gull and Burnt River Works, dams, slides, bridges, etc.	100,716 60	....	100,716 60
Haliburton Bridges, Tp. Dysart	2,000 00	....	2,000 00
Hawkers Creek Bridge, Verulam Tp. grant, 1910 ...	200 00	....	200 00
Head River improvements, Tps. Laxton and Cardon	976 82	....	976 82
Helferty Bridge, Raglan	....	380 00	380 00
High Falls, Pigeon River, slide, dam, etc., (C. L. D.)	9,706 07	....	9,706 07
High Falls Bridge, Tp. Macaulay	1,780 37	....	1,780 37
Hillardton Bridge, over White River	5,460 89	....	5,460 89
Himsworth Bridges	806 29	....	806 29
Hoeffler Bridge	3,417 35	59 85	3,477 20
Hoodstown Road Bridge, Chaffey Tp.	1,200 00	....	1,200 00
Hoodstown Road Bridge, over Big East River	800 00	....	800 00
Houseys Rapids Bridge	3,565 03	....	3,565 03
Hudson Creek Bridge, Tp. Kearns	1,792 94	....	1,792 94

STATEMENT No. 2.—Continued.

Name of Work.	Expenditure 1st July, 1867, to 31st Oct., 1912.	Expenditure Fiscal Year ending 31st Oct., 1913.	Total Expenditure to 31st October, 1913.
	$ c.	$ c.	$ c.
PUBLIC WORKS—*Continued.*			
Hymers Bridge, Whitefish River	3,000 05	....	3,000 05
Indian Point Bridge, Manitoulin Island ..	6,876 49	....	6,876 49
Indian River Works (deepening), Tps. Sarawak and Keppell	1,850 82	....	1,850 82
Ingoldsby Bridge	....	299 94	299 94
Inkerman Dam, removal of, County Dundas	1,000 00	....	1,000 00
Jean Baptiste Bridge	98 31	....	98 31
Jean Baptiste Creek Bridge (Armstrong)..	1,168 21	962 64	2,130 85
Jean Baptiste River, construction of bridge over	2,850 00	....	2,850 00
Joseph River Bridge, Medora	1,756 07	....	1,756 07
Judge Bridge, White River, Tp. of Casey ..	2,526 39	5,228 83	7,755 22
Kabuska Creek Bridge, Banfield	3,217 48	1,762 72	4,980 20
Kahshee, Morrison and Doe Lake Road Bridges	2,865 74	299 76	3,165 50
Kaministikwia River Works	22,865 02	....	22,865 02
Kaministikwia Bridge, Paipoonge	28,797 39	8,756 58	37,553 97
Katrine Bridge, Armour Tp.	1,257 23	....	1,257 23
Kearney Bridge	6,798 82	....	6,798 82
Kerr's Bridge, Co. Victoria	2,531 83	....	2,531 83
Kinmount Bridge	1,500 00	....	1,500 00
Kushog Lake Dam	300 00	....	300 00
L'Amable Bridge, Dungannon Tp.	1,271 43	....	1,271 43
La Blanche River Bridge and approaches, Casey Tp.	5,817 72	....	5,817 72
La Blanche River Bridge	2,929 87	....	2,929 87
La Blanche Bridge, Tomstown	6,326 68	....	6,326 68
La Grasse Bridge	1,500 00	....	1,500 00
Lake of Bays, dredging mouth of river at outlet of	581 82	....	581 82
Lake Nosbonsing Bridge, Nipissing District	3,497 68	....	3,497 68
Lake Scugog Works dredging at Port Perry	977 53	....	977 53
Lake Scugog Flats Road	1,500 00	....	1,500 00
Lake St. John and Sucker Creek, improving outlet ...	1,795 56	....	1,795 56
Laird Township Bridges	1,693 22	....	1,693 22
Lanark County, allowance for washout ...	....	1,225 00	1,225 00
Landing pier at Port Elgin	2,750 00	....	2,750 00
Landing pier at Southampton	2,022 63	....	2,022 63
Larder Lake Road Bridges	982 71	237 10	1,219 81
La Valley River Bridge, Woodyatt	611 40	1,763 22	2,374 62
La Vase and Boon Creek, improvements to	804 22	....	804 22
Lawrence Bridge, Gould Road	....	500 00	500 00
Leeburn Bridge, Aberdeen	....	2,174 43	2,174 43
Little Rapids Bridge, Little Thessalon	....	2,496 97	2,496 97
Madawaska Village Bridge	....	1,319 00	1,319 00
Madawaska River Bridge, near Arnprior ..	3,000 00	....	3,000 00
Madawaska River Swing Bridge at Comber-mere, bridge at Burnston and bridge Tp. Raglan	12,171 43	....	12,171 43
Madawaska River Bridge, Airy Tp.	3,498 38	....	3,498 38
Madawaska River Bridge, Murcheson Tp. ..	2,981 13	....	2,981 13
Magnetawan Works, lock, swing bridge, dam and river improvements; dam and slide, Deer Lake; swing bridge, Tp. Ryerson; dredging Burk's Falls, and removing obstructions, Ahmic Lake ..	76,778 26	....	76,778 26
Magnetawan River Bridge, Perry Tp.	3,469 47	....	3,469 47
Magnetawan River Bridge, Burk's Falls ..	12,193 78	3,808 52	16,002 30

STATEMENT No. 2.—Continued.

Name of Work.	Expenditure 1st July, 1867, to 31st Oct., 1912.	Expenditure Fiscal Year ending 31st Oct., 1913.	Total Expenditure to 31st October, 1913.
PUBLIC WORKS—*Continued.*	$ c.	$ c.	$ c.
Maintenance and Repairs, locks, dams, slides, bridges, etc. (exclusive of salaries) ..	371,775 99	30,204 18	401,980 17
Manitou Lake Works, dam at outlet, etc., Rainy River District	2,794 14	....	2,794 14
Manitowaba Bridge, McKellar Tp.	798 51	....	798 51
Maple Island Bridge, Magnetawan River, Tp. McKenzie ...	993 32	....	993 32
Magpie River Bridge...................	....	489 28	489 28
Mary's and Fairy Lakes, Lock Works and bridge over Muskoka River at Huntsville ...	80,438 37	....	80,438 37
Mary's and Fairy Lake Lock Works, to renew high bridge above lock over Muskoka River and renew cribbing above and below locks	8,389 39	....	8,389 39
Martland Tp. Bridge	1,192 90	....	1,192 90
Maskinonge Creek, Tp. Cassimer, removing obstructions	499 92	....	499 92
Matawatchin Bridge, Renfrew Co.	8,485 67	....	8,485 67
Mattawa River Bridge and Works	22,094 02	....	22,094 02
Mill Creek improvements, Co. Prescott	1,000 00	....	1,000 00
Minden Bridge	4,740 68	....	4,740 68
Minnitake Bridge ....:	....	552 34	552 34
Mississicua Lake Dam	4,989 84	....	4,989 84
Mississicua River Bridge	4,355 94	....	4,355 94
Mississauga River Bridge, Thompson Tp..	24,593 87	....	24,593 87
Mississauga River, reflooring iron bridge ..	462 60	....	462 60
Mississippi, Grant, McKenzie and Egan Bridges	2,125 26	....	2,125 26
Mississippi River improvements (obstructions)....................	7,843 08	....	7,843 08
Moira River improvements, Tp. Thurlow...	2,135 32	....	2,135 32
Monck Road Bridge, etc., Cardiff..........	774 03	....	774 03
Monroe's Rapids, Mississippi River, removing obstructions	900 00	....	900 00
Moose River Works, Co. Stormont	1,000 00	....	1,000 00
Montreal River Bridge, Elk Lake	7,820 83	24 36	7,845 19
Morley Township Bridge	742 28	....	742 28
Mountain Lake Bridge, Minden............	....	1,345 43	1,345 43
Mud Lake Works, Tp. Dalton	1,502 32	....	1,502 32
Mud Creek Bridge, Tp. Herschell	1,800 00	....	1,800 00
Mumfords Bridge, Distress River, Tp. Chapman ...	2,202 01	....	2,202 01
Muskoka Lake Works	21,915 30	....	21,915 30
" Lock, bridges and dredging at Port Carling	64,683 45	....	64,683 45
" Cut and bridge at Port Sandfield.	20,336 05	....	20,336 05
" Muskosh Falls, dams and bridges at Bala	23,567 03	....	23,567 03
" Joseph River Works, less contribution	486 87	....	486 87
" Kemp's Channel, improvements..	4,238 69	....	4,238 69
" Piers and boom, Jeannette's Channel	1,660 75	....	1,660 75
Muskoka River Works	42,670 53	....	42,670 53
Muskoka River Bridge at South Falls......	1,000 00	....	1,000 00
Muskoka River Bridge at Port Sydney ...	1,000 00	....	1,000 00
Muskrat River Improvements	1,861 98	....	1,861 98
Myers Cave Bridge, Barrie Tp.	931 38	....	931 38
McCarthy Creek Bridges, Tp. Gibbons	300 00	....	300 00
McCreight's Bridge, Kirkwood Tp.	4,814 13	825 69	5,639 82

STATEMENT No. 2.—Continued.

Name of Work.	Expenditure 1st July 1867, to 31st Oct., 1912.	Expenditure Fiscal Year ending 31st Oct., 1913.	Total Expenditure to 31st Oct., 1913.
	$ c.	$ c.	$ c.
PUBLIC WORKS—*Continued.*			
McKenzie Creek Improvement	200 35		200 35
McKelvery Creek Bridge, Crozier		1,837 67	1,837 67
Nation River Works	13,877 23		13,877 23
Nation River Dredge (contribution)	4,000 00		4,000 00
Nation River Bridge, 9th and 10th Cons. Cambridge Tp. grant	1,000 00		1,000 00
Nation River Bridge, Casselman and Cambridge Tps., grants	2,000 00		2,000 00
Neighick Lake, dredging at entrance	898 15		898 15
Neebing River Bridge, Neebing Tp.	1,800 00		1,800 00
New Liskeard Bridge, Wabis River	4,000 00		4,000 00
Nipissing Lake Works	9,182 17		9,182 17
Nogies Creek Works	2,144 57		2,144 57
Norland Bridge, Cameron Road	1,354 70		1,354 70
North West Arm Bridge	999 68		999 68
North Branch Bridge, Longford	753 35		753 35
North and Black Rivers, removing obstructions	4,535 13		4,535 13
North Road Bridge, Tp. Dymond	1,877 24		1,877 24
North River Bridge, Matchedash	3,465 89	2,060 76	5,526 65
Nottawasaga River Works	9,270 83		9,270 83
Nuggett Creek Bridge, Kenora District	963 29		963 29
Oakley Bridge, Muskoka	4,765 03		4,765 03
Onaping River Bridge	2,710 09		2,710 09
Opickinimika River Dams	1,961 11	34 22	1,995 33
Orillia Township Bridge		2,494 15	2,494 15
Otonabee River Works	9,162 91		9,162 91
Otonabee River Bridge	2,500 00		2,500 00
Otter Creek Bridge at Copp's Falls	426 32		426 32
Otter Creek Bridge, Brethour Tp.	108 60	1,003 52	1,112 12
Overhead bridges, Soo Branch, C.P.R	11,070 17		11,070 17
Oxdrift Bridge, Kenora District	656 90		656 90
Oxtongue Bridge, Muskoka District	1,058 26		1,058 26
Papineau Bridges, Boon Creek		3,074 28	3,074 28
Payne River Bridges, Tp. Finch	2,500 00		2,500 00
Payne River Works	4,000 00		4,000 00
Palmer's Rapids Bridge, Renfrew	4,629 11		4,629 11
Pautois Creek Bridge, Calvin Tp.	2,373 82		2,373 82
Peninsula Creek Improvements, bridges, cribbing, etc.	37,495 16		37,495 16
Petawawa River Bridge	3,879 25		3,879 25
Peterson, Beaumaris and Cardwell Bridges	4,311 57		4,311 57
Pickerel River Bridge, Wilson Tp.	1,846 46		1,846 46
Pickerel River Improvement		1,391 84	1,391 84
Pigeon River Works, Co. Victoria	4,999 62		4,999 62
Pinewood Bridge, Rainy River District, reflooring	375 00		375 00
Pine River Bridge, Dilke Tp.	1,322 65	200 00	1,522 65
Pine River Bridge, Rainy River District	3,241 30		3,241 30
Portage Bay Bridge, Keewatin	5,009 50		5,009 50
Portage du Fort Bridge, Ottawa River	10,747 99		10,747 99
Port Severn, Axe Lake and Cooper Bridges.	1,427 41		1,427 41
Powassan Bridge	300 00		300 00
Purchase of Rubber Boots		122 95	122 95
Rainy River Road Bridge	4,429 84		4,429 84
Rainy River Bridge	1,996 77		1,996 77
Roads, Tp. Ryerson	7,295 06		7,295 06
Root River Bridge, Tarentorus Tp., 4th Con.	3,201 50		3,201 50
Root River Bridge, Soo Trunk Road	8,104 79	11 25	8,116 04

STATEMENT No. 2.—Continued.

Name of Work.	Expenditure 1st July, 1867, to 31st Oct. 1912.	Expenditure Fiscal Year ending 31st Oct., 1913.	Total Expenditure to 31st Oct., 1913.
PUBLIC WORKS—*Continued.*	$ c.	$ c.	$ c.
Root River Bridge, Soo Trunk Road (Unpaid Accounts 1910)	101 86		101 86
Round Lake Bridge, Hagarty	500 00		500 00
Round Lake Road Bridges	2,301 90		2,301 90
Roseport Bridge, Thunder Bay District	881 75		881 75
Running Creek, dredging	1,500 00		1,500 00
Rydal Bank Bridge,	10,141 70		10,141 70
Ryerson Townline Bridge, Sprucedale Road	956 05	7 25	963 30
Sampsons and Sparks Creek Bridge, Bonfield		1,444 02	1,444 02
Sand Lake Road Bridge, Magnetawan River		2,832 15	2,832 15
Sakoose Bridges		947 68	947 68
Salter and Victoria Bridges	499 38		499 38
Sauble River Bridge, Massey	12,708 20		12,708 20
Saugeen River Bridge, Bentinck Tp.	900 00		900 00
Scugog River Works (including Lindsay lock and swing bridges	97,897 38		97,897 38
Severn Bridge, Tp. Morrison	8,350 00		8,350 00
Severn River Bridge, East Branch, Rama Tp.	1,990 00		1,990 00
Seguin River Bridge	8,754 00		8,754 00
Shadow River Bridge, Tp. Humphrey	490 90		490 90
Sherbineau Bridge, Hungerford	500 00		500 00
Shoal Lake, and Lake of the Woods, Improvement Ash Rapids	5,998 25		5,998 25
Six Mile Bridge, Shuniah		1,417 71	1,417 71
Slate River Bridge, Kaministiquia River	580 14		580 14
Sleeman's Bridge and approaches	1,044 80		1,044 80
Snake River improvements	140 65		140 65
South Channel Bridge and Dam, Bala Muskoka		5,182 95	5,182 95
South River Bridge, Nipissing Tp.	5,846 00		5,846 00
South River and Eagle Lake Bridges, Tp. of Machar	1,295 87		1,295 87
South River Bridge, Himsworth Tp.	1,987 30		1,987 30
Spanish River Bridge and approaches, Webbwood	18,364 73		18,364 73
Spanish River Bridge, Massey	28,723 08		28,723 08
Spanish River Bridge, Grant to Nairn Tp.	1,000 00		1,000 00
Spanish River Bridge, Nairn Tp.	14,302 78		14,302 78
Squaw River Works	1,688 16		1,688 16
Squaw River Works dam at Harvey	581 56		581 56
Star Lake Works	412 22		412 22
Stanley Bridge, Thunder Bay District	8,136 09		8,136 09
Steidtler Creek Bridge, Parry Sound Dis.	954 47		954 47
Stephenson Float Bridge	808 15		808 15
Still River Bridge, Byng Inlet	918 60		918 60
Stitsted. Sharpes Creek and Hoc Hoc Bridges	2,537 28		2,537 28
Stony Creek Works, Tp. Ops	4,828 25		4,828 25
Stoney Creek Bridge, Ryerson	831 68		831 68
St. Joseph Tp. Bridge, Algoma District	1,288 98		1,288 98
Sturgeon River Bridge, Tp. Field	3,616 08		3,616 08
Sturgeon River Bridge, Tp. Gibbons	2,610 35		2,610 35
Sturgeon Falls Bridge		11,596 08	11,596 08
Sudaby's Bridge, Johnson		1,794 79	1,794 79
Sunday Creek Bridge	603 00		603 00
Sunday Creek Bridge, Dack		321 11	321 11
Sunday Creek Bridge, Robillard		33 71	33 71
Surveys and Inspections, etc.	65,904 59	3,531 60	69,436 19
Swansons Creek Bridge, Van Horne	600 00	362 00	962 00
Sydenham River Works	2,156 26		2,156 26
Talbot River Works	605 95		605 95

10 P.W.

STATEMENT No. 2.—Continued.

Name of Work.	Expenditure, 1st July, 1867, to 31st Oct., 1912.	Expenditure Fiscal Year ending 31st Oct., 1913.	Total Expenditure to 31st Oct., 1913.
	$ c.	**$ c.**	**$ c.**
PUBLIC WORKS—*Continued.*			
Thessalon and Larchwood Bridges	7,769 69	....	7,769 69
Thessalon Road (horse killed)	225 00	....	225 00
Tiers Bridge, Hawkers' Creek	....	200 00	200 00
Toll Road, City of St. Thomas	3,000 00	....	3,000 00
Toll Road, London and Port Stanley, Elgin County, purchase of	3,000 00	....	3,000 00
Toll Road, Hope Township, purchase of, ..	2,300 00	....	2,300 00
Toll Road, Township of London, towards purchase of	3,666 00	......'....	3,666 00
To construct steel bridge, outlet, Lake of the Woods (Kenora)	26,455 82	....	26,455 82
To rebuild bridges in Frontenac, destroyed by fires, Clyde River, Mud Lake and Con. 1, Clarendon ....`.	3,288 06	....	3,288 06
To remove obstacles from navigable streams	513 02	....	513 02
To pay for stock injured by blasting at North River	135 00	....	135 00
Tory Hill Bridge	....	499 35	499 35
Trenough Bridge, Rama	....	1,000 00	1,000 00
Trent River Bridge and Works	2,000 00	....	2,000 00
Tunnel Bridge, Wells Tp.	5,341 54	....	5,341 54
Two Tree Bridge, St. Joseph's	....	1,802 95	1,802 95
Unpaid accounts, 1910			
Union Creek improvements	1,050 63	....	1,050 63
Veuve River Bridge, Tp. Dunnet........	918 70	....	918 70
Veuve River Bridge, Tp. Kirkpatrick	541 06	....	541 06
Veuve River Bridge, Hagar Tp............	997 95	....	997 95
Veuve River Bridge, Markstay	2,119 64	1,110 18	3,229 82
Veuve River Bridge, Tp. Verner	5,719 38	....	5,719 38
Verner Bridge	1,163 11	....	1,163 11
Vermilion River Bridge, Tp. Hanmer	662 75	....	662 75
Vermilion River Bridge, Whitefish	18,840 63	....	18,840 63
Vermilion River Bridge, Capreol	821 28	.....····	821 28
Wabigoon Bridge	2,892 79	....	2,892 79
Wabigoon Township Bridges	500 00	...~.....	500 00
Wages and expenses, supervising foreman.	....	2,022 12	2,022 12
Wahnapitae Log Canal	2,334 54	1,000 00	3,334 54
Wahnapitae River Bridge and approaches.	4,642 49	....	4,642 49
Wabis River Works, Tps. Dymond, Harris and Kearns	1,340 51	....	1,340 51
Wabis River Bridges	2,773 33	....	2,773 33
Wabis Creek, to construct bridge over	1,760 08	....	1,760 08
Watt, Ryde and Macaulay Bridges	4,094 98	....	4,094 98
Walker River Bridge, Desbarats	1,093 59	377 27	1,470 86
Warren Bridge, Veuve River	....	2,501 14	2,501 14
Wasdale Bridge, Ontario and Simcoe	1,000 00	....	1,000 00
Washago Wharf	489 22	....	489 22
Washago and Gravenhurst Road	32,792 12	....	32,792 12
Wawa Road Bridge	1,198 39	....	1,198 39
West Arm Bridge, Lake Nipissing	11,260 08	....	11,260 08
West's Bridge, Thessalon River, Plummer Tp.	3,313 84	2,081 48	5,345 32
West Channel Bridge floor, Kenora	....	962 84	962 84
Whitefish River, removing obstructions ...	249 15	....	249 15
White River Bridge, Pacaud boundary	3,423 97	....	3,423 97
White River Bridges and approaches, Marter Tp.	3,185 45	....	3,185 45
White River Bridge. Bellingham	6,737 27	200 00	6,937 27
Whitefish Bridge, Lybster	499 45	....	499 45

STATEMENT No. 2.—Continued.

Name of Work.	Expenditure 1st July 1867, to 31st Oct. 1912.	Expenditure Fiscal Year ending 31st Oct., 1913.	Total Expenditure to 31st Oct., 1913.
	$ c.	$ c.	$ c.
PUBLIC WORKS—*Continued.*			
Whitestone Bridge, McKenzie Tp.	1,395 22	....	1,395 22
Whitestone Lake Bridge, Parry Sound Dis.	706 40	....	706 40
Whitestone River Bridge	425 94	....	425 94
Widdifield Bridges	....	528 16	528 16
Wilno and Rockingham Bridges	....	499 34	499 34
Winnipeg River Bridge, Pellatt Tp.	11,089 99	....	11,089 99
Wissi-Wassa Bridge, Himsworth Tp.	1,742 60	3 00	1,745 60
Wollaston Tp. Bridge	765 73	....	765 73
Wolsley River Bridge, Mattawa Tp.	974 20	....	974 20
Wright's Creek Bridge, Tp. Casey	1,813 35	....	1,813 35
Wye River Works	5,176 98	....	5,176 98
York Branch River Bridge, Tp. of Dungannon	1,910 31	....	1,910 31
Young's Point Lock	31,192 72	....	31,192 72
DRAINAGE WORKS:			
Algoma District Drainage	....	792 57	792 57
Allan Arcand, Mountain Tp.	2,200 00	....	2,200 00
Aux Raisin River, Tps. of Osnabruck and Cornwall	7,000 00	....	7,000 00
Baldwin Drain. Mountain Tp.	290 00	....	290 00
Barkley Creek, Winchester Tp.	1,000 00	....	1,000 00
Beaver Creek Drain. Cornwall Tp.	750 00	....	750 00
Bear Lake Outlet, Macpherson (improving)	1,437 83	....	1,437 83
Becquith Creek Drain. Cumberland and Clarence Tps.	1,000 00	....	1,000 00
Big Creek Drain, Tps. West and North Tilbury	9,367 30	....	9,367 30
Big Marsh Drainage, Pelee Island	....	2,000 00	2,000 00
Black Creek, clearing, Matchedash	....	496 91	496 91
Bonfield Creek improving	955 86	....	955 86
Bonfield Creek (Unpaid Accounts 1910) ..	50 00	....	50 00
Bonfield Creek, to complete	500 00	....	500 00
Brethour Township Drainage	499 83	....	499 83
Brooke Tp. Outlet Drain for Durham Creek	1,300 00	....	1,300 00
Bromley Tp. Drainage Scheme	1,100 00	....	1,100 00
Burnett Drain, Elma Tp.	1,500 00	....	1,500 00
Capreol Drainage, Lots 5 to 10, 3rd Con. ..	800 00	....	800 00
Capreol Tp. Drainage (grant)	399 86	....	399 86
Carp River Drainage Scheme	1,000 00	1,000 00	2,000 00
Castor Extension and 8th Con., Winchester	1,600 00	....	1,600 00
Cavan Tp. Drainage Works	4,000 00	....	4,000 00
Dauphin Drainage Works, Tp. of Raleigh.	5,000 00	....	5,000 00
Dawn and Enniskillen Townline Drain ...	2,500 00	....	2,500 00
Douro Drainage Works, Tp. Douro	1,200 00	....	1,200 00
Eastnor Tp. Outlet Drain	2,480 00	....	2,480 00
Eldon Tp., Drainage	1,500 00	....	1,500 00
Elma Tp., Drainage Works	4,000 00	....	4,000 00
Elson and Crooked Creek Drainage Scheme, Tp. of Dawn	2,000 00	....	2,000 00
Evanturel Tp., Drain	749 24	....	749 24
Ferris Tp. Drain	500 00	....	500 00
Forbes Drainage Works, Tilbury East Tp..	2,000 00	....	2,000 00
Fraser Creek Drainage, Tp. of Roxborough.	300 00	....	300 00
Hagarty Creek Drain, Euphemia and Mosa Tps.	1,000 00	....	1,000 00
Hardy Creek Drainage Works, Tp. of Adelaide	1,500 00	....	1,500 00
Hardy Creek Drain, Tp. Metcalf	1,000 00	....	1,000 00

STATEMENT No. 2.—Continued.

Name of Work.	Expenditure, 1st July, 1867, to 31st. Oct., 1912	Expenditure, Fiscal Year ending 31st Oct., 1913.	Total Expenditure, to 31st Oct., 1913
	$ c.	$ c.	$ c.
DRAINAGE WORKS—*Continued.*			
Hardy Creek Drain, Warwick		225 00	225 00
Harley Township Drainage	472 33		472 33
Hanmer and Rayside Drainage	1,500 00	....	1,500 00
Henry Marentette Drain, Sandwich	....	1,500 00	1,500 00
Hilliard Tp. Drainage, 4th Con.	780 00	....	780 00
Howick Tp. Drainage	300 00	....	300 00
John Taylor Drain, Marlborough and North Gower (grant)	1,000 00	....	1,000 00
Kenyon, Charlottenburg, Cornwall and Roxborough Tps. Drainage	700 00	....	700 00
Lalonde Drainage Works, Roxborough......	900 00	....	900 00
Little River, Sandwich East	2,000 00	....	2,000 00
Little Sauble Drain, Usborne Tp..........	1,000 00	....	1,000 00
Logan North-West Drain, Tp. Logan	1,000 00	....	1,000 00
Long Swamp Drainage Works (or Davidson), Tp. Keppell	1,500 00	....	1,500 00
Long Marsh Drain, extension, Anderdon ..	....	1,500 00	1,500 00
Louise Tp. Drain, Lots 2 to 10, Con. 6	700 00	....	700 00
Luther Township Drainage	1,500 00	....	1,500 00
Lyons Creek Drain, Humberstone (grant).	800 00	....	800 00
Manitoulin District Roads, Drainage	....	750 54	750 54
Mara Tp. Drainage, Sucker Creek, etc.....	1,134 18	762 17	1,896 35
Mara Tp., Unpaid Accounts 1910	6 00	....	6 00
Maxwell Creek Drain, Chatham Tp. (grant)	4,000 00	....	4,000 00
Medonte Tp. Drain	1,800 00	....	1,800 00
Merrick Creek Drainage Works, South Sandwich Tp.	1,000 00		1,000 00
Miller Drain, Tp. of Mountain	220 00	....	220 00
Miscellaneous Drainage	27 00	....	27 00
Moira Lake Drainage, Huntingdon	....	1,000 00	1,000 00
Monklands Drainage Scheme, Tp. Roxborough	1,200 00	....	1,200 00
Mud Lake Drainage, Tp. Keppell.........	963 23	....	963 23
McDonald Robertson Drain, Lochiel	....	1,500 00	1,500 00
McGregor Creek Works, Tp. Howard	2,000 00	....	2,000 00
McIntyre Creek Drainage Works	2,200 00	....	2,200 00
Nesbitt and Rogers Drains, Tp. Bosanquet	300 00	....	300 00
Nipissing District Roads, Drainage	....	1,495 32	1,495 32
North Branch Drainage Works, Tps. of Roxborough and Cornwall	2,000 00	....	2,000 00
North Branch and McIntosh Drain, Roxborough (grant)	2,000 00	....	2,000 00
Nottawasaga River Drainage	....	455 00	455 00
Parry Sound District, Drainage	....	1,339 31	1,339 31
Pedan Drainage Works, Marlborough Tp...	1,000 00	....	1,000 00
Pelee Island Drainage	3,500 00	....	3,500 00
Pelee Drainage Works, Tp. of Mersea......	5,000 00	....	5,000 00
Perche Drainage Scheme, Sarnia (grant)..	1,500 00	....	1,500 00
Petite, Castor River and Annabel Creek Drainage Works, Tp. Winchester	7,700 00	....	7,700 00
Pike Creek Drainage Scheme, Maidstone and Sandwich	2,000 00	....	2,000 00
Pike Drainage Works, Tp. Tilbury East ..	2,000 00	....	2,000 00
Pottawatomie River Drainage Works, Tp. Derby	3,500 00	....	3,500 00
Pulse Creek Drain	....	1,500 00	1,500 00
Rainy River Roads, Drainage	....	6,052 04	6,052 04

STATEMENT No. 2.—Concluded.

Name of Work.	Expenditure, 1st July, 1867, to 31st Oct. 1912.	Expenditure Fiscal Year ending 31st Oct., 1913.	Total Expenditure, to 31st Oct., 1913.
	$ c.	$ c.	$ c.
DRAINAGE WORKS—*Continued.*			
Rama Township Road, Drainage	....	200 00	200 00
Richmond Drain, Colchester South (grant)	1,500 00	....	1,500 00
Running Creek, dredging west of 5 and 6 Side Road	3,500 00	....	3,500 00
Ruscomb Drainage Works, Tp. Rochester..	9,300 00	....	9,300 00
Rusdale Creek, Bathurst Tp. Drain	1,200 00	....	1,200 00
Silver and Castor Works, Tps. Mountain, Osgood, South Gower and Winchester..	2,400 00	....	2,400 00
Silver Creek and Castor River	1,600 00	....	1,600 00
Snake River, Tp. Bromley	7,700 00	....	7,700 00
South Branch Drain Cornwall (grant)	3,000 00	....	3,000 00
Spring Creek Drainage Works, Lochiel Tp.	2,000 00	....	2,000 00
Springer Tp. Drain	610 00	....	610 00
Springer Tp. Drain (Colonization Roads)..	115 00	....	115 00
Sturgeon Falls District, Drainage	....	997 93	997 93
Sudbury District, Drainage	....	1,440 00	1,440 00
Sundry Drainage Works (charged to Municipalities)	329,980 93	....	329,980 93
Survey and Drainage swamp lands (Prov. acct.)	36,600 51	....	36,600 51
Temiskaming District, Drainage	....	2,497 81	2,497 81
Temiskaming Railway Survey	24,823 58	....	24,823 58
Tilbury East, Outlet Drain	3,020 00	....	3,020 00
Van Camp Drainage Scheme	2,700 00	....	2,700 00
Whitebread Pumping Scheme, Dover	....	1,000 00	1,000 00
Whitebread Drainage Works, Tp. Sombra..	4,000 00	....	4,000 00
Colonization and Mining Roads	7,076,148 68	406,341 52	7,482,490 20
Aid to Railways	8,576,995 03	489,112 54	9,066,107 57

NOTE:
  Certificates issued to Railways $10,515,892 45
  Cash paid direct to Railways 2,223,362 42

  Aid granted, 2,783.197 miles $12,739,254 87
  Certificates outstanding 3,673,147 30

  Actual cash expended to
  31st Oct., 1913 .... $9,066,107 57

Totals	35,019,815 88	2,711,886 29	37,731,702 17
Recap.:—			
Total Public Buildings....................	16,502,724 39	1,636,597 56	18,139,321 95
'' Public Works and Drainage..........	2,863,947 78	179,834 67	3,043,782 45
'' Colonization and Mining Roads.......	7,076,148 68	406,341 52	2,842,490 20
'' Aid to Railways ....'..........;	8,576,995 03	489,112 54	9,066,107 57
Grand Totals	35,019,815 88	2,711,886 29	37,731,702 17

Department of Public Works, Ontario.
    Toronto, February, 1914.

                         J. P. EDWARDS,
                         Accountant, Pub. Works.

STATEMENT NO. 3.

Being a classified statement showing the expenditure on Capital Account for Public Buildings, Public Works, Roads, Aid to Railways, etc. (1) The total expenditure for thirty-seven years and six months from the 1st July, 1867, to the 31st December, 1904; (2) The total expenditure for eight years and ten months to the 31st October, 1913; and (3) The grand total expenditure from the 1st of July, 1867, to the 31st October, 1913.

Name of work.	Expenditure 1st July, 1867, to 31st Dec., 1904.	Expenditure, 1st January, 1905, to 31st October, 1913.	Total Expenditure to 31st October, 1913.
	$ c.	$ c.	$ c.
1. Hospitals for the Insane, etc., at Toronto, Whitby, Mimico, London, Hamilton, Kingston, Brockville, Orillia, Cobourg, Penetanguishene and Woodstock...............	4,774,584 48	1,818,381 87	6,592,966 35
2. Penal Institutions, viz., Reformatory for Females; Reformatory for Boys; Central Prison, Toronto; New Provincial Prison, Guelph; and Industrial Home, Fort William.	1,356,979 02	1,073,029 06	2,430,008 08
3. Educational Institutions, viz., The Ontario School for the Deaf, Belleville ; The Ontario School for the Blind, Brantford; School of Practical Science; Normal and Model Schools, at Toronto and Ottawa, and Normal Schools at London, Stratford, Hamilton, Peterborough and North Bay, and Hygienic Building, London..............	1,791,329 68	1,003,538 10	2,794,867 78
4. Agricultural Institutions, viz., Agricultural College, Guelph; Winter Fair Building, Guelph; Fruit Experimental Station, Jordan Harbour; Dairy Schools, Kingston and Strathroy; Dairy Farm, Algoma; Farm, Mimico; Ontario Veterinary College, Toronto; and Ontario Government Office Building, London, England.........	709,257 51	574,886 24	1,284,143 75
5. Buildings for Administration of Justice, being Osgoode Hall, Toronto, and Court Houses, Lockups, etc., in the Districts of Algoma, Thunder Bay, Muskoka, Parry Sound, Nipissing, Manitoulin, Sudbury, Rainy River, Kenora and Temiskaming....	459,938 26	636,627 67	1,096,565 93
6. Parliament and Departmental Buildings, and Government House..................	1,776,474 75	2,137,602 87	3,914,077 62
7. Works for the improvement of Navigation, such as locks, dams, slides, etc., and works for the improvement of Transportation, such as bridges, piers, roads, etc......	1,214,527 18	1,223,246 86	2,437,774 04
8. Drainage Works and Advances to Municipalities..................................	418,161 85	144,181 43	562,343 28
9. Miscellaneous Expenditures, viz., Brock's Monument; Niagara River Fence; Clearing of Log Houses, Township of Ryerson; Temiskaming Surveys; Immigration Offices; Lodging House; Children's Shelter, Toronto; and Boat Houses, Fish and Game Department..................................	54,590 07	15,767 50	70,357 57
10. Colonization and Mining Roads	4,059,464 44	3,423,025 76	7,482,490 20
11. Aid to Railways (actual cash expended)....	7,456,173 01	1,609,934 56	9,066,107 57
Grand Total...........................	24,071,480 25	13,660,221 92	37,731,702 17

Department of Public Works, Ontario.   J. P. EDWARDS,
Toronto, February, 1914.   Accountant.

STATEMENT NO. 4.

Being Statement of Contracts and Bonds entered into with His Majesty for the year ending 31st of October, 1913.

Date.	Work.	Subject of Contract.	Contractors.	Sureties.	Particulars.	Amount.
						$. c.
1912. Nov. 5	Parliament Buildings, Toronto.	Installing two Type A electric controllers in central passenger elevators.	Elevator Specialty Company, Limited, Toronto.			2,300 00
Nov. 20	Kenora District.	Heating and plumbing, Registry Office, Kenora.	Fraser & Magill of Winnipeg, Man.			847 00
Nov. 20	Parliament Buildings, Toronto.	Partitions, counters, fittings, etc., in north wing.	Richard Dinnis & Son, Limited, of Toronto.			2,313 00
Nov. 20	Institution for the Deaf, Belleville.	Electric wiring and fixtures, in new dormitories for girls.	Greenleaf & Son, Belleville.	J. Franklyn Wills K.C., of Belleville.		1,950 00
Nov. 23	New Government House.	Sidewalk prisms to light basement on east and west sides of building.	Luxfer Prism Company, of Toronto.			968 00
Nov. 26	Parliament Buildings, Toronto.	Acoustic treatment, etc., in Legislative Chamber.	The Canadian H. W. Johns-Manville Company, Toronto.			6,750 00
Dec. 4	Parliament Buildings (west wing).	Installing electric fixtures in corridors and vestibule entrance.	The Fred. Armstrong Company, of Toronto, Limited.	The United States Fidelity and Guaranty Company, of Baltimore, U.S.A.		3,000 00

STATEMENT No. 4.—Continued.

Being Statement of Contracts and Bonds entered into with His Majesty for the year ending 31st of October, 1913.

Date.	Work.	Subject of Contract.	Contractors.	Sureties.	Particulars.	Amount.
1913 Jan. 6.	Hospital for Insane, London.	Installing one electric dumb waiter.	Otis-Fensom Elevator Company, Toronto.	......	......	$. c. 1,250 00
Jan. 15.	Institution for the Blind, Brantford.	Installing electric wiring and lighting fixtures in new dormitory building.	The Lyons Electric Company, of Brantford.	Woods, Lyons & Robins Lyons, of Brantford.	......	2,000 00
Jan. 22.	Institution for the Blind, Brantford.	Plumbing, heating, ventilating and conduit work for new dormitory.	Drake-Avery Company, of Hamilton.	London Guarantee and Accident Company, Limited (Canadian Branch), Toronto.	......	17,984 00
Feb. 5.	Ontario Veterinary College, Toronto.	Electric wiring.	Bennett & Wright Company, Limited, Toronto.	George Clapperton, & E. S. Wright, Toronto.	......	4,516 00
Feb. 5.	Ontario Veterinary College, Toronto.	Heating, ventilating, plumbing, drainage, hanging cell-ing, tram-rail conveyor and incinerator equipment.	Purdy-Mansell, Limited, Toronto.	Fred. J. Lucas and Lewis R. Fox, of Toronto.	......	72,143 00
Feb. 13.	Ontario Veterinary College, Toronto.	Roofing, galvanized work, etc.	John McLeod Company Limited, of the City of Toronto.	Alfred Ernest Chestnut and Edwin Lister, Toronto.	......	3,195 00
Feb. 13.	Ontario Veterinary College, Toronto.	The metal lathing and plastering.	Alfred D. Grant, of Toronto.	The United States Fidelity and Guaranty Company, of Baltimore, U.S.A.	......	9,800 00

Date	Work	Description	Contractor	Sureties	Amount
Feb. 14 ...	Parliament Buildings, Toronto.	Special steel fittings in vault, of Bureau of Mines.	The Office Specialty Company, Limited, Toronto.	....	1,305 00
Feb. 14 ...	Warren Bridge (Sudbury District).	Erection of steel superstructure of bridge over Veuve River, at Warren.	Sarnia Bridge Company, of Sarnia.	....	895 00
Mar. 15 ...	La Vallee River Bridge (Rainy River District).	Erection of steel superstructure of bridge over La Vallee River.	Sarnia Bridge Company, Limited, of Sarnia.	....	945 00
Mar. 19 ..	Kenora District (New Registry Office).	Supply and placing in position metal vault fittings.	G. N. Reynolds & Company, of Toronto.	....	550 00
Mar. 19 ..	Kenora District (New Registry Office).	Supply and setting up of a metal counter, with marble top, in registry office.	Office Specialty Mfg Co., Ltd., of Toronto.	....	540 00
Mar. 29 ..	Parliament Buildings, New North Wing.	Installation of a bucket ash elevator at the Parliament Buildings.	The Canadian Fairbanks-Morse Company, Limited, of Toronto.	....	595 00
Apr. 10 ...	Temiskaming District, Monteith.	Construction of residence, at Demonstration Farm, Monteith.	Herbert W. Turney, Haileybury.	Gilbert Taylor Warr, of Haileybury. James A. Miller, of New Liskeard.	4,200 00
April 25 ..	New Government House, Toronto.	Roofing, copper work, etc.	Douglas Brothers, Limited, Toronto.	....	650 00
May 8	New Government House, Toronto.	Plastering work in basement.	T. Gander & Son, Toronto.	David Spence and James Muldoon, Toronto.	1,365 00
May 19 ...	Hospital for Insane, Brockville.	Construction of Reception Hospital.	William P. Driscoll, Brockville.	William Henry Harrison and George Ross, of Brockville.	73,577 00
May 31 ...	Normal School, Peterborough.	Construction of Tool House.	Richard Sheehy, Peterborough.	....	1,300 00
May 31 ...	Normal School, Stratford.	Construction of Tool House.	Hugh Whealey, Stratford.	....	510 00

STATEMENT No. 4.—Continued.

Being Statement of Contracts and Bonds entered into with His Majesty for the year ending 31st of October, 1913.

Date.	Work.	Subject of Contract.	Contractors.	Sureties.	Particulars.	Amount.
						$. c.
June 4......	The Ontario School for the Deaf, Belleville.	Construction and alterations to Boiler House.	Shadrack F. Whitham, Brantford.	William C. Charters, and Simon L. Slade, both of Toronto.	......	6,086 00
June 4......	School for the Deaf, Belleville.	Remodelling of power plant.	Purdy-Mansell, Limited, Toronto.	Fred. J. Lucas, and Lewis R. Fox, Toronto.	......	12,990 00
June 4......	Normal School Stratford.	Supply coal and wood. Season 1913-14.	Caspar Schneider, Stratford.	H. Pauls, and J. G. Hess of Stratford.	Small egg, per ton; Pine slabs, per cord	6 55 / 5 00
June 4......	The Ontario School for the Blind, Brantford.	Remodelling of power plant.	Drake-Avery Company, Limited, Hamilton.	Lee W. Powell, and Thos. H. Wilkinson, of Hamilton.	......	9,249 00
June 4......	Government House and Parliament Buildings, Toronto.	Supply coal and wood. Season 1913-14.	Standard Fuel Company, of Toronto.	Charles T. Logan and George Vick, of Toronto.	Stove and nut, per ton ......; Pea coal, per ton; Cannell "; Hardwood, per cord ......; Pine wood, per cord	7 40 / 5 64 / 7 25 / 8 80 / 7 40

Date	Building	Supply	Contractor	Sureties	Item	Price
June 4.....	Osgoode Hall; Normal and Model Schools, Toronto.	Supply of coal and wood. Season 1913-14.	P. Burns & Company, Toronto.	George D. McDonald, Edward A. Burns. Toronto.	Egg and stove coal, per ton ..	7 40
					Grate coal, per ton	7 00
					Soft coal, per ton	5 50
					Steam " "	5 50
					Hardwood, per cord	8 90
					Pinewood, per cord	7 40
					Pine slabs, per cord	5 75
June 5.. ..	Normal School, Ottawa.	Supply of coal. Season 1913-14.	Independent Coal Company, Limited, Ottawa.	Thomas A. Black, Fred. S. J. Slattery, Ottawa.	Egg and stove coal, per ton..	7 70
					Soft coal, per ton	5 50
June 5...	Normal School, North Bay.	Supply of coal and wood. Season 1913-14.	Lindsay & McClusky, North Bay.	B. T. Leak, James A. Smith, of North Bay.	Egg coal, per ton	7 75
					Nut " "	8 25
					Pine slabs, per cord ...... 50c. per ton extra for winter delivery.	4 50
June 5...	Normal School, Hamilton.	Supply of coal and wood. Season 1913-14.	Chas. A. Low & Co., Hamilton.	J. M. Peregrine, and John G. Sherring, of Hamilton.	Egg coal, per ton	5 79
					Nut " "	5 98
					Pine slabs, per cord	3 95
June 5...	School for the Blind, Brantford.	Supply of coal. Season 1913-14.	Daniel McDonald, Brantford.	Stephen P. Pitcher, and W. A. Hollinrake, of Brantford.	Small Egg coal, per ton	5 99
					Stove coal, per ton	5 89
					Nut coal, per ton	6 10
					Soft " "	4 35

STATEMENT No. 4—Continued.

Being Statement of Contracts and Bonds entered into with His Majesty for the year ending 31st of October, 1913.

Date.	Work.	Subject of Contract.	Contractors.	Sureties.	Particulars.	Amount. $ c.
June 5 ...	Ontario Agricultural College, Guelph, Field Husbandry Building.	Plumbing, heating and elec-tric wiring.	Stevenson & Malcolm, Guelph.	Robert D. Stewart, and Matthew Kelly, of Guelph.	......	9,770 00
June 5 ...	Normal School, Ottawa.	Supply of pine wood. Season, 1913-14.	John Heney & Son, Limited, Ottawa.	William G. Black, L. P. Sherwood, of Ottawa.	Pine wood, per cord	4 00
June 5......	Normal School, London.	Supply coal and wood. Season, 1913-14.	John Arthur McClurg of London.	Byron McKay and Arthur McClurg of London.	Small egg coal.. Pine slabs	6 55 4 55
June 10....	Normal School, Peterborough.	Supply coal and wood. Season, 1913-14.	The Peterborough Fuel and Cartage Company, Limited.	Roland Denne and William Bulley, both of Peterbor-ough.	Large egg coal.. Pine slabs	7 50 4 55
June 11....	The Ontario School for the Blind, Brantford.	Alteration to boiler house, in connection with heating and plumbing.	P. H. Secord & Sons, Limited, Brantford.	Wm. Clarke Boddy and Wm. Arthur Hollinrake of Brantford.	......	1,512 00
June 12....	Hospital for Insane, Mimico	Installation of electrical equipment.	Northern Electric and Manufacturing Com-pany, Limited.	......	......	2,547 00

Date	Institution	Description of work	Contractor	Surety	Notes	Amount
June 12	The Ontario School for the Deaf, Belleville	Erecting chimney.	The Weber Chimney Co., Chicago, Ill.	Canadian Surety Co., Toronto.		1,610 00
June 12	The Ontario School for the Blind, Brantford.	Erecting chimney.	The Weber Chimney Co., Chicago, Ill.	Canadian Surety Co., Toronto.		1,550 00
June 13	The Ontario School for the Blind, Brantford.	Installing tile floors and base in washrooms, lavatories, etc.	The Italian Mosaic and Tile Company of Toronto.		Terrazzo tile floors. Terrazzo base.	631 80 / 130 00
June 20	Ontario Agricultural College, Guelph.	Building dining hall.	P. H. Secord & Sons, Limited, Brantford.	Wm. Clarke Boddy & W. Arthur Hollinrake of Brantford.		58,703 00
July 9	New Government House, Toronto.	Wiring and electrical work.	Canadian Alexatite Co. of Toronto.	John O'Neill, Toronto.		7,100 00
July 9	Normal Schools at Stratford, London, Peterboro, North Bay, Ottawa and Hamilton.	Vacuum cleaners.	Zimmer Vacuum Machine Company, Limited, Toronto.		One plant each for 6 schools	3,500 00
July 11	The Ontario School for the Deaf, Belleville.	Supply of coal. Season, 1913-14.	N. Allen, Belleville.	Arthur P. Allen and Thomas Stewart.	Slack coal: Summer delivery / Winter delivery / Small egg coal. / Nut & stove coal / Cannel coal	4 10 / 4 50 / 6 73 / 7 49 / 8 00
July 16	The Ontario School for the Deaf, Belleville.	Construction of new dormitory building.	Thomas Manley and Thomas J. Manley, Jr., of Belleville.	Canadian Surety Co. of Toronto.		59,995 00
July 16	The Ontario School for the Blind, Brantford.	Construction of new dormitory building.	Jesse Bartle, of Brantford.	Arthur K. Bunnell & Fred. W. Frank of Brantford.		39,227 00

STATEMENT No. 4.—Continued.

Being Statement of Contracts and Bonds entered into with His Majesty for the year ending 31st of October, 1913.

Date.	Work.	Subject of Contract.	Contractors.	Sureties.	Particulars.	Amount.
						$ c.
July 16....	Ontario Agricultural College, Guelph.	Construction of Poultry Building.	Wm. E. Taylor, Guelph.	Robt. D. Stewart & George Rodgers of Guelph.	......	28,000 00
July 22....	Sturgeon Falls Bridge, Nipissing District.	Steel superstructure of a bridge over the Sturgeon River, in the town of Sturgeon Falls.	The Hamilton Bridge Works Company, Limited, of Hamilton.			13,300 00
July 23....	Two Tree Bridge, St. Joseph Island.	Steel for span and reinforcing bonding for concrete floor.	The Hamilton Bridge Works Company, Limited, of Hamilton.		Steel ...... Bonding	215 00 18 00
July 24....	Demonstration Farm, Monteith.	Installing warm air heating apparatus.	The Gurney Foundry Company, Limited, of Toronto.			397 00
July 26....	Parliament Buildings (North Wing).	Vault fittings in Education Department.	Richard Dinnis and Son, Limited, of Toronto.			448 00
July 30....	Rainy River District (Court House).	Construction of court house, Fort Frances.	Seaman & Penniman, Fort William, Ont.	United States Fidelity and Guaranty Co. of Baltimore, U.S.A.		54,719 00
July 30....	Temiskaming District (Court House).	Construction of court house, Haileybury.	P. H. Secord & Sons, Limited, Brantford.	Robt. C. Burns and Walter C. Boddy of Brantford.	......	52,452 00
July 30....	Temiskaming District (Registry Office).	Construction of Registry office, Haileybury.	P. H. Secord & Sons, Limited, Brantford.	Robt. C. Burns and Walter C. Boddy of Brantford.	......	10,638 00

Date	Work	Description	Contractor	Note	Amount
Aug. 5....	Papineau Bridges, Boon Creek (Nipissing District).	Supply of steel beam spans for bridge, Lot 9, Con. 10, and Lots 10 and 11, Con. 11, Papineau Township.	The Hamilton Bridge Works Company, Limited, of Hamilton.	each, 210.00	420 00
Aug. 5....	Boyne Bridges, Tp. Foley (Parry Sound District).	Supply of steel beam spans for bridges, Lot 134 and Lot 140, Tp. of Foley.	The Hamilton Bridge Works Company, Limited, of Hamilton.	Lot 134 Lot 140	207 00 151 00
Aug. 5....	Six Mile Creek Bridge, Shuniah Tp. (Thunder Bay District).	Steel beam spans and posts, etc., for bridge over Six Mile Creek.	The Hamilton Bridge Works Company, Limited, of Hamilton.	at per lb.	03
Aug. 13....	Ontario Agricultural College, Guelph.	Moving old barn and erection of foundation for new dairy barn.	Reuben Rogers, of the City of Guelph.	Moving barn. Building foundation.	300 00 300 00
Aug. 19....	Parliament Buildings.	Installing steel map cases in the office of the Archives.	The Steel Equipment Company, Limited, of Ottawa.		534 00
Aug. 19....	The Ontario School for the Deaf, Belleville.	Cast iron water mains to the Boys' Dormitory Building.	Purdy, Mansell, Limited, of Toronto.		324 00
Aug. 25....	The Ontario School for the Deaf, Belleville.	Supply of steel cable, insulated lead-covered, and four inside pot heads.	Canadian British Insulated Company, Ltd., of Montreal.	Cable Pot heads, each	420 00 4 00
Aug. 25....	Hospital for Feeble-Minded, Orillia.	Supply and construction two fire escapes.	Dow Wire and Iron Works of Louisville, Ky., U.S.A.		2,880 00
Aug. 26....	Kenora District.	Construction of boathouse on Lake of the Woods.	Fred. Gilbert, Kenora.		900 00
Aug. 27....	New Government House, Toronto.	Terra cotta tile, for partitions, etc.	Fred Holmes & Sons, Limited, Toronto.		600 00

STATEMENT No. 4—Continued.

Being Statement of Contracts and Bonds entered into with His Majesty for the year ending 31st of October, 1913.

Date.	Work.	Subject of Contract.	Contractors.	Sureties.	Particulars.	Amount.
Sept. 3	Rondeau Park	Construction of house for Asst. Ranger.	Watson & Taylor, Ridgetown, Ont.	W. H. Goldhue and J. M. Sheldon, of Ridgetown, Ont.		3,125 00
Sept. 4	Equipment machinery, etc., for Public Works.	Supply of tilting mixers, engine, pumps, double drum hoists, etc.	Wettlaufer, Brothers, of Toronto.			1,860 00
Sept. 4	The Ontario School for the Deaf, Belleville.	Supply of Hex tile floor, cove, Terrazzo floor and base in Girls' Dormitory.	The Lauts-Dunham Company, Limited, of Toronto.			772 00
Sept. 4	Garden River Bridge (District of Algoma).	Steel superstructure of bridge over Garden River.	Hamilton Bridge Works Company, Limited.			5,749 00
Sept. 12	Ontario Agricultural College, Guelph.	The construction of milk room in the dairy barn.	P. H. Secord & Sons, Limited, of Brantford.			1,962 00
Sept. 23	Ontario Agricultural College, Guelph.	Erection of an electric freight elevator in the Field Husbandry Building.	Turnbull Elevator Manufacturing Company, of Toronto.			995 00
Sept. 24	Temiskaming District, Judge Bridge.	Steel superstructure of bridge over White River, Tp. of Casey.	Canadian Bridge Company, Limited, Walkerville.			3,842 00
Sept. 26	Hospital for the Insane, Kingston.	Sash frames, complete, including glazing and carpentry work.	Hooper & Slater, of Kingston.			734 00

Date		Description	Contractor	Sureties		Amount
Sept. 30....	Ontario Agricultural College, Guelph.	Shingling roof, etc., of remodelled dairy barn.	The Metal, Shingle & Siding Company, Limited, Preston.	....		365 76
Oct. 3.....	The Ontario School for the Deaf, Belleville.	Building sidewalks at girls' dormitory.	A. Bellis, of Belleville.	per square ft.		14
Oct. 6.....	Ontario Agricultural College, Guelph. (Federal.)	Conduit for steam pipes, sponge filling, etc., at Field Husbandry Building, Guelph.	The Canadian H. W. Johns-Manville Company, Limited, Toronto.	12 in. conduit per ft. / sponge filling per lb.		1 50 / 08
Oct. 9.....	The Ontario School for the Deaf, Belleville.	Plumbing and heating, etc., boys new dormitory.	Purdy, Mansell, Limited, Toronto.	Fred. J. Lucas and Lewis R. Fox of Toronto.		23,589 00
Oct. 9.....	The Ontario School for the Blind, Brantford.	Plumbing and heating, etc., boys new dormitory.	Drake, Avery Company, Limited, Hamilton.	Philip H. Alexander & Lee W. Powell, both of the City of Hamilton.		20,152 00
Oct. 10.....	Hospital for the Insane, Kingston.	For extension of sewage disposal plant and underpinning partition wall of the Rockwood Hospital, Kingston.	Douglas & McIlquham, of Kingston.	extension of plant / underpinning		2,978 00 / 212 00
Oct. 23.....	Ontario Agricultural College, Guelph.	Electric wiring at the poultry building.	Stevenson & Malcolm, Limited, of Guelph.	....		750 00
Oct. 25....	Kenora District (gaol, etc.).	Installing hot water heating system in gaoler's house, Kenora.	T. G. Downard, of Kenora.	....		403 00
Oct. 28.....	The Ontario School for the Deaf, Belleville.	Electric wiring and fixtures in boys new dormitory.	Greenleaf & Son, Belleville.	Robt. Tannahill and John Franklin Wills of Belleville.		1,750 00

STATEMENT No. 4—Concluded.

Being Statement of Contracts and Bonds entered into with His Majesty for the year ending 31st of October 1913.

Date.	Work.	Subject of Contract.	Contractors.	Sureties.	Particulars.	Amount.
Oct. 30....	Ontario Agricultural College, Guelph.	Heating and plumbing, new dining hall.	Stevenson & Malcolm, Guelph, Ont.	R. D. Stewart and Matthew Kelly of Guelph.	Heating .... Conduit (per ft.) Tunnel work (per foot)	7,893 00 4 40 4 75
Oct. 30....	Ontario Agricultural College, Guelph.	Heating and plumbing, new poultry building.	Stevenson & Malcolm, Guelph, Ont.	R. D. Stewart and Matthew Kelly of the City of Guelph.	....	5,125 00

Department of Public Works, Ontario.

Toronto, February, 1914.

J. P. Edwards.

Accountant and Law Clerk, Public Works.

CANADA GROUSE

(*Canachites canadensis*)

Seventh Annual Report

OF THE

GAME AND FISHERIES DEPARTMENT

1913

PRINTED BY ORDER OF
THE LEGISLATIVE ASSEMBLY OF ONTARIO

TORONTO:
Printed and Published by L. K. CAMERON, Printer to the King's Most Excellent Majesty
1913

Printed by
WILLIAM BRIGGS
29-37 Richmond Street West
TORONTO

To His Honour SIR JOHN MORISON GIBSON, Knight Commander of the Most
Distinguished Order of St. Michael and St. George, a Colonel in the
Militia of Canada, etc., etc., etc.

Lieutenant-Governor of the Province of Ontario.

MAY IT PLEASE YOUR HONOUR:

I have the honour to submit herewith, for the information of Your Honour
and the Legislative Assembly, the Seventh Annual Report of the Game and
Fisheries Department of this Province.

I have the honour to be,

Your Honour's most obedient servant,

J. O. REAUME,

Minister of Public Works.

TORONTO, 4th December, 1913.

[3]

Seventh Annual Report

OF THE

Game and Fisheries Department of Ontario

' *To the Honourable* J. O. REAUME,

Minister of Public Works.

SIR,—I have again the honour to submit for your consideration the Report of the Department of Game and Fisheries for the twelve months ending 31st October, 1913, which I venture to hope may have your approval.

The Statistics, Reports of Inspectors, Wardens, Overseers and Deputy Wardens, and other matters connected with the administration of the Department will appear, as in the past, and I trust they will receive the generous appreciation and approval which you have accorded those of past years.

LAWS AND REGULATIONS.

The Laws and Regulations have been fairly well observed during the year, with the exception of a few whose code of ethics is not in accordance with the Golden Rule; in fact they appear to believe in those that cause the liberty of so many to be curtailed by the intervention of iron bars. These characters, who have not a proper conception of right and wrong make use of every possible subterfuge to enable them to evade the conditions of their respective licenses. These lawless, selfish characters—it would be a libel on the rest of mankind to allude to them as men—not only defraud the Government, but also injure the large majority of honest, law-abiding fishermen, who are conforming to the conditions of their licenses. There are two ways of dealing with such characters; either by cancelling their licenses or withdrawing the concessions so grossly abused and enacting more stringent laws and regulations. The latter would unfortunately result in the punishment of the innocent for the fault of the guilty. While the Government and your Department have heretofore refrained from using extreme measures against the violators of the Game and Fishery Laws, yet, in the interest of the public and the law abiding fishermen, it is imperative that these unwise and persistent lawbreakers should, in future, receive without let or hindrance the extreme punishment their wrong doing deserves. The unwise and destructive policy of abolishing close seasons for whitefish still prevails in the most valuable, and what would be the most productive fresh water lake in the world if common sense methods and nature's perfect plan of reproduction were observed and respected. Last November I procured a large tub of whitefish, supposed to be properly cured for human consumption; in a week or ten days they became discolored; a week later the entire contents were putrid. These fish would average at least five pounds each, and had been taken from the best spawning grounds in our system of lakes, during the month of November, when they were full of spawn and unfit for food. It is impossible to conjecture the millions or even billions of eggs which if not so fool-

[5]

ishly and wickedly destroyed would result in more than doubling the present supply of this much needed commodity. I venture to hope that in consequence of the scarcity of animal food, and it's almost prohibitive price, that those to whom the authority to have Nature's Laws enforced has been delegated will realize, in the interest of the general public, the urgent necessity of so doing. Faddists with absurd theories presume to ignore Nature's perfect plan of reproduction, and advocate therefor emanations from their foolish delusions. They make the absurd statement that only about one per cent. of the spawn deposited by the fish on their natural spawning grounds are fertilized or hatched. It will be apparent, even to those not conversant with fishery matters, that if, as alleged by these illusionists, this is the case, all waters not re-stocked by artificial means would have been destitute of fish ages ago. These faddists allege that spawn taken to the hatcheries are hatched to the extent of seventy-five to eighty per cent. I am not prepared to dispute this, but what means have they of knowing what becomes of the hatchery fry after being consigned to polluted or other unsuitable waters? I have seen fry deposited at the outlets of large sewers, miles from the waters which they were intended to re-stock. I have also seen large consignments of fry placed in lakes a few yards from the shore, the waters of which were infested with perch, and the fry which were not destroyed by the perch were washed ashore by the waves. With all due respect to what is alleged the hatcheries have accomplished, they are a miserable excuse, and a most unsatisfactory substitute for close seasons, which are in conformity with Nature's perfect plan of reproduction and perpetuation. I have no objection to hatcheries as an adjunct to close seasons for the purpose of aiding and assisting Nature's extensive, inexpensive, and complete system of perpetuation. If, as is so often stated, the supply of fish is inadequate to meet the demands of our somewhat limited population, what will be the result in the near future, if the present wasteful and unnatural system of abolishing close seasons continues.

The Federal Government of the United States have recently passed a most effective and far reaching measure for the protection and perpetuation of migratory birds. Though no longer young, I hope to live to see our respective Federal Governments mutually enact an equally effective and much needed measure for the protection of the fish in our international waters when migrating to their spawning grounds. I fail to see the sense of the wicked, unreasonable, foolishness in destroying either fish or birds, as the case may be, when full of eggs en route to their breeding grounds or Nature's hatcheries.

Comparisons are often made by those who are not conversant with game protection in Britain between the immense quantity of game annually killed on their restricted area and the amount killed in our Dominion. In Britain there is an average of one gamekeeper or assistant to each square mile of protected estate. I am afraid the time is far distant when our Province will be able to employ one man for each hundred square miles, who will devote his whole time to the protection of the fish and game. Gamekeepers in Britain are paid a bounty on each animal or bird, killed by them, which is destructive to the game. Bounties are not paid on foxes, they being preserved for the national sport of fox hunting; however, it is well known that they are more destructive to game and poultry than any other animal in Great Britain, one fox being known to bury about four dozen head of poultry. Another instance of the immense destruction of game by foxes is recorded —a vixen and her three cubs were dug out of her den. and in her larder beneath her den were found thirty-two rabbits. two pheasants. two partridges, and a wild duck. Our crows are similar to the carrion crow in Britain and most destructive to eggs, young game, and other birds and chickens. These marauders should be destroyed whenever it is possible to do so. The above should convince those who indulge in these unfair and unjust comparisons of the impossibility of protecting our game as effectually as is done in Britain, where the climatic conditions are also far more favourable.

I regret having again to revert to the lawless persistance and I might say criminal conduct of those owning factories situated on the banks of our rivers and streams. My attention has been called to the immense destruction of fish in the Grand River near one of the many factories located on that useful stream, which was perfectly pure until polluted and contaminated by man's unreasoning and unscrupulous greed. I feel sure that the discerning public will concur with me in regretting that there does not appear to be adequate punishment provided for those endangering human life and destroying public property, and who, for the purpose of saving the cost of properly disposing of deleterious waste from their factories, poison the waters which the public depend upon for domestic purposes. Who is the worst criminal, the miscreant who puts poison in his neighbour's well or spring, or he who insists in poisoning waters which hundreds, and in many cases thousands, have to depend on for daily use.

Some three or four years ago there was what was known as " the duck malady.". in the Salt Lake Valley, Utah. The wild ducks and geese died by thousands on the waters of those well known duck resorts. It has since been discovered that it was not a malady at all, but a well-defined case of wholesale poisoning by deleterious matter from the numerous sugar refineries and canning factories located there. The case of fish poisoning referred to above is not the first occurrence of the same thing; this Department has been trying during the last ten years to re-stock the Grand River with game fish, but our endeavours during those years have been futile, owing to the miserable action of those owning or controlling the factories causing the fish to be destroyed in that vicinity. It is an old saying that " The Lord helps those that help themselves," it is therefore reasonable to expect that unless the municipal authorities take proceedings against those responsible for this destruction and nuisance they and the Grand River in that municipality will have to do without fish.

In consequence of complaints made from various portions of the Province to the effect that fishermen refuse to supply the home market before exporting to the United States, I sent Inspector Holden to Port Stanley to investigate the matter, and the following is his report:

"Regarding the complaints received by you about the difficulties that a local buyer had at Port Stanley in procuring fish from the fishermen of that place, I beg to say that I visited Port Stanley on Monday, the 24th November. I found that something over a year ago there was a company formed known as the ' Producer's Fish Company,' to which all the fishermen from this port, with the exception of three, belong. This company has an office in the town a short distance from the harbour, where I found the Secretary, who is also the Manager, and two assistants, one of whom does not appear to have anything to do except to attend to the Canadian trade. When I asked them what I should do to get a small amount of fish, I was told, ' You can either buy them here or go to any of the docks and get them.' I found later that the men at the docks were quite willing to sell fish, no matter how small the quantity. It appears that the company does not handle these fish until the different fishermen turn them over to the company, after selling locally any that may be wanted. I do not mean that they are in the habit of making shipments, but sell any called for. The price is regulated by the market price at the time; on Monday I could buy herring at four cents a pound, no other kinds of fish were on hand that day. I did not find that there was any good reason for the complaints; possibly the price being higher than in former years may be the grievance."

(Signed) W. W. HOLDEN.

To use a hunting term, the method adopted for taking care of the Canadian demand described above appears to some extent like drawing a herring across the trail. The cognomen assumed by the company is not appropriate—nature is the producer. Port Stanley is a very small part of the Province, and it seems to me that if the so-called "Producer's Fish Company" intended to supply the home market they would appoint a manager with a distributing establishment at Toronto, the same as they have at Buffalo, where it is alleged than an ex-manager of an alien fish company, formerly operating in the Province, has been appointed. It will be interesting to learn what proportion of the fish caught by members of the "Producer's Fish Company" in Lake Erie are shipped to their Manager in Buffalo. Perhaps it may be well to remind members of associations formed for dealing in our most valuable natural product that the Government possesses effective means for dealing with those responsible for combines inimical to the public interest, whether the effect of the combination is to enhance the price or to restrict the supply.

GAME.

Moose are reported to be found as numerous as in past years, in fact, in sufficient numbers to warrant the belief that these magnificent and largest of our game animals will afford sport and recreation for many years in our northern woods. Caribou will be, in the near future, an attraction to the sportsmen in the recent addition to the Province when access thereto is facilitated by the completion of the railways now under construction.

Deer.—The wisdom of reducing the number of deer that may be legally killed in one season by each hunter, from two to one, has during the past open season been exemplified in the very large proportion of bucks killed compared with past years. The result of this in keeping up the supply of these beautiful animals will be apparent. In many portions of the Province hunters report deer as numerous as in past years, but scarce in those localities in which the destructive bush fires occurred.

Ducks.—Sportsmen have no reason to complain of the scarcity of ducks. The comparatively mild weather prevailing during the early part of the open season was not conducive to large bags. The sportsmen, not only of the Province but of the whole Dominion, are to be congratulated on the action of the Federal Government of the United States in passing a bill for the protection of migratory birds, in consequence of their far reaching and beneficial effect on the perpetuation of bird life.

Ruffed Grouse.—One of our most valued native game birds. The act of reducing the open season to one month, and limiting the number killed by one person to ten birds a day, will have a tendency to prevent the necessity of having occasional close seasons. Complaints reach me from fair weather sportsmen, who in former years were a factor in nearly exterminating these grand birds by shooting them on the ground or in the trees, when half-grown; the present open season may not be satisfactory to this class of sportsmen, but is good for the so-called partridge.

Quail are reported to have increased to some extent in consequence of last year's close season, but from a combination of circumstances I am not sanguine as to the future of these useful little natives of the South and Western Counties.

Snipe are reported to have been more numerous than usual, many large bags were made, and hunters have had excellent sport with these elusive visitors.

Woodcock.—There is hope for the future for the sportsmen of the Province who delight in killing a few brace of these, the most valued of our game birds. Their breeding grounds being the most temperate portions of Ontario and the Maritime Provinces. For a number of years they have returned from the Southern States in decreased numbers, in consequence of their being hunted and killed in their winter resorts with impunity, by negroes and others, from their arrival in October and November until March, leaving the remnants to return here to their breeding grounds. With a short open season in their winter resorts and the law effectively forced, we may reasonably expect that the threatened extermination will be delayed.

Pheasants will never be a permanent factor in our game supply in consequence of their being ground feeders, and unless fed would perish in the winter in those parts of the Province where snow covers the land for months during our long winters.

FUR-BEARING ANIMALS.

Beaver have increased to such an extent that it has been necessary to destroy their dams to prevent roads and private property being flooded by the persistent work of these intelligent dam-builders.

Otter, Mink, Muskrats, and the coarser fur-bearing animals are not decreasing to any appreciable extent.

The staff of the Department, Inspectors, Wardens, Overseers, Deputy Game and Fishery Wardens have been as in past years faithful and efficient in the discharge of their respective duties.

It is again a pleasure to extend my sincere thanks to the employees of the Department of the Honorable the Attorney-General and the Honourable the Minister of Lands and Mines for their very valuable assistance and effective co-operation during the year.

RE-STOCKING.

This important work was continued this year with good results. The experience in raising bass fingerlings is most encouraging and every year is bound to improve. Another pond was added to those already built, which was erected under the supervision of Mr. Edwards, who has been in charge of the bass ponds since they were first started. He has shown much ability in this direction, as well as in the raising of bass fingerlings, and the Department is now assured that his appointment to this position was a wise one.

It was the intention to erect a small hatchery for brook trout, for the purpose of re-stocking many of the once excellent trout streams in the Province, which have now become depleted. It is to be regretted that circumstances prevented the carrying out of these plans, but it is to be hoped that during the coming year this hatchery will be erected. It is the intention of the Department to erect this **building** in the vicinity of the Bass Ponds where ample water supply can be **obtained** and the services of the staff now employed will be available for this **important** work during the winter months, long after the raising of bass fingerlings is finished. This will enable the Department to raise these trout at a very little additional cost after the hatchery is once erected.

ANGLING PERMITS.

The sale of these permits was much greater than the year previous. It may have been partly owing to the better weather conditions, and no doubt to a great extent to the improvement in the fishing. The reports which have been received indicate that there is good angling, where in many places a few years ago the waters had become depleted. Many tourists while passing through have expressed very strongly the pleasure they derived from angling during the past summer. Others have even taken the trouble, after going home, to write to the Department, expressing their satisfaction with their summer outing. It is with much pleasure that I am able to say that the tourists have respected the Laws and Regulations in a much better manner than heretofore, and I feel satisfied that the large majority of them realize the importance of observing the same; although there are a few every year, I regret to say, who have no regard for anything but the gaining of their own selfish ends; they have found, nevertheless, that our officers have apprehended them in many instances, much to their sorrow, in the way of both expense and trouble.

PATROL SERVICE.

This service was extended by an additional boat, which patrolled the upper part of Lake Superior. On the whole the patrol service was most satisfactory. Many illegal nets were seized and the guilty parties brought to justice. There is no doubt that this service is preventing, to a considerable extent, the setting of nets which a few years ago was carried on most extensively.

It is with much regret that I am unable to publish, as I have done for years past, the excellent report furnished by Dr. B. A. Bensley, of the University of Toronto, with regard to the work carried on at the Biological Station on the Georgian Bay. It is reported that the Department of Marine and Fisheries are directing their attention to other Provinces and discontinuing for the present their important work in this Province. It is sincerely hoped that another year they will see their way clear to continue their researches.

The Railway and Steamboat Companies have rendered the Department very great assistance during the past year.

They appear to realize the importance to the interests they represent of the tourist business of the Province, which is only in its infancy, and needs for its development the active co-operation with this Department of all those interested.

My warmest thanks are herewith extended to the Railroad and Transportation Companies in the Province, for the courtesy accorded the Department and my humble self for so many years.

All of which is respectfully submitted by your obedient servant.

F. TINSLEY.

December 5th, 1913.

GAME AND FISHERY INSPECTORS.

TORONTO, Nov., 1913.

E. TINSLEY, ESQ.,
Superintendent, Game and Fisheries.

SIR,—I have the honor to submit my report for 1913.

Reports from the commercial fishermen indicate that the season has been an average one and not any improvement on former years. There is no doubt that the extremely warm weather during the Fall months caused the usual run of white fish and lake trout to be later than in some former years. It was, however, not necessary to extend the open season in order to procure spawn for the hatcheries, they having secured a fair supply before the 1st of November.

The storm that caused a great loss of life and the destruction of so many boats on the lakes also resulted in a great deal of damage to the fishermen on Lake Erie, and no doubt the catch of white fish on this lake will show a decrease, as a large number of the pound nets in the west end of the lake were completely destroyed, this happening before the Fall run of fish came on.

The catch of herring not being over I cannot say what effect this storm may have on it, but we hope it may not have any serious result, the herring being mostly caught in gill nets, and these nets being more easily replaced than pound nets would enable the fishermen to more quickly recover from any loss they may have suffered.

From the summer resorts come reports of a fairly good season, most of the anglers being satisfied with their catches, nearly all the complaints being about the insufficient protection afforded the game fish. From the trout streams of Lake Superior come reports of excellent fishing.

The German brown trout planted last spring are apparently doing well in most places. These fish appear to be particularly fitted for streams where the water has become too warm for brook trout. I had the pleasure of visiting Lake Nipigon during the summer. This is a beautiful lake, and with the C. N. R. touching the south end and G. T. P. the north will in a short time become well known. It contains numerous islands and bays, abounds with fish of nearly all the species found in our great lakes, and will in time become one of our greatest summer pleasure resorts. This lake is sixty miles long and thirty-five wide, and with the numerous bays and islands must have a shore line of about a thousand miles. I heard the islands estimated on the way from three hundred to three thousand, no one appearing to know just how many there are. The future of Lake Nipigon from a fishing point of view, if properly preserved, will be a great one.

Returns from the hunters of large game not being complete it is impossible to know how this year compares with last. No doubt the fires of last summer will have changed the feeding grounds, and we may expect to hear of a scarcity of game from some places where it has been plentiful in past years; this should be made up by the greater number in other parts.

Allow me to make a few recommendations most of these have been mentioned in former reports but will stand repetition.

A Resident Trapper's License.—A great many trappers are asking for this, they wish to protect the animals and at the same time improve their own business.

A Resident Angling Permit.—This is not being asked for, but we should have it.

A Gun License or a License to Hunt Small Game.—At present the hunters of large game are the only ones paying anything towards the expense of protection.

A size limit for Sturgeon; or, better still, a close season for them of five years. —As we have no way of propagating these fish they need more protection than is now given them.

A size limit for Perch, Blue Pickerel, and Herring.—Too many small fish of these species are being caught.

The Game and Fisheries Laws and Regulations have been fairly well observed throughout the Province, and your overseers and officers on the different patrol boats have been diligent in the discharge of their duties.

Respectfully submitted,

Your Obedient Servant.

WM. W. HOLDEN,

Inspector.

BELLEVILLE, November 18th, 1913.

E. TINSLEY, ESQ.,

Superintendent.

SIR,—I herewith beg to submit my annual report.

During the past season I have visited the greater portion of the Province and find that the laws are being better observed.

I find that deer and moose are increasing in number and are becoming more tame; that ducks are plentiful, but partridges, I am sorry to say, are reported fewer in number. I would suggest to close season for at least two years.

A great number of non-resident tourists visited our waters last year and reported excellent angling, caused, no doubt, by your frequent re-stocking the different lakes from the Brantford Bass Ponds, which I am glad to note are proving so successful.

The different patrol boats are doing good work and are manned by efficient crews.

Commercial fishermen report an average year. I would recommend the issuing of a special Sturgeon license, as a large number of Sturgeon are accidentally caught in Gill and Pound Nets each year and no revenue is derived by your Department. I would also recommend a resident trapper's and gun license, also a license for resident anglers who go more than ten miles from their home to fish.

I am glad to note that the licensed guides are giving good satisfaction. I would again call your attention to the fact that commercial fish buyers should be licensed.

Your obedient servant,

ALF. HUNTER,

Inspector.

GAME AND FISHERY WARDENS.

Warden William Burt, of Simcoe, reports:

SPECKLED TROUT.

He is glad to state that these fish are still increasing but the increase is only noticed in those streams where the fry supplied by the Department were planted. The fry supplied by the Department last spring were more widely distributed than in any previous year, and it is hoped that the increase in numbers of these fish will be noticed in the other streams. The experiment of planting the fry in Norfolk County streams has proved so successful that he would strongly recommend that it be continued from year to year, as the brooks of Norfolk County are particularly well adapted for the propagation of this game fish.

BASS.

The bass fishing in Long Point Bay has been good, but not up to the previous year or two. The fish did not commence to bite freely until about the 1st of July. It was thought, however, by the sportsmen that while the fish caught were less numerous, they seemed to be larger than in former years. He is pleased to report that the hatchery at Mount Pleasant has proved to be an unqualified success. An ample supply of bass fry or minnows has been obtained from it. Mr. Edwards, the manager of this hatchery, has proved to be a very efficient and active officer. Not only does he make a success of the hatchery, but he keeps the grounds in an artistic manner so that all visitors are very much struck with the beauty of the spot.

COMMERCIAL FISH.

The fishermen report that the gill net fishing has been good. The seines have been successful. The experiment with the carp ponds continues successful, the fishermen being able to catch the carp when they are plentiful and at a low price, and preserve them in the ponds until the fish are scarce and the price higher. The carp in Long Point Bay have very much increased in numbers, and the price during the year has been much higher than ever before, so that this coarse fish is now one of the best paying commercial fish.

QUAIL AND RUFFED GROUSE.

The quail are still very scarce in his district, the number being practically the same as at the time of his last report.

The ruffed grouse have again increased materially. The birds are more numerous than they have been for a number of years.

MONGOLIAN PHEASANTS.

A few of these game birds have been seen in Norfolk County from the eggs hatched last spring, but the experiment is on such a small scale that no great result has yet been attained. The birds seem to be healthy specimens, and he would recommend that, if possible, some mature birds be sent into the County to responsible persons who will undertake to keep them, and raise the young, turning them loose as soon as they are able to take care of themselves. He has had no report as to the condition of the Mongolian Pheasants in the Niagara District so cannot report upon how well they are succeeding.

WOODCOCK.

These are still very scarce, but are reported to be slowly increasing in number.

BLACK SQUIRRELS.

Where sufficient woods has been left there has been a decided increase in the numbers of these squirrels. The sportsmen attribute this to the short season in which they are allowed to be shot. In the County of Norfolk, where it is against the law to shoot them, they have very materially increased in number.

WILD GEESE.

The conditions with regard to these birds are the same as in his last report.

WILD DUCKS.

The Long Point District continues to have more ducks than formerly, the Black ducks, Mallard and Pin Tail being very numerous. An increasing number of Black ducks and Wood ducks have bred in the marshes about Long Point Bay, and it has been reported to him also that some young broods of Pin tails were seen. The Canvas-back, Redhead and Blue Bills seem to be here in about as large numbers as in his last report.

FUR-BEARING ANIMALS.

. The muskrat continues to rate highest among these animals in his district. The trappers report a very good catch last spring, better than for several years past. This is attributed to the fact that some of the game companies and others prohibited the trapping in their marshes during the previous season, thus leaving a larger breeding herd than usual in the marshes. The owners of the marshes find that the fur of the rats trapped in December is of an inferior quality. None of the owners of the marshes trap until spring, the consequence being the only rats killed in December are those taken by poachers, and he would again most strongly recommend that the killing of muskrats in the month of December be prohibited. and that the use of dogs, spears and guns in the taking of muskrats also be prohibited.

The game laws in his district have been well observed. The Deputy Wardens and Overseers have performed their duties well, so that there have been very few complaints of infringements of the law.

There are two matters where from his experience, he would suggest that game laws be amended. The first is that the form of license adopted should contain the date on which it is issued. He has had one case in which, on issuing a search warrant, the body of a deer was found on a farm. The owner of the farm said he had a license but could not find it at the time the constable made the search. It was afterwards produced, and was issued by one of the party who had been deer-shooting with the killer of the deer. This man, it appears, has the issuing of licenses at one point in Warden Burt's district and he has very grave suspicions that the deer was killed without a license, and that the license was afterwards purchased.

The other respect in which he thinks the Act should be amended is by striking out of Section 63, Chapter 69, Act of 1913, that part of the section which provides that no person shall be compelled to go more than ten miles before a magistrate. From long experience and endeavoring to enforce the game laws, he finds that it is impossible to find a magistrate living in the vicinity of shooting grounds who does not sympathize with the offenders. The consequence is that unless he takes a magistrate from outside the ten-mile radius to try the case, he can only secure a nominal fine in each case, and as the law-breaker often secures $30.00 to $40.00 worth of game in a day, a fine of $5.00 and costs has no effect in deterring him or others from again breaking the law. It appears to him that this provision in the game law is totally wrong on principle. In effect, it amounts to saying to the public that an infraction of the game law is such a trivial matter that an offender cannot be taken more than ten miles from his residence or where the offence is committed, while the case of a most petty assault may be taken anywhere within the jurisdiction of the magistrates in the County in which the offence is committed.

Warden V. Chauvin, of Windsor, reports, that he has visited all the fishermen in his district during the season and found that they made good catches of fish in the spring and up to the time of writing, with the exception of white fish, which have been very poor and the catches very small on Lake Erie and Detroit River.

There should be a limit put on the size of perch, white bass and blue pickerel caught; they should be not less than ten inches in length.

Sturgeon were plentiful in Lake St. Clair. There should also be a regulation made regarding the size of these fish as they are now being caught as small as two pounds.

Anglers were satisfied with the bass angling in St. Clair Flats, Mitchell Bay and other places.

The law was very well observed by the fishermen throughout the district.

With regard to game, quail have been reported to be very plentiful by the farmers, and woodcock were plentiful early in the season, but very few have been killed. Partridges are about the same as other years, they are not increasing. Hungarian partridges are doing well, the Leamington farmers say that they have seen a great many young ones during the summer. English pheasants are about the same as other years.

Black and grey squirrels are scarce in Essex County; otherwise there is no change, they are plentiful east of this County.

Muskrats are doing well this fall, there are plenty of houses being built in the marshes.

Wild geese are not very plentiful at present though they were more numerous in the spring.

The Mallard duck black and grey are very numerous in the Detroit River and marshes round Lake Erie and Lake St. Clair. River ducks are more plentiful this year than other years. Snipe are rather scarce.

Open season for quail should be from November 1st-15th.

The sportsmen were very pleased with the bag they secured during the day, and have observed the game laws fairly well.

Warden J. H. Metcalfe, of Kingston, reports, that as far as the eastern portion of the Province is concerned, from a commercial standpoint, the season just closed has been a fairly good one.

Tourist visitors came in greater numbers than last year, and most of them reported excellent catches of game fish.

Bass fishing in the St. Lawrence River and adjacent waters of Lake Ontario, has been unusually good throughout the past season.

At several points on the River St. Lawrence law-breakers from the State of New York made futile attempts at trapping muskrats.   The vigilance of the Overseers prevented this illegal work, and a large number of traps were seized and confiscated.

He visited the greater part of his district and is pleased to state that the Officers of the Department were uniformly diligent and energetic in the performance of their various duties.   The laws and Regulations of the Department have been observed fairly well in most places.   The patrol boats with their energetic and able officers have been most effective in punishing the law-breakers and enforcing the regulations.

He has been greatly aided in his work by the cheerful and willing co-operation of all the officers of these boats, as well as by all the overseers of the Department, whom he called to aid him in his efforts to maintain the laws and regulations.

He is very pleased to hear of the Department's continuous efforts to exterminate lyng in the Rideau and adjacent lakes, which will very much benefit the waters.

Refuse material from saw-mills has been properly disposed of at most places, in accordance with the requirements of the Department.

Partridges are plentiful.

Ducks though arriving late, owing to the mild weather are numerous.

Muskrats show an increase.   He is still of the opinion that trappers licenses should be issued by the Department.

He suggests that the bounty on wolves should be increased to $25 each.

He is pleased to report that many sportsmen and others have very materially aided him throughout the past season, by giving him information and assistance, which prevented violations of the laws of the Department.

Warden G. M. Parks, of North Bay, reports that he has been travelling extensively over his district during the past year, and is pleased to say that he has found a great improvement in the general conditions regarding game and fishery laws.

The imposing of severe penalties on those who have committed violations has had the desired effect.

During the past season, the angling has been exceedingly good, and he finds a great improvement in all the angling waters, especially the French River and west arm of Lake Nipissing.   The restocking of a number of lakes in the north has met with great favor among the residents of that district, and they are very pleased to learn that net fishing has been done away with in Lake Temiskaming for the next five years.

Regarding game, he finds that moose are very plentiful this year, and he has never before seen so many fine specimens. Deer are rapidly increasing in number, and almost every hunter has secured a deer in his vicinity.

Beaver and otter are also increasing in number, and many a colony of beaver are to be found in the immediate vicinity of North Bay.

Mink, ermine and muskrats are also very plentiful.

Ducks have been very plentiful in the vicinity of Lake Nipissing this season, as are also partridges.

Warden J. T. Robinson, of Sault Ste. Marie, reports that commercial fishing has been as good as the season of 1912, and when the full returns come in he thinks the catch will be much larger, in spite of the season not being a favourable one for the fishermen, as there have been very high winds on Lake Superior. The fishing regulations have been well observed.

Speckled trout are very plentiful, and the tourists say that this was the best season for angling that they have ever had in this district.

Bass are increasing in the rivers and inland lakes, he has seen some very fine specimens taken by the anglers during the season.

Rainbow trout should be protected, as they are a good, game, fish, and the anglers have good sport with them in Ste. Marie's rapids, but if they are not protected there will soon be none left. The close season for these fish should be the same as for speckled trout.

The grey trout which are in the inland lakes should also be protected, as they are a good food fish, and are easily taken as they put up no fight when hooked. Their close season should be from the 15th September to the 1st May. If these fish were protected it would give the officers a better chance to protect the speckled trout.

Maskinonge are scarce in this district.

Sturgeon are increasing in Lake Superior, but not to any great extent.

Pickerel are increasing in Lake Superior.

Wild ducks of all kinds are plentiful in this district.

Wild geese are scarce.

Woodcock and quail very scarce.

Partridges are plentiful, but if great care is not taken this beautiful game bird will become extinct in a few years. The open season should be from 1st November to 15th, and the open season for hares should be the same as for deer, then all game could be better protected.

There are quite a number of wolves in this district, and there is no doubt but what they kill a lot of deer in the winter. If the bounty were raised to $25, and a license put on trappers to make up the difference in the bounty, the trappers would then take an interest in catching the wolves.

Bears are becoming quite plentiful.

Red deer and moose are plentiful, they seem to be on the increase, considering the numbers that are taken by the hunters in the open season. They are well protected, and the law is well observed.

Mink are holding their own in some localities, but in other parts they are decreasing in number.

Muskrats and otter are about the same as usual.

Beaver are becoming very numerous, and are doing a great deal of damage to timber and public highways. He would suggest that the Department have an open season for one or two years to get rid of some of them. If this plan

2 G.F.

were carried out, he would suggest that it be done in the following manner. Each trapper should pay $10 for a license, with which he receives ten tags, so that the license would allow him to catch ten beaver, and one tag must be put on each skin and cancelled by a Government Official, before the skin is sold.

There are no black squirrels in his district.

It is his opinion that trappers should pay for a license. Trapping means money making for the trapper, and why should he be allowed to make so much money and pay nothing to help to keep up the expense of looking after the game. He suggests that each trapper should pay five dollars for a license to trap any fur-bearing animals except beaver and otter.

With regard to the work done by patrol Boat "Jessie T," which has been good this season. She is constantly patrolling the waters. No violations of the law have come to his notice this summer, the people are beginning to realize that it does not pay to break the law and get caught.

It is his opinion that the Order-in-Council passed on August 28th, 1913, is a decided improvement to the game laws, but he hopes to see lumber camps included in another Order-in-Council, and then he would feel that the Game Laws were perfect. Guns in lumber camps are the hardest things he has to contend with in the north country, as he cannot watch all the camps.

In concluding his report he says that he thinks it has been a successful year financially.

Warden C. N. Sterling, of Kenora, Reports that during the year 1913 he has visited the district under his charge several times, and found a large portion of his work has been to look after the northern part of the district, along the line of the Transcontinental Railway. There is a large foreign population in that part of the district who are not complying with the Fish and Game Laws. He would suggest that an overseer be placed at Sioux Lookout to assist in looking after that part of the district where game and fish are very plentiful, and if protected would be of great value to the Province and a revenue to the Department.

FISH.

During the year fishing in the greater part of the district has been much better than the previous year. He would suggest that nothing smaller than a five inch mesh be allowed, as most of the fishermen in the district of Kenora are using five and five and a half inch mesh and are getting a better grade of fish. In fact, some of them are using a six inch mesh.

Black bass fishing has been much better than the previous year. In Long Lake (off the Lake of the Woods) quite a number have escaped into the Lake of the Woods, caused by the dam being defective at the outlet, although a number of good catches have been made this season. Fox Lake (off the Lake of the Woods to the west) was stocked with black bass fingerlings during the month of August, this year. He would suggest that one or more of such lakes be stocked with black bass next season as there are a number of fine lakes such as Fox Lake which are adjacent to the Lake of the Woods.

MOOSE.

Moose were more numerous than they were last year. Nearly every week he receives a report that one or more have been killed by trains along the lines of the Trancontinental, Canadian Pacific and Canadian Northern Railways.

Caribou.

The number is about the same as last year. There is a big herd now north of English River in the District of Patricia.

Red Deer.

Red deer have increased more than any of the big game. They can be found in nearly any part of the woods.

Beaver and Otter.

Beaver is increasing very rapidly and the number can be clearly determined by the dams they are constructing in the different parts of the district. As to otter it is very difficult to obtain any information regarding them.

Mink and Muskrat.

Mink and muskrat are fully up to the standard of last season. The principal difficulty that he has to deal with is the fact that the Indians break open the muskrat houses during the closed season as well as the open season.

Grouse and Partridge.

Partridge are much more numerous than last season. Good bags have been secured. Grouse are up to the standard of last year.

Ducks and Geese.

Ducks and geese have been very plentiful in the western part of the district. In the eastern part of the district have been very scarce.

The wild celery which was sent by the Department to this point has all been placed at different points on the Lake of the Woods, and should be of value in increasing the number of ducks.

Wolves.

Since his last report he finds that the bush wolves are becoming very numerous, and are just as destructive with regard to red deer as the timber wolf. Unless some means are provided for destroying them they will drive the red deer out of the district in a few years.

In conclusion he would suggest that all trappers whether residents or non-residents should have a license which would be of great assistance to the Officers, also a revenue to the Department.

Warden J. H. Willmott, of Beaumaris, reports that there is an annual increasing influx of tourists, principally from the United States, who are as a rule strict observers of the laws of the land, and a boon to the settlers of the lake districts, both as to the provisions they purchase and the guides they hire.

The fishing during the early summer months was not so good as usual, but towards September there was a noticeable improvement. The Department is to be congratulated on the success attained in the propagation and distribution of bass fingerlings. Those sent up to the Muskoka Lakes this year arrived in the best possible condition, thanks to the untiring care of Mr. Edwards of the Brantford Fish Hatchery, who took charge of them in transit. It is gratifying to note the desire of the Department to make arrangements with the Dominion Government with regard to the lengthening of the close season for pickerel and lake trout, the former should be prolonged to June 15th, and the latter should begin three weeks earlier that it now does.

As the Department is already aware a fish hatchery has been started at Port Carling, which is supported by the Hotel Keepers' Association, and subscriptions kindly contributed by others who are interested. This year they successfully hatched out and distributed 1,500,000 fry in the Muskoka Lakes, the spawn being procured at the Bracebridge Falls. There appears to be an almost unanimous feeling that this hatchery is not in the best locality as they are dependent for their water supply to a pump worked by a gasoline engine. The general feeling is that Bracebridge is the proper location for this hatchery, as at that place they would have a never failing flow of water from the falls for hatching purposes, and would also be right on the spot for procuring spawn at the right season, and they would be so situated that the fry could be shipped by rail to any point required for stocking purposes. It is thought possible that arrangements could be made with those who are interested in this hatchery to hand it over to the Government for a moderate sum and the building could be moved on a scow to the proposed site. The acquisition of this plant would undoubtedly be an immense advantage to the Department, it would be difficult to estimate the number of fry which could be hatched out, certainly many millions.

Deer are holding their own, but the stock in the older portions of Muskoka and Parry Sound is lamentably short of that existing some years ago, this is no doubt caused by the ever increasing number of sportsmen who visit these districts annually. It was grievous to note the numbers of does and fawns which were shipped last season. If it were possible, the whole of these districts would be the better for a two or three years close season.

Partridges are plentiful in the newer districts, but in the older sections the large covies which were met with years ago are of rare occurrence, had it not been for the two close seasons a few years ago, the stock would be at a minimum.

Beaver have increased to an enormous extent through the northern sections, in many instances have become a real nuisance, it is thought that an open season for one year would not materially injure the stock.

Otter are fairly plentiful in places. It seems rather a mistake to preserve these animals, as it is known that otter and loons are more destructive to fish than any other animal or bird.

The laws have been well observed in this district on the whole, of course there have been, and always will be infractions, but it is the aim and desire of all who are interested in game and fish to keep these at a minimum.

Warden D. D. Young, of the Quetico Reserve, Kawene, reports that moose are very plentiful.

Red deer increasing rapidly, a great many more seen this fall than last.

WOOD DUCK
(*Aix sponsa*)

Wolves, timber, brush and coyote, are increasing in an alarming degree, and are very destructive to small game.

Lynx very numerous.

Bears scarce.

Foxes increasing.

Hares scarce.

Beaver, mink, weasels (or Canadian ermine) increasing very rapidly.

Musckrats scarce.

Otter, saw a few.

Grouse (partridges) are not so plentiful as last year, owing to the large number of wolves, foxes, owls, hawks, crows, red squirrels, and weasels.

Ducks scarce, there are no feeding grounds, he saw a few mallards and ruddy ducks.

Geese, a few flocks passed over.

Fish of all kinds are plentiful; viz., whitefish, pickerel, lake trout, pike (northern), suckers.

Lyng in most of the lakes.

Black bass in a few small lakes in the south of the Reserve.

He is pleased to say that the law has been well observed in a general way. Two dead moose were found and reported last spring. He imagined that they had been drowned while breaking through the ice near the shore, one had his leg caught between two rocks.

RAINY RIVER DISTRICT SOUTH OF C.P.R.

Game, fur bearing animals and fish are plentiful.

He is sorry to report that the Game Laws have been broken ruthlessly. He has heard of several dead moose having been seen, some not touched, merely shot for pleasure, and others with the hind quarters cut off and the rest left to rot. Several moose have been killed on the railway track.

Near Banning and Mine Centre the wolves are increasing in an alarming manner.

This district is completely different from those in Eastern Ontario, because it has to be patrolled by canoes in summer and on snow shoes in winter. The Indians come in from Savanne, as far south as Banel Lake, trying to sell moose meat to the section men on the railroad.

Last winter there was a great deal of trapping done near Atikokan and Banning.

Since Overseer Aymer has had authority to lease a launch he has done good work on Rainy Lake.

All the fishermen he has seen were satisfied with their catch this summer. He thinks it a pity that Eva Lake was leased as it is a good lake for angling and easy to get at. The trout are very gamey. He is glad to report that the lessee has not netted this lake. Over twenty people visited it for angling this summer, and he strongly recommends that it should not be leased again.

He has made several trips up the Big Turtle River, Little Turtle River, Elbow, Mink, Banel and Sleep Rock Lakes, and the fish seem to be plentiful in all these lakes.

He strongly recommends that trappers should be obliged to take out licenses, and that a district be allotted to them for five years, it would then be to their interest to protect the fur bearing animals and game, and they should send in a return of what they have trapped.

He also recommends that wild celery be planted in selected lakes and bays. If this were done he feels sure that the ducks would remain in there and breed.

He would suggest that the open season be changed for mink in this district, viz., from November 15th to March 15th, as they are in young in April. Also that the bounty on wolves be raised, and a bounty given for brush wolves and coyotes, as they are more destructive with deer and smaller game than their larger brother (timber wolves). They hunt in packs and a deer has a very poor chance of escaping.

He recommends that a close season be put on marten and fisher for two years.

SPECIAL GAME AND FISHERY OVERSEERS.

Overseer Daniel Blea, of South River, reports, that the fishing in the northern part of the Province has not been as good as last year.

The deer appear to be very plentiful, the reason for which he attributes to the reducing of the number from two to one for each man. He strongly recommends that the sale of venison be discontinued; this is the opinion of many others who earnestly hope that some action will be taken in the matter. Partridges do not seem to be so plentiful as last year; he recommends that the season for the northern hare does not come in before the partridge.

It is his pleasure to state that the settlers and inhabitants are giving what assistance they can in enforcing the game laws.

Overseer A. Drouillard, of Walkerville, reports, that the Game and Fishery Laws have been exceedingly well observed in his district, as he only made one seizure during the year.

He suggests that some regulation should be made defining the size of perch and blue pickerel caught in Lake Erie, and shipped to the stations in his district; in many instances he has observed that they were very small, and in his opinion should not have been allowed to be caught.

The fishermen in Lake St. Clair and Lake Erie, suffered considerable loss by reason of the recent storm. Pound nets and hoop nets were almost entirely lost, so he does not anticipate that much fish will be shipped during the fall.

Overseer Henry Watson, of Toronto, reports, that the past season has been the worst ever known for the licensed fishermen in this district. Salmon trout and whitefish appear to become fewer every year, the small amount of restocking that takes place does not make any perceptible increase in the catch.

Herring fishing also decreases every year and this may be attributed to the small meshed nets used at this end of the lake.

Rod fishing has improved a little, the water in the Bay is not quite so putrid as formerly, thanks to the trunk sewer, and if it continues to improve the Government might be justified in re-stocking Toronto Bay with small mouthed black bass.

The number of illegal shipments of game, furs. and fish coming to and passing through Toronto decrease slightly each year.

Most of the fishermen respected the fishery laws and regulations.

Returning deer hunters report that deer are as plentiful as ever and from the number of large ones with horns that were brought out, shows that they are not decreasing; a smaller proportion of does and fawns came through this year than last.

Partridges were reported fairly plentiful, during the first two weeks of the open season, but after that all the hunters say they were very scarce, and in some places none were found. Either the weather conditions caused them to take to the swamps or they have got to the vanishing point in a great many places.

ADDINGTON COUNTY.

Overseer W. J. Donaldson, of Donaldson, reports, that there have been no fishing licenses issued in his district during the past year.

The Game and Fishery Laws have been well observed.

Deer are quite plentiful. Partridges and ducks are scarce.

All fur-bearing animals are very scarce.

Overseer John E. Irish, of Vennachar, reports, that the Game and Fishery Laws seem to have been well observed during the past year, he has made enquiries and there have been no violations brought to his notice.

Deer appear to be plentiful.

Partridges are on the increase.

Ducks are scarce.

Muskrats, mink and fish are scarce.

Black squirrels on the increase.

Mill owners are being careful with regard to their sawdust and rubbish.

Overseer H. R. Purcell, of Colebrook, reports, that quite a number of tourists came to Beaver, White, Bass and Shirtluf Lakes, and report very good angling.

Trapping for muskrats last spring was fairly good. He thinks that all trappers should be obliged to take out a license, as they are more trouble than the hunters.

Partridges are becoming more numerous, and ducks were plentiful this year.

He seized five traps and fined one man $20 for killing deer out of season.

The law has been very well observed with a few exceptions.

Overseer William Young, of Cloyne, reports that the fishing in his district was very good, grey trout and bass being the principal fish in the division.

There were not so many angling permits sold this year as in 1912, but all those who purchased the same report as good catches as in previous years.

Deer seem to be still plentiful.

There are a number of partridges, ducks and rabbits; wolves and bears are very numerous in the north-west end of his district, which he presumes were driven there from the west by the bush fires. Bears are very bold, two having been trapped in the settlement within two miles of the village.

The close seasons have been very well observed, as far as he can ascertain. He sold a few more resident deer licenses than last season. All hunters returning home report plenty of game.

ALGOMA DISTRICT.

Overseer J. R. Bradbury, of Blind River, reports, that the catch of fish in his district has been about the same as last year, that of whitefish being larger. The size of the fish shows a large percentage of jumbo white over five pounds. Trout are slightly more numerous than last year, but smaller in size. The pickerel catch was not so large, about 20 per cent. less than last season, but the fish are a fair size, and the Regulations regarding them have been well observed. Blind River is the principal point in his district for sturgeon and there have been more caught this year than last.

There has been a very heavy catch of mullet, the price was good and a great many were shipped from the district, which added very materially to the cash receipts of the fishermen, as mullets are great destroyers of salmon spawn, a double purpose is served by catching them.

The catch of pilots in the vicinity of St. Joseph's Island also show that they are full of trout spawn, though the number caught has been about average; the catch has been somewhat scattered, owing no doubt to the strong winds which probably drove the fish into different localities.

Pike are about average, but perch seem to be falling off.

Pickerel and bass angling in the smaller lakes and streams inland was good. Tourists are becoming more numerous during the summer, they go to the small streams, which have proved to be good fishing grounds.

Deer and moose are fairly numerous, and mink, martin and muskrat are likely to give good trapping. Beaver are becoming very numerous, and are building dams in the farming settlements. Ducks and geese are not plentiful in his district, but partridges are quite numerous and some fine birds to be seen.

He would advise that the deer season be changed from Nov. 1st-15th, to Nov. 15th-Dec. 1st, for the reason that for several seasons a great deal of game meat has been wasted because the weather is too warm, during the first part of the season, and hunters who come from a distance and kill their deer or moose on or soon after Nov. 1st, must either leave before their party has got its complement of game or see their deer or moose spoil while they wait for their friends; this has a tendency to induce them to kill other animals in excess of their licenses, if they are to have any game fit to take home at the end of the season.

As his district has about one hundred by fifty miles of timber land, the people are left a great deal to their own honour. with regard to keeping the Game Laws. The majority of the farmers consider that they have a right to shoot what game they require regardless of close or open seasons; and the lumber jacks say that if the settler who lives there does not respect the law, why should they who have no interest there? Some claim that they might as well have the sport as allow the wolves to kill the game. The wolf bounty has been so reduced by the Government taking the skins that it has ceased to be an inducement to hunters to destroy the wolves.

He only made two convictions this year; both of which were for killing moose out of season.

If the Department had the support of the people for whose benefit the laws were made, it would be an easier matter to protect the game.

Overseer Fred. Eddy, of Carterton, reports, that game has increased on St. Joseph's Island, especially moose, deer, partridges and beaver. Ducks are about the same as they were last year, and muskrats not quite so plentiful.

The fishermen report that there are not quite as many fish as there were last year, but this he can quite understand, as there are so many fishermen near the international line fishing with trap nets who are continually catching all kinds of small fish, and it does not give the fishermen in his district much chance; and there is so much poaching done at night near Detour. He has confiscated a few of the nets belonging to these law-breakers, but nothing to the number used by them, he feels that he needs a better equipment to cope with them.

More tourists visited this district than usual.

He thinks it would be an improvement if the deer season opened on the 15th instead of the 1st November, as the farmers are busy getting out roots and ploughing, and many deer are wounded, and there is no snow to track them.

There is much more work to be done than a few years ago, and he hopes next year to be able to devote more of his time to the work and obtain better results.

Overseer Herbert Edwards, of Nairn Centre, reports, that the fishing was not good this season, there being only nine tourists visiting there during the summer.

There were plenty of deer last November, and the hunting was good; every one went away very pleased with their sport. Muskrats and mink are very plentiful and beaver are increasing. Partridges are very numerous but ducks are scarce.

The Game laws have been well observed in his district, but on the outskirts of his division he has made three convictions. One for shooting partridges illegally, and two for illegal trapping. He finds that it is necessary to keep a sharp watch on the boundary of his division as there are a lot of deer there.

There are a number of hunters already in the district, and there is every indication of a good hunting season.

Overseer V. J. Jewell, of Batchawana Bay, reports, that he found the fishermen in his district on Lake Superior a most law abiding people in every particular, and he has not had any reason to complain of the non-fulfilment of the laws.

He thinks the law might be amended in one respect, i.e., fishermen are not allowed to retain fish under 1½ lbs. dressed, and he finds that during the season he has had to reject from one to two hundred of such fish every day as they would not come up to the requirements of the law, and the major portion of the same would weigh 22 or 23 oz. He advises that this be looked into as it is such a serious matter and one that should be placed very strongly before the Department. The fishermen have to depend solely upon the Dominion Fish Co., for an outlet for their fish market, from whom they get the very best treatment, and this is one of the stipulations laid down, and the fishermen have to abide by the same.

Fishing has been about the same as it was last year. Speckled trout and bass fishing has been very satisfactory during the past season.

Another matter of vital importance which has come to his notice is the protection of red deer from the wolves, which are their greatest enemies, and he does not think that the deer are sufficiently protected from them. It is his opinion that the bounty on wolves should be $25 for each one killed. If this were the case he feels confident that there are a number of people who would make a business of exterminating these animals. He is satisfied that there are ten red deer killed by the wolves for every one killed by the hunter who has procured a license for same. It is a common occurrence for the fishermen to report that they have seen the bones of a deer on the beach, or else a pack of wolves run a fawn down and devour it before they could get to shore to give any assistance. He feels sure that, with the splendid laws which are made for the protection of the game from the hunters, in a few years they would have a hunter's paradise on Lake Superior, if something were done to exterminate the wolves.

Partridges are much more plentiful this year than he has known them to be for years.

BRANT COUNTY.

Overseer W. W. Jackson, of St. George, reports, that he has kept a watch over his district and finds that most of the game such as partridges have increased. Black and grey squirrels and rabbits are very plentiful, and ducks were more numerous than they have been for years.

There is promise of an abundant quantity of muskrats.

The Game Laws have been well observed. he still recommends that guns and traps should be licensed.

Overseer Henry Johnson, of Brantford, reports, that the game fish angling in his district has been better than in former years, especially in the vicinity of Paris, but it was not quite so good in the Brantford district; the reason for this is that considerable construction work has been going on this season in that vicinity. Trout fishing has been reported good, and plenty of coarse fish.

With regard to game. Black and grey squirrels and partridges are still on the increase, and he recommends that a limit should be put on the number of black and grey squirrels killed, his reason for this is that he knows of two people who killed forty black and grey squirrels in one afternoon.

Woodcocks are about the same. and ducks more plentiful.

Fur-bearing animals. Muskrats and mink are on the increase, and rabbits are becoming a nuisance to farmers.

The Grand River is still a cesspool for sewage.

With a few exceptions the Game and Fishery Laws have been well observed, and he wishes to thank the Deputy Game Wardens and the public for the assistance they have given him.

He has made several visits to the hatchery at Mt. Pleasant and each time was greatly impressed with the developments there.

BRUCE COUNTY.

Overseer J. W. Jermyn, of Wiarton, reports that this has been a very poor season for fishing, on account of the rough weather.

The fall run of trout did not come on until very late, just as the season was about at an end. The stormy weather was also a handicap to the fishermen.

Some fishermen still insist on fishing hooks and he has pulled miles of them out of the water during the past season.

There are no deer to be shot on the Peninsula this fall.

Partridges and rabbits are plentiful.

Ducks fairly plentiful.

Fur-bearing animals scarce.

Overseer Daniel Kehoe, of Millarton, reports, that the fishermen state that the catch of fish was light during October, owing to the rough weather.

He has made no convictions during the past year, and no infractions of the law were brought to his notice.

Game is scarce in this part of the county but more plentiful in the eastern portion.

Overseer John Trelford, of Southampton, reports that the fishermen had a good season up till Sept. 1st, but after that date the fishing was light until the 15th October when it became fairly good again. The fishermen attribute this falling off to the warm weather during September and October.

He has had very little trouble with the licensees in his district, as they all seem to observe the laws well.

There were a great many tourists camping in his division this season, who were also careful not to break the laws regarding the fishing. They mostly camp between Southampton and Stokes Bay, and state the bass and perch fishing has been good.

There are a great many rabbits this year, but partridges and pheasants are scarce, and there do not appear to be many black squirrels.

Ducks and wild geese are plentiful round the small lakes.

Muskrats are very plentiful. The trapping is done mainly by the Indians, very few white men are engaged in this business.

There are no beaver in his district and very few mink.

Last year a great many deer were shot in the northern part of his division, and he has noticed that the law provides a close season for three years, which he thinks a good thing. He also thinks that hunting with dogs should not be permitted.

CARLETON COUNTY.

Overseer Adam Greene, of Diamond, reports that the fishing was good this season, bass and pickerel were plentiful, also all kinds of coarse fish.

Partridges have not increased. Ducks were plentiful late in the season.

Deer are scarce, he thinks the construction of the C. N. R. and so much rock cutting was the cause. Bears are increasing on Mississippi River also on Carp River.

There were no seizures or convictions made.

Overseer E. T. Loveday, of Ottawa, reports that during 1912 and the beginning of 1913 he made a number of seizures of illegal fur amounting to somewhere in the neighbourhood of $2,000, and in nearly every case he was successful in tracing the owners, who were prosecuted and paid fines ranging from $50 to $200. One offender being fined twice in a short time $100. While on a trip which took him through Peterborough, where he was delayed a couple of hours, he visited the express office and seized a bag of fur valued at $250, which was sent to the Department at Toronto, who traced the owner and fined him $50.

During the year two licenses for non-residents were sold, one for hunting and for fishing. Hotel, game dealers, and cold storage licenses have been taken out; and night line licenses have been issued.

Angling has not been so good as other years, not because there are less fish, but because the river is so full of minnows, and the fish are too well fed.

With regard to the game he thinks if he saw one he saw five thousand ducks on Lake Deschenes one evening, but they keep out in the lake and it is hard to get near them. Partridges are reported to be plentiful. Moose have been seen within three miles of the city limits, and bear a short distance further. One farmer reports having seen eight deer among his cows.

Mr. Loveday recommends that the non-resident license for deer be reduced from $50 to $25, to correspond with Quebec Province, as Americans are going to Quebec who might come to Ontario if the license fee were the same.

Overseer William Major, of Woodlawn, reports that the law was well observed in his district. There was no Sunday shooting done.

Fish are plentiful, especially pike, perch, sunfish and bullheads.

Ducks are plentiful. Geese are scarce in the fall, but plentiful in the spring. There are not many muskrats in his district. Partridges are also scarce.

DUFFERIN COUNTY.

Overseer George Moffatt, of Glen Cross, reports that the law has been well observed in his district, no violations of the same having come to his notice.

The fish under his supervision are mostly trout and suckers. The trout were rather small this year, but were very plentiful. On account of the extremely dry summer the streams have been very low.

Rabbits are quite numerous, red fox are about the same as last year, but mink are getting a little scarce on account of their fur being so valuable.

Overseer John Small, of Grand Valley, reports that the fishing was fairly good this season.

Deer is on the increase, on account of the close season in Dufferin County.

Ducks and geese are not so plentiful this season.

Mink very scarce.

Muskrats very plentiful.

The law has been well observed in his district, no infractions having come to his notice.

DURHAM COUNTY.

Overseer Robert Elliott, of Port Hope, reports that there have been no violations of the laws in his district.

Whitefish have been more plentiful this summer than they have for some years past, while salmon trout are not so plentiful. Angling in the harbour has been very good, carp, eels, bullheads and perch, being caught mostly. Speckled trout fishing has been about the same as it was last year.

With regard to the game, partridges are on the increase, and muskrats plentiful, while mink and black squirrel are scarce. There have been a few ducks but not many, cotton-tail rabbits are quite numerous, but wood hare scarce. Trappers report that weasels and skunk are quite plentiful.

Overseer S. G. Pickell, of Bowmanville, reports that the speckled trout, pike and herring fishing were about the same as last year.

Ducks were very plentiful this fall. Wood-hare and cotton-tail rabbits are increasing every year owing to the short open season. Partridges are the same as last year.

He thinks that the sale of ducks, partidges and rabbits should be prohibited.

Black squirrels are more numerous than ever.

The laws have been well observed with the exception of a little trouble which he had on March 28th, regarding illegal duck shooting, and again in the latter part of February when muskrat houses were opened and traps set in them. He took the traps and stopped further trouble, but was unable to apprehend either of the law-breakers.

Overseer C. Twamley, of Cavan, reports that the speckled trout were not so plentiful this year, owing to the low water. He strongly recommends that the close season should begin on September 1st.

Bass are more numerous, they came up early to spawn and remained up the creek all the summer on account of the sewerage at Peterborough.

Black ducks were very plentiful, also partridges. The Italians working on the C.P.R. gave him a great deal of trouble. Black squirrels are plentiful. Mink are scarce, and muskrats becoming more plentiful.

The law was well observed.

Overseer John Watson, of Caesarea, reports that the Game and Fishery Laws have been fairly well observed in his division, with the exception of the one regarding shooting before sunrise and after sunset, which has been violated to a great extent at the Cartwright and Port Perry bridges. He has also heard of some shooting at other places, but not very much.

With regard to the fish, he would suggest that speckled trout fishing be prohibited for at least two years, and that a limit should be put on the number of bass and maskinonge caught daily by each person, *i.e.,* two maskinonge and four bass.

It is his opinion that the fishing will never amount to very much in Scugog Lake, unless the water is kept up to the top of the dam at Lindsay. He thinks some steps should be taken to have this done, as it would improve the fishing, shooting, and trapping and it would be more healthy for the general public.

Ducks, partridges and rabbits are very plentiful, there were also a number of geese in the spring. He would suggest again that the open seasons should be as follows:

Rabbits—October 15th, to January 1st.

Ducks—September 15th to December 15th.

Mink—November 1st to January 1st.

Muskrats—April 1st to May 1st.

And as far as he can find out from the hunters and trappers they would approve of the change.

He thinks that trappers should be obliged to take out a license, also that guns should be licensed except those carried by farmers on their own land. Further that all dogs that chase rabbits during the months of April, May, June and July should be kept tied up. It would also improve the shooting if a limit were set on the number of ducks killed each day by any one person, he thinks 25 would be a fair limit.

ELGIN COUNTY.

Overseer K. McClennan, of Aylmer, reports that whitefish and herring fishing was exceptionally good, in fact, it was better than in 1911, and the prices were good. The spring fishing this year was not so good as it was last, but the prices have been better. The laws have been well observed: there was, however, one infraction in the early spring when three East Elgin fishermen set their nets in West Elgin, but as soon as it was brought to Overseer McClennan's attention he warned them, and this appeared to be sufficient as the violation was not repeated

Coon, black squirrel and partridges appear to be more numerous than in 1912. He suggests that the season for killing partridges, quail, black and grey squirrel should open on the same day. He has received reports that some hunters are out in the woods as soon as the partridge season opens and they shoot both partridges and squirrels regardless of the law, but he has not got sufficient evidence to convict these people, and if the seasons opened simultaneously, there would be no excuse for the hunters to be shooting in the close season. The law was well observed until the partridge season opened.

Essex County.

Overseer H. A. Henderson, of Pelee Island, reports that the catch of fish has been a little better than last season.

The angling has not been quite so good as usual.

There is little game on the island.

The Game and Fishery Laws have been fairly well observed.

Overseer Remi LaFramboise, of Canard River, reports that during the month of November last, fishing for whitefish was better than it has been for years, though it has become lighter towards the end of the year.

Carp fishing has been rather discouraging on account of the high water, they stayed in the marsh where the fishermen could not get them, all other fish such as black bass, pickerel and perch seem to be about the same as they have always been.

With regard to the game, quail seem to be very numerous this fall, he has seen several bevies himself. Ducks have also been very plentiful, especially marsh ducks, such as black mallards. River ducks are also quite numerous. Black and grey squirrels are very scarce, rabbits and muskrats are very plentiful.

The Game and Fishery Laws have been fairly well observed in his division.

Overseer M. W. Scott, of Leamington, reports that quail are very scarce all over his territory, black squirrels are also almost extinct. He tried to ascertain if anyone was breaking the law by shooting quail or squirrels, but could find no evidence of illegal work.

The Hungarian pheasants which were sent to this district for propagation purposes are doing well and increasing in number.

Ducks are fairly plentiful, but the number killed was not up to the average.

Frontenac County.

Overseer James B. Angrove, of Kingston, reports that at the beginning of November, 1912, he went on a special trip to North Frontenac, for the purpose of aiding the proper carrying out of the Laws and Regulations of the Game and Fishery Department, in the sparsely populated portions of the County. Deer were plentiful and wolves very destructive. He came across several carcases of deer which had been destroyed by wolves. He strongly recommends that a larger bounty be paid for killing these destructive animals than that given at the present time; he saw several of them during his trip.

The amount of fish shipped from his district compares favourably with the quantity exported other years.

The tourist season opened somewhat late this year, yet the number of visitors at the principal summer resorts in the district exceeded that of 1912.

Owing to the very warm weather the duck shooting was poor at the opening, but as it became cooler the number of ducks increased. There are more black squirrels to be seen than last year. Red squirrels are numerous and muskrats plentiful; for the benefit of the future supply of these useful fur-bearing animals he would suggest that hunters should be obliged to take out a license for killing same.

He is pleased to report that the Laws and Regulations have been well observed in his district.

Overseer M. Avery, of Sharbot Lake, reports that the fishing has been good this season.

He finds that by keeping a close watch over his division he is able to prevent the people from breaking the law.

He did not find any nets during the fall or summer, and thinks those he seized last year was a sufficient lesson to them. He saw some people carrying guns out of season, and gave them a sharp warning, which had the desired effect.

Deer are quite plentiful and if the wolves were hunted out of the district they would be still more numerous. He thinks that a higher bounty on wolves would help to dispose of them.

Overseer George Barr, of Harrowsmith, reports that angling for bass and pickerel in Fourteen Island Lake was not good, but in Rock, Long and Silver Lakes anglers report good results.

Last year he reported that the pike in Rock, Long and Silver Lakes were infected with cancerous sores; the disease has now spread to Napanee Lake. If the water were lowered he thinks they would soon be rid of the disease.

Herring last fall was good in Desert Lake, but the fishermen were not quite so successful in Knowlton Lake.

Muskrats were plentiful this season, but he thinks it would be advisable to charge a small license fee for muskrat and mink and have the trapping season for both open at the same time.

Ducks and partridges continue to increase.

Rabbits are quite plentiful, but he would advise that a limit be put to the number killed each day by one man, as there is a needless waste.

Black and grey squirrels are numerous, he recommends that no boy under eighteen should be allowed to hunt, if a small license fee were charged this would make it easier.

He has examined Fourteen Island Lake and Petworth Dams. At the former one inch of water was flowing over the top of the dam, and pickerel were being carried over and killed by being dashed on the rocks at the bottom. There is no fishway in the Petworth dam either.

The number of tourists who visit this district is increasing rapidly.

There have been no fines imposed in his district this year.

Overseer Matthew Cox, of Howe Island, reports that as there is no fishing being done in his district the coarse fish are becoming plentiful.

Trolling has been very good this year.

Ducks are plentiful.

There have been no violations of the law come to his notice.

Overseer J. W. Davis, of Sydenham, reports that the fishing in his district has been good, bass in particular have been very plentiful.

Owing to cold weather at the beginning of the season, very few visitors came to his division.

Game is decreasing. Ducks were not plentiful, the hunters only secured a very few. Muskrats are more plentiful this year than last. Mink are very scarce.

There are still a few deer in the district, if they were left alone for a few years they would become plentiful. Partridges and rabbits are very plentiful and foxes are increasing.

The pickerel which were placed in Sydenham Lake are doing well, the people in his district do not understand catching them.

The Game and Fishery Laws have been well observed.

Overseer Henry Drew, of Long Lake, reports that he has kept a careful watch over his district during the past year, and believes that the laws have been strictly observed.

Fishing was very good in the small lakes, with the exception of Eagle Lake. Herring seem to be plentiful, but salmon and bass very scarce. He has examined the bars and found very little sign of salmon. The water in this lake is splendid and the spawning grounds are good, with plenty of feed. He would advise that the lake be stocked with salmon and black bass.

Partridges are very plentiful, and deer more plentiful than they have been for years. Mink are very scarce.

Overseer James Fisher, of Sunbury, reports that with regard to the fishing in his district the farmers are making complaints about the scarcity of bass in Loborough and Dog Lakes, due to the tremendous number of tourists who visit that neighbourhood during the summer. Salmon seem to be more plentiful, some good catches having been reported.

He recommends that a license be granted to some reliable man to catch the whitefish and coarse fish in Loborough Lake, as they are harmful.

Ducks are not very plentiful. Black squirrel and mink are very scarce, and mink not so plentiful as in former years.

The Game and Fishery Laws have been fairly well observed in his district. A few complaints have come to his notice, which upon investigation proved to be false.

Overseer George Gates, of Kingston, reports that as far as he is aware the laws have been well observed in his district.

Bass fishing has been as good or better than during former years, and other fish were about average.

Ducks were not so plentiful as other years, on account of the weather being so mild they have not come south yet.

LAKE TROUT
(Cristimover namaycush)

There seemed to be about the same number of tourists visiting the district as there have been other years.

He thinks that trappers of muskrats should be licensed as it would stop outsiders from setting traps and muskrats are becoming extinct.

Overseer Henry Holliday, of Wolfe Island, reports that the fishing has been good in his district, with the exception of bass which were not very plentiful during July, but later in the season they improved and some large fish were caught. Pike, pickerel and maskinonge were plentiful and the anglers had a good season. Salmon were very plentiful, but whitefish were very scarce in this district.

The fishermen have had no fault to find with the hoop net fishing, as it has been good, some good catches were made.

There was one case of illegal fishing, but he was unable to apprehend the law-breaker, otherwise the law has been well observed by both net fishermen and anglers.

Wild ducks have been very scarce this fall, owing to the warm weather, as they stay farther north. Muskrats are becoming very scarce, he would advise that the season should not open until the end of March, as then there would be no breaking into the houses.

Overseer J. A. Kennedy, of Tichborne, reports that the residents are taking an interest in seeing that the law is observed.

He sold thirty-eight permits to non-residents of the Province.

The anglers state that they have had a good season, bass and pickerel fishing has been good all through.

Partridges which were hatched in large quantities seem to have died during the summer for some reason, and they have become very scarce. Ducks were more numerous than they have been for some years past. There are a few deer in his district, and they raise their young there. Muskrats were quite plentiful.

Overseer William Truelove, of Fermoy, reports that there have been very few violations of the Act during the last year. He confiscated two gill nets which were illegally set in the fall of 1912, but was unable to find the offender.

There were not quite so many tourists this year as last. Bass fishing was good but pickerel fishing in Wolf Lake was not so good. He attributes the reason for this to be the Derbyshire dam, which was built in 1912; as the fish go down in the spring and cannot get back, there being no fish slide, and he prophesies that in a year or two there will be no pickerel in Wolf Lake. Herring fishing was good in all the numerous lakes in the township of Bedford, and there was plenty of pickerel in Bobs Lake.

He transplanted some parent pickerel in Clear Lake and a pond near Fermoy, last May, which were taken from Bobs lake, and he is expecting good results therefrom, as those waters are full of suckers, which will give them plenty of food.

He recommended fifty resident fishing licenses for the fall of 1912, and twenty-one hunting licenses. Very few deer are killed, but the sport is good.

Red deer are on the increase. Ducks are scarce and partridges plentiful. Black squirrels are becoming very numerous, and there are a few grey ones. Raccoons are on the increase, mink are scarce, but muskrats plentiful. Some trappers made $100 in the spring. The foxes are still after the farmers' turkeys.

3 G.F.

Overseer H. E. Wartman, of Portsmouth, reports that the fishing in his district was not so good as it was last year, although some fine bass fishing was reported in October, which was no doubt owing to the fine weather as this is very late in the season.

Ducks, especially black, are as plentiful as they were last year. As yet, blue bills and winter ducks are not very numerous, but it is early in the season for them.

A large flock of wild geese was seen flying early in September, which was exceptionally early, as November is the month during which they are usually to be seen.

Muskrats and mink are quite as plentiful as they were last year.

The laws have been well observed in his district, he has interested some good men in the protection of the game, who have proved a great help.

Overseer F. L. Wormworth, of Arden, reports that there were quite a lot of non-resident fishermen this year, who stated that on the whole the fishing was good, with the exception of Cross Lake which was not so good as other seasons. Every one seemed to be careful not to break the law with regard to catching under-sized fish. A few black bass were put in Big Clearwater Lake, but he thinks they need more; the lakes near the town need re-stocking more especially, as they are fished most.

The deer hunting for the fall of 1912 was the best that has been known for years. He had some trouble with people hunting without licenses, and made one conviction. Duck shooting was not so good as usual, but partridges are quite plentiful. On the whole the game laws have been well observed, some people tried to trap out of season, and he managed to seize the traps though he could not trace the owners.

GRENVILLE COUNTY.

Overseer J. H. Boyd, of Merrickville, reports that the fishing has been excellent this year, there was quite an increase in pike, pickerel and bass. Several large maskinonge were also caught.

A number of nets were seized and a few fines imposed.

Ducks and partridges have increased wonderfully.

Muskrats are about the same as they were last year. The hunters would like to see them protected more, and he thinks the trappers should be licensed as the fur is so valuable. He further advises that the hunting of muskrats should be prohibited during the fall and winter, as the skins are not so valuable during these seasons.

Deer are quite numerous this year, more so than last. The dogs do not seem to bother them and they are quite tame.

The Game and Fishery Laws have been much better observed this year.

Overseer James A. Fraser, of Prescott, reports that things have been very quiet in his district this year, fishing has not been so good as usual. A few of the more experienced men believe that the high water was responsible for it.

Bass are very scarce, pickerel about the same, and there have been only a few maskinonge. Perch was the only species of fish that were plentiful. Rock bass were plentiful in the early spring.

Partridges and ducks are the only game in his district. Partridges were only fair, but ducks were very plentiful both in the spring and the fall.

Violations of the law are becoming fewer on the river. Poachers are afraid of the patrol boat and give it a wide berth, as is proved by the small number of seizures he has made this season. He only seized one boat and net and two or three spears with one small set line.

GREY COUNTY.

Overseer James Gillespie, of Berkeley, reports that with regard to the Fisheries his duties were more especially to watch the inland lakes and small streams to prevent the illegal taking of speckled trout.

Early in the season he had the Regulations posted round the lakes and streams and in public places. He went to Markdale and Chatsworth in order to post up these Laws, and mailed several copies to be put up by friends.

During the summer quite a number of people camped round Ewart's and Bell's Lakes, mostly for pleasure, and he often used to visit these lakes, sometimes taking a boat at night and dragging for nets, and sometimes watching from the shore, but he found no illegal work being carried on.

Early in May he, with Mr. Watson, of Toronto, deposited thirty thousand speckled trout fry in Ewart's Lake, which connects with Bell's Lake and many others, making a chain of several miles in length.

He thinks the law is being fairly well observed round Chatsworth, as there have been very few complaints. In June he received an anonymous letter from Massie, stating that sawdust was being allowed to run into the river in that vicinity. He investigated the matter and found the mill running, and the owner was using a blower so that the sawdust did not fall into the stream. The matter was reported to the Department at the time.

Acting upon instructions from the Department, in August he visited the Mad River, in Osprey, to find out if possible if any illegal fishing was being carried on, and forwarded a report on his inspection the following day to the Department.

He did not sell any Angling Permits.

In November he received instructions to go to the vicinity of Markdale and find out if the Indians were trapping muskrat and beaver, as a report had reached the Department that this was the case, but he could find nothing to lead him to believe that they had been trapping beaver; they may have caught some muskrats, but this he could not prove. He explained the law to them and they left the district.

During the winter he visited the lakes several times to see if there was any evidence of anyone fishing through the ice, but could find none.

With regard to the game, he thinks the law has been fairly well observed. Last December he heard of one instance, when it was reported that a partridge was shot out of season, but if this was the case, he is satisfied that the person did not know it was close season. He supplied them with a copy of the Game and Fishery Laws. It is a rule of his to supply these Laws to anyone whom he knows to be in the habit of hunting or trapping.

He is of the opinion that great damage is done in the spring by hounds running hares, as they can be heard in the swamps every day.

Partridges are said to be more plentiful this season.

Overseer Thomas McKenny, of Thornbury, reports that the fishing was fairly good for part of the year, and that the average weight of the fish was greater than last year.

The laws have been fairly well observed, but he regrets to say that night line fishing is still carried on to some extent in Owen Sound Bay and round Griffith's Island.

When in Owen Sound last summer he visited a fish-freezing establishment and found a quantity of fish with the marks of hooks in their mouths and no marks of gill nets, which made him feel sure that lines were being used. He spent nearly a week trying to locate them, but regrets to say that he failed to discover any. He states that it is almost impossible to find them owing to the new method of setting them, *i.e.,* they take double ranges, one at right angles to the other, then ascertain the depth of the water at that point and measure out that depth less 3 or 4 feet, thereby leaving the buoy that distance under the water and making it almost impossible for officers to detect them. He feels sure, however, that the seizures made by himself and Overseer Jermyn last year have had good effect and lessened line fishing.

He thinks it advisable to refuse to grant herring net licenses as they are not fished to any great extent for public use, and they are better for line fishing.

Fall fishing was unusually late this season in his district and some fishermen only got one good catch before the close season commenced. The fish seem to come to spawning grounds very much earlier up the lake and gradually come to the lower end of the bay, so that men in his district get but poor fishing compared with those further north.

Overseer James Myers, of Holstein, reports that the chief fish in his district are speckled trout and bass.

The catches were fairly good this year.

He has had his district well posted with game and Fishery Laws, and only two violations of the Fisheries Act came to his notice, these were for taking under-sized trout and were settled out of court.

There was one violation of the Game Laws; this was killing hares out of season, also settled out of court.

Deer are becoming more plentiful, partridges are also doing better.

He thinks that the mink and muskrat seasons should open on the same date, either November 1st or December 1st.

HALDIMAND COUNTY.

Overseer James Vokes, of Nanticoke, reports:

Black squirrel appear to be slightly on the increase. Several complaints reached him about the shooting of squirrel out of season, and he was fortunate enough to catch two persons. The fine inflicted in each case will, no doubt, be a warning to others.

Muskrat are quite as plentiful as in the previous year or two, and the law is fairly well respected now, previous convictions having had good effect.

Mink are very scarce.

Quail are on the increase, he has heard of several being seen in different parts of the county. The close season for these birds is evidently having the desired effect.

Woodcock and plover were plentiful, and good bags were secured for a few days after the season began.

Partridge appear to be slightly on the increase. He strongly recommended that the open season for partridges and black squirrel be made to run concurrently. As things are now, the season for squirrel opens when the season for partridge closes. He finds that this is a great temptation for hunters who are after birds to shoot the squirrels also, as their haunts are much the same. It is this fact that has caused most of the complaints he has received about shooting squirrels out of season, and it also makes it very difficult to track up the guilty parties.

A number of pheasants have been seen at the lower end of the county this Fall. This, no doubt, is owing to the fact that the taking of pheasant is prohibited in the neighbouring counties of Lincoln and Welland. It seems a pity that these birds should be shot whilst they are yet so scarce. He would suggest that the taking of pheasant be also prohibited in the county of Haldimand for two or three years.

He fined a man for shooting along the Grand River on Sunday.

The fishery laws have been well observed this year, and no serious infractions of the law have come to his notice.

Both gill-net and pound-net fishermen report an average season.

Herring were not quite so plentiful as last year, but perch, pickerel, and coarse fish were quite up to the average.

White fish were very plentiful at the lower end of the county last Fall, but did not come so strong as usual at the upper fisheries. Owing to the continued mild weather this Fall, they have not come on shore in any large quantities as yet. A large amount of spawn was taken care of last Fall, and the fishermen are strongly of the opinion that the hatcheries are doing a good work.

Sturgeon has been coming in steadily all summer, but no big hauls were taken at any one time.

Angling in the Grand River was not very good.

Duck have been quite plentiful in the River district, but he understands they are somewhat scarce this Fall in the Long Point Bay district.

HALIBURTON COUNTY.

Overseer Manley Maybee, of Cameron, reports that the maskinonge and bass fishing has been as good as usual, and he recommends that their close season be from January 1st—June 15th.

Frogs are scarce.

The trapping was good this spring, muskrats were plentiful but mink not quite so plentiful as last year. He thinks it would be a good thing if the close season for mink began on March 1st, as the March sun fades the fur and reduces its value. Partridges are increasing slowly, and he suggests that the first half of November be made an open season for them. Ducks are very plentiful, especially black ducks. He thinks that they should not be allowed to be sold, and that shooting between sunset and sunrise should be prohibited. Rabbits are plentiful. There are no deer or black squirrels in his district.

The Game and Fishery Laws have been well observed in his territory.

He states that it would be a fine thing if some wild rice was distributed along McLaren's Creek, as there are thousands of acres of marsh land.

Overseer M. W. Switzer, of Gooderham, reports that the close season for fish was well observed, no reports of illegal fishing having come to his notice.

There are some salmon trout, speckled trout, brook trout, and black bass in his district; he visited several of the lakes and saw some fine catches of fish. As far as he could tell, all the fish caught were used for home consumption.

There are no fish ways in his division, and the mill owners have observed the law fairly well.

No tourists visited this district. There are some fine lakes, but they have no game fish in them; if these were stocked with salmon trout, bass, and pickerel, it would be a fine thing for the settlers and they would soon have their share of tourists during the season.

The Game Laws were well observed, he did not hear of any illegal hunting going on with the exception of one instance.

Deer was not up to the average, if dogs were prohibited from chasing them they would soon increase. There are also beaver, otter, mink and muskrats in this district, but no black or grey squirrels.

HALTON COUNTY.

Overseer R. M. Brown, of Milton, reports that the speckled trout are gradually being fished out in his district and will soon be a thing of the past.

Partridges having been protected for three years, they have increased wonderfully; in fact, in some parts of the county they are quite plentiful.

Black and grey squirrels are more numerous than they have been during the last few years.

Cottontail rabbits are very plentiful.

Wood hare are becoming very scarce.

Mink are very scarce; he has not seen one this year.

Coon seem to be holding their own; they are about the same as they were last year.

Muskrats are not as plentiful as other years.

Red foxes are fairly numerous.

The law has been fairly well observed. The farmers have taken to protecting their own properties, and a great many have notices posted up. He states that they have been troubled with Italians, and suggests that licenses be issued for carrying guns, as it would enable the wardens and others employed in the service to obtain the names of the hunters. A great many are in favour of a license and would willingly pay one or two dollars a year. The Western Provinces have this, why not Ontario?

Overseer W. Sargent, of Bronte, reports that he has been over his division a number of times and has always found that the law is well observed.

He regrets to say that the herring fishing has not been so good as other years. He would judge it to have been about 15 per cent. less than last year, but the prices have been much better, so the fishermen will not feel any loss.

Whitefish are about the same as former years, and the prices are much better.

There is a small decrease in the number of trout caught, about 10 per cent. less than last year. This he attributes to the bad weather and so much easterly wind that the fishermen could not lift and set their nets regularly.

He was pleased that the extension of the open season for whitefish and trout was not allowed this year, as has been the case other years. He is convinced that it would have been harmful to the whitefish and trout.

Angling in the twelve and sixteen mile creeks was about the same as during former years. All the fish are sold at the home market, and good prices are realized.

There is not a great deal of game in his division, but he has noticed quite an increase in black and grey squirrels and partridges.

HASTINGS COUNTY.

Overseer H. C. Armstrong, of Glen Ross, reports that he has had a successful season as an overseer. He fined three people who gave quite a lot of trouble about an eel rack which was set in Trent River. He has inspected several shipments of fish and found them all satisfactory. He heard reports of nets set in Trent River, but could not find any trace of them. Game fish are increasing.

Cottontail rabbits are becoming very numerous, so much so that they are destroying orchards and gardens, and he would advise that they should be shot during any season of the year. Black squirrels, partridges, muskrats and winter ducks are increasing, but mink are scarce.

Overseer Robert Bonter, of Marmora, reports that he has kept as close a watch as possible over his district; it being practically a fishing and hunting township it requires most of the overseer's time to stop all illegal fishing and hunting.

Fishing has been good this season.

He has travelled many miles to investigate reports of deer being killed illegally, but was unable to find sufficient evidence to make any convictions.

Ducks were plentiful but partridges not so numerous as last year. He recommends that they should be protected for at least two years.

Overseer Thomas Gault, of Deseronto, reports that the bass fishing has been particularly good; the whitefish are slow in coming up. Hoop net fishing was good.

Ducks and small game were plentiful, more so than for many years.

He made two seizures for duck shooting.

The laws have been very well observed by the fishermen in his district.

Overseer John Haggerty, of Gilmour, reports that the fishing has been very good this season.

Deer are plentiful. Partridges very scarce.

Wolves were thick through Central Grimsthorpe.

Beaver quite plentiful.

Muskrats and mink rather scarce.

He does not know of any violations of the Game and Fishery Laws.

Overseer James McCaw, of Bancroft, reports that brook trout are as plentiful as they have been other years. Lake trout were more numerous this season, some very fine catches being made in Baptiste Lake and Clear Lake. Bass have been caught in Trout Lake and York River, but the size was not large.

Partridges were very scarce, he thinks this was on account of the bush fires during the hatching season. He would suggest that their open season be shortened to Nov. 1st-15th, the same as deer, or else give them another three years close season, in order to increase the number once more.

Ducks have not been so plentiful this season. Rabbits are very scarce on account of the fires.

Deer seem to be more plentiful, he has seen several himself this summer, bears also have not been so numerous for years as they have been this season. They have been doing considerable damage to the farmers. sheep; some very large ones were caught, quite a few during the summer, when their fur was useless.

Muskrats are very plentiful, and a few beaver have been reported, some on Bently and Bird's Creeks and along the York Branch of the River, where a few otter have also been seen.

Some moose were seen round Baptiste Lake.

On the whole he thinks the settlers are taking a keener interest in protecting the game as very few complaints have been made.

Overseer J. A. Moore, of Trenton, reports that game and fish have been very scarce in the Bay of Quinte and all the adjoining waters this present season, and he would recommend that fry, especially bass, be deposited therein in order to replete the same. Tourists were quite numerous in his district during the present season. The professional fishermen had not very successful catches this year; the spring season being very short, and the weather during the early autumn so warm the fish did not appear to be running.

Ducks have been very plentiful in some of the waters in his neighborhood but have been unmercifully slaughtered by what are known as pot hunters, comprising retired farmers, retired business men and professionals who hunt for the market. Under the present regulations, which allow shooting from monitors, these pot hunters use very large flocks of decoys, making it almost impossible for the ordinary person to obtain any game whatever; the result is that the sport has been left almost entirely to these gentry, who have slaughtered and shipped great numbers. This state of affairs is very annoying to the people at large and if continued for a few years more there will be no ducks in this vicinity, but they will be shot or driven away. He would recommend strongly, and he states that he is supported by all the people, except the pot hunters, in his district that the sale of ducks be prohibited, and also that shooting from monitors, which in reality is a sunken punt, be prohibited, and that the distance from the shore or natural blind where decoys may be set be decreased to sixty yards. These regulations, if enforced, would give the fowl a chance and not drive them from the waters or subject them to such a slaughter as at present.

Partridges have been scarce, probably owing to the great number of forest fires in the Hastings District, which apparently destroyed a large number of them. He would consider it most advisable that a close season be again declared for a period of three years; also that a limit of not more than fifteen birds to each gun during the season be allowed, and that the season be shortened from the 15th October to the 1st November, or from 1st November to the 15th. Black squirrels have been very plentiful in this district, but there is great difficulty in preventing them from being shot owing to the fact that hunters are able to shoot partridge during part of the closed season for squirrels, and the report is that a great many have been shot by partridge hunters, but he has been unable to obtain any direct evidence of the fact. He would, therefore, recommend that the season for black squirrels be changed to the same as partridge and that both be made from the 15th October to the 1st November.

Overseer J. W. Morton, of St. Ola, reports that the fishing has not been very good this summer. Trout and bass which are the principal fish were very scarce.

Not many angling permits were sold this season.

Partridges and ducks were quite plentiful. Deer, wolves, squirrels and rabbits are very plentiful, and a few bears and moose have been seen, also black squirrels which are uncommon in that part of the country.

As far as he can tell the Game and Fishery Laws have been well observed.

Overseer Charles St. Charles, of Madoc, reports, that there are fish of the following species in Moira Lake, maskinonge, pickerel, black bass, white suckers, red fin suckers, rock fish, sun fish, eels and mudcats. The fishing this year has been good, a great many maskinonge have been caught. The dam at the foot of the lake has been blown up and the lake lowered over four feet, this has improved the fishing. Mudcats are very plentiful, black bass, pickerel and pike are also plentiful. No fish caught in his district are exported they are all used for home consumption.

Deer are very plentiful this year, and are quite commonly seen in the northern district. There are also a great number of wolves, and there are more bears to be seen than usual. Beaver and otter and grey squirrels are scarce, but skunks and black squirrels are very numerous. Partridges are also plentiful.

The fishing and hunting is done by local people who like to see the law enforced, so no violations of the Act have taken place.

Overseer E. A. Wootton, of Maynooth, reports that this has been a most favourable season with regard to the way in which the laws have been kept.

He strongly recommends that some way should be found to destroy the wolves which have been very plentiful in his district. The opinion of old hunters is that they could be easily poisoned in the summer when they cannot get the deer so easily. If some reliable men could be chosen to put out the poison and the wolves got rid of, it would make a vast difference to the deer, whereas if nothing is done there will soon be few left. From reports received from those who have seen where the deer have been killed in the winter one would judge that the wolves kill ten deer to the hunter's one. He states that the settlers in that locality think that $2 is too much to pay for a deer license, for many of them can ill afford it, and may perhaps only desire to go out for a day or two; if the license fee were 50c,. it would save many a man from breaking the law and more licenses would be sold thereby bringing in a good revenue to the Department.

Beaver are getting more plentiful but mink and muskrats are scarce. Partridges are about the same as they were last year. Ducks are scarce as the feeding grounds are not good. Bears have been very plentiful on account of the bush fires in the north which have driven them south.

HURON COUNTY.

Overseer Robert McMurray, of Bayfield, reports that the fishermen in his division have had a fairly good season. The pound net fishing was not so good as in 1912. The catch of trout has been fairly good, but the bass fishing was not up to the average. Perch were plentiful in April, May and October.

No illegal fishing was brought to his notice and the close seasons were well observed.

Some non-residents of the County desired tug licenses to fish gill nets during 1913, and he thinks the Department did right in not granting these licenses.

The Game Laws have been well observed during the past year.

Black squirrels are becoming plentiful.

KENORA DISTRICT.

Overseer W. G. Muncer, of Minaki, reports that the fishing season has been one of the best for many years, throughout his district very good catches of lake trout have been made. Fox Lake, Vermillion Lake, and Red Deer Lake are excellent trout waters. Good catches of maskinonge have been made in Winnipeg River, some of the fish turning the scale at 25 lbs. He strongly recommends that the close season for lake trout be from October 1st, to November 15th, as he has examined several doe trout during the month of October and found them full of spawn and in every way too far advanced to be taken.

Game, large and small, is good. Moose, caribou and deer are plentiful. Partridges are very much more numerous than last year. Ducks are scarce. Fur-bearing animals are plentiful.

The Game and Fishery Laws have not been well observed, several violations having occurred; three convictions were made and there are others pending.

He recommends that the wolf bounty be increased, as the timber wolf is increasing very quickly; also that residents and non-residents should be obliged to take out a license for guns, as this will check the carrying of guns during the close season; and prevent boys and girls under the age of 15 years from carrying guns at any time.

Fur-bearing animals are very plentiful throughout the G. T. P. line, and trapping is very much on the increase.

KENT COUNTY.

Overseer John Crotty, of Bothwell, reports that there was a decrease in the amount of fish caught this year. There were fewer fishermen, some of whom did not use their nets at all on account of the water being so high. No fish were exported, all that were caught were used for home consumption.

The law was well observed during the season, no infractions having taken place, there were therefore no fines imposed or nets, etc., confiscated. The close season was strictly observed.

Quail and black squirrels are more plentiful owing to the protection given to them. Cottontail rabbits are very plentiful, and in some localities are somewhat destructive.

Overseer John Featherston, of Renwick, reports that owing to the late spring and the presence of the ice late in the season, the pound nets were set about three weeks later than usual. The catch during last fall and the past season has only been fair. Herring have been much larger this year, and a much finer and better fish. Whitefish are on the increase, the catch has more than doubled during the last three years, which speaks well for the work done by the hatcheries. Blue pike also seem to be increasing, but he notices a large quantity of these fish being shipped which he thinks are too small to be of commercial value, and recommends that some regulation should be made setting a definite size or weight on the fish caught. Fishermen with tug licenses have had only a fair season, chiefly owing to so much rough and stormy weather and the fish being nearer the shore, but some fine catches of whitefish were made in the early spring. He estimates that about seventy-five per cent. of the fish caught are exported to the United States.

Game is very scarce, and it will soon be a rare thing to see a game bird Quail have not increased in number and are quite scarce, owing to the lack of cover which enables the hunters to completely annihilate any game birds they should find.

The regulations have been carefully observed and he. is pleased to report that he did not find it necessary to make any prosecutions.

Overseer Richard Little, of *Wallaceburg,* reports that the commercial fishing in his district has been exceptionally good this season.

Angling for bass has been better than last season and pickerel have been fairly plentiful.

On Good Friday last, a terrific wind storm from the south and south west prevailed over the Lake St. Clair district—the wind throughout the day, maintaining a velocity of eighty miles an hour—and as a result the fishermen lost all their nets. Prior to this storm, there were in use eight sets of nets and since the storm but three sets have been used and the catch of fish with the three sets has been greater than it ever was with the eight sets; he is inclined to believe that the storm changed the "bottom" conditions of the fishing grounds, causing the feed to be more plentiful and more fish came into these waters.

The Indians on the Walpole and St. Ann's Island Indian Reserve have, for many years, been engaged in catching carp with seines in waters on and adjoining the reserve, which fish they sell to the commercial fishermen of the district.

Complaints have been made in the past that the drawing of these carp seines damaged the bass spawn on the spawning beds; this year, these Indian fishermen have adopted a new plan to get carp. Instead of travelling over the waters until the carp are located, they now have selected a certain tract where the water is shallow on which they deposit boiled oats as bait for the carp and when a school of carp get on this specially baited feeding ground, the seine is hauled and the Indians have never failed to make a good catch on the baited ground.

The same ground is baited over and over again and these Indians fish almost no where else, so that no damage is done to the bass spawning grounds.

Geese were quite plentiful last spring also ducks, especially canvas-back, redheads and mallard and black ducks are very plentiful.

Snipe and woodcock seem to be increasing slightly and quail are reported to be holding their own in some localities, although there are not nearly so many of these game birds as there were a few years ago.

The Game and Fishery Laws have been fairly well observed in his district during the past year.

Overseer James McVittie, of Blenheim, reports that the fishing in East Kent and Lake Erie was very good, the catch being large and consisting mostly of herring. Not many whitefish were caught in East Kent, but a good catch was reported at times off Point aux Pines. The fall was very rough and many fishermen lost all their stakes and some of their twine, this was a big loss to the fishermen as stakes are hard to get and have to be brought from the north of Michigan. Fall fishing for carp in Rondeau Bay was light, no big catches being reported as has been the case other years. It is generally thought that carp fishing is falling off, they are hard to keep track of as at times they go off into the lake and then come back again like a flock of sheep. The spring of 1913 proved to be very good, although the catches have not been large, the prices were good and have continued so all the season. During July and August there were a tremendous number of fish caught, mostly herring, but they fell off in September and October, and there were scarcely anything but blues and perch caught. There was an improvement again towards the end of October but no herring were caught. White bass or white perch as they are called were very scarce and hardly any to be seen, while some years they are extremely numerous. Carp fishing has not paid expenses all the season. The fishermen are having a great deal of trouble with their ice, last year it did not keep good and it is expensive to have it shipped from other places.

Ducks were very plentiful in the fall of 1912, but the water was rough and it was hard to get at them, quite a number of them stayed in the district all through the year, and are now very plentiful. Deer in the Government Park were getting so thick that the Department had a man shoot 98 and they were sold at 10c. per lb.

The laws have been well observed, no one being fined, and all license fees were paid early in the season.

Angling season was good, quite a number of permits were sold to Americans.

Overseer T. Peltier, of Dover South, reports that the number of fish caught by the licensed fishermen has been about average.

Dredging operations in the River Thames and mouth thereof has interfered with angling in that locality and there have been no non-resident anglers.

The roll nets used by the farmers along the river have proved satisfactory, sufficient being taken for their own use, but not in large enough quantities to interfere with the run of fish in the river, and none have been used for commercial purposes.

Ducks are plentiful this fall, but quail and other game birds are scarce and would warrant continued restriction in hunting.

LAMBTON COUNTY.

Overseer H. A. Blunden, of Sarnia, reports that the fishing season opened very much as usual with periods of high winds which made it hard for pound net fishermen to set their nets.

By keeping a close watch he is able to see that the law regarding undersized fish is being well observed.

The fishermen report rather a light catch this year, but it is difficult to estimate till the close of the season.

Quail and partridges are not so plentiful in the more settled parts of the County as they are further inland.

Black squirrels are more plentiful this season. Muskrats are holding their own in spite of the high price of pelts. Wild geese do not seem to be so numerous as usually but wild ducks are more plentiful than former years.

LANARK COUNTY.

Overseer George Burke, of Perth, reports that last November he was on the Rideau Lake assisting Mr. Phillips and Mr. Best look after the whitefish. If the inland lakes were as well looked after as the Rideau Lake the law-breakers would not find much opportunity of committing infractions. Mr. Best and he seized one gill net. They patrolled every night from dark until day break, using a drag, and there was no illegal work done while they were there.

Bass fishing in Otty Lake was very good, this is the best lake for bass in the district. Pike, pickerel and bass were good in the Tay River. Pickerel were biting well at the lower end of Christies Lake.

He thinks there should be a hatchery on the Rideau Lake, as they could furnish pickerel spawn from the Tay River, and salmon spawn from the Rideau Lake.

There were quite a few deer seen at the end of the town. Ducks and partridges are about average. Muskrafs and mink were plentiful last spring.

Very few complaints of law-breakers have reached him, and those which have come to his notice have not resulted in convictions as he was unable to obtain any evidence.

Overseer Ephraim Deacon, of Bolingbroke, reports that the close season for the fish was well observed. There have been no violations of the law this season.

The fishing has not been so good as in former years. He cannot understand why this should have been so.

He sold quite a number of angling permits during the season, but many of the visitors were provided with permits before they arrived.

Muskrats seem to be plentiful, but mink were scarce. Partridges were more plentiful than they have been other years. Ducks are quite scarce. Deer are more numerous, which fact he attributes to the hunters only being allowed one deer each.

Overseer William Pepper, of Lanark, reports that there have been no violations of the law during the year, of which he could obtain evidence, but several rumours have reached him, which upon being investigated, he could get no one to swear to the veracity of their statements.

With regard to the fish, the Mississippi River seems to be becoming well stocked with pickerel; they are now taken quite easily, whereas a year or two ago, it was difficult to catch one. Black bass are gradually becoming more scarce.

With regard to game, deer seem to be more plentiful this year than they have been for several years. Partridges are also more plentiful. Whilst driving along the road they are continually to be seen getting up in front of the rig. Ducks are not so plentiful as they were a few years ago; only some isolated flocks are to be seen occasionally.

Overseer J. H. Phillips, of Smith's Falls, reports that during the month of November he patrolled the Rideau Lake with a row boat, in order to see that the laws regarding the close season for whitefish and salmon trout were observed. Gill net licenses were granted from Dec. 1st to 10th, and during that time he remained at the lake to see that no illegal fishing was done. It was reported that few fish were caught in the deep water. It was a wise move on the part of the Department to change the close season to Oct 5th to November 5th, as this gives the salmon better protection.

During February and March he spent his time taking lyng from Otty Lake. In March, he made frequent trips to see that no rat houses were interfered with, and during April he watched to see that no spearing was done or dip nets used.

On April 16th, he received a report that muskrat houses were being broken into, and the rats shot. He went to Chesterville to investigate the matter, and secured sufficient evidence to convict the offenders, who were fined $25.

May was spent in the same way as April.

On June 5th he went to Kingston with his crew to fetch the Patrol boat "Ella C." After having the boiler tested they left Kingston and commenced the season's patrol work between Smith's Falls, Newboro and Merrickville.

The fishing on the Rideau has been good on the whole this year. In the early part of the season, salmon fishing was never better, and remained fairly good all the summer. Bass fishing was good, many large fish being caught, some of which weighed five or six pounds. He thinks it would be a good thing if a limit were put on the number of salmon caught each day by one person, as he knows of a man who caught as many as 29 in one day. The consequence is the tourists cannot get guides as they say they can catch all the fish they want without rowing the visitors.

He did not sell as many permits as usual this year, but the Rideau was crowded all the summer by residents of the Province and Ottawa people. Every boarding house was full. Many new cottages were built and the lake is becoming very popular.

He thinks it would be wise to stop shooting on duck grounds during the close season, as anyone can go into the marsh with a gun and pretend they are shooting black birds. He kept a close watch on the duck grounds and found none being shot before the season began.

The laws and regulations were fairly well observed in his district during the past year. In May he had some people fined for spearing with a jack-light and fishing with a dip-net without a license. He also had a man fined for using a drive net at Pike Falls. On October 19th, he seized three gill nets in Big Rideau, containing nine salmon. These latter he turned over to the hospitals, and had the owners of the nets and his assistant fined $25 and $15, respectively. He seized one other gill net, but was unable to find the owner.

Wild ducks and partridges are very plentiful this year, and there were quite a number of muskrats to be seen in the spring.

Overseer Fred Stanzel, of Carleton Place, reports that he has been over his district a number of times during the past year, and has always found the law well observed. He has received a few complaints, which when investigated, proved to be incorrect, he has, therefore, made no conviction.

Rough fish are plentiful and the catch of bass has been about normal.

During the early part of the duck season, they were a little scarce, but there is now an abundance of game. The partridge season opened with plenty of game, but they are getting pretty well thinned out now. Muskrats have not been quite so plentiful and mink are very scarce.

Overseer Hugh Wilson, of Elphin, reports that the fishing in his district was very poor.

Partridges were scarce.

Deer appear to be quite plentiful.

The Game and Fishery Laws were well observed during the year.

LEEDS COUNTY.

Overseer W. J. Birch, of Delta, reports that he made frequent trips by water over Upper and Lower Beverly Lakes, during November, and continued them until the water froze over and he was obliged to stop. This is the time of the year when rod fishing is done and illegal fishing with nets or spearing with torch lights carried on, but he found none of this, although several reports reached him of such work.

Bass fishing in Lower Beverly Lake was not so good as it has been other years, but Upper Beverly was much better, some fine catches being made. This lake has been licensed for coarse fish for thirty years and more, which is improving the bass fishing.

Ducks were quite numerous last November, and large numbers shot; he would like to see a limit set on the number shot by each man, the same as for partridges.

He made several trips to inspect the grounds where muskrats build their houses, and found some of them disturbed, but he was able to find the offender and brought him before a Justice of the Peace, who fined him. This did a considerable amount of good as he heard of no other trouble during the season, and when spring came the muskrats seemed to be more plentiful than the previous year; he would, however, advise that their close season begin on May 1st, and continue until March 1st, and that trappers should be obliged to take out a license.

There are very few mink left, and if there is not a close season provided for them for at least three years they will become quite extinct. Black squirrels are quite plentiful, but he considers that the season opens a month too late for them. Partidges are increasing slowly.

There is no summer hotel or boarding house there, so they get very few tourists, and there are not many angling permits or Guides' licenses sold.

The cottage owners report that the season has been a good one.

The Laws and Regulations have been very well observed in this district.

Overseer Gordon H. Clark, of Westport, reports that the fishing has not been so good this year as in former years.

Muskrats, black squirrels and partridges are very plentiful, but mink are very scarce. Ducks have been unusually numerous, and very few have been shot. Deer is quite plentiful, but he thinks people owning dogs should keep them shut up during the close season, as they chase the deer and do much harm.

Overseer H. N. Covell, of Lombardy, reports that he has kept a close watch over his territory this year, and there have been no violations of the Fishery Laws.

There have been no tourists in his division this season, as the accommodation round the lake is very poor.

Black suckers are very thick in Otter Creek in the spring, but they do not last very long.

Black squirrels are getting very plentiful also partridges. Black ducks are not so plentiful as they were other years. Mink are very scarce and he thinks the open season for muskrats should be shorter as they are getting scarce.

Overseer John McGuire, of Jones Falls, reports that during the month of November, 1912, he and his assistant kept up a constant patrol of the waters in his district with the launch "Mermaid." During January, February and March, he spent his time seeing that the fishermen got their licenses renewed, and made trips to the different fishing grounds to see that bass fishing through the ice was not being carried on. He found it rather difficult to stop some of the fishermen from doing this, as they did not like being deprived of the fish they had previously been allowed to catch.

On March 17th, he found a great many muskrat houses cut open and traps set in them. He seized eleven traps, and although he called on a number of the trappers they all denied ownership to the traps and he was unable to prove anything.

Last winter being an open one, trapping commenced early. Muskrats were very scarce, this, he thinks, was caused by some unprincipled trappers catching them during the winter. He thinks this should be prohibited and the close season continued until March.

On May 15th he began to get the "Mermaid" in order for the season. He had the engine thoroughly over-hauled, and the boat generally painted and varnished; by June 1st she was ready to commence patrol service, and throughout the summer he and his assistant kept up a constant patrol of the Rideau Canal waters from Newboro to Kingston.

The fishing was good, and the visitors were pleased with their sport. During July, the hotels and boarding houses were filled to over-flowing, and all agreed that the fishing was never better. Not many tourists brought in the limit that they are allowed to catch, i.e., 8 daily, they preferred to return the fish to the water after they were caught, as they were anxious for the sport, and did not want to spoil it for another year. This keen interest in the welfare of the fisheries is probably the reason for the large improvement of the fishing in this district. After eight year's experience as a Game and Fishery overseer he notices the difference in the appearance and size of the bass spread out on the hotel lawns in Jones Falls and Chaffeys Lock; where 7 lb. bass were sometimes to be seen, and 6½ lb. bass were quite a frequent occurrence. A salmon caught by J. G. Morton, of Peekskill, N.Y., weighing 22½ lbs. was on view in the store at Jones Falls. The next largest which was caught weighed 17½ lbs., and the next 9½ lbs., and so on. Eight years ago fish of this size were unknown in his district, so it is encouraging to notice the improvement, and the waters show no signs of becoming depleted.

During August, one man acting as a guide without a license was brought before a Justice of the Peace and fined $5 and costs.

A great quantity of salmon were caught all along the Rideau Canal, mainly trolling. They have never been known to bite the hook as they have done this season. It was difficult at times to get guides, they found they could make more money by catching salmon and selling them, and it is his opinion that unless some restrictions are put on salmon they will soon be a thing of the past. He thinks four salmon to each rod would be a fair restriction; he knows of one man who caught 30 salmon one morning, during the beginning of October, in Devil Lake, and at the end of two days fishing he had 70 salmon, weighing from 2½ lbs. to 10 lbs. each. During this part of the season there were about 20 boats on Devil Lake, and if they had the same luck it would not be a very good thing for salmon. He knows other instances of a similar nature occurring on Dog, Loughboro and Rideau Lakes.

The duck season opened on October 15th, with very few ducks about. Partridges are also very scarce. Black squirrels were very plentiful, and did considerable harm to the farmers' crops during September and October. He thinks it would be an improvement if the 15 days open season were placed a month earlier.

On October 25th, it was reported that the laws regarding the close season for salmon were being violated in a barefaced manner, so he went to Battersea

ROCK BASS
(*Ambloplites rupestris*)

for tl
l.m
l.gil
no
begi
day
fad
feh
wa1
in
Ov
a
He
th
m

g
n

for the purpose of carrying on a night patrol on Loughboro Lake, taking with him J. L. Sears, who is well acquainted with the lake. They grappled nearly all night with no result. The three following nights they were out again but with no better result. However, on Wednesday, they noticed that the salmon had begun spawning, and at about midnight they came across a large net, and by daylight they had grappled 500 yards of extra heavy gill net. They could not find out who had set these nets, as they waited until after daybreak when the fishermen usually come for their nets, and no one appeared; either they had been watching the operations of the "Mermaid," or else they intended leaving them in until the following night. The launch left for Battersea with the nets, and Overseer McGuire intended returning again the following night, but he contracted a heavy cold and was unfortunately unable to follow up the seizure of the nets. He thinks there must have been seven or eight men operating these nets, as they were all different from each other, and he intends to follow up any clues he may have as soon as possible.

Overseer George M. Slate, of Rockport, reports that the season has been a good one. Black bass have been quite plentiful, but pike and maskinonge have not been so good as other years.

Black squirrel are plentiful, but ducks are scarce.

There have been a great many guide licenses sold.

Overseer William Spence, of Athens, reports that he has kept a close watch over his division, and has found that the Game and Fishery Laws have been very well observed. There being only four cases of illegal fishing at the beginning of the year.

More tourists visited the lake this summer than last, and everybody agreed that the salmon fishing was better than it has ever been. He thinks it would be a good thing to set a limit of four salmon to be caught during one day by each angler, as has been done other years. Bass fishing was about the same.

There were plenty of ducks and partridges. He recommends that there should be a limit set on the number of ducks killed by each person to stop hunters coming from other places to shoot. Mink, black squirrel and muskrats are scarce. He thinks there should be a close season for fox, coon, and skunk, the same as there is for mink.

Overseer J. H. Stewart, of Brockville, reports that the fishing has been better this year than it has been for many years, especially black bass, pickerel and maskinonge on the St. Lawrence River.

The fishing laws have been well observed, no cases of illegal work having come to his notice.

Ducks and partridges were plentiful this fall.

He made five convictions for illegal hunting; two for shooting deer, and three for shooting ducks out of season.

Overseer George Toner, of Gananoque, reports that game and fish have been very plentiful during the past year. Many excellent game fish have been caught. Both partridge and ducks are increasing in number and have been very plentiful, as well as black and grey squirrels. Muskrats have not been so plentiful as in former years.

4 G.F.

He recommends that the close season for trapping muskrats be extended to March 1st, and the season for trapping be from March 1st to May 1st, he also recommends that a small license fee of about $2 be charged those who engage in trapping. His reason for this is, that it would prevent small boys and others from trapping and catching muskrats during the early part of the season when the' fur is not very valuable. He has found many rat houses which have been cut open in January and February, and if trapping were prohibited during those two months it might put some check on the practice.

There were not as many tourists as usual visiting the district this season, he thinks this is accounted for by the great increase in the number of automobiles in use.

He recommends that non-residents in his district should be obliged to take out a license to fish, the same as in other districts, as, during the spring, he has found as many as thirty Americans fishing in Canadian waters for bullheads, and as it is impossible for him to watch all the sections both day and night, they may have resorted to methods of fishing which are strictly prohibited to residents.

Overseer James Townsend, of Long Point, reports that the law has been well observed, and the season was a very successful one. He sold more permits than during any previous year.

Fishing has been fair and the prospects are good for another year for the tourists say they are coming again.

He recommends that the lake be re-stocked with bass, and that a day's catch be reduced to six instead of eight.

Some very fine catches of salmon were made during the warm weather by deep trolling. He recommends that their close season be changed to October instead of November, as this is their spawning season.

Game is fairly plentiful, there are quite a number of partridges and black squirrels, it is his opinion that trappers should be licensed, also guns.

During the summer the Department of Public Works expended about $400 in clearing the rapids from Lyndhurst to Marble Rock, making them navigable for motor boats, which is very beneficial as it will probably increase the number of visitors, and it is very much appreciated by the motorists.

Overseer J. R. Wight, of Newboro, reports that the fishing has been good this season, if anything, bass have been larger and more plentiful. The only falling off in the fishing which has been reported this year is that the herring have been completely fished out, this he thinks is due to the warmer weather during the fall. There has been a great decrease in the number of American tourists, a large number of anglers come from Ottawa. The high water favoured the fish this year, allowing them to reach feeding beds which they were unable to get to last year. With regard to black bass, a great many tourists catch too small fish, he suggests that they should weigh at least two pounds or be thrown back into the water. The lakes have been well stocked with fish, and there is not much danger of their being over fished.

He thinks the muskrat season should not open until April, otherwise it gives the hunters a chance to destroy the rats' houses. It is reported that the season has been a good one for game, and the people seem interested in the preservation of the fish and game. Ducks have been scarce, mink were also scarce last winter, but partridges and black squirrels were plentiful.

LENNOX COUNTY.

Overseer P. W. Dafoe, of Napanee, reports that the fishermen seem contented with their catch.

The law has been well observed, no real complaints have reached him with the exception of one case, though this he believed to be an unintentional, though careless mistake in the date of the open season for ducks.

Fish.

It is his opinion that the close season for pickerel in the southern part of Ontario is a week or two too late as the run is nearly over before the close season begins, and there is no way to protect them as they pile up at the falls.

There have been more maskinonge caught in Napanee River this season than there ever were in any one season before.

Game.

Deer are plentiful and about 45 hunters have gone north from Napanee.

Partridges are plentiful, and ducks are holding their own. Muskrats are a little scarce.

Raccoons are plentiful, but they need a little better protection.

Overseer E. M. Huffman, of Hay Bay, reports that the season has been a quiet one, and on the whole the laws have been well observed by the fishermen. The close season for whitefish was the busiest time as the people seemed determined to catch them, and the mouth of Hay Bay is a great fishing ground. Twice he was out nearly all night; the first time he found about a thousand yards of gill net, and the second night he discovered ten nets which had just been lifted, concealed in some bushes. He had one party fined. It is usually holders of domestic licenses who do this work, as they find October too early to keep fish for the winter. He does not favour the extension of time given to the close season as the fishermen always want a little longer.

Game has been very good this season. He thinks that it would be a good thing if the sale of ducks were prohibited, as some people simply shoot them for sale, and it would improve the sport if this were not allowed. Muskrats are not so plentiful, he recommends a shorter season for them and also that trappers should be required to take out a license.

LINCOLN COUNTY.

Overseer J. C. May, of St. Catharines, reports that the fishermen have begun their fall fishing, and are well satisfied with the catches they make, as herring are still plentiful, more so than any other species of fish.

There is very little game in his district, pheasant being the principal bird, and they are not very numerous.

Fur-bearing animals are very scarce.

The Rules and Regulations have been well observed by the fishermen in his district.

Overseer Oliver Taylor, *of Niagara-on-the-Lake*, reports that this has been the poorest fishing season at the mouth of the Niagara River that the fishermen have ever known. Having discussed the matter with the fishermen, they have come to the conclusion that it must be on account of the polluted water coming down the river, as the fish will not come into this water.

Owners of trap nets above Queenston have done nothing.

♦ The Fishery Laws were well observed, with the exception of several lines which he found illegally set and which he seized early in the spring.

He only sold eight angling permits as the season was a very poor one.

There is very little game in his district beyond pheasants and they are very plentiful this fall.

Muskrats were quite plentiful round the ponds last spring.

MANITOULIN DISTRICT.

Overseer J. J. Avis, *of Cockburn Island*, reports that the season this year has been an average one, very much the same as it was in 1912, except that there were no pound nets set, no American tourists came, and therefore there were no angling permits sold. He states that he does not think the trout spawn should be conveyed from the waters in his district to stock the lakes in the east, but that the spawn which is taken from those waters should be raised to young fry to re-stock Lake Huron or the North Channel of the Georgian Bay. It is his opinion that the reason for the scarcity of whitefish is because the spawn is destroyed by other kinds of fish, and that the fishermen in that district agree with him in saying that the close season through November should be abolished, and one or two hatcheries established. It is their firm belief that if this were done the lakes would, in the course of a few years, be once more teaming with fish. When these hatcheries have been established he would suggest that the fishermen's twine should be reduced to half the present length.

With regard to the game, partridges, ducks, rabbits and deer are numerous, and there are a few stray moose.

The Game and Fishery Laws have been well observed.

Overseer W. M. Boyd, *of Kagawong*, reports that the season just closed has been an exceptionally pleasant and profitable one for the tourists who visited Kagawong in order to fish in the lake. Never does he remember such a successful season for angling, when such splendid catches were made; the fish were large and in many cases the limit was caught in a couple of hours.

The Game and Fishery Regulations were well observed.

Ducks were very plentiful, but partridges do not seem to be so numerous, they are perhaps the most difficult bird to protect. He thinks still fewer should be allowed to be shot during the day, half a dozen should be enough to satisfy any sportsman, and it would help to increase the numbers for another year.

He never remembers deer being so plentiful on Manitoulin Island as they are this year, the farmers are getting their limit apparently all over the island.

Mink and muskrats are increasing, especially the latter.

Overseer Andrew Hall, *of Gore Bay*, reports that brook trout have been very plentiful, although they do not seem to be as large as usual.

If mill owners were compelled to build proper slides at their dams it would be a great benefit.

Commercial fishing has been good.

Bass have been very plentiful, large numbers having been caught. The law regarding angling has been well observed; and he has visited the different fishing stations several times.

Partridges have been fairly plentiful, large numbers were killed during the open season, and he believes that the law regarding the limit on the "bag" is being strictly observed.

Ducks seem to be more scarce than usual, and not many were killed.

Red deer are becoming more plentiful every year, in spite of the large number killed each season.

A great many farmers take advantage of the Order-in-Council of April 20th, 1911.

Muskrats are plentiful, but mink rather scarce. Very few people except the Indians are engaged in the trapping business. He would suggest that those engaged in trapping fur-bearing animals protected by Game Laws should be obliged to pay a small sum for a license to permit them to do so.

To the best of his knowledge the Game and Fishery Laws have been well observed, only two cases of illegal work having come to his notice. One for taking mink and muskrat and the other was an Indian who shot partridges out of season.

Overseer Joseph Hembruff, of Manitowaning, reports that the angling for bass has been fairly good, but there were not so many large fish caught as there were last year. He thinks that the open season for bass should begin on July 1st, as they have not finished spawning by June 15th. Speckled trout are not very plentiful.

Partridges are very scarce this year, and ducks verey plentiful. Deer are about the same as last year.

There have been a great many tourists visiting the district this summer, and they have all observed the laws well.

Overseer David Irwin, of Little Current, reports as follows:

Commercial Fishing.—The season just closed has been fairly successful from a commercial point of view; all fishermen report as good a season as last year, and some better than for many years.

Game.—Big game, moose, deer, etc., according to reports are as plentiful as last season, and on the Manitoulin many state that there is an increase in the number of red deer.

Partridges in general are as plentiful as last season.

Angling for black bass and other game fish was better than last season and more tourists have visited the district.

Ducks were more plentiful than last season.

The Game and Fishery Laws have been well observed throughout the district.

Overseer James Lewis, of Shequiandah, reports that the commercial fishing has been much better at the majority of places in his district this year. The fish packers are more careful not to pack undersized fish, and very little illegal fishing is done. Black bass are numerous but not easily caught. He recommends that the size of sturgeon caught be limited, as they are getting very scarce, and if something isn't done there will be no sturgeon in most of the fishing grounds in a very short time. He thinks the ten days extension given in November is a mistake, as the trout are all spawned by November 10th.

Deer are quite plentiful, but moose are moving further back. Ducks are plentiful, but partridges are very scarce; he recommends that there should be no open season for partridges for 1914.

Overseer David Pyette, of Tehkummah, reports that he has made many trips along the streams under his jurisdiction and has seen no illegal fishing.

Speckled trout have been reported to be very scarce all through the district, very few good catches having been made. He strongly recommends that there should be one year's close season for speckled trout on the Manitoulin Island.

Partridges are exceedingly scarce, and he considers ten birds a day for each person far too many, and recommends that, if not closed altogether for two or three years, the season should be shortened to from November 1st to November 15th.

He considers it a grave mistake to have the hare season open two weeks sooner than the partridge, as it allows unscrupulous persons the liberty of carrying guns in the bush and killing young partridges under the pretence of hare hunting.

Deer are reported more plentiful than they were a few years ago, and he thinks they would be comparatively safe on the Manitoulin Island until November 1st, if the partridge and hare seasons opened at that time also.

Finally he recommends that the season for deer, partridge, and hare should open on November 1st, and that the deer and partridge should close on November 15th and hare on December 1st.

Overseer James Ramesbottom, of Little Current, reports that the commercial fishing has been good this season.

Pickerel were more plentiful than they have been for many years.

Bass was about the same as last year.

More tourists visited his district this summer than other seasons.

Partridges were about the same as other years.

Deer and moose were plentiful.

MIDDLESEX COUNTY.

Overseer William Boler, of Byron, reports that the laws have been very well observed, no violations came to his notice.

Squirrels are more numerous than last year. Partridges and quail are nearly extinct, he only saw one of each this year. Geese and ducks are around in small flocks. There were several sea-gulls on the river late last Fall.

He recommends that guns should be licensed, as it would put a stop to a number of people who come out from the towns to shoot anything.

On Thanksgiving Day he was making his rounds, when he came upon an Italian who threatened to shoot him if he came any nearer and pointed his gun at him. Overseer Boler was alone, but the Italian had a companion.

It is his opinion that there should be two overseers in that district during the shooting season.

Overseer J. D. Campbell, of Sylvan, reports that the law has been well observed in his division, some few reports of illegal work came to his notice but nothing to warrant a conviction.

The catch of fish in inland waters has increased and they are very plentiful, but in the lake the fishing has not been up to the average.

The two fishways in this division are in good repair.

Small game have increased, ducks, partridges, and squirrels being very plentiful. He would recommend a greater restriction on ice fishing, as he deems it to be very injurious to the fisheries.

Overseer W. E. Collins, of Strathroy, reports that the law has been fairly well observed in his district.

The fishing was about the same as usual, pike, bass and pickerel being quite plentiful.

There are hardly any quail or partridges in this district, as there is so little cover for them. Squirrels are plentiful, but mink and muskrats are scarce, and he thinks the coons should be protected.

Overseer Arthur Corsant, of Masonville, reports that the law has been well observed in his district, no illegal fishing having come to his notice.

There were more coarse fish caught this year, but bass was about the same as it was last year.

Quail and partridges are very scarce, also mink and muskrats. Black squirrel are more plentiful this year, they seem to be on the increase, but he thinks it would be wise to prohibit the killing of squirrels for at least two years.

Overseer J. M. Temple, of Dorchester, reports that the Game and Fishery Laws have been fairly well observed by the country people, as their time is occupied by the care of their farms; but there are a certain number of people in the small villages and larger cities who own guns, and who, with the excuse of shooting woodcock, take their guns and dogs, and if a partridge gets up within range it is shot. Numbers of them come from the city, some drive and others motor, but those who come in by the train are watched more easily.

Game is scarce in his district, with the exception of black squirrel, and there are a number of them. Mink is almost extinct, and muskrats very scarce; there are a few houses being built, but not many. He only noticed one that had been destroyed last winter, but could not find out who did it.

He would recommend that everyone should be obliged to take out a license for carrying a gun in the game districts, also for trapping, as it would stop the boys from interfering with the game and fur animals, also insectiverous birds and birds of song. The overseers should be allowed to sell the licenses, as they would then know who had them, and they should be obtained before game comes into season. He thinks $5 for each rifle or shot gun would be a fair price to charge.

There are no fox, otter or beaver in his district, and ducks are very scarce.

Overseer S. Turner, of London, reports that the Fish Laws have been very well observed in his district this season, which is no doubt owing to the close watch he has kept.

Fishing is not as good as it should be, and he thinks this is owing to the shallowness of the water and the unusual number of fishermen who participate in the sport. Saturday being a half-holiday most of the manufacturers and their employees spend the afternoon angling.

With regard to the Game Laws, he would like to see the season for partridge, quail and squirrel all come at the same time, viz., November 15th—December 15th, as he thinks it would save much confusion and many birds.

MUSKOKA DISTRICT.

Overseer F. A. Hanes, of Huntsville, reports that bass and speckled trout are increasing and coming up the rivers and creeks more, as he has taken the trouble to find out where they are.

There are several lakes which should be stocked with bass and speckled trout, this could be done at a very small cost.

Deer are increasing very fast, and he has seen more this year than he has seen for the last five years; another man who has been out a great deal says the same thing.

When the season opened there were a great many partridges round the lakes, but ducks are scarce as there is not much feed for them.

Mink are plentiful and beaver seem to be increasing; he has seen several in the lakes.

Muskrats are decreasing.

Overseer William Robinson, of Kilworthy, reports that the law has been fairly well observed in his division this season. The tourists have had a good summer and there have been more campers this year than for many seasons.

The fishing was good at the beginning of the season, but during the last two weeks in July and the month of August it was astonishing what a number of undersized dead fish were floating on the water. A fish which has swallowed the hook cannot be saved, and Overseer Robinson thinks that if there was no restriction as to size there would not be so many fish destroyed. He thinks the restriction as to the number caught a good thing, so that if an undersized fish is caught that would count as one, and not be thrown back to die and another one caught in its place.

Deer seem to be plentiful. Partridges and ducks are about the same as last year. Muskrat, otter, and beaver are increasing fast, and mink are more plentiful this season than last.

There are three mills in his division, but they are keeping their refuse out of the rivers and lakes.

Overseer William Smith, of Gravenhurst, reports that he has made a diligent patrol of the Muskoka Lakes throughout the year, five months of which—June to October—he was in charge of patrol boat "Meenagha."

During this time all the summer resorts were visited frequently and all back channels and islands which could not be reached by steamer were thoroughly patrolled.

He found that the Game and Fishery Laws were well observed, there being only one violation of the Fishery Regulations, which was the setting of a net in Lake Rosseau, but he failed to apprehend the owner.

There were two violations of the Game Laws, a conviction was made in one case, but the other was dismissed.

The fishing in June and July was better than during previous years, but in August the very hot and smoky atmosphere kept the anglers from the water.

Two car loads of bass fingerlings were deposited in the lakes during the season, which he feels sure will add greatly to the stocking already done.

He thinks the partridges and ducks will compare favourably with last year, although the great territories which were swept by fires destroyed many partridges.

It is reported that beaver are on the increase round the waters in his district, also muskrats and mink.

It is difficult to estimate the number of deer, as the bush fires scattered them and they went to search for green bush to live in.

Overseer John Traves, of Fraserburg, reports that there are four townships in his district. He found that the hunters succeeded in obtaining their number of deer. He visited quite a number of hunting parties and inspected their licenses. They say that deer and partridges have increased considerably.

Ducks were fairly plentiful last fall, mink is scarce but slightly on the increase.

The fishing last spring was not so good as it was the previous year, owing to the cold, and then to the height of the water after the fine weather. Angling for bass and trout was fairly good.

He has patrolled the woods carefully every month in the year and has found that during the last six or seven years beaver and muskrats have been very plentiful; there are also quite a number of otter. Mink is scarce but on the increase since the close season was provided for them.

No violations have occurred in his district this year, and he is satisfied that the settlers in and around the neighbourhood have observed the laws well.

He is a faithful servant and takes great pleasure in improving the game in every way.

NIPISSING DISTRICT.

Overseer Joseph Rivet, of Sturgeon Falls, reports that the fishing was not so good this year as it has been other years.

There has been no illegal fishing in Lake Nipissing and its tributaries.

The Game and Fishery Laws have been well observed to the best of his knowledge.

NORFOLK COUNTY.

Overseer J. S. Smith, of Port Rowan, reports that the seine fishing in the Bay was not up to the average this season. Bass fishing was very poor, and there were not as many tourists in his district as there were last year. Gill net and pound net fishing has been about average. There have been several violations of the law and fines have been imposed.

Plover and snipe are very scarce, but wild ducks are as plentiful as usual. Partridges and woodcock are scarce, but in some sections black squirrels are extremely plentiful.

NORTHUMBERLAND COUNTY.

Overseer C. H. Cassan, of Campbellford, reports that the fishing has been fairly good in some parts of the river. A good deal of dredging was carried on which made the water dirty and he thinks that accounts for the fishing not being so good. The water has been lowered so often that it has interfered with the fishing; he recommends that something be done to keep the water at a regular height during the spawning season, as during the last two springs it was lowered to such an extent that it was possible to walk along the shore and see the spawn lying on the swamps all dried up, which is of course a very bad thing for the fish.

There have not been so many tourist visitors this year as there were last. He recommends that the waters be stocked with bass as they give the best sport, and something must be done to keep up the supply of fish. He thinks it would be a good thing if a bass hatchery were established in his district, as the contract for the Trent Valley Canal is nearly through and there would be no trouble in getting a dredge to clean out a place.

The Trent waters from Campbellford to Trent Bridge are good and there is every accommodation for those seeking sport in that neighbourhood.

He had some trouble watching the district where the contract for the Trent Valley Canal is being carried out, as there are so many foreigners working there.

He suggests that there should be a close season for frogs, and thinks that the prohibition of fishing through the ice an excellent regulation.

He finds it difficult to get guides, and thinks that the license they take out for this work should also entitle them to hunt deer.

Ducks are more plentiful this year than last, partridges also seem quite numerous. He recommends that the open season for hare and partridge should begin on the same day, as people hunting hares are apt to shoot partridges.

He thinks the close season for muskrats a good thing, but that it would be an improvement if the open season were for the months of March and April.

Overseer Thomas H. Cheer, of Brighton, reports that the laws have been well observed in his district this season.

The catch of trout and whitefish has been very good, much better than last year, the rougher varieties have been exceptionally good, especially pike, which have been more than double what they were last year.

Ducks of all species were very scarce early in the season. He thinks it was owing to the very mild fall, however of late they have been very numerous, more so than in previous years.

Partridges are still very scarce, about the same as last season, but black and grey squirrels are becoming more scarce every year. He thinks the season should be made very short. Muskrats are becoming very scarce, he attributes this to the winter trapping, as their dens and houses are destroyed and they are left to perish, and he suggests that the open season be from March 15th to April 30th.

Mink are almost extinct in this district, he thinks this is on account of the long open season, and the very high price paid for the fur, which causes them to be hunted relentlessly, he would advise a much shorter open season for them or stop them from being trapped for two or three years.

Deer are reported to be very plentiful this season, the limit of one deer for each man has been a means of improving the quantity.

Overseer H. W. Hayes, of Trenton, reports that herring are very plentiful, but whitefish seem to be scarce in Lake Ontario.

Ducks are very plentiful. He was informed that two men killed as many as 150 in a day.

Mink and muskrats are scarce. He would still advise that there be a close season for them for two years.

Black and grey squirrels seem to be increasing.

There have been no violations of the law in his district this year.

Overseer J. H. Hess, of Hastings, reports that the Game and Fishery Laws have been well regarded in his district. He thinks that the public have come to the conclusion that it is necessary to protect the game and fish.

The fishing was good at the beginning of the season and some excellent catches were made, the quality being above the average, but for some reason, later in the season it was almost impossible to catch a fish.

Ducks were plentiful this season, and very little illegal work was done.

Overseer W. H. Johnson of Harwood, reports that the Game and Fishery Laws have been fairly well kept in his district, with the exception of "shooting before sunrise and after sunset." He thinks that if the overseers could work together in a different manner from what they have been doing, the Game and Fishery Laws would be better observed.

The water in the lake was higher than usual during the spawning season, but it fell quite rapidly, leaving the spawn and little fish to perish in the marshes. Maskinonge fishing was not quite so good as it was last year, but bass fishing was better and the tourists were well pleased.

Black and wood ducks were not so plentiful, but the other species of duck were about the same as last year.

Black and grey squirrels and partridges are very scarce. He thinks that either the season should be closed for three or four years or the open season shortened.

Rabbits are quite plentiful. Mink very scarce, and muskrat trapping not so good as last year. He strongly recommends that there be only one month of trapping and that the month of April.

Overseer A. J. Kent, of Bewdley, reports that the laws were well observed with regard to the fish. The past season was a record one, the fishing being the finest that has been known for many years.

Muskrats were not very plentiful last spring, and he recommends that the open season be shortened. Ducks and black squirrels are very numerous and partridges seem to be on the increase.

Tourists are beginning to find this district a good one for sport, and it is expected that next season there wil be an increase in the number of visitors, as a summer hotel has been erected for the accommodation of those seeking good fishing and shooting.

Considering everything, he is well satisfied with the result of the season.

Overseer J. R. McAllister, of Gore's Landing, reports that during April and May bass and maskinonge were as plentiful as other years, but except for the first two weeks of the open season, maskinonge fishing was very poor. During the first week in September when the fishing should be good, two men from Sodus, New York, fished for six days, mostly for maskinonge, and caught one fish. Bass fishing was a great deal better.

Ducks are as plentiful as last year. At the time of writing there are a great many round the lake.

Other game, such as grouse, rail, squirrels, rabbits, are the same as last year.

The law regarding both fish and game has been well observed in his division, but he heard that the Indians are doing pretty much as they like on the rice beds near the mouth of the Indian River.

There were not so many visitors as last year on account of the poor fishing.

Muskrats were very scarce as usual, and will continue to be until the season for trapping them is shortened; he considers that from March 15th–May 1st, quite long enough for the open season.

The people are not satisfied with the change in the law with regard to the time of day when ducks may be shot. They want it as it was before, half an hour before sunrise and half an hour after sunset. He himself thinks that the shooting should begin as soon as ducks can see the decoys and the hunters can see to shoot properly.

He took a note of this on October 31st, when he was on Spook Island facing the east, and by his watch it was 40 minutes from the time that it was possible to see to shoot until sunrise.

Overseer F. H. Meneilley, of Warkworth, reports that the fishing in the waters of the Trent River was good during the past summer. All kinds of fish seem to be increasing, this he attributes to the use of nets being abolished.

All the fish caught in his district is used locally.

The close seasons have been well observed, although there are always some who would not observe them if it were not for fear of the law. He has spent a good deal of time in seeing that the law was observed.

He caught one man spearing illegally and prosecuted him and had him fined.

He warned all mill owners not to throw refuse in the rivers or creeks.

There are fishways left in the new dams on the Trent Canal for the free passage of the fish.

Overseer James Redfearn, of Lakeport, reports that on the whole the fishing was up to the average, some of the fishermen doing better at Cobourg than during past seasons.

During the season he visited his district many times, and on all occasions found everything in order. He also watched Cobourg Harbour and interior and found no illegal fishing being carried on, although he thought several people were that way inclined, and that his presence put a stop to anything of the kind.

He thinks that there is no doubt that whitefish and trout are increasing in Cobourg, but fishermen did not catch any very great quantity of herring. There was no one fishing at Lakeport this season.

Ducks of all kinds were up to the average, also muskrats and mink.

There is a considerable amount of trapping done throughout the district, which requires careful watching.

Overseer Amos Shearer, of Roseneath, reports that there is no doubt that the fish are decreasing in Rice Lake every year. This can be accounted for in several ways: the maskinonge, the wolf of the fresh water, kill smaller fish for the sake of killing them. There are two bands of Indians on Rice Lake, some of whom fish all the time in season and out of season. He is able to stop a good deal of their illegal work, but not all; he does not think that any nets are being used there.

He suggests that for a reasonable time before sunrise and after sunset, duck shooting should be allowed, as after sunset is about the only time that it is possible to get black ducks and they are just raising and fattening them to go south to be shot.

He is of the opinion that the open season for muskrats should begin a month later, as a great many rats are caught round the houses before the lake freezes up.

Partridges and black squirrels are quite plentiful.

Overseer D. C. Stuart, of Codrington, reports that the law has been very well observed from Percy Boon to Chisholm's Rapids on the Trent River, the only trouble he has had was in keeping the mill refuse and sawdust from running in Salt and Cole Creeks, as there are a number of trout in these streams.

There seemed to be quite an increase in the fish, and the people were better satisfied with their catches.

With regard to game, he never saw as many ducks as there were this year, partridges are also plentiful, and there are a good many black squirrels.

Muskrats are about the same as usual, and mink are rather scarce.

ONTARIO COUNTY.

Overseer Gilbert Gillespie, of Brechin, reports that the laws have been well observed in his district. He heard no reports of illegal net fishing, and he himself did not find anyone breaking the laws in this respect.

The winter fishing was not good, and there was no spearing done on account of the mud which was from three to ten feet deep. Bass are scarce, but trout were plentiful in May and June. The weather during October was rough for trolling. The reports from the Islands were good, some fine catches being made.

Ducks are not plentiful, but there a great many partridges and muskrats are increasing. There are a few mink to be seen.

Overseer Charles E. Halward, of Cannington, reports that this has been a very favourable year for the game. He has had little or no trouble in enforcing the laws, and game has been unusually plentiful, especially ducks and partridges.

He would like to see two regulations added to the Game Laws which he thinks woud do much to preserve some of the most valuable game. First that there should be a limit to the number of ducks shot in the day by each hunter, and secondly that trappers should be obliged to take out a license.

Overseer George Hood, of Scugog, reports that maskinonge were very scarce, only a few were caught on the east side of the lake.

There were a few bass caught on the west side.

Small fish were very plentiful.

Ducks are very plentiful, more so than they have been for years. Partridges are increasing. Geese are very numerous.

Muskrats are very plentiful. Mink are scarce and rabbits very plentiful.

Overseer Thomas Mansfield, of Pickering Harbour, reports that during the early part of the season the fishing was not so good as it might have been. The fishermen did not get such large hauls as it was their fortune to catch last year, they did not seem to get on the track of the fish until late in the season and when their nets were becoming worn, and they themselves were perhaps discouraged at their previous efforts, and did not push the business enough to renew their nets, as they would have done had they made a little money earlier in the season. The angling also was not so good as it usually is.

The law has been well observed in his district. He has followed up several reports of illegal work but always found them to be false. On one occasion he grappled most of the night with a man who had told him that he knew where a net was set, but they could find nothing.

Ducks, mink and muskrats have been quite up to the average.

Overseer H. McDonald, of Beaverton, reports that during the winter and summer the Game and Fishery Laws were very well observed in his district; but on October 20th some gill nets were found set, these were promptly taken up by Captain Carson who discovered them. Again on the 24th he found some more.

Salmon are becoming more plentiful in Lake Simcoe each year. Bass and whitefish are also increasing.

There were quite a number of tourists in his district during the season, but they had all been supplied with permits, so he was unable to sell any.

Game seems to be about the same as it has been other years.

The people all appreciate the work being done by the Department for the protection of the Game and Fish.

Overseer Donald McPhee, of Upthegrove, reports that in Lake Simcoe the trout are plentiful and still increasing, also whitefish. Good catches of bass have been reported, but the size has been small. Maskinonge have been plentiful and carp very numerous.

The fish are numerous in Mud Lake, particularly maskinonge and pickerel.

With regard to the game in the vicinity of Lake Simcoe, partridges are more numerous than usual, and ducks are also plentiful. Mink are very scarce and muskrats very plentiful.

Ducks, partridges and muskrats are very numerous in the vicinity of Mud Lake.

Overseer Michael Timlin, of Atherley, reports that the Fishery Laws have been well observed during the past year, and no infractions came to his notice.

Fishing was about the same as last year, bass and pickerel being much the same.

There are four saw-mills in his division, but they were careful not to let the sawdust and refuse go into the river.

The Game Laws were well observed.

Ducks were plentiful in Mud Lake, also partridges. Mink were scarce, but muskrats plentiful.

PARRY SOUND DISTRICT.

Overseer J. G. Duncan, of Callendar, reports that last November he decided to explain the Game Laws to the inhabitants of his district as far as he could, so that he could obtain their co-operation in his work. He visited his district with this purpose, and as far as he can judge he thinks he was fairly successful, he has observed no infringements of the law himself, and has had no direct complaints made to him.

The spring was cold, and yet the plover (killdeer) and wood duck appeared earlier than he has known them do for a number of years.

There was no fishing done through the ice during the winter, and very little spearing of fish in the spring.

The visitors during the summer were mainly Canadians, very few coming from across the border, they all had a good season, and some fine specimens of pickerel and bass were caught. Pike on the whole were large. There was only one camp, and they did not make any record.

Ducks were scarce during the summer, and the Wilson snipe were numerous in the latter part of the season. He saw very few partridges in his district, and it is his opinion that they are about all killed off.

He saw no illegal shooting being done before the season opened, although he did see parties with power launches, who made off before he could get near them.

There were quite a few of the yellow-legged plover about the end of October. The sportsmen have not had much success in shooting fowl, though they have had good luck with deer. Four bears were shot in this district, but they were small.

Altogether it has been a very successful season, those people who fished near the shore caught a good many perch and sunfish, and some very fair sized pickerel and pike. Those who went further afield to shoot game also had good sport.

He finds the work both congenial and instructive, and is pleased that the Government are looking into the protection of the wild animals as well as they are.

Overseer John Dunk, of Kearney, reports that on account of the game laws being so well observed in his district there has been an enormous increase in beaver; there are some in every creek and river, and in some cases the roads are flooded through the backing up of the water by their dams. Deer and partridges show no decrease, but mink and muskrat are almost extinct, owing to the demand for these furs at a very profitable figures.

Overseer T. H. Johnston, of Royston, reports that the season of 1913 has been a very successful one, and the law has been well observed. There have oeen plenty of fish in all the lakes on the Magnetewan River. Many of which have had fry deposited in them by the Department.

Deer hunting was good in the fall, no less than 350 left Burke Falls wharf. Beaver are plentiful; it is wonderful what a number of dams they have built.

He states that he has collected about $50 for angling permits.

Overseer Richard Lambkins, of Loring, reports that during the past winter and summer the Game and Fishery Laws have been well observed.

He reported last year that improvements were to be made on the Pickerel River. These improvements consist of deepening the outlet of Wauquigamog Lake, some four feet, removing Wilson Dam, which is ten miles down river, and raising Dollars Dam four feet; this dam is at the foot of Kawigamog Lake. When these improvements are completed it will give an average depth of eight feet of water for some thirty miles, and will not only allow fish of all kinds to come up into Wauquigamog Lake from the lake below, but will also be a great benefit to the people living in this vicinity, besides the lumbermen and tourists who use these waters in the summer. He would strongly recommend the Department to urge the Government to put in a fish slide at Dollar Dam, as ever since this dam was built (thirty years ago) it has completely blocked these waters and prevented fish from coming up from the Georgian Bay. He states that the river improvements referred to above were started in August last, and Mr. D. H. McIntosh is still working at same.

With reference to fish he would say that pickerel, pike, bass, of which there are three kinds, *i.e.,* small mouth black bass, silver bass, and the small rock bass, also large lake trout are fairly plentiful. At the head of all the waters in his district, speckled trout are plentiful, but so far none have ever been taken in this vicinity. He would suggest that the Department stock some of the numerous spring lakes with these beautiful fish. With reference to partridges, at the time of hatching, the weather was very bad for the young, being very wet; he thinks this accounts for these being a little more scarcer this season than last. Ducks have never been very numerous in the inland lakes, on account of there being no wild rice or other food grown in this part of the district, but if wild rice were sown in some of the waters, he feels confident that in a short time they would have ducks of all kinds in large numbers.

Deer are holding their own very well, considering the number taken by hunters each year, also the number killed by wolves. In his travels about this part of the district, he has seen many deer during the past summer, and believes that they are more numerous this fall than they were last.

With reference to wolves, these are the most destructive animals they have, as he believes that they kill more deer than all the hunters put together. He has known one wolf to kill seven deer in one week, and only suck the blood from their cut throats; of course this was when the crust was on the snow, but if one wolf will do this much, what will hundreds do? He is of the opinion that it is time that something was done to destroy these pests, and would suggest that a straight bounty of twenty-five dollars be given by the Government for each pelt, or if the trapper were allowed to keep the skin, then give a bounty of twenty dollars. It is a positive fact that if wolves are allowed to increase, as they have been doing for the past few years, in a short time they will be in such numbers that they will practically clean out the deer; at the present time the bounty is only fifteen dollars, which does not pay a man to go after them as they are very hard to get. Sometimes a trapper will work two or three months without getting a single wolf, then he may get one or two, but what is thirty dollars to a man for two or three months' work? The result is that very few of the trappers will bother with wolves at all, while, if as suggested, the bounty were raised to $25, it would pay a man to begin poisoning or trapping them.

There are a few colonies of beaver in his section, he thinks otter are holding their own. Muskrats are increasing slowly. Mink are about the same. There are no marten in this district, they used to be fairly plentiful years ago, but of late none have been seen.

From all reports there will be more hunters this fall than usual. From careful observation he finds that in nearly all cases hunters as a rule live up to, and try to obey the Game Laws.

Overseer H. W. Reid, of Parry Sound, reports that the fishermen state that the spring and summer fishing was very good, but during the fall it was very poor owing to the stormy weather; in October, it was very hard to get out to the nets, many of which were destroyed in the storms, and some of the men with small rigs were unable to fish at all.

On Nov. 23rd, he went to Moon River on the "Katharine C," and found a large trap net hung up in the bush newly tarred ready to set. He destroyed it by burning it.

During the summer he found part of a trap net on a small island near Copper Head and took it to Parry Sound and burned it.

There have been a large number of tourists in his district this summer, and they appeared to be well pleased with the bass fishing, he did not hear of any complaints and did not find any of them breaking the laws.

He reports that partridges have been very scarce during the hunting season, although there seemed to be plenty of young birds in the spring, but they disappeared. It is his opinion that the weather and bush fires were the cause of the young birds' death.

Ducks are very plentiful, and hunters report good bags.

Mink and muskrats are numerous.

On October 31st he went to Partridge Bay, 12 miles from home, and found several mink traps set, which he confiscated.

There have been a very large number of hunters in the woods this year, and a great many deer were killed. One car which he inspected at the C.N.O. station contained over 300 and another 135, these deer were being shipped south.

He states that he has not made any convictions this year, and it is his opinion that the Laws and Regulations are being fairly well observed.

PEEL COUNTY.

Overseer Alex Clunis, of Claude, reports that the speckled trout have been up to the average this year, some good catches were made.

Bass are steadily decreasing, and it is his opinion that the waters need re-stocking again.

Coarse fish such as suckers are very plentiful.

Partridges are quite plentiful. The spring was a good one for hatching.

Fur-bearing animals are becoming quite scarce, there are almost as many hunters and trappers as there are animals.

The law has been well observed, and he has no reason to complain.

Overseer James Johnston, of Orangeville, reports that the speckled trout were very good this year, and some fine catches were made. Bass fishing in Green Lake was also good, and some excellent specimens were caught.

With regard to mink and muskrats they are becoming very scarce, and he strongly recommends that trapping these animals should be prohibited for a few years. Rabbits are plentiful and partridge fair.

The laws were well observed in his district as far as he could tell from the reports received by him.

Overseer R. J. Walker, of Port Credit, reports that the trout fishing has not been up to the average, the fish were very late in coming into the spawning ground.

Whitefish have been about average. Angling has been about the same as other years. Carp are falling off.

There is not very much game in his division, cotton-tail rabbits are becoming very numerous.

There are a few black and grey squirrels, and partridges are very scarce, he thinks the clearing of the woods has caused this.

The Game and Fishery Laws have been well observed. He finds that some people make their complaints to the Department instead of to him, if they would inform him he would investigate the trouble.

5 G.F.

PERTH COUNTY.

Overseer Charles Jickling, of St. Mary's, reports that bass have been more plentiful than usual, some of the local anglers having made some fine catches.

The German brown trout which were placed in Otter Creek seem to be growing splendidly, and the pickerel placed in the lake at Lakeside are also doing well.

He thinks it would be a good thing if the overseers could devote more of their time to stocking the small streams. He would like to experiment by sowing wild rice and see if he could not entice the ducks to stay near the home streams.

In his opinion it is a mistake to give the partridges so long an open season. They seem, however, to be on the increase, he has put them up in places where he has not seen any for a number of years. This year being a dry season they have hatched well and raised their young.

Black and grey squirrels are more numerous than they have been for years, they seem to be scattered in the orchards and around the buildings in search of food.

Ducks seem to be quite plentiful on the small streams, he has also seen wild geese in the fields in May. There is an abundance of cottontail rabbits. Muskrats and mink are becoming scarce since the prices were raised.

He considers that there is too much shooting being done by young boys with small rifles, and thinks that guns should be licensed.

He has been approached by several members of the different hunting clubs as to the advisability of forming a Fish and Game Protective Association all over the district.

There are so many people interested in the protection of the fish and game in his district that there is very little chance of an infraction being committed without the law-breaker being caught.

He thinks there should be a limit set on the number of squirrels caught by each person.

PETERBOROUGH COUNTY.

Overseer William Clarkson, of Lakehurst, reports that during the past year the Game and Fishery Laws were fairly well observed.

The fishermen in his district were apparently pleased with the season. There was an increase in the number of bass and maskinonge caught this year. Trout are becoming scarce in the lakes situated in the north of his district, and he recommends that the close season should last for two months, from October 1st to November 30th.

The number of tourists who visit this district is increasing every year.

Ducks are not so plentiful this fall. Partridges and mink are plentiful, and he recommends that trappers should be obliged to take out licenses to kill muskrats.

After patrolling the waters he finds that beaver are very numerous. Deer are holding their own well.

The laws regarding mill refuse have been well observed. There are no fish slides in his division.

Capt. Carson and crew with the " Naiad " are doing good work in giving information and enforcing the laws.

Overseer Edward Dulmage, of Oak Lake, reports that owing to the terrible fires, which destroyed everything, it is hard to give a correct statement of the quantity of game.

Deer have had to hunt for food and shelter, and are not so plentiful. Partridges are not so numerous as they were some years ago. Muskrats and mink are about the same as previous year.

Bass in Oak Lake are more numerous, and the surrounding lakes are as well stocked as other years. Trout are increasing in Oak Lake. All the other fish in the district are about the same as in former years.

The Game and Fishery Laws have been fairly well observed.

Overseer Edward Fleming, of Hastings, reports that he has not heard of one fish being speared illegally in his district during the season so well has the law been observed. The illegal fishers did not go up to Hastings in the spring as they have done other years.

There have not been so many fish caught this summer as during previous seasons.

There are plenty of ducks on the river this fall. Muskrats are not so plentiful, and partridges are getting very scarce.

Overseer Wellington Lean, of Apsley, reports that the Game and Fishery Laws have been well observed in his district during the past year. Very few tourists visited the lakes this summer on account of the forest fires, which were raging in the best fishing season. On the whole fishing has been about average.

Partridges seem scarce owing to the forest fires. Deer are as plentiful as they have been for a number of years. He advises that the dogs should not be allowed to chase the deer, as they are the cause of more being wounded and left to die than the hunters kill. Beaver are becoming quite numerous, and are to be found on nearly all the lakes and creeks in his district; if they are protected for a few years they would be as plentiful as they have been in past years. He thinks it would be a good thing if a larger bounty were put on wolves, viz., $25, which would encourage people to kill them, as they are the worst enemies the deer have.

There are only two mills in his district, and the owners are observing the law with regard to the sawdust, etc.

Overseer John McFarlane, of Keene, reports that the fishing in his district has been fairly good, especially bass angling, and the law has been fairly well observed. He does not think that there were any fish taken through the ice, as most of the people are in favor of the regulation prohibiting this. There may have been a few fish taken with the hook and line during the close season, but not many.

Trapping was very good considering the number of trappers in his district, many of whom come from the other side of the lake to catch muskrats in the spring, and they all did well. Mink are very scarce.

Ducks were very plentiful on the lake in the spring, more so than they have been for many years, and they were not molested, but in the fall the hunters are difficult to watch, as they will break the game laws if they can; there has been more moonlight than usual, and they will shoot after sunset and before sunrise if they are not watched.

He found some hunters shooting by moonlight, but they got away, leaving their decoys behind, which he seized. He also had to tear down some blinds which were beyond the limit.

He made one conviction for shooting hares in close season.

Partridges and black squirrels were plentiful.

There was a good crop of rice this season. About twenty tents of Indians and their families were camped on Sugar Island, at the mouth of Keene River, from the other side of the lake. These, with a number of Indians from Hiawatha, gathered rice through September, for which they received a good price.

The mill owners were careful about their sawdust and rubbish.

He thinks the guides should be obliged to get their licenses from the Overseer of their district, as he would then know who had licenses and who had not without making enquiries. As it is, a number of the guides from his district go to some other Overseer for his license and vice versa. In talking this matter over with the other Overseers they were of the same opinion, and would like to see the change made for Rice Lake.

Overseer Henry Melville, of Havelock, reports the fishing for bass, maskinonge and speckled trout has been good this season.

Deer are scarce, but mink, muskrat and other fur-bearing animals seem to be on the increase. Game birds of all kinds are plentiful.

Overseer F. J. Moore, of Lakefield, reports that during the past year the Game and Fishery-Laws have been fairly well observed, spearing and netting of fish being almost stamped out. Last spring was a fairly good season for bass and maskinonge to spawn, as the water was high until the season was well over, which gave the small fish a chance to get out into deep water. Tourists have had very good luck fishing with rod and spoon, particularly those who employed guides. He recommends that Stoney Lake be re-stocked with bass, as it is becoming a great summer resort for tourists from all parts of the United States, as well as from our own Provinces; he thinks the fishermen would be willing to pay more for their licenses if they were sure of good fishing, as they seem very taken with the lakes. Many anglers went further up the lake this year, as the fishing seemed to be better. He suggests that this Department co-operates with the Dominion Government to keep the water as nearly one height as possible during the spawning season in the spring. He further recommends that the close season for bass and maskinonge be from April 1st—15th June

Partridges are plentiful but ducks are scarce. Trappers have had a fairly good season with the muskrats, but mink are not so plentiful.

He suggests that the carrying of firearms be prohibited as far as possible during the close season, as there are so many people on the waters in the summer that it is very dangerous, and there is no need to carry them.

Overseer W. H. Thompson, of Bailieboro, reports that the laws have been fairly well observed in his division.

Maskinonge were not so plentiful in the river during spawning season, as the weather was cold and they probably spawned in deeper water. Maskinonge fishing has therefore not been so good as it was last season, although some large fish have been caught. Overseer Thompson thinks that fishing from gasoline launches should be stopped.

Black and wood ducks are scarce, particularly the latter. Partridges and black and grey squirrel are also scarce. Muskrats are about the same as last year, they are very closely hunted, and he thinks it would be better if the season started on March 1st and closed on April 15th. Mink are very scarce, and he proposes that skunk and raccoon should have a close season.

He thinks that the discharging of guns on Sunday should be stopped. The people who do this cannot be fined unless they are shooting game, but it is very annoying for the residents to hear guns being discharged on Sunday.

He further proposes that all overseers between Peterborough and Hastings meet once a year to talk things over, with a view to improving the fish and game.

Overseer John Wall, of Peterboro, reports that bass and maskinonge have not been so plentiful in his territory, at least they have not been biting so well as usual. This, he thinks, is due to the quantity of natural feed, as all the fish caught are in such fine condition. He has never seen so many large, fat maskinonge as have been taken this year. He thinks it must be an off season, as he has heard the same complaint in other parts.

The muskrat catch was fairly good, but the mink are becoming very scarce, and he suggests that their season should not open until December 1st.

Partridges are very plentiful all round his district, and there is the usual good supply of ducks.

A great many deer hunters have gone north for the hunt this year, and he is awaiting their return to hear the result of their chase.

PRESCOTT COUNTY.

Overseer F. Dupuis, of Hawkesbury, reports that the Game and Fishery Laws have been fairly well observed, only one fine being imposed during the year. Owing to his having such a large territory to look after, i.e., the County of Prescott and a part of the County of Glengarry, he finds that it keeps him pretty busy looking out to see that there are no violations of the law.

More fishing licenses were sold this year than usual.

Mixed and coarse fish, perch, eels, pike and catfish were very good this season.

Partridges are scarce, but muskrats and mink are fairly plentiful.

PRINCE EDWARD COUNTY.

Overseer Angus Brisbin, of Picton, reports that there have been about the same number of gill-net fishermen as usual, but there have been a greater number of night lines set.

Fishing in South Marysburg has been about average, but it has not been so good in North Marysburg waters. He is pleased to report that black bass are becoming very plentiful at Main Ducks.

Black squirrels are also becoming more plentiful, and ducks are about the same as usual.

He has no fault to find with the ways the laws have been observed, as he has had no trouble with any of the fishermen.

Overseer David Conger, of West Lake, reports that the catch of whitefish and salmon trout has been satisfactory to the fishermen, and he is satisfied that the licensees observed the laws.

Angling has been the same as it was last season in West and East Lake.

He seized one set of hoop nets in West Lake and delivered them to Overseer Brisbin, of Picton, but could not find out who the offender was who set them.

With regard to the game, ducks are very plentiful, and muskrats are holding their own, but mink are very scarce. Black squirrels are increasing.

The Game Laws have been fairly well observed.

Overseer E. R. Fox, of Northport, reports that fish of all kinds are quite plentiful, some species more so than last year. Bass are more numerous than last season, and the non-residents report them to be very large; many of them say that if all is well they will return next year and bring others with them.

Whitefish are more numerous than last year; one fisherman lifted his hoop nets after being set for two nights, and dressed 1,000 bullheads of 7 lbs., from six sets of nets, which is sufficient evidence to prove that there are plenty of bullheads.

Ducks were very plentiful during August and the first week of September, but they seemed to leave the district after this. He thinks they had finished all the wild rice, and had to go to look for other feeding grounds. Partridges are increasing, but there is no great quantity of them. Muskrats and mink are quite scarce in most of the marshes, and he recommends that the trappers should be licensed or that there should be a close season for two years.

Overseer E. A. Titus, of Wellington, reports that this has been a very favourable season for the fishermen, although it was not quite up to 1912; this was probably caused by the weather conditions, which were not so good. Salmon and whitefish were as plentiful as last year, but on account of so much windy weather they did not do quite so well as the year before. Hoop-net fishing was good during the spring, but the carp are becoming so numerous in Wellers Bay that the fishermen are afraid they will destroy the hoop-net fishing entirely.

Ducks are very numerous; he does not think he ever saw so many Fall ducks as there are this season. Muskrats were quite scarce last spring. Mink, beaver and black squirrels are very scarce in his division. Partridges are plentiful this Fall.

The law has been fairly well observed, with one or two exceptions. There were only two convictions made for. illegal shooting at Wellers Bay. There was some illegal shooting being done on West Lake beach, but the law-breakers escaped without being caught.

RAINY RIVER DISTRICT.

Overseer William Aymer, of Fort Frances, reports that the fishing in Rainy Lake was better than last year, lyng and other worthless fish are increasing, especially in the small inland lakes; he would suggest that more of them be licensed for winter fishing.

He recommends re-stock of Baffin and Nickle Lakes, two small lakes near Fort Frances with bass.

Partridges are not so numerous as last year. Prairie chickens are increasing, especially along the railway line. Ducks are not so plentiful as last year, as there is no wild rice.

Moose and deer are about the same as last year.

The game laws have been fairly well observed, with the exception of those regarding moose, as these were killed during the summer around Rat and Pipestone Rivers, 50 miles south-east of Fort Frances on Rainy Lake He counted eight carcasses in a distance of ten miles. Some were shot for their heads, and some were left untouched. Reports of this work do not reach him until weeks after it has happened, and it is too late to do any good; a steady patrol of the lake would be the only way to stop it.

The trappers had an exceptionally good season last winter, a large quantity of fur being obtained. He strongly recommends that there should be a resident trapping license in the country not open to free homestead entry; the trappers themselves would like to see this, as it would enable them to check illegal trapping.

Wolves are becoming very numerous, especially the brush wolf, which some claim is more destructive than the timber wolf.

A large number of tourists have visited his district this year, coming from places as far off as Texas and California; they all report a splendid trip. This will mean a fine thing for the district in a few years if it is properly looked after.

As his district is so large, he has found it impossible to travel over much of it. With the exception of Rainy Lake, it can only be travelled by canoe, and one man cannot manage alone.

Overseer George S. Cates, of Emo, reports that he has watched his territory as closely as possible, and as far as he can tell the people living along the river on the older settled part are observing the laws better every year. He has been informed that some of the settlers twelve or fifteen miles north do kill game out of season, but on visiting that portion of the district he has never found anything killed beyond a rabbit or a woodchuck.

There are many settlers who have no means of getting in provisions unless they carry them on their backs over some very bad trails.

Deer are becoming more numerous each year, and moose seem to be holding their own in the north. The large timber wolf is not so plentiful, but quite a few farmers have given up keeping sheep on account of the small brush wolf or coyote. Partridges are not quite so plentiful as they were last year. Prairie fowl are scarce, but ducks seem to be plentiful. Beaver are increasing fast, and many new dams are being built all over the territory. Rabbits have been becoming more and more scarce since last winter, and there are now few to be seen. Mink, fox and skunk are increasing slowly.

RENFREW COUNTY.

Overseer Samuel Andrews, of Micksburg, reports that he has kept a close watch over his division, and found that the game and fishery laws have been fairly well observed this year. He destroyed one net, which he found illegally set in Mud Lake, during the month of April, but was unable to find the owner.

He was not able to discover any other violations of the law, there were therefore no fines imposed

Angling has been fairly good this season, pike and suckers were very plentiful early in the season.

Ducks and partridges are scarce, also mink and muskrats.

He thinks it would be a good thing if the Department were to protect muskrats for a couple of years in this county, as they are very scarce and will soon become extinct, which will be a serious loss to the county.

Red deer are plentiful, and are often to be seen in the more settled parts of the county.

Overseer W. L. Briscoe, of Killaloe, reports that he has kept a close watch over his territory during the past year, and states that the game and fishery laws have been well observed, as very few reports of illegal work have come to his notice.

Trout are very scarce.   He thinks they have gone to Round Lake, as the fishing in that lake is reported to be much better this year than during previous years.   There is a considerable amount of black bass in the Bonnechere waters. Pike is very plentiful in Golden Lake.

Red deer are plentiful along the Bonnechere waters owing to the large area of burnt country, which has driven them to the front. Partridges are very scarce owing to the hard spring, and the fires have burnt a large quantity of them.   He would urge the Department to prohibit partridge shooting for a period of two years to prevent their becoming extinct. Rats seem to be on the increase.   Mink is very scarce.   Beaver are increasing in the back small lakes, as the fires on the Upper Bonnechere burnt their feed and they left for better feeding grounds.

Overseer D. E. Burns, of Pembroke, reports that the fish and game laws have been fairly well observed in his district.   The people who took out licenses for domestic purposes only say that the season was a fairly good one.

He has had considerable trouble with people hunting on Sunday.   He had some of them brought before the Police Magistrate, who imposed fines on them, which had the desired effect.

Beaver are still very numerous, and doing considerable damage in some parts of the district.

Overseer John Devine, of Renfrew, reports that the game and fishery laws still continue to be fairly well observed in his division.   With the exception of eight parties whom he had fined by resident Magistrates for violation of the game laws, he does not think there is much to complain of with regard to infractions.

There were no fishing licenses issued for nets this year, and in consequence the angling was very much improved.

Partridges are scarce, owing to a great extent to the continued cold weather last spring.   Deer do not appear to be so numerous as last year, owing to the increased number of wolves, and he thinks that unless something can be done to lessen the number of wolves along the valley of the Madawaska River and Black Donald Creek the deer will certainly decrease in number.

Overseer A. H. G. Wilson, of Eganville, reports that the game and fish in his district are about the same as they were last year.

Fish were very fair this summer, especially the pike in Lake Dore, Mink Lake and Lake Clear.

He received a report that there were dead fish on Lake Clear, but upon investigation he discovered that the fish had gone up the creek during the dry season and had become stuck in the mud, and on September 22nd had floated down, dead, with the flood to the lake. On going to the lake he only found three dead fish, which were pike, and upon examining them he concluded that there were no diseases among the fish, but that their death was caused by the very dry weather before September 22nd.

Partridge are very plentiful, but the bush fires have made them very wild and hard to get at. Ducks are also plentiful, more so than last year.

Wild geese seem to be very scarce, as he has only seen a couple of flocks.

There were a few mink and quite a number of muskrats in the creeks and along the Bonnechere.

Deer are still fairly plentiful in the back country and among the mountains.

There are a couple of families of beaver on Constant Lake, as he saw their work around the lake and up the creeks. He did not see the beaver himself, but some farmers informed him that they had seen them at work.

Red squirrels are very numerous, but black and grey squirrels are very scarce. Skunk are fairly plentiful.

He only imposed one fine during the year, the people are becoming more observant of the law.

RUSSELL COUNTY.

Overseer J. B. Bourgon, of *Rockland,* reports that about the same number of licenses were issued as other years in the Ottawa River of the county of Russell. Catfish, bullheads, pike and perch are chiefly taken in the Ottawa River.

The county is well settled, so there is no game.

Fines amounting to $35 were imposed on people fishing without licenses.

About the same quantity of fish was taken as during the year 1912.

SIMCOE COUNTY.

Overseer John Beatty, of *Midland,* reports that the season of 1913 has been a successful one for the game and fish. There have been more maskinonge and black bass caught than for a number of years.

Black squirrels are very scarce. Partridges are more plentiful than other years; ducks are also plentiful, but sportsmen have had poor luck on account of the warm weather. Muskrats are scarce; there are few houses to be seen this season.

On June 22nd he found 700 yards of gill net which he destroyed, but could not find the people to whom they belonged. During May he also destroyed one punt, two jack lights and two spears, but the owners got away across the marsh land. He thinks on the whole the laws have been fairly well observed.

Overseer Samuel Coulter, of *Gilford,* reports that the Game Laws have been well observed in his district. The people seem to keep the Regulations much better than they have done other years. It is only a short time since everyone shot just when they have done other years. It is only a short time since everyone shot just when they felt like it all the year round, but now it is a rare thing to hear a gun fired out of season.

There has been very little trolling done in his division. A few maskinonge were caught in the river this fall by trolling. Angling for bass has been very good.

The Bradford Fish Company have had a fair summer, and obtained a very large haul on October 8th.

Ducks have been very scarce this fall. There were quite a number before October 1st. The hunters were all ready to start the night before, and they seemed to frighten all the ducks away. He recommends that the open season for that particular district be from October 15th, as it would give the ducks a better chance to come round. At it is they are scared away just as they come, and do not get a chance to locate a feeding ground.

Cotton-tail rabbits and hares are very numerous. Wild geese seem to be about the same as usual. There have been a few partridges, but they are always scarce.

There are quite a number of muskrat houses, which have been built on the marsh, but he never saw them build in the lake so far from the shore.

Mink are not very plentiful. On a little reserve belonging to Sir Edmund Walker there are upwards of 1,000 black squirrels, which shows what a little protection of the game will do.

Overseer B. A. Dusang, of Waubaushene, reports that maskinonge have never been known to be so plentiful as they were this year. He knows one man who has caught over forty during the season. Speckled trout are about the same as last year; there are not many in his district. Pickerel have increased about fifty per cent. in the last two years. Whitefish and salmon trout are about the average; there were not so many caught this year owing to the rough weather. Bass, pike and coarse fish are about the same as last year; he has received no complaints about the fish from anglers. It is thought that two maskinonge is sufficient for one man each day.

Partridges and ducks are more plentiful than they have been for years. Deer about the same as usual. Muskrat and mink not so plentiful as other years, and there are no otter or beaver. The tourists' trade was not so good as it was last year.

He has been on patrol work since spring. He took seven trips—along the north shore as far as Parry Sound, and along the south shore as far as Christian Island and Nattawasaga River, Hope Island, Beckwith and the Tombs.

Overseer Charles G. Gaudaur, of Atherley, reports that whitefish were very scarce in the fall of 1912, compared with other years. Fishermen who were spearing for trout through the ice last winter, state that they were very scarce, but the trout run has been good this year. Herring are very plentiful in Lake Simcoe, and many of them are caught with the fly through June. Sportsmen say that fishing for herring with flies is the finest sport of the season. Maskinonge are not so numerous as they have been other years at the Narrows and on the different spawning beds, but trolling through the open season was fairly good, some fine catches having been reported. Black bass have been very scarce, and he thinks that something should be done with regard to stocking Lakes Simcoe and Couchiching with black bass fry. Carp are very plentiful at the Narrows and rush beds in this district; it is possible to see them by hundreds where the black bass and maskinonge spawn. They are very destructive to fish that spawn in muddy grounds, as they eat up the spawn as soon as it is deposited. Fish such as rockbass, suckers, sunfish, perch, catfish and carp are very plentiful in Lakes Simcoe and Couchiching.

On October 17th he seized one trout net on Strawberry Island.

Fur bearing animals, muskrats, mink and foxes, were plentiful last fall and the trappers had a good season. Rabbits were very numerous during the winter. There are indications of a good season for muskrats this year, as there are numerous houses around the Narrows, Lake Couchiching and Mud Lake.

Partridges and ducks are very plentiful; the hunters report having had good sport and are well satisfied with the Game Laws. Snipe, woodcock and plover are not so plentiful as they have been other years.

Very few reports of illegal work have reached him, although he has friends at various points in his division, who would inform him of any infractions. The Laws have been well observed.

Overseer G. G. Green, of Bradford, reports that the season has been a very quiet one, practically no illegal fishing having been done, and there was no trouble with the shooting.

With regard to the fishing, the run was over very quickly; he cannot account for this unless it was the condition of the season and the water.

He only succeeded in seizing one small net, about 15 feet long.

The shooting was no good, owing to the low water. Quite a lot of black ducks nested in the district, but when the season opened up they went away. There are no snipe, but squirrels are reported plentiful.

The operations of the Bradford Fish Company have not been very successful in the carp industry, but they have taken a lot of suckers, and the quality of these are greatly improved over last year. Perch have been a very light run.

He again advises the placing of a close season on all fur bearing animals in his district. He notices an increase in muskrats, and if a little protection were given them there is no doubt that the section would again become a good producer.

Overseer T. J. Hornsby, of Penetanguishene, reports that the Game and Fish Laws have been fairly well observed in his district, no complaints having come to his notice.

The fishing was moderately good in the early part of the season, but the fishermen complained during the latter part, as the season seemed to be later than usual. Bass fishing was good, but pickerel only fair.

With regard to the game, partridges are plentiful compared with last year. Black and grey squirrels very scarce, but ducks more plentiful than last year.

Overseer J. H. Laughlin, of New Lowell, reports that he has been over his territory a good many times during the past season, and has found that the Game and Fishery Laws have been fairly well observed. He has had some trouble over the dogs chasing the deer in the winter time, but it is hard to stop them.

Deer are increasing, but partridges are not so plentiful as they were last year. He thinks it would be a good thing if the rabbit season opened the same day as the partridge. He suggests that there should be a close season for raccoon, as he knows of six instances when raccoons were killed when their pelts would not bring 25 cents, while in the winter when they are prime they would be worth from $3 to $4. He is very much in favour of seizing every unprime muskrat pelt, as it would stop the trappers from catching them out of season, and people would get value for their money.

Overseer Robert Leadley, of Barrie, reports that whitefish and herring are as plentiful as other years, but there have not been so many trout caught, although they are coming farther into Kempenfeldt Bay than they have done for some years.

Deer are increasing in the north-west portion of the Township of Vespra. He has only heard of one complaint of dogs running them.

Partridges are increasing.

Overseer Harry Mayor, of Painswick, reports that trout, whitefish and herring are as numerous as they were last year, the two last named being particularly plentiful.

Anglers report that the bass fishing was worse than last season, which was extremely bad, and he thinks something should be done to stop this rapid decrease of these fish. The only thing would be to re-stock Lake Simcoe and prohibit the catching of black bass for three years.

There are quantities of the coarser varieties of fish, as they are not much sought after. This seems to prove that too many black bass have been taken, owing to the fact that Lake Simcoe is fast becoming a summer resort for tourists from all parts of America, who devote so much of their time to angling; the problem of preserving the best fish in this lake will be a difficult one to solve.

With regard to game, partridges have increased in a most encouraging manner, and they are now quite up to the standard of former years. Duck and other water fowl are quite plentiful.

Squirrels and hares are to be found at any time, and he is pleased to say that the black squirrels are being well protected by the residents of the neighbourhood.

Considering the limited natural wood protection they have it is astonishing the way the fur bearing animals, such as raccoon, fox, mink, skunk and muskrat are holding their own.

He is pleased to say that when performing his duties he has always received most courteous treatment from both residents and tourists, and any assistance or information required has been given willingly.

Overseer William McGinn, of Orillia, reports that bass fishing in Lake Couchiching has been very poor, especially during the early part of the summer, but during the latter part of September and October it was better and the sample was larger.

The smaller kinds of fish, such as rock bass, perch and sunfish are very plentiful. Maskinonge fishing has been very good. He knows one man who caught twenty-three this season. He caught five in one week, averaging eighteen pounds each.

Trout fishing in Lake Simcoe during the spring and fall was exceptionally good. They are becoming more plentiful every year. Great credit is due to the crew on Patrol Boat "Naiad," who keep the nets out of the water at the head of the lake.

Bass fishing in Lake Simcoe has been poor this season in the north end of the lake.

There are a few ducks about, but not many as there is no feed for them. Partridges are plentiful.

Game is becoming more scarce in this district every year.

He has had very little trouble with the poachers, either with the fish or game. There were a few reports of shooting out of season, but it is almost impossible to catch a poacher in the bush, as the farmers and settlers refuse to give any information other than that they hear reports.

The bush fires in this district have done much damage to rabbits and partridges. The farmers say that they have seen partridges with their wings so badly burned that they could not fly, and rabbits with their fur burned off their bodies and blinded by the smoke. One settler reports having seen two deer burned to death in Matchedash.

Overseer Samuel Patterson, of Dunkerron, reports that he has done his duty during the past year, particularly during the close season, and he found no one violating the law.

With regard to the game and fish they seem to be more numerous than during the year 1912.

STORMONT COUNTY.

Overseer W. A. Anderson, of Cornwall, reports that the Game Laws were fairly well observed in his district. Sunday shooting which was a very common occurrence has been stopped.

Most game is plentiful especially ducks.

He thinks the present Game Laws are all that could be desired, except that there should be a limit put on the number of ducks shot, as there are many people making a business of shooting them for sale, especially in Lake St. Francis.

THUNDER BAY DISTRICT.

Overseer Fred. Gammond, of Slate River, reports that he has been over his district a number of times during the year and finds that moose are becoming more scarce every year, and he thinks that in five years, if they continue to decrease at the same rate, they will all have been killed or driven out of the district. He suggests that the hunting season be reduced to two weeks duration, or else that there should be a close season for two years.

Red deer are about the same as in former years. Caribou are very scarce; he has not seen, or heard of one being killed for a number of years.

Beaver are very plentiful owing no doubt to the close season which they have. Muskrats seem to be on the increase, while otter, mink and lynx are practically extinct. It is his opinion that they should be protected by a close season of at least three years.

The coyotes or brush wolves are becoming so numerous that they are a menace to sheep raising throughout the district. One man had so many killed that he sold the remainder of his flock and gave up the business. He recommends that a bounty be placed on these wolves to induce trappers to kill them.

Overseer W. H. S. Gordon, of Port Arthur, reports that during the season he has used every available source to ascertain information as to the fisheries under his supervision in the District of Thunder Bay.

Lake Superior.

Thunder Bay District.—From all information to be gleaned the fishing in this section has not fallen off at all. The gill-net fishermen all report an excellent season. As a large amount of the fishing is done in the sheltered sections, the fishermen working out of Port Arthur and Fort William have not suffered so much as the eastern men by the rough weather. Large catches have been reported, especially of whitefish. The pound net fishermen also report favorably, the fishing being equally good as last year. The herring fishing of last fall was bigger than ever—many very large catches being made.

Rossport District.—The Rossport fishermen do not report quite as good a season as last year. They, however, do not attribute this to the fact that the fishing was lighter, but to the rough weather. They experienced a stormy summer, and there were days at a time when they could not make a lift or set a net. The lifts, however, were equal to last season.

Some of the Rossport fishermen have experienced quite a little loss the past month, when a slide took place at the village. The docks and fish houses were moved out into the bay and considerable expenditure was sustained in refitting them.

Port Coldwell, Jackfish and Heron Bay.—At these different points the reports are to the effect that the fishermen have had a good season. There has been a good catch of trout.

Inland Lakes.—For some unaccountable reason the catch at Whitefish Lake has not been as good as former years. This is not attributed to the fact that the lake is being depleted, but evidently the fish have been running to a different section of the lake. The licensee has been giving the lake the same diligent attention as in the former years.

Shebandowan Lake has not been up to the mark this season, that is, there has not been a big catch. However, the lake has not been fished very much, and consequently the season has not been as good as usual.

At Lac Mille Lac, however, there has been a good season. The whitefish from this lake are now better market fish. The coarse grades are being all fished out. The netting of this lake has certainly been beneficial to the waters.

The reports from the inland lakes along the line of the C. N. R. west of his district are to the effect that the fishing has been up to the average, and the class of fish is improving.

General.—There have been no saw mills in operation on any of the lakes in his district, therefore, there has been no sawdust, etc., deposited in the waters.

VICTORIA COUNTY.

Overseer William Adair, of Norland, reports that he has been over his territory several times during the season and is pleased to say that Game and Fishery Laws have been fairly well observed, no violations of the Act having come to his notice this year.

No sawdust has been dumped in the waters.

No fish are exported from his district. Maskinonge and bass fishing have been very good, and tourists report that the trout fishing in the Upper Lakes is as good as usual.

Fur-bearing animals are still plentiful, especially beaver. Deer and partridges are both plentiful, ducks more so than usual.

Overseer J. R. Boate, of Fowler's Corner, reports that the fishing has been very good in his division. Bass and maskinonge have been very plentiful.

Muskrats were very plentiful.   •

Mink very scarce.

Raccoon very scarce.

Black and grey squirrels scarce.

Ducks have been plentiful this season, some good bags were taken.

The law was well observed in his district, no violations having come to his notice.

Overseer A. Bradshaw, of Lindsay, reports that the catch of bass and maskinonge in his district was not so large as that of last year. He is of the opinion that the low water during the summer caused this, as the fish were in marshes and weedy places where trolling could not be done.

At the opening of the season good catches were made and the anglers were well satisfied.

Frogs do not seem to increase as fast as they should considering the protection given them in Victoria County.

Ducks are very plentiful, and the wonderful yearly increase is most satisfactory.

Muskrats were caught last spring in large quantities by local trappers, and good prices were paid for their skins.

Mink were also plentiful and the prices good.

The prohibiting of fishing through the ice for bass and maskinonge was a wise and much needed act, and will enable overseers to keep a strict and vigilant watch on poaching.

The law has been well observed in his division as far as he could find out, and he is of the opinion that with one or two exceptions the people want the laws protecting the game and fish properly enforced.

Overseer C. H. Burtcheall, of Coboconk, reports that this has been a poor season for fishing, there being only one or two good catches made during the summer. He cannot account for the scarcity of fish, there seem to be very few good sized ones, they are mostly too small to be caught legally. He states that there was no spearing done. On one occasion he saw lights on the water belonging to people fishing illegally, but it was too windy for him to get near them and they soon had to come in themselves.

Very few deer were killed in his district as they are very scarce. Muskrats are also scarce, he thinks it would be an improvement if the trapping season ended on the first of April instead of the thirtieth. There are very few mink, beaver or otter, in fact he might almost say there are none, as only one or two have been caught, and he himself never sees any trace of them. During the early part of the summer he saw some nice flocks of duck, but later in the season no ducks or partridges were to be seen. He thinks the latter were killed off too closely last year and that a two years close season would be a good thing for them.

Overseer J. J. Irwin, of Dalrymple, reports that there have been principally carp in the canal waters and in the spring an abundance of suckers. Maskinonge and bass are not very plentiful in those waters.

The Bradford Fish Co. shipped about 31 tons of carp from the lift lock.

Angling on Mud Lake was not quite so good during the months of July and August, as it was last year. Maskinonge fishing was good during September and October.

Mink and muskrat are increasing on the canal waters and Talbot River, they are also improving on Mud Lake. Otter are about the same as last year. Ducks were plentiful at the beginning of the season, and partridges have been fairly numerous. Deer are not very plentiful.

Only one violation of the law was brought to his notice.

Overseer John Jones, of Fenelon Falls, reports that the fishing has been better than in previous years and some good catches have been made.

Ducks have been very plentiful this fall but not many have been killed.

Muskrats are fairly plentiful but mink are scarce.

Frogs are becoming more plentiful and no doubt the close season is having good effect.

Deer are about the same as other years, although there were not many killed, they were hard to get.

Overseer H. B. Parker, of Bobcaygeon, reports that the fishing this year was very fair but not so good as it was last year.

Maskinonge are decreasing owing to such a large number being taken each year; besides this last spring was a very bad one for hatching, as the fish spawn in the marshes when the water is at its height, and then when it drops, the eggs are left stranded. There are two reasons for the loss of maskinonge spawn which are hard to control. They spawn in water from six inches to two feet deep as soon as the ice leaves the lake, and by the time they have finished spawning the water begins to drop. It falls from two to three feet in the lower lakes below Bobcaygeon and from one to two feet in the upper lakes. It is a difficult matter to control the water at that time of the year as the whole country is flooded and it would be unwise to hold it back although it can sometimes be reasonably aided.

Another reason for the loss of maskinonge is that sometimes there will be just a few of this species of fish in a marsh with an area of 20 acres. These fish swim all over the marsh in about six inches to two feet of water, depositing their spawn as they swim and then they go to the deeper water, leaving the eggs to be devoured by minnows and perch.

Maskinonge spawn from April 20th to May 10th and bass from May 20th to June 20th. Unlike the maskinonge the bass watch their spawn until they have been hatched a few days and are able to swim about. They spawn in from three to six feet of water on rocky or sandy shores, and it has better opportunities of fertilizing than the maskinonge spawn.

He recommends that the Department have a qualified person to investigate a suitable site for a fish hatchery on the Karwartha Lakes, especially for maskinonge as he thinks the bass will hold their own.

The early fall ducks were more numerous than other years but up to the time of writing the late fall ducks are scarce.

Partridges are very numerous, and it is an easy matter to attain the limit.

Deer are more plentiful this fall than other years.

Muskrats are very numerous, their houses are very thick in the marshes and bays, owing to the water being so very low in the creeks and ponds in the woods. They have all come to the lakes to spend the winter where there is plenty of water.

Mink are about the same as usual. Beaver are increasing, and if left alone they would abound in the north country as there are thousands of acres of waste land which is of no value except for the game and fur found thereon, which if protected would be a paradise for game.

Overseer Charles W. Parkin, of Valentia, reports that maskinonge and bass were very scarce throughout his division during the past season: but now that winter fishing is prohibited and the Government has recently deposited a large number of black bass fingerlings in the Scugog waters they should again enjoy good angling.

Muskrats were more plentiful last spring. Partridges and mink are increasing. Hares are very numerous. Wild geese were very plentiful in the spring, but they did not reach the lake until late so very few were killed in his district.

Snipe and plover are increasing and ducks are becoming more plentiful every year. There are thousands of red heads, blue bills and black ducks on the lake.

He has watched his division very closely during the past year and has taken an interest in the protection of the game and fish, and is pleased to say that the laws have been well observed.

He only made four convictions during the year. Two for shooting ducks in the spring. He confiscated the guns one being an automatic one. The other two convictions were for shooting on Sunday.

Overseer Ira Toole, of Omemee, reports that the maskinonge fishing has been excellent in Pigeon River, this season in fact he states that it has never been equalled in his time. Bass are very plentiful, but not many people fish for them as they are of the large mouth or mud variety, and not to be considered when the lunge fishing has been as good as it was this season. Owing to the large number of people who come to fish in that district from the surrounding towns and villages, he finds his work very much increased, as the fishermen will take all they can catch and are not particular how they catch them. Frogs are getting quite plentiful again, owing to the protection they have received during the last few years.

Muskrats are holding their own remarkably well considering the numbers which are caught. Mink were so scarce when they received protection that their chances of ever amounting to anything again in that district are very slight. Fox, coon and skunk, which at the present time are fairly valuable, are also becoming scarce as they receive no protection and are caught when the fur is of very little use. Partridges are as plentiful this year as they have been for some time. Black ducks were very plentiful when the season opened on September 1st, and nearly everyone seemed to be well satisfied with the shooting, which was much better than last year.

WATERLOO COUNTY.

Overseer Edwin F. Scherer, of New Hamburg, reports that the Game and Fishery Laws have been much better observed this year than last when there was no one to protect the game.

Last year when there was plenty of food for the squirrels they seemed to be scarce, but this season there is very little food for them and in consequence they seem to be more plentiful as they have to come some distance to find food.

Cottontail rabbits are very plentiful, and it would not hurt them if the open season were made to extend a month longer. Muskrat and coon are plentiful but mink and water fowl are scarce.

WELLAND COUNTY.

Overseer T. J. Briggs, of Bridgeburg, reports that on November 20, 1913, he seized four deer which had been shot illegally by non-residents and shipped to Fort Erie with Canadian Coupons. On April 10th, 1913, he fined an American citizen $25 for setting baited hooks in the waters of Niagara River, illegally. Four men were found violating the law at Fort Erie by drawing a seine in the Niagara River. They were brought before the magistrate and found guilty, and in consequence the seine and boat were confiscated and the men fined.

6 G.F.

A large number of Angling Permits were sold but the angling was very poor, but for a short time large catches of pickerel and sturgeon were made.

Game is very scarce in this division, but the laws are being well observed. Boys with .22 rifles do a lot of harm to the song birds, and Overseer Briggs thinks that these rifles should be licensed, as it would benefit the people in the neighbourhood, also the game.

The Erie County Society of the Birds, Fish and Game, in sympathy with the protection, makes the Niagara River fishing better than other years. This society is a great help to the Canadian Game and Fishery overseers on the borders. The American State Division Chief, F. W. Hamilton, Game Protector, is a very prompt and willing officer on his side of the river.

Overseer H. G. A. Cook, of Niagara Falls, reports that the Game Laws have been very well observed by the hunters in this district, and he has had no complaints.

Overseer David Jones, of Welland, reports that last year was a very fair one for pickerel and black bass in his district; there was not so many carp as usual.

Complaints of illegal work were not very bad; there was only one case, which was satisfactorily settled by Inspector Hunter.

Muskrats were plentiful, but other fur-bearing animals scarce; he recommends that trappers should be licensed, as he could deal with them better.

Black and grey squirrels are scarce.

Partridges are about the same, and pheasants on the increase; the farmers have come to the conclusion that it is better to protect the game and report all infractions of the laws.

Ducks were plentiful; he caught one man shooting illegally and had him fined.

Laws were fairly well observed in this district.

WELLINGTON COUNTY.

Overseer Colin Robertson, of Hillsburg, reports that he has been over his territory several times during the season and finds that the Game and Fishery Laws have been fairly well observed.

The chief fish caught are brook trout, and he would strongly recommend that the close season for this species of fish begin on September 1st instead of the 15th.

Anglers report a fair season, but not nearly as good as a few years ago.

The laws regarding sawdust, etc., have been well observed by the mill owners; there are several mills in his district, which he has visited from time to time during the year, and always found them to be in a satisfactory condition.

Foxes and rabbits are plentiful. Mink, muskrat, partridges and wild ducks are scarce.

There are not many deer, otter, beaver, bear or other big game in his district.

WENTWORTH COUNTY.

Overseer O. J. Kerr, of Hamilton, reports as follows:

Transportation Inspection.—This part of his duties has taken up a good deal of his time, as he found that a great deal of illegal shipping of undersized fish was being carried on, and it required a great deal of work to detect them. He is pleased to say that owing to the close watch he kept few illegal fish got through to the United States.

Deer and moose heads, which when mounted go to adorn the homes of the rich in the United States, make a good trade, and it is his opinion that the purchasers of these heads should be obliged to obtain a license for procuring them from Canada. The taxidermists who are in this trade reap a bountiful harvest all the year round. He also found during the deer season that the deer shot were extra large and the sportsmen came home well satisfied.

Furs.—He seized a lot of furs shipped in the close season; he was on the look out for these as he knew there were law-breakers in the back woods. He also had some trouble with the Toronto fur dealers in the way they shipped their furs.

The industry of fur farming is in its infancy here, but is carried on with great profit in Prince Edward Island, particularly the fox; he would advise the Department to pay particular attention to this business.

As far as he can tell there is a great quantity of fur in the Counties of Wentworth and Halton; the number of muskrats, mink, coon, skunk and foxes is surprising. The trappers do their best to clean them up, but the next year they are as plentiful as ever. The ground hog is not so useless an animal as it appears to be. He digs a hole in the hill side and banks himself in for the winter, while the skunk comes and occupies the outer portion of the hole and makes it his home for the winter. Coons are also taking to the ground as the forest disappears.

Fishing.—Fishing by licensed fishermen has not been up to the average, but it is hoped that by the close of the year their catch will have improved. He is very strongly opposed to the extension of the open season for whitefish.

Angling in Burlington Bay during the year was fair, and some fine black bass were caught at the Beach Canal Piers and in other parts of the bay by those who are skilled in the art of catching black bass. Trollers for pike did fairly well, and considering that Hamilton has a population of 100,000, and so much dredging and other work being carried on, the bay is doing splendidly. Carp fishers have done well, about 50 tons of carp being taken out of the west end of the bay and Dundas Marsh.

Fines, Seizures, and Forfeitures.—Illegal netting in Burlington Bay is a thing of the past, only one man, a foreigner, using an umbrella net, was fined $5.

He made a great many seizures, and, in spite of the careful investigations which are always made by him at his point, and by the Department whenever reports of illegal work reached them, there have been a great number of infractions of the law.

Duck Shooting in Burlington Bay.—Burlington Bay can give good sport to those who do not wish to go further afield for good shooting grounds, and who have time to go to the east end of the bay. If the so-called screening were not allowed, and the decoy limit made to be 50 yards from the shore, then the genuine sportsman would stand on equal terms and not be monopolized by the screener. The shooters are getting to be too many for the bay, and on holidays every place of vantage on the beach is taken up the night before, so that it is plainly seen that this sport is appreciated by young and old, and they all seem to enjoy sleeping out in their boats all night in order to secure their position.

The early fall duck was not so plentiful in the marshes this year, but they are coming in by hundreds now, and the shooting promises to be very good, if it is not spoilt by the screeners.

Wild ducks are the only game birds that are allowed to be sold. and some people argue that they should not be sold. but he is of opinion that it would not do to change this, as, in the first place, the duck is a migratory bird, and in the second, about 7 per cent. of the people shoot. and it would be unreasonable to keep the 93 per cent. from procuring them.

It is beginning to be understood more generally now that the game does not belong solely to those who take out licenses to go hunting, but that 95 per cent. of it belongs to the people who do no shooting or killing, and when it is decided to protect any particular bird or animal it is the decision of those people which will prevail. The true sportsman will concur, but the man who shoots for the sake of killing all he can will object. But the game bird does not belong to him. and the question of what this class of hunter will agree to in the line of real conservation is now only a matter of academic interest. Through their greed and selfishness in shooting to the limit and beyond the heedless hunters of this land have brought the once bountiful supply of game to an alarmingly low point. The way to bring back the birds is to stop them being killed. and if this spells prohibition, then prohibition let it be, for the game birds must and shall be saved.

There is a drove of five deer in the County of Halton which have been there since spring, and have been seen several times in the woods near Lake Medad.

He was obliged to fine a man $20 for shooting a deer in the Township of Ancaster, without a license. last November.

YORK-COUNTY.

Overseer Albert E. Tarry, of Toronto. reports that the fishermen of Lake Ontario have informed him that the fishing has been very poor. and continues to get worse. There have been very small catches of trout and whitefish made, and no herring at all of any account. Angling has been equally poor.

There seems to be plenty of carp, but very little fish of any other species.

The close season has been very well observed in his district. There have been four convictions made for illegal fishing.

Ducks are not so plentiful as last year; he does not know how to account for this. Muskrats are practically extinct, and there have been very few mink caught.

There have been two convictions made under the Game Act and one under the Insectivorous Bird Act.

Overseer Robert Tillett, of Roach's Point, reports that the bass fishing was not very good at the beginning of the season, but there were some good catches made later. There seemed to be plenty of whitefish and salmon, but very few maskinonge and pickerel.

He did not come across any Americans this year. He has taken up some nets but could not find who had set them. He thinks the spearing license in the winter a good thing for the protection of the fish during the close season.

There are plenty of wild ducks and geese, and partridges are quite numerous. Black squirrels are becoming more plentiful each year.

The Fish and Game Laws have been well observed on the whole.

Overseer C. West, of Holland Landing, reports that the Game and Fishery Laws have been well observed in his division, and he has had no occasion to prosecute anyone.

He has every reason to believe that there is a satisfactory increase in all kinds of game fish.

Carp are becoming very scarce. The Bradford Fish Company report very poor catches.

Ducks are more plentiful this fall, and the shooting has been good; there has been more wild rice grown for the game.

He would suggest that mink should have the same protection that the musk-rats have.

Overseer G. W. West, of Holland Landing, reports that he finds that maskin-onge are on the increase in Cook's Bay, but very few were caught owing to the large quantity of natural food.

Black bass are plentiful, especially the smaller ones; they are following the streams more than he has ever known them to do. Judging from the large amount of food, all other game fish are doing well.

Ducks and snipe are scarce; in fact, this is the case with most of the game, owing, he thinks, to the dry season, and the bush and march fires which have destroyed the food. Wild rice is growing more plentiful, but there is not sufficient food yet for the ducks.

The law has been very well observed; he only saw that some trapping had been done out of season; he destroyed the traps, but could not find out who had set them; this was however sufficient to stop the law-breakers.

Mink and muskrats are quite as plentiful as they were last year.

MOHAWK, October 21, 1913.

MR. E. TINSLEY,

Superintendent Game and Fisheries, Toronto, Ont.

Dear Sir,—I beg to submit to you my fifth annual report in connection with the construction of bass ponds and the propagation of fish, and the results thereof.

One bass pond, one trout pond, and one minnow pond were completed this year, some five hundred feet of pipe line laid, a considerable amount of rip rapping and sodding of banks was also done. A terrace was made and lettered, grading and lettering and underbrushing also occupied a great portion of my time throughout this season. This work was done subject to the approval of Chief Engineer Halford, of the Public Works Department, and was carefully figured out.

As to propagation and results: Four ponds were made use of this year, the output of which exceeded that of former years by many thousands, and the many lakes that were re-stocked have received an adequate supply, which if allowed to mature and no unlawful fishing is done, will give them ample stock of parent fish for many years to come. The transportation of these fish was very successful, very few having died. The distance travelled in transporting fish amounted to about six thousand miles. The average size of fingerlings sent out this year were three inches in length, and they were in first class condition. The flowers were very fine and many people visited the Hatchery this year who were very loud in their praise with regard to its general appearance.

With the beginning of shipping of the advanced fry earlier in the season next year, and five ponds ready for use, the output, with favourable weather conditions, should be increased to over three times the amount of this year.

I remain, your Obedient Servant,

J. T. EDWARDS,

Superintendent, Mount Pleasant Hatchery.

REPORT OF WORK PERFORMED BY THE PATROL BOAT "NAVARCH ' ON THE RIDEAU WATERS AND BAY OF QUINTE DURIING THE YEAR 1913.

The first ten days in May were spent in fitting out the boat and on the 10th patrolled to Trenton, the boat running well. The following week visited Picton, Glen Island, Amherst Island, Kingston, Wolf Island, Simcoe Island, Horse Shoe Island, Deseronto, Belleville, Nigger Island.

On the 22nd patrolled the Gananoque with Warden Metcalfe on board. On the 26th patrolled from Kingston to the Brothers Island, Amherst Island, and through the Upper Gap to Willards Dock, and on the 30th to Picton and Hay Bay, interviewed Overseer Huffman and patrolled to Belleville.

On June 2nd patrolled between Belleville and Brighton with Capt. Hunter on board. On the 6th patrolled from Grenadier Island to Brockville and on to Prescott, then back to Brockville. The following week visited Grenadier Island, Jones Creek, Gananoque, Howe Island (patrolling all the bays between Gananoque and Kingston), Wolfe Island, Brothers Islands, Collin's Bay, and Upper Gap. On the 23rd patrolled from Belleville to Brighton and Presque Isle Point, seized set of hoop nets in the south-west end of Brighton Bay.

During July patrolled to Ottawa along the Ottawa River (with Overseer Loveday on board), Merrickville, Newboro, Kingston, Picton, Brothers Islands, Amherst Island, Pryners Cove, Collin's Bay, Brockville, Grenadier Island, Gananoque, Howe Island, Wolfe Island, Simcoe, Upper Gap, Belleville, Trenton, Brighton, Presque Isle (met Overseer Cheer), Mosquito Bay, and Horse Shoe Island.

From August 1st to 4th patrolled from Belleville to Kingston, Newboro, Portland, Smith's Falls, and back to Newboro, with Mr. Cox and Capt, Hunter on board. The following week patrolled to Brockville and Gananoque, then Mate Taylor patrolled with motor boat, as the boiler of steamer needed repairing.

On September 8th patrolled from Kingston to Gananoque with Mr. Pegg and Capt. Hunter on board. On the 10th seized about 3,000 yards of gill net set in the Gap, chased the men who set them, but they had too fast a boat and got away. On the 11th patrolled from Amherst Island to Belleville, seized over 2,000 yards of gill net set just off Adolphustown, in the Bay of Quinte. On the 20th patrolled from Kingston to Snake Island and Lower Gap. Seized two and a half sets of hoop nets in Bateau Channel close to Simcoe Island. On the 24th seized about 1,000 yards of gill net in Wellers Bay.

During October patrolled the Upper Gap, Amherst Island, Brothers Islands, Collins Bay, Kingston, Howe Island, Gros Creek, Wolfe Island, Bateau Channel, Simcoe Island, Snake Island, Bath (met Overseer Davy), Pryners Cove, Picton, Belleville, Emerald (Capt. Hunter on board), Deseronto, Trenton, Mosquito Bay, Shannonville River, Baker's Island, Nigger Island, Big Bay, Massassaga, Murray Canal, Wellers Bay, Fish Point, and Brighton Bay.

On the 1st seized about 3,000 yards of gill net, and again on the 30th seized about 1,000 yards of gill net in Wellers Bay.

On November 1st patrolled from Belleville to Massassaga Point with Mr. Holden and Capt. Hunter on board. The 4th, 5th, and 6th were spent going over the seining grounds with the Inspectors. On the 6th seized about 1,000 yards of gill net. On the 8th patrolled from Pryners Cove to Belleville, watching carefully for nets.

Capt. Carson joined the boat for a day or two on the 11th, patrolled between Belleville and Pryners Cove, and the following day seized a quantity of gill net between Deseronto and Picton, near Foresters Island. The season's work was finished on November 15th.

REPORT OF THE WORK PERFORMED BY THE PATROL BOAT "NAIAD" ON LAKE SIMCOE AND KAWARTHA LAKES DURING THE YEAR 1913.

On Tuesday, 15th April, left Peterboro and went to Talbot to fit out steamer and begun patrol work on the 24th, went to Beaverton, Thora Island, Georgina, Fox, Roaches Points, Mouth of Holland River, Bradford, Strawberry Island. On the 29th broke a piston in low pressure cylinder, but managed to run high pressure to Atherley, could not get through G. T. R. Bridge, obliged to go to Long March for repairs. During May patrolled to Eight Mile Point, Hawkston Shanty Bay, Barrie, Strath Allen, Big Bay Point, Sandico Bay, Fox Island, Roaches Point, Bradford, Holland River, Cook's Bay, Georgina and Thora Islands, Atherley, Grape Island, Shanty Bay, Orillia, Longford Mills, Washago and Severn Rivers, Beaverton, Jackson Point, Balsover, Balsam Lake, Rosedale, Fenelon Falls, South Bay, Coboconk, Gull River, Burnt River, Gun Point, Lindsay, Pleasant Point, Emily Creek, Bobcaygeon, Cameron Lake, Gamebridge, Kirkfield Lift Lock, Simcoe, Allandale, Oak Orchard, Buckhorn, Lovesick Lakes, Burleigh Falls, Mount Julian, Chemong Village, McCrackens Landing, Youngs Point, Lakefield, and Peterboro. On the 24th seized one boat, a trolling line and lunge. During the month communicated with Overseers West, Gaudaur, Bradshaw, Parker, and Leadley, and Inspector Holden. During June patrolled to Jubilee Point, Gore Landing (took on Overseer McAllister), Harwood, Idle Wild (saw Overseers Johnston and Shearer), Mouth of the Trent River, Rice Lake, Hiawatha, Otonabee River (met Overseer Thompson), Halls Bridge (saw Overseer Bonter), Peterboro, Lakefield, Youngs Point, Clear Lake, Sandy Point, McCrackens Landing, Jumper Island, Glenwood and Bellevedere, Boschink Narrow (met Overseer Moore), Mount Julian, Gilchrist Bay, Burleigh Falls, Lovesick Lake, Beer Bay, Buckhorn Lake, Chemong Lake, Bridgnorth, Huron Island, Sandy Creek (met Overseer Clarkson), Bobcaygeon, McCombs Island, Sturgeon Point, Fenelon Falls, Bauld and Pleasant Points, Moose Lake, Lindsay, Coboconk (saw Overseer Burtcheall), Jackson's Point, Strath

Allan, Sebastopol, Four Mile Point, Orillia, Washago, Genoa, Park, Longford Mills, Rama, Turner's Grove, Belle Ewart, Point Mara, and Thompson's Point. A great deal of dragging was done, and several fish and licenses examined. The first week in June was spent in repairing the boat. On the 16th Capt. Hunter was taken on board *re* Robinson case. During July patrolled to Barrie, Beaverton, Balsam Lake, Coboconk, Fenelon Falls, North Bay, South Bay, Rosedale, Gull River, Burnt River, Bobcaygeon, Emily Creek, Sturgeon Point, Ball Point, Lindsay, Gammons Narrows, Oak Orchard, Henningtons Island, Chemong Park, Indian Village, Herons Island, Lancasters Bridge, Buckhorn, Lovesick, Burleigh Falls, Mount Julian, McCrackens Landing, South Beach, Youngs Point, Lakefield, Juniper Island, Crows Landing, Monaca Camp, Gamebridge, Lake Simcoe, Thora Island, Longford Mills, Genoa Park, Orillia. Eight Mile Point, Hawkeston, Big Bay Point, Sebastopol, Jackson's Point, Fox Island, Roaches Point, Holland River, Shanty Bay, Port Bolster, Georgina Island, Sandico Bay, Birch Point. Duclose Point, West Bay, and Gulf River. Several Angling Permits were sold during the month and many of the Overseers interviewed. In August patrolled to Bobcaygeon, Nogies Creek, Eels Creek, Big Ball and Little Ball, Lindsay, Peterboro, Halls Bridge, Bensfort, Jubilee Point, Gore Landing, Harwood, Idyl Wild, Shearers Point, Hastings, Trent Bridge, Healy Falls, Birdsall, Foleys Island, Point Widlocks, South Beach, Sandy Point, Stoney Lake, McCrackens Landing, Bellevedere, Glenwood, Gilchrist Bay, Burleigh Falls, Lovesick, Buckhorn, Chemong Park, Henningtons Island, Oak Orchard, Sandy Creek, Bobcaygeon, Nogus Creek, Bald Lake, Sturgeon Point, Pleasant Point, Scugog, McLanes Creek, Gull River, South Bay, Thora Island, Strawberry Island, Atherley, Beaverton, Jackson Point, Holland River, Shanty Bay, Sebastopol, Lake Simcoe, Eight Mile Point. Longford, Rama, Lakefield, and Balsam Lake. The following overseers were communicated with during the month: Parker, Shearer, Macfarlane, Gaudaur, Green. Tillett, Johnson, and Forsythe. On the 5th the boiler was inspected at Peterboro. Capt. Hunter was on board from the 6th—8th. Several angling permits were sold, and many boats, licenses and fish were examined. On Monday, Sept. 1st, patrolled from Peterboro to Hastings with Mr. Cox on board. During the month visited Trent Bridge. Healy Falls, Foleys Island, Keene, Roaches Point, Idyl Wild. Gore Landing, Bewdley, Jubilee Point, Tick Island, Otonobee River, Widlock. Campbelltown, Bensford Bridge, Halls Bridge, Lakefield, Youngs Point. South Beach. Kawartha Park, McCrackens Landing, Bellevedere, Mount Julian. Burleigh Falls, Lovesick, Buckhorn, Chemong Village, Bridgenorth. Oak Orchard. Gammons Narrows.

On October 10th patrolled from Beaverton to the Kirkfield Canal and on to Balsam Lake, Cameron Lake to Fenelon Falls, then into Sturgeon Lake and Bobcaygeon. The following day patrolled to Gammons Narrows and Buckhorn, and there met Overseer Clarkson. The 12th, 13th, and 14th were spent in laying up the steamer for the winter.

REPORT OF THE WORK PERFORMED BY THE PATROL BOAT "LOTUS"
ON THE WATERS OF THE NORTH CHANNEL OF LAKE
HURON AND GEORGIAN BAY DURING THE YEAR
1913.

Left Little Current on May 7th for the season's patrol work, calling at Sheguiandah and Killarney, then back to Little Current and on to Whitefish River
and home again, spending Sunday in Little Current. On Monday took Overseer
Ramesbottom to McGregor Bay, and during the rest of the week called at Manita-
waning, Killarney, and Beaverstone, and patrolled among the islands with small
boat and picked up a seine net, then on to Byng Inlet, calling at the Bustards,
where they had to remain for a few days on account of the stormy weather. The
following week they went to Parry Sound, where they took Overseer Dusang on
board, and went to Indian Harbour and on to Penetang and Midland. The rest
of the month patrolled to Collingwood, Wiarton, where they took Overseer Jermyn
on board, Cape Commodore, Griffith Island and Tobermory. Lifted about two
miles of night line on the way. During June they patrolled to Fitzwilliam Island,
South Bay, Killarney, Little Current, Whitefish River (with Overseer Ramesbottom on board), Gore Bay, Duck Islands, Murphy's Harbour, Smith's Bay, Byng
Inlet, The Bustards, Parry Sound, and Point au Baril. On the 16th they broke
a small wheel and were obliged to go to Blind River to have it mended. On July
4th they took Capt. Hunter on board and patrolled to Minnicoy, calling at Santa
Lusia and Copper Head, and again on the 24th of that month they went to Blind
River and the Soo with the Inspector on board. On the 22nd they took Overseer
Andrew Hall and Constable Shields round Barrie Island and in to Bayfield Sound,
and on the 25th they took Overseer Bradbury to Thessalon. The rest of the month
they patrolled to Collingwood, Meaford, Owen Sound, Tobermory, Little Current,
Fitzwilliam Islands, South Bay, Gore Bay, Kagawong, and John Islands. On
the 7th and 8th of August they took up three trap nets which they burnt. Round
the 19th and 20th the weather was stormy. They patrolled to Killarney, Beaverstone, Toad Island, Little Current, Round Island, Fitzwilliam Island, Tobermory,
Johnston Harbour, Pike Bay, Southampton, Griffith Island. Penetang, Parry
Sound, Point au Baril, Byng Inlet, and The Bustards. On September 4th they
took Overseer Ramesbottom to McGregor Bay, and the rest of the month was spent
in patrolling the West Bay, Bedford Island, Whitefish Bay, Little Current, Claper-
ture Island, Spanish and John Islands, Gore Bay, and Sheguiandah. They broke
a small wheel in the engine during the patrol work and spent the first week in
October fitting her up again, after which they patrolled to Sheguiandah, Round
Island, Killarney, Scarecrow Island, Papoose Island, Little Current, Beaverstone,
Grondine Point, Kagawong, McGregor Bay, and Bay Finn. They found two trap
nets at Scarecrow Island and Papoose Island which they burnt, and picked up a
seine near Grondine Point. There was a good deal of stormy weather during
this month. On October 30th and 31st they laid the boat up at Little Current for
the winter.

REPORT OF WORK PERFORMED BY THE PATROL BOAT "JESSIE T" ON THE WATERS OF LAKE SUPERIOR DURING THE YEAR 1913.

From May 1st to 7th was spent in preparing boat for patrol work, and on the 8th, patrolled to Richard's Landing, and from there went to Sault Ste. Marie the following day. During the remainder of the month, patrolled Goulais Bay. Batchawana, Maple Island, Sandy Island, Copper Mine Point, Gargantua Harbour, Lizard Islands, Agawa Rocks, Michipicoten Harbour, Pilot Harbour, Otter Head. Ganley's Harbour, Pucksaw River, Indian Harbour, and Mamaise Point.

June was spent patrolling the vicinity of the above places.

The beginning of July was spent in repairing the engine. On the 16th and 17th, patrolled Goulais Bay and Batchawana Bay, and the remainder of the month patrolled to Parisian Island, Maple Island, Sault Ste. Marie, Groscap, Pancake Bay, Batchawana Bay, Lizard Island, Copper Mine, Agawa River, Sandy River, Copper Point, and Mamaise Point.

August and September were spent patrolling Lake Superior in the vicinity of Sault Ste. Marie.

During October, the following places were patrolled. Goulais Bay, Batchawana Harbour, Gargantua Harbour, Michipicoten Harbour, Indian Harbour, Agawa River, Sault Ste. Marie, Groscap, Echo Lake, Whiskey Bay, Hilton Landing, Copper Mine Point and Garden River.

On November 12th, patrolled to Goulais Bay and fetched a boat which had been seized. The 15th, 16th and 17th were spent laying up "Jessie T" for the winter.

REPORT OF WORK PERFORMED BY PATROL BOAT "GLADYS R" ON THE WESTERN PORTION OF LAKE SUPERIOR DURING THE YEAR 1913.

Left Sault Ste. Marie on June 20th, arriving at Rossport on the 28th. The first three weeks of July were spent in making repairs and painting boat, etc., and getting ready for patrol work.

On the 21st, patrolled to Flower Island, Moffatt Strait, Bead Island, Otter Bay, and Duncan's Cove, thence to Silver Islet, Black's Dock, Trombly's Dock and Point Magnet the following day, and on the 23rd patrolled to Port Arthur: when within two miles of Welcome Island calking came out of seams, water stopped engine, leaving boat in sinking condition. Called boat to tow them to Welcome Island. The remainder of the month was spent in making repairs and having engine overhauled.

On August 1st patrolled to Trombly's Dock, called at Point Magnet. The next day went to Rossport, calling at Black's Dock, Nepigon Strait, and Nepigon Bay, south shore. The following week patrolled to Vert Island, Gravel River, Cyprus River, Mazokama River, Burnt Harbour, Otter Bay, St. Ignace Island, French Harbour, Duncan's Cove, Moffat Strait, Woodbine Harbour, McKay's Harbour, Simpson Harbour, Battle Island, Jackfish, Black River, Steel River, Battle Island and Blind Channel.

Found Moose very plentiful along Moffat's Straits.

On September 4th, patrolled to Battle Island, called at all bays and harbours round Simpson Island, and found plenty of moose in Morn Harbour. On the 8th, patrolled to Little St. Ignace Island, calling at Otter Bay, French Harbour and Burnt Harbour. Went to meet Mr. Holden at Nepigon on the 11th, returning the following day. On the 17th, patrolled to French Harbour, and on the 18th returned to Rossport, calling at Woodbine Harbour, McKay's Harbour, Morn Harbour, found ducks plentiful at several places. The remainder of the month patrolled to Mazokama Bay, Cyprus River, Gravel River, Flower Island, Black's Dock, Trombly's Dock, Point Magnet and Port Arthur, calling at Silver Islet.

Met Mr. Holden, Inspector of Fisheries, at Port Arthur on the 9th October, and on the 13th had boat loaded on car and shipped to Fort Frances for the winter.

REPORT OF WORK PERFORMED BY THE PATROL BOAT "ELLA C" ON THE RIDEAU WATERS DURING THE YEAR 1913.

On June 6th left for Kingston to take charge of boat, and after having the boiler tested the following day, patrolled down the Rideau to Jones Falls, and then on to Smith's Falls. The following week patrolled the south shore to McDonald's Bay, Portland, Bungalow, Garrett's Rest, German Bay, Oak Island, Horseshoe Bay, Bass Bay, Noble's Bay, McLean Bay, Gem Island, Adam's Lake, Oliver's Ferry and Poonahmalee.

The following places were visited during July: German Bay, Rideau Ferry, Horseshoe Bay, Bass Bay, Garrett's Rest, The Bungalow, Murphy's Cove, McLean's Bay, Gem Island, Adam's Lake, Front and Grindstone Islands, McDonald's Bay, Portland, Little Boy's Camp, Hog's Creek, McVeety's Bay, Newboro, Long Island, Rocky Narrows, Perth, and Oak Island.

On the 27th, took Warden Metcalfe on board and patrolled down the Rideau Ferry.

The above places were visited during August, and on the 18th, patrolled the south shore to Portland, Narrows Locks and Westport to see Overseer Clarke. On the 29th patrolled McVeety's and McLean's Bay with row boat to see that there was no illegal shooting being carried on.

During September, patrolled to McLean's Bay, Perth Tay Canal, Rideau, Smith's Falls, Portland, Adam's Lake, McDonald's Bay, Gem Island, German Bay, Garrett's Rest, Tar Island, Newboro, Noble's Bay, Murphy's Cove, Bungalow, Horseshoe Bay, Gould's Wharf, Westport, Front Island and Long Island, keeping a careful watch all the time to see that no one was shooting.

On October 6th, patrolled to Kilmarnock and Merrickville, and called to see Overseer Boyd. The next day went back to Kilmarnock and took row boat, patrolled Irish Creek. On the 10th, patrolled to Hutton's Lock, and with row boat patrolled Otter Creek, but found no illegal fishing.

On October 12th, seized one gill net in Noble's Bay, and on the 19th seized three gill nets. On the 22nd took row boat and patrolled at night to Rocky Narrows and back along the north shore to Guinea Point, and the following day patrolled round Star and Birch Islands.

On November 4th, patrolled to Kingston, and left steamer in charge of Warden Metcalfe to be laid up.

REPORT OF THE WORK PERFORMED BY THE PATROL BOAT
"ATHENE" ON THE DETROIT RIVER DURING THE YEAR 1913.

On May 6th, patrolled to Amherstburg, and the 8th patrolled to Livingston,
with the Game Warden on board, found two trespassers who ran away before
they could be caught, but on the 10th, discovered one man fishing without a
permit; compelled him to pay $2 for license.

On the 14th, patrolled the Thames River with Warden Chauvin and Overseer
Drouillard on board.

On the 17th, patrolled to Sandwich and Windsor, took up two boxes of black
bass which had been seized, left Windsor for Lower Detroit River and Livingston
Channel.

The remainder of the month patrolled to Peach Island, Lake St. Clair,
Detroit River, Sandwich, Amherstburg, and the last few days of May were spent
in dry dock making repairs.

On June 10th, patrolled to Pelee Island and Kingsville, and the following
day went down Detroit River, Canard River and Sandwich. On the 22nd,
patrolled Lower Detroit River, and west side of Fighting Island, found four
people trespassing, made them take out licenses.

During July, visited Livingston Channel, Amherstburg, Sandwich, Fighting
Island, Grosse Island, Grey Duck Bay and Turkey Island, Detroit River, Lake
St. Clair, Pike Creek, Thames River, Mitchell's Bay, Walkerville, Chappers Canal,
River Canard, Peach Island, Grassy Island. Several fishermen were discovered
angling without a license, compelled them to take out permits. On the 20th, found
two boats, owners fishing without licenses, seized the boats and took them to
Walkerville.

On August 6th, patrolled to Rondeau Provincial Park with Warden Chauvin
on board, remained there three days on account of the rough weather. On the
17th, patrolled Upper Detroit River and Lake St. Clair with Warden on board.
Found one poacher, compelled him to take out license. The remainder of the
month was spent installing new engine in the boat.

During September, found a number of people fishing without licenses, all
of whom were obliged to pay $2 for same. Watched carefully throughout the
month to see that no illegal shooting was done.

During October, patrolled to Fighting Island, River Detroit, Belle Isle,
Canard River, Lake St. Clair, Peach Island, Thames River, Kirsch Wharf, Grey
Duck Bay, Mitchell's Bay and Wallaceburg. A number of permits were sold
during the month to people fishing without them.

On November 4th, season's work was finished, and boat put away for the
winter.

REPORT OF THE WORK PERFORMED BY THE LAUNCH "HELEN" ON
THE WATERS OF THE ST. LAWRENCE RIVER DURING
THE YEAR 1913.

On March 22nd, patrolled to Grindstone Island, upon reports of illegal
shooting, but was unable to catch the lawbreakers. The following week patrolled
to Ivy Lea, Landon's Bay, (seized 24 traps set to catch muskrats) Rockport and
Longbridge Creek, Grappling all the time for nets. On April 1st, seized one

set of hoop nets and gill net, and on the 2nd, took up about 60 traps set in the rat houses. On the 4th, went to Lansdown Dock and took up some more rat traps.

On the 6th, seized four sets of gill nets near Tar Island, and on the 7th and 9th, seized one set of gill nets and some more traps.

Left Gananoque on the 13th, upon receipt of reports that there were some Americans trapping in Jones Creek. Discovered five of them; drove them out and seized their traps; went out on the river and grappled, took up four night lines, there were about 2,000 hooks on them and 14 sturgeon.

On the 15th, seized six sets of gill nets in Black Duck Bay. The remainder of the month visited Grenadier Island, Mallorytown Creek, Howe Island, Grasses Creek, Rockport, Jones Creek, Longbridge Creek, Thompson's Creek, and Tee Island. Seized four more night lines, one of which was about three-quarters of a mile long.

On May 3rd, took up two sets of hoop nets in Landon's Bay, and on the 7th seized two sets of gill nets in South Lake. On the 17th, patrolled to Grenadier Island, and watched some Americans as they ran their nets at night, but they got away as they had a fast boat, however, their nets were seized. Took one night line on the 20th. Out all night on the 24th, watching some American from a Thousand Islands, but their boat was too fast, and they escaped.

During June patrolled to Howe Island, Grenadier Island, Wolfe Island, Tar Island, Jones Creek, Big Bay, Landon's Bay, Hickory Island, Leak Island, Tay Island, Mud Island, Rockport.

On June 8th, seized seven sets of gill nets, and on the 10th, two sets of gill nets and one night line. On the 12th, patrolled down the river and found a fisherman drying nets, tried to seize them, but was driven off with a shot gun. Had him summonsed and fined $101 and costs, and bound over to keep the law in bonds of $700. On the 18th, seized one gill net.

July was spent in carefully patrolling the river, grappling for nets, and watching for illegal fishing.

During August, patrolled to Longbridge Creek, Rockport, Wolfe Island, Jones Creek, Howe Island, Ivy Lea, Float Island, Marble Rock, Tar Island, and all the small islands in the Gananoque River.

The first week or two in September, was spent in watching to see that no illegal shooting was done. On the 18th, seized one net in Longbridge Creek.

On October 11th, seized one set of trap nets and half a mile of gill nets. During the month patrolled to Grenadier Island, Wolfe Island, Howe Island, Rockport, Sugar Island, Jones Creek, Tar Island, Thompson Bay, and finished the season's patrol work on November 4th.

REPORT OF WORK PERFORMED BY THE LAUNCH "SWALLOW" ON THE WATERS OF LAKE NIPISSING DURING THE YEAR 1913.

On May 8th, commenced patrol work by going to Callender upon instructions from the Department, re illegal shipping of fish. On 14th, patrolled along north-east shore of Lake Nipissing to Callender Bay, saw no sign of illegal fishing. On 17th, made trip to Beaucage to search railway construction camp. During June, patrolled to Fish Bay, saw no sign of any violations of the laws; to Beaucage to inspect the railway construction camp; to Manitou Islands, patrolled all round the group, but found no illegal fishing being done; to the Callender Bay along the north-east shore of Lake Nipissing, no sign of any nets; and to Goose Islands, patrolled all round, but saw no signs of any violations. During the week of July 14th, patrolled to Callender Bay, Fish Bay, Mouth of South River and Goose Islands, but saw no evidence of illegal work. Left for French River the following week on the 22nd, patrolled to Frank's Bay, Restoule Bay, round Sand Island Channel, Little Chaudiere, Wigwam Point and Big Chaudiere Falls. On Aug. 5th, left Frank's Bay for west arm of Lake Nipissing, patrolled west arm, seized one rifle and two guns, returned to Frank's Bay. On 12th, patrolled Frank's Bay to Chaudiere Falls, saw no signs of any violations, returned along south shore of lake to Cross Point. On 16th, round Sand Island Channel, and during the last week patrolled to Fish Bay as per instructions from the Department to investigate complaint. On the 30th, went to South East Bay, saw no signs of any illegal duck hunting. During September, patrolled to Fish Bay, round the islands in that vicinity, and to South-East Bay with Overseer Drouillard, re testing for net fishing, also to Manitou Islands and Lavaes River, but saw no signs of illegal hunting or fishing. On October 1st, patrolled round Manitou Islands, no signs of any nets, and on the 4th, went to Frank's Bay to investigate complaint of illegal net fishing, no evidence for conviction.

REPORT OF WORK PERFORMED BY THE LAUNCH "AUDREY C" ON THE WATERS OF THE NORTH SHORE OF THE GEORGIAN BAY DURING THE YEAR 1913.

On June 2nd, began to fit up "Audrey C" for patrol work, and worked at the engine for two or three days. On the 9th, left Waubaushene for Parry Sound and on to Penn House on the 11th, and the following day patrolled to Moon River, Crawfords, Summersett and Yank Canuck. On the 14th, patrolled to Fesserton. The following week was spent in patrolling to the Christian Islands, Cave Island, Musquash, Tomahawk Point, Midland, Coldwater, Copperhead, Parry Sound and Indian Harbour.

During July patrolled to Parry Sound, Fesserton, Copperhead, Sans Souci, Whalens, Martin's Island, Gorby's, Minnicog, Tomahawk, Honey Harbour, Musquash, Frances, Yank Canuck, Moon River, Quivive, Iona, Drummonds, Jubilee Island, and Split Rock. On the 22nd, seized one trap net, and again on the 29th raised the remainder of a trap net, and seized one gill net with one black bass and two dog fish.

August was spent in much the same manner as July. On the 18th, went to Penetang and took Overseer Hornsby on board, patrolled to Christian Islands, and there seized one trap net and burned it.

September was spent in patrolling Honey Harbour, Whalens, Mitchell, Christian Islands, Giant's Tomb, Musquash, Quarry Island, Sturgeon Point, Copperhead, Sans Souci, Moon River, Buffalo House, Midland, Port McNicoll, Waubaushene, Victoria Harbour, Frances, Cove Island, Salt Harbour and Parry Sound. During October, patrolled the above places, and on the 2nd November, seized 16 decoys and discovered two men shooting ducks on Sunday. The following day patrolled to McCrae's Lake and to Midland on the 3rd. Laid boat up for the winter on the 15th November.

REPORT OF THE WORK PERFORMED BY THE LAUNCH "BESSIE G".
ON THE ST. LAWRENCE RIVER DURING THE YEAR 1913.

On June 3rd patrolled to Brown's Bay, and from there to Simcoe Island and Reed's Bay, and on the 12th to Big Bay and Point Alexander, but found no illegal fishing.

The 14th, 16th, and the last week of June were spent patrolling Barrot's Bay, Simcoe Island, Reed's Bay, Big Bay, Alexander Point and Big Sand Bay

July 1st and 2nd were spent in the vicinity of Point Alexander, Big Sand Bay, Simcoe Island and Reeds Bay, and on the 8th, patrolled to foot of Wolfe Island and Big Bay, then on through the Canal to Barrot's Bay. The 14th and 15th were spent around Point Alexander, and during the last week of the month patrolled to Simcoe Island, Reeds Bay, and Point Alexander, but found no illegal fishing being carried on.

During August, patrolled the neighbourhood of Big Sand Bay at the head of Wolfe Island, Simcoe Island, Reeds Bay and vicinity, Point Alexander and Horseshoe Island.

On Sept. 2nd, patrolled to Point Alexander and Big Sand Bay, then to Simcoe Island and Reeds Bay and vicinity the following day. The 10th and 13th were spent in the neighbourhood of Big Bay, and the 17th, 26th and 27th around Simcoe Island, Reeds Bay and Point Alexander.

On October 2nd, patrolled from Wolfe Island to Barrot's Bay, then on to Simcoe Island and Reeds Bay, found everything quiet, no illegal shooting or fishing. The following day patrolled to Simcoe Island and back to Barrot's Bay, and on the 4th to Brown's Bay. The next week and again on the 16th and 18th went to head of Wolfe Island and Simcoe Island, Big Bay and Button Bay. On the 25th patrolled to Barrot's Bay, Simcoe Island and Reeds Bay, and on the 30th to Big Bay, Button Bay and Alexander Point, which finished the season's work.

REPORT OF WORK PERFORMED BY LAUNCH "LIBBY" ON STONEY
LAKE DURING THE YEAR 1913.

In April patrolled to Stoney Lake to see that the Fishery Laws were well observed, again on May 27th, June 9th and 16th visited Stoney Lake.

On June 25th, patrolled to Burleigh Falls, Lovesick Lake, Mt. Julian and Young's Point, and to Lakefield, on the 27th.

During July, patrolled to Stoney Lake, Mt. Julian, Burleigh Falls, Crow's Landing, McCracken's Landing, Clear Lake, Young's Pt., Ketchawanooka Lake, Lakefield, Lovesick Lake, and Deer Bay.

The beginning of August was spent on Stoney Lake, visiting Lovesick Lake, Victoria House, Burleigh Falls, Lakefield, and Deer Bay, and during the last two weeks visited Eel's Creek, Glenwood, Crow's Landing, Juniper Island, Viamded, Burleigh Falls, Lovesick Lake, Lakefield, and Brooks.

The above places were visited in September, and a close watch was kept to see that no illegal fishing or shooting was carried on.

On October 8th, patrolled to Lovesick Lake, Stoney Lake, Clear Lake, Young's Pt., to see that no trapping was done. Also out on patrol work on the 18th, 20th, 27th and 29th of this month.

WORK PERFORMED BY LAUNCH "LAURA" IN THE NORTH CHANNEL OF LAKE HURON DURING THE YEAR 1913.

On June 3rd, left Mud Lake for Hay Marsh and Old Fort, dragged round some islands until evening, then went on to Whiskey Bay for the night. The following day patrolled round Duncan and other small islands, and back to Hay Marsh and home.

On the 13th left home for Mud Lake, patrolled to Sailor's Encampment and Richard's Landing, then on to Kensington Point and Hilton, and back to Lake George for the night, returning home the next day, after patrolling the lake.

On the 17th, patrolled the full length of Hay Marsh, and spent the night at Old Fort. The following day went to Whiskey Bay, Milford Haven, Beef Island, Big Point and on to Richard's Landing for the night. On the 19th patrolled to Nebesh Encampment, then home. On the 30th, went to Dickens' Mills to see the damage done by the beavers and blow them out with dynamite.

On July 8th, patrolled Mud Lake, Hay Marsh, Old Fort, and dragged round some islands in Sterling Bay, and spent the night in Whiskey Bay. The next morning went to Milford Haven and Beef Island, where we spent the night, leaving for Big Point, Hilton and Richard's Landing the next day, and on the 11th patrolled to the Encampment, Mud Lake and home.

On the 16th and 17th patrolled Hay Marsh, Old Fort, Whiskey Bay, Mud Lake, Encampment and Lake George, where the wheel broke; procured another one from the Soo. On the 21st patrolled to Lake George and Richard's Landing, then on to Kensington Point, and back to Richard's Landing for the night. The following day left for Encampment and Nebesh, then on to Mud Lake and home.

On August 12th, left Mud Lake for the Soo, wind very high, stayed there all night and the following day, leaving on 14th for home.

During the week of the 21st, made two trips, one to Richard's Landing via Mud Lake, Lake George, and Campmadours, and home again by Kensington Point and Encampment; the other one to Whiskey Bay by Hay Marsh, and Old Fort, returning home through Milford Haven and Beef Island, and back to the Old Fort and Hay Mash. On the 27th and 28th went to the Soo, on the way patrolling Encampment, Lake George and Richard's Landing, returning home on the 30th.

On September 2nd, left Mud Lake for Whiskey Bay and spent the night there. The following day found five boat loads of Indians from the other side, some were fishing and others picking blackberries; sent them all away; remained on Hay Marsh until all the American Indians had disappeared. On the 9th, 10th and 11th went to the Soo for gasoline.

On the 18th, left Mud Lake for Hay Marsh, Old Fort, and spent the night at Raines Point, found two nets. The following day patrolled Whiskey Bay, Milford Haven, Beef Island and back to Hay Marsh for the night, returning home on the 30th.

Patrolled to Edward Island on the 24th.

During the week of the 30th, went to Mud Lake, and Richardson's Point; had trouble with the launch on account of poor gasoline, returned home by Whiskey Bay.

Patrolled to Kentville on the 30th October for gasoline, and on the 31st went to Hay Marsh and other places, but it turned very cold and stormy and had to return home.

REPORT OF WORK PERFORMED BY THE PATROL BOAT "MEENAGHA"
ON THE MUSKOKA LAKES DURING THE YEAR 1913.

The 2nd and 3rd June was spent in the vicinity of Gravenhurst, patrolling Brydens Bay, Hackrock River, Muskoka River, Dennison's Island, Montcalm, Walker's Point and Port Carling. Received report of illegal fishing on the 4th at Clarks Falls, took row boat but found nothing.

The remainder of the week patrolled Breckinridge Bay, Windermere, Tobins Island, Waskada, Rostreavar, Muskoka, Juddhaven, Morgans Bay, Rosseau, Sandy Bay, Cape Elizabeth, and Skeleton Bay.

The next fortnight was spent patrolling to South Falls, Gull and Silver Lakes, Montcalm, Walker's Point, Beaumaris, Milford Bay, Port Carling, Breckenridge Bay, Windermere, Dee Bank River, Waskada, Tobins Island, Horseshoe Island, Fairview Island, Mortimer's Point, Smith's Bay, Big Island, St. Elma, Narrows, Gravenhurst, Hackrock River, Steven's Bay, Gerry Lea Island, Gowan's Island, Shanty Bay, Acton Island and Rossclair.

The week of the 30th was spent in patrolling Breckenbridge Bay, Windermere, Dee Bank River, Juddhaven, Royal Muskoka, Waskada, Minett, Pinelands, Ferndale, Milford Bay, Beaumaris, Walker's Point and Montcalm.

On Monday, 7th July, patrolled Gull and Silver Lakes, calling at Pine Dale House and the cottages by row boat.

The remainder of the month was spent in making a thorough patrol of the different lakes and bays in the vicinity of Port Carling and Gravenhurst.

On August 1st left Royal Muskoka for Skeleton Bay, but the wind was very high, had to take shelter until evening and returned to Royal Muskoka. On the 4th patrolled Gull and Silver Lakes, calling at the cottages and Pinedale House by rowboat. The next two or three weeks were spent patrolling St. Elmo, Big Island, Beaumaris, Woodington, Nepawin, Joseph River, Painton House, Tobins Island, Port Carling, Rossclair, Fairview, Mortimers, Bala Park, Dudley, Acton Island, Montcalm, Walker's Point, Windermere, Waskada, Dee Bank River, Port Sandfield, Craigielea, Breckenridge, Gravenhurst, Milford Bay, Shanty Bay, Gerry Lea Island, Hackrock River, and Juddhaven.

September was spent in much the same manner as August, patrolling the different rivers and lakes in the vicinity of Port Carling. There were one or two reports of illegal work received, but no convictions were made.

On October 4th, patrolled to Big Lake and Loon Lake in search of nets, etc., but found nothing. On the 21st summoned two men who had partridges in their possession during the close season. They were brought before the magistrate on the 24th, and it was proved that they both had the partridges out of season; one case was dismissed and the other adjourned while the evidence was submitted to the Attorney General.

On October 30th, lay the patrol boat up for the winter.

---

7 G.F.

WORK PERFORMED BY PATROL BOAT "MADELINE" ON THE RIVER
ST. LAWRENCE AND LAKE ONTARIO DURING THE YEAR 1913.

The early part of May was spent fitting out the boat for the season's work,
and the remainder of the month in patrolling the waters of the St. Lawrence
and Rideau Rivers, and Lake Ontario.

During the beginning of June patrolled the St. Lawrence River and Cataraque.
The following week proceeded to Brother's Island and Collins Bay, then up the
St. Lawrence River to Howe Island, Grass Creek, McKenzies Island and Milton
Island. On June 20th, left for Brother's Island, Simcoe Island and Cataraque
Creek, and the last week of June was spent on Lake Ontario and River St.
Lawrence.

During July patrolled the St. Lawrence River, the Rideau River to Kingston
Mills, then to Howe Island, McKenzies Island, Brophy's Point, Milton Island and
Kingston. Brother's Island, Collins Bay, Simcoe Island, Reeds Bay, Bateau
Channel, Deadman's Bay, Navy Bay, Cedar Island and Grass Creek were also
visited.

The first two weeks in August were spent in patrolling the Rideau and St.
Lawrence Rivers, and Lake Ontario, after which visited Howe Island, Long
Island Park, Grass Creek, Oak Point, McKenzies Island, Milton Island, Cedar
Island, and all the bays and shoals as far as Fort Henry. All points on the
Rideau River as far as Kingston Mills, were visited, also Brother's Islands,
Collins Bay, Simcoe Island and Reeds Bay.

At the beginning of September he went to Collins Bay, Brother's Islands,
Simcoe Island, Milton Island, Cedar Island, Dead Man's Bay, Navy Bay and
Rideau River; after which patrolled Lake Ontario to Collins Bay, St. Lawrence
River to Howe Island and Rideau River to Kingston Mills.

During October patrolled the St. Lawrence to Howe Island, Long Island
Park, Grass Creek, McKenzies Island, Milton Island, Cedar Island, also Lake
Ontario, and the St. Lawrence and Rideau Rivers.

THE FOLLOWING ARTICLES WERE CONFISCATED DURING THE
YEAR 1913 ON ACCOUNT OF FISHERIES.

11,484 yards of gill net; 36 boxes of fish; 12 trap nets; 9 seines; 46 hoop
nets; 800 hooks; 8 spears; 5 dip nets; 5 row boats; 1 gasolene boat; 20 fish
traps; 5 jacklights.

On the Pickerel River.

1

A Four Days' Hunt in the vicinity of Lake of the Woods.

Near Curtain Falls, Rainy River District.

Stepping onto a Bull Moose, in the Rainy River District.

Landing a Big One on the Rideau Lakes.

Indians drying Moose Meat at Fort Matachewan, on the Montreal River.

On the Pickerel River, in Parry Sound District.

Hudson Bay Company Factor and crew at dinner, Indian Chutes, Montreal River.

Key Rapids, near Key Inlet Crossing, in the Parry Sound District.

Lake Rosseau, in the Muskoka District.

Hudson Bay Factor and Fur Press at Fort
Matachewan, on the Montreal River.

LIST OF GAME AND FISHERY WARDENS.

Name.	Residence.	District.
Burt, William........	Simcoe	Niagara Peninsula.
Chauvin, Victor.......	Windsor	South Western District.
Metcalf, J. H.........	Kingston	Eastern District.
Parks, G. M..........	North Bay.........	Districts of Nipissing, Sudbury and Timiskaming.
Robinson, J. T........	Sault Ste. Marie....	Districts of Algoma and Manitoulin.
Sterling, C. N........	Kenora	Districts of Kenora and Thunder Bay.
Willmott, J. H........	Beaumaris	Districts of Muskoka and Parry Sound.
Young, D. D. (Col.)....	Fort Frances.......	Rainy River District.

LIST OF OVERSEERS.

Name.	Residence.	District.
Adair, William	Norland	Townships of Laxton, Digby and Somerville, in the County of Victoria.
Anderson, W. A.	Cornwall	Counties of Stormont and Glengarry, with jurisdiction over so much of the River St. Lawrence as lies in front of said counties.
Andrews, Samuel .	Micksburg ...	For the Tps. of Bromley, Stafford, and Ross, in the County of Renfrew, with joint jurisdiction over the Tp. of Westmeath.
Angrove, James ...	Kingston	City of Kingston, and waters fronting Co. Frontenac, with joint jurisdiction over the Rideau waters between St. Lawrence and Kingston Mills.
Armstrong, H. C. ..	Glen Ross ...	The Trent River, from its mouth to Chisholm's Rapids, and tributaries thereto, and to Trenton Junction.
Avery, Melzar	Sharbot Lake	Township of Oso, with joint jurisdiction over the Township of Hinchinbrook, in the County of Frontenac.
Avis, J. J.	Cockburn Island..	Cockburn Island, in the District of Manitoulin.
Aymer, William ...	Fort Frances.	Fort Frances, from mouth of Rainy River to Emo and District of Rainy River.
Barr, George	Harrowsmith	Tp. Portland, in Co. Frontenac, with joint jurisdiction over Desert and Knowlton Lakes.
Beatty, John	Old Fort, Midland	With jurisdiction, with other overseers, over Tps. Tay and Matchedash, Co. Simcoe.
Birch, W. J.	Delta	Upper and Lower Beverley lakes and rivers.
Blea, Daniel	South River .	Province of Ontario.
Bliss, L. E.	Nepigon	The River Nepigon, Lake Nepigon, and waters tributary to the said river and lake.
Blunden, H. A.	Sarnia	County Lambton, exclusive of Walpole and St. Ann's Islands.
Boate, J. R.	Fowler's Cors.	Tp. Emily, in Co. Victoria.
Boler, William	Byron	River Thames, between London and boundary line between Townships Delaware and Westminster, County of Middlesex.
Bonter, Robert	Marmora ...	Tp. of Marmora, County of Hastings.
Bourgon, J. B.	Rockland	County of Russell.
Boyd, J. H.	Merrickville .	Rideau River and tributaries, fronting on County of Grenville.
Boyd, W. M.	Kagawong ..	Kagawong Lake, with jurisdiction over North Channel, in vicinity of Kagawong Village.
Bradbury, J. R.	Blind River ..	District of Algoma.

LIST OF OVERSEERS.—*Continued.*

Name.	Residence.	District.
Bradshaw, A.	Lindsay	Townships Mariposa and Ops, Co. Victoria.
Briggs, T. J.	Bridgeburg ··	County of Welland.
Brisbin, Angus	Picton ·······	For the waters of Lake Ontario, fronting Tps. North and South Marysburg, including all waters surrounding islands in said townships, also Main Duck Islands, and that portion of Bay of Quinte fronting these townships, as well as the waters of the Bay of Quinte, known as Picton Harbor, in Tp. Hallowell.
Briscoe, W. L.	Killaloe Stn...	Townships of Jones, Sherwood, Hagarty, Radcliffe, Brudenell, Raglan, and Lynedoch, Co. Renfrew.
Brown, R. M.	Milton ....,	Townships of Nassagaweya and Esquesing in the County of Halton.
Burke, George	Perth	For the Town of Perth, Townships of North Elmsley, Drummond, North Burgess, and the first two concessions of the Township of Bathurst, County Lanark.
Burns, D. E.' ...:..	Pembroke ····	The waters between Allumette Rapids and Deux Joachim.
Burtcheall, C.	Coboconk ····	Balsam and Mud Turtle Lakes, County Victoria.
Campbell, John	Sylvan	River Aux Sables and tributaries.
Carson, R. W.	Peterboro' ...	Counties Simcoe, Ontario, Victoria, Peterboro', Durham, Northumberland, and York.
Cassan, C. H.	Campbellford	Trent River and tributaries, Co. Northumberland, from Campbellford to Trent Bridge.
Cates, Geo. S.	Emo	Rainy River District, between Emo and the Town of Rainy River.
Cheer, T. H.	Brighton	For the waters of Lake Ontario, fronting Co Northumberland, also inland waters tributary to said lake in said county.
Clark, Gordon	Westport ····	Township of North Crosby, in the County of Leeds, and with joint jurisdiction with any other overseer over Wolf Lake, in said Township, and the Township of Bedford, in County of Frontenac.
Clarkson, William ..	Lakehurst ···	West half of Township of Smith, Township of Ennismore, west half of Tp. Harvey, Tps. of Galway and Cavendish, Co. Peterboro'.
Clunis, A.	Claude	In and for the Townships of Chinguacousy, Caledon and Albion, in the County of Peel.
Collins, W. E.	Strathroy ...;	Townships of Adelaide, Metcalfe, and with joint jurisdiction over Tp. Caradoc, Co. Middlesex.
Conger, David	West Lake ...	Lake Ontario, fronting Townships Hallowell and Athol, also for the Village of Wellington, in the Township of Hillier, and for the inland lakes and streams in said Townships of Hallowell and Athol.

LIST OF OVERSEERS.—*Continued.*

Name.	Residence.	District.
Conway, Richard	Madawaska	Townships of Airy, Murchison, Sabine and Lyell, in the District of Nipissing.
Cook, H. G. A.	Niagara Falls.	County Welland.
Corsant, A.	Masonville	County Middlesex, east of boundary line between the Townships of Westminster and Delaware, London and Lobo.
Coulter, Samuel	Gilford	Lake Simcoe, from the 10th concession, Township Innisfail, to the mouth of the Holland River.
Covell, H. N.	Lombardy	Township South Elmsley, County Leeds.
Cox, Matthew	Howe Island	The waters of St. Lawrence River around Howe Island.
Crotty, John	Bothwell	River Thames, between Village of Wardsville and easterly limits of County of Kent, in County of Middlesex.
Dafoe, P. W.	Napanee	Tp. Richmond, with joint jurisdiction over Tp. N. Fredericksburg, and for the waters known as Napanee River, fronting Tps. Richmond and N. Fredericksburg.
Davis, J. W.	Sydenham	Township of Loughboro.
Davy, Charles B.	Bath	Townships of Ernesttown and South Fredericksburg fronting Lake Ontario and the Bay of Quinte, but not Hay Bay, and with joint jurisdiction with any other Overseer or Overseers who have been or may hereafter be appointed over any of the townships fronting those waters in the County of Lennox.
Deacon, Ephraim	Bolingbroke	In and for the Townships of Bathurst and South Sherbrooke, in the County of Lanark, including Christy's Lake, and with joint jurisdiction over the Township of Bedford, in the County of Frontenac.
Devine, John	Renfrew	Townships Horton, McNab, Admaston, Bagot, Blythfield, Brougham, Griffith, and Matawatchan, in the County of Renfrew.
Donaldson, W. J.	Donaldson	Townships of Palmerston, Clarendon, Barrie, Miller, North Canonto, and South Canonto, electoral district of Addington.
Drew, Henry	Long Lake	Townships Olden and Kennebec, with joint jurisdiction over Hinchinbrooke.
Drouillard, Arsas	Walkerville	County of Essex.
Dulmage, Ed.	Oak Lake	Townships Methuen and Belmont, with joint jurisdiction in Co. Peterboro.
Duncan, J. G.	Callender	Districts of Parry Sound and Nipissing, with jurisdiction on and over Lake Nipissing.

LIST OF OVERSEERS.—*Continued.*

Name.	Residence.	District.
Dunk, Jno., Sr.	Kearney	Tps. Perry, Bethune, Proudfoot, and Armour. in District of Parry Sound, with jurisdiction over Parry Sound.
Dupuis, Ferdinand ..	Hawkesbury .	County of Prescott.
Dusang, B. A.	Waubaushene .	Tps. of Freeman, Gibson, Baxter, Wood and Morrison, in District of Muskoka, also over Severn River.
Eddy, Fred	Carterton ...	The whole of St. Joseph's Island.
Edwards, Herbert ..	Nairn Centre .	Townships Merritt, Nairn, Lorne, and Baldwin, in the District of Algoma.
Elliott, Robt.	Port Hope ...	Tps. Hope and Cavan, in County Durham, with joint jurisdiction over County of Durham.
Featherstone, John .	Renwick	Townships Romney, East Tilbury and Raleigh, in Co. Kent.
Fisher, James	Sunbury	Townships Storrington, including Rideau waters from Brewer's Mills to south limit of the township, with jurisdiction over all of Loughboro Lake and the lakes of Township of Storrington.
Fleming, E.	Hastings	Village of Hastings.
Fleming, John	Newboro' ..	Cos. Leeds, Frontenac, Lennox and Addington, Hastings, Prince Edward, Northumberland, Lanark, Carleton, Russell, Prescott, Glengarry, Stormont, Dundas and Grenville.
Forsyth, John	Bridgenorth .	The waters of Chemong Lake and Lovesick Lake.
Fox, Eben R.	Northport ...	For that portion of the Bay of Quinte fronting Township Ameliasburg, east of Belleville Bridge, and also Township Sophiasburg, and over all the inland waters within Township Sophiasburg, and with joint jurisdiction, with any other overseer, over all inland waters in Township of Ameliasburg.
Fraser, J. A.	Prescott	St. Lawrence River, from the head of Cardinal Rapids west to Union Park.
Gammond, Fred ...	Slate River ..	Tps. of Neebing, Paipoonge, Pardee, Crooks, Scoble, Blake, Pearson, Gillies, Marks, and Lybster, in the Fort William District.
Gates, George	Kingston	Rideau waters between Kingston Mills and Brewer's Mills, with joint jurisdiction over the Rideau waters between Kingston Mills and the River St. Lawrence.
Gaudaur, C. G.	Atherley	Lake Couchiching and the waters of Lake Simcoe as far as Uptergrove, with joint jurisdiction over Mud Lake, in the County of Ontario.

LIST OF OVERSEERS.—*Continued.*

Name.	Residence.	District.
Gault, T. G.	Deseronto	Bay of Quinte, East Riding County of Hastings, and for Moira River and other waters in said riding.
Gillespie, G.	Brechin	Lake Simcoe and tributaries fronting Tp. Mara, in Co. Simcoe.
Gillespie, James ...	Berkeley ····	Electoral District of Centre Grey and for Township of Glenelg in South Grey.
Gordon, Walter	Port Arthur ·	In and for the District of Thunder Bay.
Green, Adam	Diamond ····	Townships Huntley and Fitzroy, County Carleton.
Green, Geo. G.	Bradford ····	Holland River, on the north side in Township West Gwillimbury, westward to the forks of the river in County Simcoe.
Haggerty, John	Gilmour P.O. ·	Tps. Grimsthorpe and Cashel, in Co. Hastings, and with joint jurisdiction over Tps. Tudor, Lake, Wollaston, Limerick, Faraday, Dungannon, and Mayo, in said Co.
Hall, Andrew	Gore Bay	West end of Manitoulin Island, including the Tps. of Gordon and Mills, in the District of Manitoulin.
Halward, Chas.	Cannington ··	Beaver River, running through the Townships of Brock and Thorah, and the Villages of Sunderland and Cannington, in the County of Ontario.
Hanes, F. A.	Huntsville ...	Townships Stephenson, Stisted, Chaffey, Sinclair, and Brunel, in District of Muskoka.
Hayes, Henry	Murray	Bay of Quinte, as lies in front of the East Riding of Northumberland, for that portion of the River Trent lying between the Townships of Sidney and the Bay of Quinte, and for the inland waters of the Townships of Murray, Dreyden, Cramahe and Haldimand.
Hembruff, Jos.	Manitowaning.	Lake Manitou, on Manitoulin Island, and the streams tributary thereto.
Henderson, H. A. ····	Pelee Island .	For Pelee Island and the other islands in Lake Erie, south of the County of Essex.
Hess, James	Hastings	Trent River and tributaries in County Northumberland, from Trent Bridge to Rice Lake.
Holliday, Henry	Wolfe Island .	Township of Wolfe Island and for the islands of Simcoe, Garden and Horseshoe, and any other islands comprised in the Township of Wolfe Island.

LIST OF OVERSEERS.—*Continued.*

Name.	Residence.	District.
Hood. Geo., Sr	Scugog	For the Township of Reach, in the County of Ontario, and for the Township of Mariposa, in the County of Victoria, and over so much of the waters of Lake Scugog as lies in front of the said townships, and for the westerly half of Scugog Island, and over the waters of Lake Scugog fronting thereon.
Hornsby, T. J.	Penetang	Tps. Matchedash, Tay, Medonte, Tiny, Flos, Sunnidale, and Nottawasaga, in the County of Simcoe, and over Christian, Bethwick, and Giant's Tomb Island.
Huffman, E. M.	Hay Bay	Tps. N. Fredericksburg, Adolphustown, and S. Fredericksburg, fronting on Hay Bay and Bay of Quinte as far as Cole's Point, but not including the Napanee River, in the County of Lennox.
Irish, John E.	Vennachar	Tps. of Anglesea, Effingham, Ashley, Denbigh and Abinger, in the County of Addington.
Irwin, David	Little Current	In and for that portion of the District of Algoma lying east of the Village of Algoma Mills, and for Cockburn and Manitoulin Islands, and in and over the waters that lie in front of the said District and which surround the said islands, and with joint jurisdiction with any other overseer who has been or may hereafter be appointed.
Irwin, Charles W.	Birkendale	Townships of Maclean, Ridout, Franklin and Brunel, in the District of Muskoka, and the Townships of McClintock, Livingstone, Sherbourne and Havelock, in the District of Haliburton.
Irwin, J. J.	Dalrymple	Township Carden, in County Victoria, with jurisdiction over Mud Lake, in County Victoria.
Jackson, W. W.	St. George	South Dumfries, lying south of the Grand River, in the County of Brant.
Jermyn, J. W.	Wiarton	Georgian Bay, County of Bruce, lying east and south of Tobermory Harbor, but exclusive of the said Harbor.
Jewell, V. J.	Batchawana	Lake Superior, in the vicinity of Batchawana.
Jickling, Chas.	St. Paul's Stn.	County Perth and for Townships East Nissouri and East and West Zorra, in County Oxford.
Johnson, Henry	Brantford	That part of Grand River lying between the southerly boundary of Town of Galt and the boundary line between Tuscarora and Onondaga Townships in County Brant and the Townships of Seneca and Oneida in Haldimand County; also concurrent jurisdiction with Overseer Kern over tributaries to the Grand River in Burford, Oakland and Brantford Townships west of Grand River.

LIST OF OVERSEERS.—*Continued.*

Name.	Residence.	District.
Johnston, James ...	Orangeville ..	Townships of Caledon and Albion, in the County of Peel.
Johnston, Thos. H. .	Royston	Townships of Lount, Machar, Laurier, Croft, Chapman, Strong, Jolly, Spence, Ryerson, Armour, Proudfoot, Monteith, McMurrich, Perry and Bethune, District of Parry Sound.
Johnston, W. H. ...	Harwood	Rice Lake, in the Townships of Hamilton and Alnwick, County Northumberland.
Jones, David	Welland	County of Welland.
Jones, John	Fenelon Falls .	For the north end of Sturgeon Lake, and Cameron Lake to Rosedale Locks, Burnt River and Rosedale River, in the County of Victoria.
Kehoe, D.	Millarton	That portion of County Bruce lying south of Indian Reserve and Township of Amabel, with jurisdiction over Lake Huron in front of said county, south of Southampton.
Kennedy, J. A.	Tichborne.....	Eagle Lake, in the Townships of Hinchinbrooke and Bedford, and with joint jurisdiction over the Township of Bedford, in the County of Frontenac.
Kent, A. J. ....,	Bewdley	Rice Lake from Ley's Point on the south shore of said lake around the head of lake to Barnard's Bay on the north shore of Rice Lake.
Kern, Jacob	Burford	County of Brant, comprising Townships of Burford, Oakland and Brantford, west of Grand River, but exclusive of said river.
Kerr, C. J.	Hamilton	County of Wentworth.
Laframboise, Remi..	Canard River.	Detroit River, fronting Townships of Sandwich, West Anderdon and Malden, and also Canadian islands in said river, County Essex.
Lambkin, Richard ..	Loring	Townships of Harrison, Burton, McKenzie, Ferrie, Wallbridge, Brown, Wilson, Mills, Pringle, Gurd, Himsworth, Nipissing, Patterson, Hardy, McConkey, Blair, and Mowat, in the District of Parry Sound.
Laughlin, J. H.	New Lowell ..	Townships of Nottawasaga, Sunnidale and Flos. in County Simcoe, with joint jurisdiction over the Township of Vespra in said county.
Leadley, Robt.	Barrie	For the Township of Vespra and the Town of Barrie, in the County of Simcoe, and over so much of the waters of Kempenfeldt Bay as lies in front of the said town and township: also, that portion of Kempenfeldt Bay, lying in front of the Township of Oro.
Lean, Wellington ..	Apsley	Townships of Anstruther and Chandos, County of Peterboro.

LIST OF OVERSEERS.—*Continued.*

Name.	Residence.	District.
Lee, James W.	Wellandport .	In and for the Townships of Moulton, Sherbrooke and Wainfleet in the Electoral District of Monck, with jurisdiction over so much of the waters of Lake Erie as lies in front of said townships.
Lewis, James	Sheguiandah ·	North Channel of Lake Huron, from the Soo to the Bustards.
Little, Richard	Wallaceburg ·	County of Kent, fronting on Lake St. Clair, exclusive of Dover West Township, also Walpole and Ste. Annes Islands, County Lambton.
Loveday, E. T.	Ottawa	In and for the Townships of Nepean, Gloucester, North Gower and Osgoode, in the County of Carleton, with jurisdiction over so much of the River Ottawa and the River Rideau and The Rideau Canal as lies in front or within said Townships, and over the tributaries to the said rivers and canals.
McAllister, J. R.	Gore's Landing	Rice Lake, between Jubilee Point, and Lower Close's Point and the waters tributary thereto, in the Townships of Hamilton and Alnwick, County of Northumberland.
McArthur, John, ...	Ice Lake	Tp. of Allan, in the District of Manitoulin.
McCaw, James	Bancroft	Townships Farraday, Dungannon and Herschell, in the County of Hastings.
McClennan, Kenneth	Aylmer	Townships of Yarmouth, Malahide and Bayham, with jurisdiction over so much of the waters of Lake Erie as lies in front of the said townships and the tributaries thereto.
McDonald, Hector.	Beaverton	Waters of Lake Simcoe and tributaries thereto fronting the Tp. of Thorah, in the County of Ontario.
McFarlane, J. S.....	Keene	Townships Otonabee and Asphodel, in Co. Peterboro, with jurisdiction over so much of Rice Lake as lies in front of said townships, and joint jurisdiction over said lake.
McGinn, Wm.	Orillia	Townships of Orillia and Oro, in the County of Simcoe, and over so much of Shingle and Carthews Bays and Lakes Couchiching and Simcoe as lies in front of said townships, and over River Severn.
McGuire, J.	Jones Falls ..	Rideau River, fronting on the Township of South Crosby, County of Leeds, with jurisdiction as far as Kingston Mills, and also over Crippen Lake, in Leeds Township.
McKenny, Thos. ...	Thornbury ...	Co. Grey, exclusive of the Tps. of Proton, Egremont and Normanby, with jurisdiction over so much of the waters of the Georgian Bay as lies in front of said county.
McMurray, R.	Bayfield	County of Huron.
McPhee, D.	Uptergrove ..	Lake Simcoe, fronting on Township of Mara and the tributaries thereto, and for Mud Lake in the Townships of Mara and Carden.

LIST OF OVERSEERS.—*Continued.*

Name.	Residence.	District.
McVittie, James	Blenheim	Townships Orford, Howard and Harwich, Co. Kent.
Major, William	Woodlawn	Townships of March and Torbolton, County Carleton.
Mansfield, Thomas	Pickering	Electoral District of South Ontario, exclusive of the Township of Reach.
May, J. C.	St. Catharines	County of Lincoln and over so much of the waters of Lake Ontario as lies in front of the said county, and with jurisdiction over the Niagara River between its mouth and the Falls.
Maybee, Manly	Cameron P.O.	Sturgeon Lake, beginning at Day's Landing and running south for five miles, including McLaren's Creek, Sturgeon Point and Pleasant Point in Co. Haliburton.
Mayor, Harry	Painswick	Lake Simcoe, from Lovers' Creek, near Barrie, on Kempenfeldt Bay, to concession 10 of the Township of Innisfil.
Melville, Henry	Havelock	Townships of Belmont and Bethuen, County Peterborough.
Meneilly, F. H.	Warkworth	River Trent and tributaries, in Co. Northumberland, from Percy Boom to Campbellford Bridge.
Moffatt, George	Glencross	Townships of Mulmur, Mono and East Garafraxa.
Moore, F. J.	Lakefield	Townships of Douro, Dummer, east part of Smith, Tp. of Burleigh and east half of Harvey, Co. Peterboro'.
Moore, James A.	Trenton	That portion of Co. Hastings fronting Bay of Quinte from City of Belleville west to the Trent River as far as Trenton Junction, with joint jurisdiction over the waters of the Bay of Quinte between bridge at Belleville and Murray Canal and also Weller's Bay.
Morton, John	St. Ola	Townships Limerick, Tudor, Wollaston, Cashel Lake and Grimsthorpe, County Hastings.
Muncer, W. G.	Minaki	That portion of the Rainy River District, between Reddittt and the boundary line between the Province of Ontario and the Province of Manitoba.
Myers, James	Holstein	Townships of Proton, Egremont and Normanby, County Grey, and Townships Minto, Arthur and West Luther, County Wellington.
Parker, H. B.	Bobcaygeon	In and for the Township of Verulam, in the County of Victoria and the Tp. of Harvey, in the County of Peterboro'.
Parkin, C. W.	Valentia	Townships Mariposa and Ops, County Victoria.

LIST OF OVERSEERS.—*Continued.*

Name.	Residence.	District.
Patterson, S.	Dunkerron ...	Holland River known as the north and west branches in Tps. Tecumseh, and West Gwillimbury, in Co. Simcoe.
Peltier, Theo.	Dover South..	River Thames from Lewisville to its mouth, also the tributaries of said river between these points; also the Township of Dover West, County Kent.
Pepper, Wm.	Lanark	Townships Drummond, Lanark, Darling, and Lavant, in Co. Lanark, with joint jurisdiction over waters in Tp. Drummond.
Phillips, J. H.	Smith's Falls.	County Frontenac lying north of the Townships of Kingston and Pittsburg, the Townships of North and South Crosby, Bastard, South Elmsley and Kitley, County of Leeds, and the County of Lanark.
Pickell, S. G.	Oshawa	Co. Durham, with jurisdiction over so much of the waters of Lake Ontario as lies in front of said county.
Purcell, H. R·	Colebrook	Townships Camden and Sheffield, the County Addington.
Pyette, David	Tehkumah ...	Manitoulin Island, in Lake Huron.
Ramesbottom, John.	Little Current.	District of Manitoulin.
Redfearn, Capt. Jas..	Lakeport	Town of Cobourg and the Townships of Hamilton and Haldimand, in the County of Northumberland.
Reid, H. W.	Parry Sound..	Townships Shawanaga, Ferguson, Carling, McDougall, McKellar, Christie, Foley, Parry Island, Cowper, and Conger.
Rivet, Jos.	Sturgeon Falls.	That portion of the District of Nipissing lying west and north of the Townships of Widdifield, Merrick, Stewart and Osborne, exclusive of Lake Timiskaming and its tributaries.
Robertson, C.	Hillsburg	Townships of Erin and West Garafraxa, County of Wellington.
Robinson, T. W. ...	Collingwood ..	Townships Collingwood and Osprey, County of Grey, and the Townships of Nottawasaga and Sunnidale, County of Simcoe.
Robinson, Wm.	Kilworthy ...	Severn River and Sparrow Lake.
Sargent, W. J.	Bronte	County of Halton.
Scherer, Edwin F...	New Hamburg	Township of Wilmot, in the County of Waterloo.
Schliehauf, Albert ..	Rodney	Townships of Southwold, Dunwich and Aldborough, exclusive of the River Thames, with jurisdiction over so much of Lake Erie as lies in front of the said townships and tributaries thereto, in the County of Elgin.

LIST OF OVERSEERS.—*Continued.*

Name.	Residence.	District.
Scott, M. W.	Leamington	Tps. Malden, North and South Colchester, North and South Gosfield, and Mersea, in the County of Essex, with jurisdiction over so much of the waters of Lake Erie as lies in front of said townships, but not for the Detroit River.
Senecal, John	Stormont	The counties and waters fronting the Counties of Stormont and Glengarry in the Province of Ontario, and with joint jurisdiction with any other Overseer or Overseers in the County of Dundas, in the Province of Ontario.
Shearer, Amos	Roseneath ...	That portion of Rice Lake in the Townships of Hamilton and Alnwick, between Rock Island and Webb's Landing, with waters tributary thereto.
Slate, George	Rockport	River St. Lawrence between Jackstraw Light and Mallorytown Landing.
Small, John	Grand Valley.	Townships of Melancthon, Amaranth and East Luther, County Dufferin.
Smith, J. S.	Port Rowan...	For the County of Norfolk.
Smith, William	Gravenhurst .	Lakes Muskoka, Rosseau and Joseph, in the Districts of Parry sound and Muskoka.
Spence, William ...	Athens	Charlestown Lake and its tributaries, County Leeds.
Stafford, William ..	Byng Inlet ..	River Magnetawan, and for the waters of the Georgian Bay lying between the said river and French River.
Stanzel, Fred.	Carleton Place	Townships Beckwith, Drummond, Ramsay and Pakenham in County Lanark, and Townships Fitzroy, Huntley and Goulbourn in County Carleton, with joint jurisdiction over the waters of the Township Drummond with any other overseer.
St. Charles, C.	Madoc	Townships Madoc and Huntington, County Hastings.
Stewart, Jas. H. ...	Brockville ...	Townships of Elizabethtown and the Front of Escott and Yonge, in the County of Leeds.
Stuart, D.	Codrington ...	Trent River and tributaries, County of Northumberland, from Chisholm's Rapids to Percy Boom.
Switzer, W. H.	Gooderham ..	Townships of Snowdon, Glamorgan, Monmouth, Cardiff, and Harcourt, District of Haliburton.
Tarry, A. E.	Toronto	Townships of Etobicoke, York and Scarboro, and for the City of Toronto, in the County of York, with jurisdiction over the inland waters of said townships, and also over Toronto and Ashbridge's Bays, and so much of the waters of Lake Ontario as lies in front of the County of York.

LIST OF OVERSEERS.—*Continued.*

Name.	Residence.	District.
Taylor, Oliver	Niagara-on-the-Lake	Niagara River, between Niagara Falls and the mouth of the river.
Temple, Jas. M. ...	Dorchester Stn	Thames River, easterly to boundary line between Oxford and Middlesex, and joint jurisdiction over Oxford.
Thompson, W. H. ..	Baillieboro ...	The Otonabee River, from Bensfort Bridge to Rice Lake.
Tillett, R.	Roach's Point.	North York; with jurisdiction over Holland River and that portion of Lake Simcoe lying in front of North Gwillimbury and Georgina Townships.
imlin, M.	Atherley	Lake Couchiching and tributaries fronting Townships Mara and Rama.
itus, E. A.	Wellington ...	For that portion of the Bay of Quinte fronting on Tp. Ameliasburg lying west of Belleville Bridge, also for the waters of Lake Ontario fronting on Tps. Ameliasburg and Hillier, with the exception of Village of Wellington, and including Weller's Bay, Consecon Lake, and all inland waters in said townships.
oner, George	Gananoque ...	River St. Lawrence, from head of Howe Island to Union Park, and with joint jurisdiction with any other overseer or overseers over the Gananoque River from Gananoque to Marble Rock.
oole, Ira	Omemee	Township of Emily, County of Victoria.
ownsend, J.	Long Point ..	Lyndhurst waters south of Lyndhurst; also South and Gananoque Lakes.
raves, J. A., Sr...	Fraserburg ...	For the District of Muskoka, with joint jurisdiction with any Game and Fisheries overseers who have been or may be appointed over the District of Parry Sound.
elford, John	Southampton .	That portion of the County of Bruce fronting on Lake Huron, and lying between the Town of Southampton and Tobermory Harbor, both inclusive.
ruelove, Wm.	Fermoy	The waters in the Tp. of Bedford, in County Frontenac.
urner, S.	London	City of London, with joint jurisdiction over the County of Middlesex with any other overseer or overseers who have been or may hereafter be appointed.
amley, C.	Cavan	Townships Cavan and Manvers, Co. Durham.
okes, James	Nanticoke ...	For the Townships Walpole, Rainham, South Cayuga, and Dunn, in Co. Haldimand, and the waters of the Grand River, fronting the Townships of Oneida, Seneca, S. Cayuga, N. Cayuga, Canborough, and Dunn.

LIST OF OVERSEERS.—*Continued.*

Name.	Residence.	District.
Walker, R. J.	Port Credit ..	Lake Ontario, fronting County Peel, and for Rivers Credit and Etobicoke, tributary to said lake.
Wartman, H. E. ...	Portsmouth ..	For the Township of Kingston, in the County of Frontenac
Watson, Hy.	Toronto	Province of Ontario.
Watson, J.	Cæsarea	Townships of Cartwright and Manvers, the waters of Lake Scugog fronting on said townships and the waters tributary to said lake.
Watt, John	Peterboro	For that portion of the River Otonabee and tributaries between Lakefield and Bensfort Bridge.
West, Chas.	Holland Ldg..	Joint jurisdiction along the east bank of the Holland River, through the Township of East Gwillimbury and along the shore of Lake Simcoe, through Township of North Gwillimbury, in the County of York.
West, Geo. W.	Holland Ldg..	With joint jurisdiction along east bank of Holland River, through Township of Gwillimbury, and along the shore of Lake Simcoe, through Township of North Gwillimbury, in the County of York.
Wight, J. R.	Newboro	Rideau Waters, between Chaffeys Lock and Newboro, including Indian, Benson, Mosquito, Clear, Mud and Loon Lakes, and also the Upper Rideau, with jurisdiction over the inland lakes and streams between these two points in the vicinity of the Rideau waters.
Wilson, A. H. G. ...	Eganville	Townships S. Algona, N. Algona, Wilberforce, Grattan, and Sebastopol, in Co. Renfrew.
Wilson, H.	Elphin	Townships of Dalhousie and North Sherbrooke, County of Lanark.
Wootton, E. A.	Maynooth	Townships of Bangor, Wicklow and McClure, in County Hastings.
Wormworth, F. L. .	Arden	Townships Kennebec and Barrie, Co. Frontenac.
Young, William ...	Cloyne	Tps. of Kaladar and Barrie, in the County of Addington, and with joint jurisdiction over the Townships of Anglesea and Effingham.
Younghusband, D...	South March..	Townships March and Nepean, County Carleton.

8 G.F.

STATEMENT of Revenue received from Game and Fisheries during the year ended October 31st, 1913.

GAME.	$ c.	$ c.
Trappers' Licenses	160 00	
Non-resident Hunting Licenses	6,750 50	
Resident Deer Licenses	21,257 60	
Resident Moose Licenses	5,160 00	
Game Dealers' Licenses	694 00	
Hotel, Restaurant and Club Licenses	294 00	
Cold Storage Licenses	175 00	
Guides' Licenses	1,644 00	
Fines	4,005 82	
Sales	2,912 67	
		43,053 59

FISHERIES

District.	Name of Overseer.	Amount.	Total.
		$ c.	$ c.
Kenora and Rainy River District	Aymer, Wm.	562 00	
	Muncer, W. G.	248 00	
	Sterling, C. N.	1,984 50	
	Young, Col. D. D.	16 00	
			2,810 50
River Nepigon	Bliss, L. E.		1,155 00
Lake Superior	Armstrong, F. C.	42 00	
	Boon, Charles	16 00	
	Fitzsimon, Ch.	42 00	
	Gordon, W.	1,876 60	
	Jewell, V. J.	44 00	
	Oliver, J. A.	4 00	
	Robinson, J. T.	2,046 00	
			4,070 60
Lake Huron (North Channel)	Boyd, Wm.	144 00	
	Bradbury, J. R.	2,555 00	
	Eddy, Fred.	48 00	
	Hembruff, Jos.	88 00	
	Irwin, David	6,492 00	
	Lewis, James	140 00	
	Ramesbottom, J.	681 00	
	Vincer, Wm.	13 00	
			10,161 00
Georgian Bay	Dusang, B. A.	677 00	
	Hornsby, T. J.	246 00	
	Jermyn, J. W.	706 80	
	McKenny, Thos.	903 55	
	Newell, Chas. E.	2 00	
	Oldfield, Miss E.	58 00	
	Reid, Henry W.	1,585 00	
	Robinson, T. W.	462 00	
	Stafford, J. W.	49 00	
	Watts, Murdoch	580 00	
	Lamorandiere, P. R.	50 00	
	Wood, P. V.	78 00	
			5,397 35
Lake Huron (proper) and River St. Clair	Blunden, H. A.	3,640 00	
	Karr, Richard	62 00	
	Kehoe, D.	215 00	
	McMurray, Robt.	530 00	
	Trelford, John	1,276 00	
			5,723 00
	Carried forward		29,317 45

STATEMENT of Revenue received—Continued.

District.	Name of Overseer.	Amount. $ c.	Total. $ c.
	Brought forward		29,317 45
Lake St. Clair, River Thames and Detroit River	Campbell, J. D.	28 00	
	Chauvin, Victor	2,015 88	
	Crotty, John	12 00	
	Laframboise, R.	325 00	
	Little, Richard	1,535 50	
	Osborne, Hy.	17 00	
	Peltier, Theo.	781 00	4,714 38
Lake Erie, Grand River, and Niagara River	Briggs, T. J.	927 00	
	Buckley, G. E.	1,178 00	
	Burt, Wm.	10 00	
	Eyers, Jacob	4 00	
	Featherstone, J.	4,528 00	
	Greenwood, T. D.	78 00	
	Harrison, L. S.	56 00	
	Henderson, H. A.	1,277 00	
	Johnson, Henry	25 00	
	Jones, David	44 00	
	Lee, Edward	679 00	
	McClennan, K.	5,150 25	
	McEwen, A.	2,925 35	
	McVittie, James	3,844 50	
	Phemister, Geo.	726 00	
	Schliehauf, A. C.	725 00	
	Scott, William	9,698 25	
	Smith, J. S.	4,229 00	
	Vokes, James	3,740 00	39,844 35
Lake Ontario and Bay of Quinte ...	Brisbin, Angus	1,112 00	
	Cheer, Thomas	304 00	
	Clark, G. F.	38 00	
	Conger, David	325 00	
	Dafoe, P. W.	219 00	
	Elliott, Robt.	25 00	
	Fox, E. R.	691 00	
	Gault, Thomas	766 00	
	Hayes, H. W.	161 00	
	Higginbottom, F. V. ..	204 00	
	Holliday, Henry	740 00	
	Horning, C. E.	52 00	
	Huffman, E. M.	1,872 50	
	Kerr, C. J.	318 50	
	Lang, W. A.	6 00	
	Mansfield, Thos.	48 00	
	Maughan, W.	62 00	
	May, J. C.	494 00	
	MacDonald, J. K.	2 00	
	Moore, James A.	138 00	
	Morgan, H. M.	296 00	
	Pickell, S. G.	3 00	
	Pitney, P. O.	1 00	
	Purser, M. W. G.	2 00	
	Radcliffe, J. H.	74 00	
	Reeves, H. J.	136 00	
	Sargent, Wm.	433 00	
	Tarry, A. E.	232 00	
	Taylor, Oliver	16 00	
	Telfer, J. A.	76 00	
	Titus, A. E.	379 00	
	Walker, R. J.	60 00	
	Wartman, H. E.	50 00	9,336 00
	Carried forward		83,212 18

STATEMENT of Revenue received—Continued.

District.	Name of Overseer.	Amount.	Total.
		$ c.	$ c.
Counties Addington, Carleton, Frontenac, Grenville, **Lanark**, Leeds, **Lennox**, Prescott, **Renfrew**, and **Russell**	*Brought forward*		83,212 18
	Augrove, Jas.	388 00	
	Avery, M.	121 00	
	Barr, Geo.	44 00	
	Birch, W. J.	75 00	
	Bourgon, J. B.	186 00	
	Briscoe, W. L.	10 00	
	Burke, Geo.	5 00	
	Chapman, C. E.	14 00	
	Clark, Gordon	114 00	
	Davis, J. W.	44 00	
	Deacon, Ephraim	26 00	
	Devine, John	2 00	
	Donaldson, W. J.	2 00	
	Drew, Henry	17 00	
	Dupuis, F.	94 00	
	Fisher, James	627 00	
	Fleming, Capt. J.	12 00	
	Gates, Geo.	214 00	
	Kennedy, J. A.	93 00	
	Loveday, E. T.	39 00	
	Mallett, W. H.	6 00	
	McGuire, J.	765 00	
	Metcalfe, J. H.	15 00	
	Pepper, Wm.	25 00	
	Phillips, J. H.	377 00	
	Spence, Wm.	168 00	
	Townsend, Jas.	409 00	
	Truelove, Wm.	74 00	
	Wight, J. R.	435 00	
	Wormworth, F. L.	40 00	
	Young, Wm.	40 00	
			4,481 00
Northumberland, Peterboro', Victoria, and other inland Counties	Adair, Wm.	12 00	
	Armstrong, H. C.	6 00	
	Bennett, E. C.	36 00	
	Best, S. G.	10 00	
	Blea, Daniel	4 00	
	Bonter, Robt.	15 00	
	Boyd, J. H.	26 00	
	Bradshaw, A.	10 00	
	Burtcheall, C.	66 00	
	Carson, R. W.	166 00	
	Cassan, C. H.	88 00	
	Clarkson, Wm.	239 00	
	Crump, C. J. C.	12 00	
	Doolan, J. T.	10 00	
	Dunk, John	18 00	
	Edwards, Herbert	18 00	
	Fenton, M. H.	214 00	
	Forsythe, J. H.	4 00	
	Gouldie, W. D.	36 00	
	Green, R. J.	62 00	
	Haggarty, John	24 00	
	Hanes, F. A.	180 00	
	Hess, Jas. H.	4 00	
	Hood, George	2 00	
	Howard, Thos.	2 00	
	Hunter, Capt. A.	398 50	
	Ireland, Dr.	4 00	
	Carried forward ..	1,616 50	87,693 18

STATEMENT of Revenue received—Continued.

District.	Name of Overseer.	Amount. $ c.	Total. $ c.
	Brought forward ..	1,616 50	87,693 18
Northumberland, Peterboro', Victoria, and other inland Counties —Continued.	Irwin, Chas. W.	62 00	
	Irwin, J. J.	4 00	
	Johnson, W. H.	100 00	
	Johnston, Thos.	49 00	
	Jones, John	125 50	
	Keller, Rod.	56 00	
	Kent, A. J.	18 00	
	Killen, Wm.	36 00	
	Lambkin, Richard	6 00	
	Lean, Wellington	14 00	
	McAllister, J. R.	128 00	
	McArthur, J. R.	20 00	
	McFarlane, J.	8 00	
	Menielly, F. H.	3 00	
	Metcalf, Fred.	6 00	
	Moore, F. J.	444 00	
	Morton, J. W.	30 00	
	Myers, James	10 00	
	Parker, Henry	489 00	
	Purcell, H. R.	30 50	
	Remey, John	68 00	
	Rice, M. A.	28 00	
	Robinson, Wm.	349 00	
	Roche, W.	16 00	
	St. Charles, Ch.	5 00	
	Shearer, Amos	2 00	
	Smith, Wm.	172 00	
	Stinson, F. S.	84 00	
	Thompson, W. H.	26 00	
	Uren, John	2 00	
	Watson, John	2 00	
	Watt, John	88 00	
	Weldon, Jas. O.	282 00	
	Widdup, J.	24 00	
	Willmott, J. H.	144 00	
	Woods, John	4 00	
	Wootton, E. A.	8 00	
	Yates, Wm.	2 00	4,561 50
River St. Lawrence	Senecal, John	22 00	
	Slate, Geo.	6 00	
	Stewart, J. H.	5 00	
	Toner, George	234 10	267 10
Lakes Couchiching, Simcoe and Sparrow	Coulter, Sam.	83 00	
	Gaudaur, C. G.	68 00	
	Green, G. G.	25 00	
	Leadley, Robt.	11 00	
	Mayor, Harry	6 00	
	McDonald, H.	66 00	
	McGinn, Wm.	21 00	
	McPhee, Donald	36 00	
	Tillett, Robt.	112 00	
	Timlin, M.	6 00	
	West, G. W.	50 00	484 00
Nipissing	Duncan, J. G.	20 00	
	Elder, W. A.	22 00	
	Hindson, C. E.	890 00	
	Parks, G. M.	393 50	
	Woods, H. G.	436 00	1,761 50
	Carried forward ..		94,767 28

STATEMENT of Revenue received—Concluded.

District.	Name of Overseer.	Amount.	Total
	Brought forward ..	$ c, ...	$ c. 94,767 28
Rondeau Provincial Park	....	44 05	44 05
Unclassified	....	499 39	499 39
	Total Fisheries	....	95,310 72
	Total Game	....r.......	48,053 59
	Total	....	138,364 31

WATERS STOCKED FROM 1901 TO 1913, WITH THE NUMBER AND KINDS OF
FISH PLANTED IN EACH.

1901.

Waters stocked.	Species.	Number.
Muskoka Lake	Bass	1,205
Lake Rosseau	Bass	700
Lake Joseph	Bass	1,052
Fairy and Vernon Lakes	Bass	244
Lake of Bays	Bass	693
Thames River at Ingersoll	Bass	225
Thames River at Woodstock	Bass	225
Bear Creek at Strathroy	Bass	396
Thames River at Dorchester	Bass	696
Lake Couchiching	Bass	436
Stoney Lake	Bass	751
Lake Simcoe at Jackson's Point	Bass	603
Holland River	Bass	387
Golden Lake	Bass	372
Severn River	Bass	526
Grand River at Cayuga	Bass	400
Grand River at Brantford	Bass	274
Kempenfeldt Bay	Bass	300
		9,841

1902.

Waters stocked.	Species.	Number.
Muskoka Lake	Bass	246
Lake Joseph	Bass	256
Lake Rosseau	Bass	227
Lake Couchiching	Bass	285
Bear Creek at Strathroy	Bass	395
Stoney Lake	Bass	330
Huntsville Lakes	Bass	265
Winnipeg River	Brook Trout	55
		2,059

1903.

Waters stocked.	Species.	Number.
Bear Creek at Strathroy	Bass	926
Lake Rosseau	Bass	1,130
Lake Joseph	Bass	500
Muskoka Lake	Bass	1,002
Lake of Bays	Bass	371
Sparrow Lake	Bass	650
Lake Couchiching	Bass	258
Long Lake at Rat Portage	Bass	460
Golden Lake	Bass	100
Mink Lake	Bass	85
Clear Lake	Bass	85
White Lake	Bass	100
Lynn River at Lake Simcoe	Bass	355
Grand River at Brantford	Bass	425
Thames River at Ingersoll	Bass	75
Thames River at London	Bass	200
Thames River at St. Mary's	Bass	205
Grand River at Fergus	Bass	100
Grand River at Grand Valley	Bass	70
Grand River at Paris	Bass	130
Musselman's Lake	Bass	200
Lake of Bays	Bass	500
		7,927

WATERS STOCKED FROM 1901 TO 1913, WITH THE NUMBER AND KINDS OF FISH PLANTED IN EACH.—Continued.

1904.

Waters stocked.	Species.	Number.
Credit River	Bass	115
Lake Rosseau	Bass	380
Green Lake	Bass	135
Opinicon Forks	Bass	50
Lake near Barry's Bay	Bass	30
Barry's Bay	Bass	100
Gorman Lake	Bass	75
Golden Lake	Bass	565
Mink Lake	Bass	60
White Lake	Bass	160
Clear Lake	Bass	50
Snell's Lake	Bass	100
Lake Joseph	Bass	725
Bass Lake	Bass	200
Lake Couchiching	Bass	230
Lake Joseph	Bass	415
Lake of Bays	Bass	530
Lake Simcoe at Jackson's Point	Bass	785
Beaver River at Cannington	Bass	250
Balsam Lake	Bass	400
Lake of Bays	Bass Fingerlings	5,000
Oxbow River at Komoka	Bass Fingerlings	1,200
Lake Scugog	Bass Fingerlings	1,400
		12,955

1905.

Waters stocked.	Species.	Number.
Lake Scugog	Bass	400
Stoney Lake	Bass	600
Muskoka Lake	Bass	500
Thames River at Stratford	Bass	250
Thames River at Mitchell	Bass	350
Lake Couchiching	Bass	500
Gull Lake (near Gravenhurst)	Bass	100
Lake of Bays	Bass	400
		3,100

1906.

Waters stocked.	Species.	Number.
Lake Simcoe	Bass	450
Lake of Bays	Bass	700
Gull River	Bass	610
Grand River	Bass	575
Lake Scugog	Bass	400
Muskoka Lake	Bass	700
River Nith	Bass	600
Lake Simcoe	Bass	700
Lake Simcoe	Bass	700
		5,435

1908.

Waters stocked.	Species.	Number.
Sparrow Lake	Bass	500
Haliburton Lake	Bass	520
Puslinch Lake	Bass Fingerlings	725
River vicinity Kenora	Trout, Speckled, fry	2,000
		3,745

WATERS STOCKED FROM 1901 TO 1913, WITH THE NUMBER AND KINDS OF
FISH PLANTED IN EACH.—Continued.

1909.

Waters stocked.	Species.	Number.
Mohawk Lake	Bass Fingerlings	1,000
Lake Rosseau	Bass Fingerlings	1,500
Lake Muskoka	Bass Fingerlings	1,500
Lake Joseph	Bass Fingerlings	2,000
Lake of Bays	Bass Fingerlings	2,000
Stoney Lake	Bass Fingerlings	3,500
Gull Lake	Bass Fingerlings	200
Whiteman's Creek	Bass Fingerlings	200
Cooley's Pond	Bass Fingerlings	150
Sparrow Lake	Bass Fingerlings	2,500
		14,550

1910.

Waters stocked.	Species.	Number.
Rideau waters (near Merrickville)	Bass Fingerlings	3,000
Lake Rosseau	Bass Fingerlings	3,000
Lake Joseph	Bass Fingerlings	3,000
Lake Muskoka	Bass Fingerlings	4,000
Gull Lake	Bass Fingerlings	100
Sturgeon Lake	Bass Fingerlings	4,000
Cameron Lake	Bass Fingerlings	3,000
Pigeon Lake	Bass Fingerlings	3,000
Fairy Lake and vicinity of Huntsville	Bass Fingerlings	8,500
Victoria Lake	Bass Fingerlings	2,000
Grand River (at Brantford)	Bass Fingerlings	300
Clear Lake	Bass Fingerlings	2,000
Long Lake (vicinity of Utterson)	Bass Fingerlings	1,725
Grand River (at Brantford)	Parent Bass	50
Oakland Pond	Parent Bass	25

Total Bass Fingerlings 37,625
Total Parent Bass 75

Grand Total 37,700

1911.

Waters stocked.	Species.	Number.
Lake of Bays	Bass Fingerlings	12,000
Lake Rosseau	Bass Fingerlings	20,000
Lake Joseph	Bass Fingerlings	20,000
Wagner Lake	Bass Fingerlings	2,500
Gull Lake	Bass Fingerlings	3,000
Fairy Lake	Bass Fingerlings	5,000
Peninsula Lake	Bass Fingerlings	5,000
Maitland River at Brussels	Bass Fingerlings	2,000
Stoney Lake and Big Cedar Lake	Bass Fingerlings	10,000
Sand Lake	Bass Fingerlings	3,000
Trout Lake	Bass Fingerlings	7,000
Grand River at Brantford	Bass Fingerlings	500
Oakland Pond	Bass Fingerlings	200
		90,200

WATERS STOCKED FROM 1901 TO 1913 WITH THE NUMBER AND KINDS OF
FISH PLANTED IN EACH.—Continued—1912

Waters Stocked and Location.	Species.	Number.
Muskoka Lake in Muskoka District	Bass Fingerlings	12,000
Rosseau Lake " " "	" "	11,000
Gull Lake " " "	" "	4,000
Joseph Lake " " "	"	10,000
Vernon Lake " " "	"	2,500
Fairy Lake " " "	"	2,500
Mary Lake " " "	"	2,500
Peninsula Lake " " "	"	2,500
Cache Lake " Algonquin Park	"	10,000
Sturgeon Lake " Kawartha District	"	4,000
Balsam Lake " " "	"	3,000
Cameron Lake " " "	"	2,000
Loughboro and Collins Lakes in Frontenac County	" "	2,000
Long Lake on Timiskaming and Northern Ontario Railway	" "	2,000
Kenogami Lake " " "	" "	5,000
Sesekinika Lake " " "	" "	5,000
Grand River	Parent Bass	300
Belle and Ewart Lakes in Grey County	Trout (Speckled)	20,000
Streams in Norfolk County	" "	50,000
	Total Bass Fingerlings	80,000
	" Parent Bass	300
	" Trout (Speckled)	70,000
	Grand Total	150,300

1913.

Waters Stocked and Location.	Species.	Number.
Fox Lake in Kenora District	Bass Fingerlings	15,000
Muskoka Lake in District of Muskoka	" "	10,000
Joseph Lake " " "	"	8,000
Rosseau Lake " " " "	"	7,000
Gull Lake " " " "	"	5,000
Windy Lake " Sudbury District	"	5,000
Rumsey Lake " " "	"	5,000
Horse Shoe or Pah-She-Gong-Ga Lake in Parry Sound District	"	5,000
Trout Lake on the Timiskaming & Northern Ontario Ry.	" "	5,000
Moose " " " " " " "	" "	5,000
Rib " " " " " " "	" "	5,000
Scugog Lake in the Kawartha District	"	5,000
Charleston Lake in Leeds County	"	5,000
Grand River in the vicinity of Breslau	"	5,000
Grand River in the vicinity of Brantford	" "	400
Streams in the vicinity of King, York County	Parent Bass	200
Rib Lake on the Timiskaming & Northern Ontario Railway	" "	25
Gull Lake in Muskoka District	" "	20
Muskoka Lake in " "	" "	20
Sharbot " " Frontenac County	Pickerel	100
Clear " " " "	" "	50
Speed River in vicinity of Hespeler	Trout (Brown)	1,000
Streams in the vicinity of Simcoe, Norfolk County	" "	1,000
Streams " " " St. Paul's, Perth County	" "	1,000
Bell and Ewart Lakes in Grey County	" (Speckled)	30,000
Utterson Lakes in Muskoka District	" "	20,000
Squires Creek, in the vicinity of Spring Brook, in Hastings County	"	20,000
Streams in the vicinity of Simcoe, Norfolk County	" "	10,000
	Total Bass Fingerlings	90,400
	" Parent Bass	265
	" " Pickerel	150
	" Trout (Brown)	3,000
	" " (Speckled)	80,000
	Grand Total	173,815

Statement showing the number of fry distributed in the waters of the Province by the Federal Government from Dominion hatcheries.

Years.	Newcastle Hatchery.	Sandwich Hatchery.	Ottawa Hatchery.	Wiarton.	Sarnia.	Total.
1868-73	1,070,000					1,070,000
1874.........	350,000					350,000
1875.........	650,000					650,000
1876.........	700,000	8,000,000				8,700,000
1877.........	1,300,000	8,000,000				9,300,000
1878.........	2,605,000	20,000,000				22,605,000
1879.........	2,602,700	12,000,000				14,602,700
1880.........	1,923,000	13,500,000				15,423,000
1881.........	3,300,000	16,000,000				19,300,000
1882.........	4,841,000	44,000,000				48,841,000
1883.........	6,053,000	72,000,000				78,053,000
1884.........	8,800,000	37,000,000				45,800,000
1885.........	5,700,000	68,000,000				73,700,000
1886.........	6,451,000	57,000,000				63,451,000
1887.........	5,130,000	56,500,000				61,630,000
1888.........	8,076,000	56,000,000				64,076,000
1889.........	5,846,500	21,000,000				26,846,500
1890........ ●	7,736,000	52,000,000	5,732,000			65,468,000
1891.........	7,807,500	75,000,000	7,043,000			89,850,500
1892.........	4,823,500	44,500,000	4,909,000			54,232,000
1893.........	9,835,000	68,000,000	6,208,000			84,043,000
1894.........	6,000,000	47,000,000	4,480,000			57,480,000
1895.........	6,000,000	73,000,000	3,210,000			82,210,000
1896.........	5,200,000	61,000,000	3,950,000			70,150,000
1897.........	4,200,000	72,000,000	4,100,000			80,300,000
1898.........	4,325,000	71,000,000	3,020,000			78,345,000
1899.........	4,050,000	73,000,000	3,700,000			80,750,000
1900.........	5,175,000	90,000,000	3,450,000			98,625,000
1901.........	5,900,000	67,000,000	3,410,000			76,310,000
1902.........	650,000	100,000,000	1,245,000			101,895,000
1903.........	2,500,000	90,000,000	1,201,000			93,701,000
1904.........	1,475,000	75,000,000	877,000			77,352,000
1905.........	1,480,000	106,000,000	1,103,000			108,583,000
1906.........	1,550,000	88,000,000	1,123,000			90,673,000
1907.........	1,807,000	103,000,000	1,152,000			106,359,000
1908.........	2,600,000	79,000,000	2,010,000	4,955,000	51,000,000	139,565,000
1909.........	1,881,000	66,500,000	1,575,000	8,100,000	159,500,000	237,556,000
1910.........	1,520,400	76,000,000	1,478,000	12,088,000	74,000,000	165,086,400
1911.........	1,543,816	77,000,000		12,249,500	113,500,000	204,298,316
Totals...	153,456,916	2,143,000,000	64,976,000	37,392,500	398,000,000	2,657,225,416

ONTARIO

Return of the number of fishermen, tonnage and value of tugs, vessels and boats, the
industry during

		Fishing material.							
Number.	District.	Tugs or Vessels.				Boats.			Gill-Nets.	
		No.	Ton-nage.	Value.	Men.	No.	Value.	Men.	Yards.	Value.
	Kenora and Rainy River.			$			$			$
1	Lake of the Woods	3	61	2,220	8	21	6,235	49	76,000	4,475
2	Shoal, Dogtooth and Sandy Lakes	....	....	....	....	2	450	5	3,000	500
3	Lost, Minnitaki, Pelican and Vermilion Lake	....	....	....	....	4	400	8	7,000	875
4	Clay, Lac Suel and One Man's Lakes	....	....	....	....	4	1,525	9	8,000	1,225
5	Dinorwic, Loon, Pipestone, Upper Manitou, Wabigoon.	....	....	....	....	8	450	6	4,000	440
6	Black Hawk, Clearwater, Good, Nannikan, Raleigh and Sand Point Lakes									
7	Rainy Lake	....	....	....	....	2	650	4	3,250	325
8	Kariskong, Orang Outang and Sturgeon Lakes	....	....	....	....	11	2,525	18	16,000	1,400
9	Abraham, Buckety, Crow and Trout Lakes	....	....	....	....	1	150	4	4,000	350
		....	....	....	....	4	475	9	7,500	1,025
	Totals	3	61	2,220	8	52	12,860	112	78,750	10,615

Return of the kinds, quantities and values

Number.	District.	Herring, salted.	Herring, fresh.	Whitefish, salted.	Whitefish, fresh.	Trout, salted.	Trout, fresh.	Pike.	Pickerel or Dore.
	Kenora and Rainy River.	brls.	lbs.	brls.	lbs.	brls.	lbs.	lbs.	lbs.
1	Lake of the Woods........	.....	.....	.....	717,297	....	18,230	366,043	492,346
2	Shoal, Dogtooth and Sandy Lakes	.....	.....	.....	1,700	1,000	1,700	1,300	370
3	Lost, Minnitaki, Pelican and Vermilion Lake	.....	.....	.....	30,292	....	12,900	4,584	10,050
4	Clay, Lac Suel and One Man's Lakes	.....	.....	.....	152,742	....	4,700	980	36,164
5	Dinorwic, Loon, Pipestone, Upper Manitou, Wabigoon.	.....	.....	.....	18,600	....	3,500	2,600	7,300
6	Black Hawk, Clearwater, Good, Nannikan, Raleigh and Sand Point Lakes	.....	.....	.....	4,250	....	1,365	4,840	3,654
7	Rainy Lake	.....	.....	.....	46,761	....	50	63,890	62,896
8	Kariskong, Orang Outang and Sturgeon Lakes	.....	.....	.....	4,100	....	2,900	5,050	800
9	Abraham, Buckety, Crow and Trout Lakes	.....	.....	.....	23,686	....	10,298	7,757	5,730
	Totals	.....	.....	.....	994,428	1,000	55,643	456,994	669,311
	Values				$ c. 99,442 80	$ c. 10,000 00	$ c. 5,564 30	$ c. 36,559 52	$ c. 66,931 10

FISHERIES.

quantity and value of all fishing materials and other fixtures employed in the fishing
the year 1912.

													Fishing material.						Other fixtures used in fishing.			
Seines.			Pound nets.		Hoop nets.		Dip nets.		Night lines.		Spears.									Freezers and Ice Houses.		Piers and Wharves.	
No.	Yards.	Value.	No.	Value.	No.	Value.	No.	Value.	No. Hooks.	Value.	No.	Value.								No.	Value.	No.	Value.
		$		$		$		$		$		$									$		$
...	......	......	28	9,000	6	1,025	....	....	....	....	....	....								6	4,900	10	2,850
....	......	......																					
....	......	......																					
....	......	......																		3	9,500	....	....
....	......	......																		1	200	....	....
....	......	......																		4	1,150	....	....
....	......	......																					
....	......	......																		1	500	1	100
...	......	......	28	9,000	6	1,025	....	....	....	....	....	....								15	9,250	11	2,450

of fish caught during the year 1912.

Sturgeon.	Eels.	Perch.	Tullibee.	Catfish.	Mixed and coarse fish.	Caviare.	Sturgeon Bladders.	Carp.	Buffalo fish.	Value.
lbs.	lbs.	lbs.	lbs.	lbs.	lbs.	lbs.	No.	lbs.	lbs.	$ c.
113,912	....	....	69,730	28,450	....	2,756	213	....	91,076	185,787 22
....	....	....	....	....	....	....	....	....	....	10,481 00
....	....	....	....	....	....	....	....	....	....	5,684 92
....	....	....	1,249	....	7,255	....	....	....	....	24,876 69
....	....	....	....	....	860	....	....	....	....	2,691 00
2,000	....	....	4,000	....	....	40	....	....	....	1,894 30
2,021	....	....	30,600	....	25,778	....	....	....	....	19,509 85
....	....	....	....	....	....	....	....	....	....	1,184 00
....	....	....	....	....	....	....	....	....	....	4,598 96
117,983	....	....	105,579	28,450	33,893	2,796	213	....	91,076	256,702 94
$ c. 17,639 95	....	....	$ c. 6,334 74	$ c. 2,276 00	$ c. 1,694 65	$ c. 2,796 00	$ c. 127 80	....	$ c. 7,286 08	$ c. 256,702 94

ONTARIO

Return of the number of fishermen, tonnage and value of tugs, vessels and boats
fishing industry

		Fishing material.							
Number.	District.	Tugs or vessels.				Boats.			Gill-Nets.	
		No.	Ton nage.	Value.	Men.	No.	Value.	Men.	Yards.	Value.
	Lake Superior.			$			$			$
1	Pigeon River to Thunder Cape (including Thunder Bay)..	4	37	8,300	22	15	735	20	133,500	4,925
2	Black Bay					1	35	2	....	....
3	Nepigon Straits to Simpson Island	11	110	13,175	26	3	90	8	59,000	1,530
4	Rossport	5	59	5,900	12	5	275	8	82,000	4,7..
5	Jackfish and Port Coldwell..					2	50	3	6,000	22
6	Sturgeon Kashabowie and Lac des Milles Lac	3	......	1,800	24	11	740	8	22,000	1,45..
7	Michipicoten	3	50	9,500	14	6	550	11	105,900	1,50..
8	Gargantua	1	25	7,500	10	4	290	8	14,000	525
9	Lizard Islands					8	400	6	12,500	45..
10	Agawa and Mica Bays	1	30	6,000	6	1	50	2	65,000	750
11	Batchawawa Bay					12	875	22	31,800	1,18..
12	Richardson's Harbor	1	30	7,500	10				60,000	....
13	Goulis Bay					15	1,550	30	47,000	1,60..
14	Gros Cap					5	425	6	9,500	325
	Totals	28	341	58,675	124	88	6,065	124	652,200	19,81..

Return of the kinds, quantities and values

Number.	District.	Herring, salted.	Herring, fresh.	Whitefish, salted.	Whitefish, fresh.	Trout, salted.	Trout, fresh.	Pike.	Pickerel, or Dore.
	Lake Superior.	brls.	lbs.	brls.	lbs.	brls.	lbs.	lbs.	lbs.
1	Pigeon River to Thunder Cape (including Thunder Bay)..	....	728,215	....	175,250	....	329,270	13,858	18,262
2	Black Bay	....	222,000	....	26,600	....	47,400	....	21,65..
3	Nepigon Straits to Simpson Island	....	550,000	....	69,137	....	334,600	3,180	10,14..
4	Rossport	....	260,000	....	30,278	....	163,588	600	2,00..
5	Jackfish and Port Coldwell..	....	....	....	1,350	....	10,260	....	....
6	Sturgeon Kashabowie and Lac des Milles Lac	....	....	....	114,727	....	27,778	106,443	165,77..
7	Michipicoten	....	....	....	24,872	180	185,796	....	....
8	Gargantua	....	....	....	18,920	175	89,848	....	....
9	Lizard Islands	....	....	....	16,705	13	21,840	....	....
10	Agawa and Mica Bays	....	....	....	16,500	50	87,000	....	....
11	Batchawawa Bay	....	....	....	11,480	....	13,535	100	30..
12	Richardson's Harbor	....	....	....	10,555	182	123,165	....	....
13	Goulis Bay	....	....	....	45,800	90	32,200	....	....
14	Gros Cap	....	3,100	....	12,000	....	10,600	....	....
	Totals	....	1,763,315	....	573,674	690	1,475,924	122,631	217,56..
	Values		$ c. 88,165 75		$ c. 57,367 40	$ c. 6,900 00	$ c. 147,592 40	$ c. 9,810 48	$ c. 21,784 70

FISHERIES.

the quantity and value of all fishing materials and other fixtures employed in the
during the year 1912.

	Fishing material.														Other fixtures used in fishing.			
Seines.			Pound Nets.		Hoop Nets.		Dip Nets.		Night Lines.		Spears.		Freezers and Ice Houses.		Piers and Wharves.				
No.	Yards.	Value.	No.	Value.	No.	Value.	No.	Value.	No. Hooks.	Value.	No.	Value.	No.	Value.	No.	Value.			
		$		$										$		$			
			28	5,500									9	9,300	4	3,100			
			5	1,500															
			18	2,900									2	1,400					
													2	1,500	1	2,000			
													4	1,000	1	2,000			
													2	1,500	2	2,000			
													1	200		500			
													1	1,000	1	2,000			
													1	500	1	500			
													1	300	1	500			
			46	9,900									20	16,700	12	12,600			

of fish caught during the year 1912.

Sturgeon.	Eels.	Perch.	Tullibee.	Catfish.	Mixed and coarse fish.	Caviare.	Sturgeon bladders.	Carp.	Value.
lbs.	lbs.	lbs.	lbs.	lbs.	lbs.	lbs.	No.	lbs.	$ c.
1,867									90,085 64
									90,646 50
1,700									69,393 60
									32,684 80
									1,161 00
									89,065 44
			270						22,883 00
			90						12,681 50
									3,964 50
									10,850 00
									2,554 50
			190						15,108 40
									3,900 00
									2,415 00
5,567			550						832,188 78
$ c. 535 05			$ c. 88 00						$ c. 832,188 78

ONTARIO

Return of the number of fishermen, tonnage and value of tugs, vessels and boats,
fishing industry

		Fishing material.							
		Tugs or vessels.				Boats.		Gill-Nets.	
Number.	District.	No.	Ton-nage.	Value.	Men.	No.	Value.	Men.	Yards.	Value.
	Lake Huron (North Channel).			$			$			$
1	Bruce Mines and Thessalon...	2	......	500	9	9	1,900	18	27,000	1,525
2	Cockburn Island and Meldrum Bay	5	......	1,150	10	......	....	......	26,000	900
3	Blind River and Jollette Islands	......	......	......	......	19	1 175	24	6,500	400
4	Algoma Mills, Spragge and Cutler	......	......	......	......	5	375	8	8,250	75
5	John's Island and Spanish:..	3	69	8,800	13	13	1,150	20	56,400	2,75
6	Gore Bay and Kagawong....	4	......	10,225	11	......	....	......	51,100	3,500
7	Little Current	1	......	400	2	2	....	2	2,200	....
8	Manitowaning and Fraser Bay	3	20	6,500	11	1	....	1	100	....
9	Killarney, Squaw and Rabbit Islands	28	459	21,100	56	5	250	6	338,800	162,500
10	Fitzwilliam Island and South Bay	4	51	7,000	19	12	1,875	......	222,000	112,200
11	Missassagi Straits and Providence Bay	6	107	22,500	35	2	100	4	244,200	12,625
12	Duck Islands	9	39	12,200	25	......	....	......	174,000	2,900
	Totals	60	745	90,375	193	69	6,725	83	1,150,550	449,145

Return of the kinds, quantities and values

Number.	District.	Herring, salted.	Herring, fresh.	Whitefish, salted.	Whitefish, fresh.	Trout, salted.	Trout, fresh.	Pike.	Pickerel, or Dore.
	Lake Huron (North Channel).	bris.	lbs.	bris.	lbs.	bris.	lbs.	lbs.	lbs.
1	Bruce Mines and Thessalon...	......	......	......	26,156	....	25,495	17,899	106,565
2	Cockburn Island and Meldrum Bay	......	......	......	10,136	....	18,287	....	....
3	Blind River and Jollette Islands	......	......	......	19,200	....	15,672	2,788	54,000
4	Algoma Mills, Spragge and Cutler	58	200	....	380	....	6,085	580	580
5	John's Island and Spanish...	225	200	4	3,075	2	70,818	15,594	158,657
6	Gore Bay and Kagawong....	......	......	......	29,216	....	42,188	1,998	22,006
7	Little Current	......	......	......	890	....	1,964	527	....
8	Manitowaning and Fraser Bay	......	......	......	39,421	....	27,764	11,847	45,434
9	Killarney, Squaw and Rabbit Islands	......	......	½	333,367	½	317,885	11,580	36,294
10	Fitzwilliam Island and South Bay	......	......	......	53,297	....	353,756	500	....
11	Missassagi Straits and Providence Bay	......	......	......	144,630	1,000	550,257	....	....
12	Duck Islands	......	......	......	1,392	....	464,978	....	....
	Totals	276	400	2½	660,160	1,002½	1,690,706	68,516	424,556
	Values	$ c. 2,760 00	$ c. 20 00	$ c. 25 00	$ c. 66,016 00	$ c. 10,025 00	$ c. 169,070 80	$ c. 5,481 28	$ c. 42,455 60

FISHERIES

the quantity and value of all fishing materials and other fixtures employed in the
during the year 1912.

															Other fixtures used in fishing.			
	Seines.			Pound nets.		Hoop nets.		Dip nets.		Night lines.		Spears.		Freezers and Ice Houses.		Piers and Wharves.	
No.	Yards.	Value.	No.	Value.	No.	Value.	No.	Value.	No. Hooks.	Value.	No.	Value.	No.	Value.	No.	Value.
		$		$		$		$		$		$		$		$
			19	6,500									2	500		
			1	300												
			14	2,800									2	1,000	2	700
			12	3,800									5	1,400	2	800
			8	4,000												
			15	4,000												
			15	5,250												
			6	2,000												
			16	7,500												
			106	35,850									9	2,900	4	1,500

of fish caught during the year 1912.

Sturgeon.	Eels.	Perch.	Tullibee.	Catfish.	Mixed and Coarse fish.	Caviare.	Sturgeon Bladders.	Carp.	Value.
lbs.	lbs.	lbs.	lbs.	lbs.	lbs.	lbs.	No.	lbs.	$ c.
5,567		3,114		266	8,293	10			18,693 80
									2,842 80
7,677					94,845	266			15,226 04
100		1,000			10,820				1,889 20
5,736		5,450		200	180,870	64			37,088 92
1,116									9,798 06
									827 56
948					6,663	65			12,784 01
660		1,800	500	2,000	1,500				70,049 50
									40,745 8
314			2,760						79,555 R
									26,802 6
22,016		11,454	3,260	2 486	302,491	405			315,658 11
$ c.		$ c.	$ c.	$ c.	$ c.	$ c.			$ c.
2,302 70		572 70	195 60	196 88	15,124 55	405 00			315,658 11

9 G.F.

ONTARIO

Return of the number of fishermen, tonnage and value of tugs, vessels and boats, the
industry during

Number.	District.	Fishing material.								
		Tugs or vessels.				Boats.			Gill-Nets.	
		No.	Ton-nage.	Value.	Men.	No.	Value.	Men.	Yards.	Value.
	Georgian Bay.			$			$			$
1	Byng Inlet	9	......	4,000	8	6	1,600	14	86,000	450
2	Parry Sound	5	......	7,000	27	11	1,795	19	367,100	11,683
3	Waubaushene	......	......	......	......	17	1,295	24	45,600	3,500
4	Penetanguishene	......	......	......	......	8	95	10	23,200	1,082
5	Collingwood	1	35	3,000	6	13	5,925	26	109,000	6,210
6	Meaford (including Owen Sound Bay)	7	172	20,100	25	22	4,655	38	447,950	9,745
7	Colpoy's Bay to Tobermory...	3	41	9,200	14	47	3,790	84	195,100	10,575
	Totals	18	248	43,300	80	124	19,065	215	1,261,950	43,185

Return of the kinds, quantities and values of

Number.	District.	Herring, salted.	Herring, fresh.	Whitefish, salted.	Whitefish, fresh.	Trout, salted.	Trout, fresh.	Pike.	Pickerel or Dore.
	Georgian Bay.	brls.	lbs.	brls.	lbs.	brls.	lbs.	lbs.	lbs.
1	Byng Inlet ....:.....	49½	....	....	62,542	....	30,800	14,896	40,218
2	Parry Sound	....	....	15	186,706	....	241,488	....	4,944
3	Waubaushene	15	700	13	16,466	25	2,516	19,300	12,750
4	Penetanguishene	19	500	12	5,525	89	12,115	....	100
5	Collingwood	....	18,200	....	11,300	....	91,839	100	....
6	Meaford (including Owen Sound Bay)	1,000	38,750	....	750	700	425,200	....	....
7	Colpoy's Bay to Tobermory...	49	9,200	....	3,872	99½	214,069	100	....
	Totals	1,123½	67,350	40	287,161	913½	1,027,027	34,396	58,012
	Values	$ c. 11,235 00	$ c. 3,367 50	$ c. 400 00	$ c. 28,716 10	$ c. 9,135 00	$ c. 102,702 70	$ c. 2,746 08	$ c. 5,801 20

FISHERIES

quantity and value of all fishing materials and other fixtures employed in the fishing
the year 1912.

Fishing material.																	Other fixtures used in fishing.			
Seines.			Pound nets.		Hoop nets.		Dip nets.		Night Lines.		Spears.			Freezers and Ice Houses.		Piers and Wharves.				
No.	Yards.	Value.	No.	Value.	No.	Value.	No.	Value.	No. Hooks.	Value.	No.	Value.		No.	Value.	No.	Value.			
		$		$				$		$		$			$		$			
.....	... .	....	9	3,500	....	....	..	....	....	....	...	....		4	2,700	3	1,700			
.....	....	....	...	....	12	605	....	....	....	....	....	....		3	375	2	500			
.....	....	....	...	....	...	....	....	....	....	....	...	....		1	75	....	....			
...	....	....	...	....	...	....	....	....	....	....	...	....		5	650	....	....			
...	....	....	......	....	...	....	....	....	....	....	....	....		6	3,700	2	1,135			
...	... .	....	9	3,500	12	605	...	....	....	....	....	....		19	7,500	9	3,535			

fish caught during the year 1912.

Sturgeon.	Eels.	Perch.	Tullibee.	Catfish.	Mixed and coarse fish.	Caviare.	Sturgeon Bladders.	Carp.	Value.
lbs.	lbs.	lbs.	lbs.	lbs.	lbs.	lbs.	No.	lbs.	$ c.
976	....	....	....	376	7,095	100	....	....	16,497 59
....	....	....	....	....	4,368	....	....	....	43,682 20
....	....	....	....	700	29,700	....	....	8,100	6,965 20
....	....	....	600	....	....	....	....	....	3,035 00
....	....	3,000	....	....	1,200	....	....	....	11,441 90
....	....	....	....	....	....	....	....	....	61,582 50
....	....	....	34,814	....	....	....	....	....	26,885 94
976	....	3,000	35,414	1,067	42,863	100	....	8,100	168,990 33
$ c. 146 40	....	$ c. 150 00	$ c. 2,124 84	$ c. 85 36	$ c. 2,118 15	$ c. 100 00	....	$ c. 162 00	$ c. 168,990 33

ONTARIO

Return of the number of fishermen, tonnage and value of tugs, vessels and boats,
fishing industry

Number.	District.	Fishing material.								
		Tugs or vessels.				Boats.			Gill-Nets.	
		No.	Ton-nage.	Value.	Men.	No.	Value.	Men.	Yards.	Value.
	Lake Huron (Proper).			$			$			$
1	Cape Hurd to Southampton..	7	866	10,500	35	36	3,437	68	404,735	15,715
2	Southampton to Pine Point..	2	......	3,700	9	7	210	10	69,785	407
3	County of Huron	1	19	1,500	5	11	3,290	44	62,685	3,827
4	County of Lambton (including the River St. Clair	......	......	......	......	58	9,285	86	10,000	220
	Totals	10	885	15,700	49	112	16,222	208	547,205	23,141

Returns of the kinds, quantities and values

Number.	District.	Herring, salted.	Herring, fresh.	Whitefish, salted.	Whitefish, fresh.	Trout, salted.	Trout, fresh.	Pike.	Pickerel, or Dore.
	Lake Huron (Proper).	bris.	lbs.	bris.	lbs.	bris.	lbs.	lbs.	lbs.
1	Cape Hurd to Southampton..	87	4,078	....	9,010	623½	452,516	154	4
2	Southampton to Pine Point..	....	150	....	....	15	55,620	....	....
3	County of Huron	....	20,425	....	10,968	....	102,954	....	9,312
4	County of Lambton (including the River St. Clair	30	125,871	....	18,740	....	20,135	598	177,861
	Totals	117	150,524	....	38,738	638½	631,225	752	187,177
	Values	$ c. 1,170 00	$ c. 7,526 20	$ c.	$ c. 3,873 80	$ c. 6,385 00	$ c. 63,122 50	$ c. 60 16	$ c. 15,717 70

FISHERIES.

the quantity and value of all fishing materials and other fixtures employed in the
during the year 1912.

												Fishing material.									Other fixtures used in fishing.			
	Seines.			Pound nets.		Hoop nets.		Dip Nets.		Night Lines.		Spears.									Freezers and Ice Houses.		Piers and Wharves.	
No.	Yards.	Value.	No.	Value.	No.	Value.	No.	Value.	No. Hooks.	Value.	No.	Value.									No.	Value.	No.	Value.
		$		$		$		$ c.		$		$										$		
....	....	....	2	200	....	....	8	12 25	....	....	....	....									7	5,700	....	....
....	....	....	....	....	....	....	....	....	....	....	....	....									1	200	....	....
....	....	....	8	1,800	....	....	....	....	....	....	....	....									9	225	....	....
5	873	215	68	17,500	1	20	....	....	....	....	....	....									7	840	....	....
5	873	215	78	19,600	1	20	8	12 25	....	....	....	....									24	7,065	....	....

of fish caught during the year 1912.

Sturgeon.	Eels.	Perch.	Tullibee.	Catfish.	Mixed and coarse fish.	Caviare.	Sturgeon Bladders.	Carp.	Values.
lbs.	lbs.	lbs.	lbs.	lbs.	lbs.	lbs.	No.	lbs.	$ c.
350	....	21,390	277,000	....	505	20	....	....	71,286 47
....	....	....	....	....	600	....	....	....	5,749 50
1,354	....	33,058	200	....	11,155	16	....	....	15,788 40
46,959	405	6,551	....	146	78,113	1,741	11	100	41,377 62
48,663	405	61,499	277,200	146	90,373	1,777	11	100	134,201 99
$ c. 7,299 45	$ c. 24 30	$ c. 3,074 95	$ c. 16,632 00	$ c. 11 68	$ c. 4,513 65	$ c. 1,777 00	$ c. 6 60	$ c. 2 00	$ c. 134,201 99

ONTARIO

Return of the number of fishermen, tonnage and value of tugs, vessels and boats,
fishing industry

Number.	District.	Fishing material.								
		Tugs or vessels.				Boats.			Gill-Nets.	
		No.	Ton-nage.	Value.	Men.	No.	Value.	Men.	Yards.	Value.
	Lake St. Clair.			$			$			$
1	River Thames	.....	......		.....	42	149	42	....	....
2	Lake St. Clair	12	......	2,825	15	84	13,078	166	....	....
3	Detroit River					85	1,606	95	....	....
	Totals	12	......	2,825	15	161	14,828	303	....	....

Return of the kinds, quantities and values

Number.	District.	Herring, salted.	Herring, fresh.	Whitefish, salted.	Whitefish, fresh.	Trout, salted.	Trout, fresh.	Pike.	Pickerel or Dore.
	Lake St. Clair.	bris.	lbs.	bris.	lbs.	bris.	lbs.	lbs.	lbs
1	River Thames	......	....	....		....	....	....	825
2	Lake St. Clair	......	....	....	49,277	....	....	18,264	53,692
3	Detroit River	......	....	....	109,165	....	....	19,075	3,900
	Totals	... ...	....	....	158,442	....	....	37,339	57,917
	Values	......	....	....	$ c. 15,844 20	....	....	$ c. 2,987 12	$ c. 5,791 70

FISHERIES.

the quantity and value of all fishing materials and other fixtures employed in the
during the year 1912.

Fishing material.														Other fixtures used in fishing.			
Seines.			Pound nets.		Hoop nets.		Dip nets.		Night Lines.		Spears.			Freezers and Ice Houses.		Piers and Wharves.	
No.	Yards.	Value.	No.	Value.	No.	Value.	No.	Value.	No. Hooks.	Value.	No.	Value.		No.	Value.	No.	Value.
		$		$		$		$ c.		$		$			$		$
17	2,433	1,390	12	3,550	154	7,380	84 2	453 50 10 00	1,000 4,900	59 1,470	....	....		9	2,550	15	2,350
32	2,905	1,410	....	....	1	10	....	....	1,000	36	....	....		....	....	1	200
49	5,338	2,800	12	3,550	155	7,390	86	463 50	6,900	1,565	....	....		9	2,550	16	2,550

of fish caught during the year 1912.

Sturgeon.	Eels.	Perch.	Tullibee.	Catfish.	Mixed and coarse fish.	Caviare.	Sturgeon bladders.	Carp.	Value.
lbs.	lbs.	lbs.	lbs.	lbs.	lbs.	lbs.	No.	lbs.	$ c.
44,888	....	69,499	75	8 50,638	16,545 392,683	....	970	9,760	860 39 46,743 56
4,450	....	11,150	....	750	53,650	65	....	65,800	18,128 00
48,818	....	80,649	75	51,396	462,828	1,035	....	75,060	65,731 95
$ c. 7,522 70	....	$ c. 4,032 45	$ c. 4 50	$ c 4,111 68	$ c. 23,141 40	$ c. 1,035 00	....	$ c. 1,461 20	$ c. 65,731 95

ONTARIO

Return of the number of fishermen, tonnage and value of tugs, vessels and boats,
fishing industry

Number.	District.	Tugs or vessels.				Boats.			Gill-Nets.	
		No.	Tonnage.	Value.	Men.	No.	Value.	Men.	Yards.	Value.
	Lake Erie.			$			$			$
1	Pelee Island	5	80	15,000	26	9	1,150	19	49,950	5,450
2	Essex County	8	481	9,000	9	63	20,964	128	8,000	2,250
3	Kent West	2	50	12,750	13	48	17,700	59	17,500	3,700
4	Kent East					31	10,810	73		
5	Elgin West	2		15,000	18	32	8,450	60	24,000	5,550
6	Elgin East	17	517	100,000	61	6	8,200	17	283,000	52,010
7	Houghton, Norfolk County...	2	38	6,000	12				16,000	8,000
8	Walsingham, Norfolk County..	1	15	2,000	6	20	500	32		
9	Long Point (including Outer Bay)	1		4,000	6	19	540	34		
10	Charlotteville, Norfolk County	2	28	4,600	8	24	1,528	42	48,933	5,156
11	Inner Bay, Norfolk County..	1	20	4,000	6	33	1,018	75		
12	Woodhouse, Norfolk County..	2	20	10,000	17	5	200	5	9,500	4,051
13	Haldimand County	9	180	31,600	41	27	2,258	47	75,500	6,710
14	Pt. Maitland to Pt. Colborne..	5	42	7,050	20	15	231	15	32,170	4,606
15	Pt. Colborne to Niagara Falls.	1		2,500		29	116	33	12,200	
	Totals	58	1,566	223,500	243	347	68,686	628	569,753	100,943

Return of the kinds, quantities and values

Number.	District.	Herring, salted.	Herring, fresh.	Whitefish, salted.	Whitefish, fresh.	Trout, salted.	Trout, fresh.	Pike.	Pickerel, or Dore.
	Lake Erie.	bris.	lbs.	bris.	lbs.	bris.	lbs.	lbs.	lbs.
1	Pelee Island	25	567,096		37,514			12,204	6,172
2	Essex County	2,594	809,943	1,730	876,331			334,688	277,758
3	Kent West		2,197,113		176,056			406,197	52,796
4	Kent East		2,050,888		105,982			241,306	20,078
5	Elgin West		1,688,000		145,800			46,900	259,000
6	Elgin East		4,362,891		523,569			69,978	82,843
7	Houghton, Norfolk County...		97,784		40,675		195	980	71,235
8	Walsingham, Norfolk County..		3,475		1,932		145	11,404	35,288
9	Long Point (including Outer Bay)	2,000	336,524		71,149		336	102,387	24,143
10	Charlotteville, Norfolk County		147,073		32,196			15,187	18,109
11	Inner Bay, Norfolk County..		194,715		18,200			4,447	4,185
12	Woodhouse, Norfolk County..		294,000		26,405			27,000	2,775
13	Haldimand County		218,874		288,546		1,413	52,394	142,813
14	Pt. Maitland to Pt. Colborne..		160,791		22,841		400	140,207	638
15	Pt. Colborne to Niagara Falls.		12,475		1,012			20,890	5,343
	Totals	4,619	13,041,413	1,730	2,368,428		2,489	1,485,166	975,190
	Values	$ c. 46,190 00	$ c. 652,070 90	$ c. 17,200 00	$ c. 223,642 80		$ c. 248 90	$ c. 118,813 28	$ c. 97,518 90

FISHERIES.

the quantity and value of all fishing materials and other fixtures employed in the
during the year 1912.

Fishing material.																Other fixtures used in fishing.			
Seines.			Pound Nets.		Hoop Nets.		Dip Nets.		Night Lines.		Spears.		Freezers and Ice Houses.			Piers and Wharves.	
No.	Yards.	Value.	No.	Value.	No.	Value.	No.	Value.	No. Hooks.	Value.	No.	Value.	No.	Value.		No.	Value.
		$		$		$		$		$		$		$			$	
....	......	....	5	1,000	....	....	....	....	....	....	....	....	2	8,500		1	4,000
9	2,500	1,395	130	45,700	....	....	11	110	....	....	....	....	27	15,500		....	......
1	100	25	10	41,480	....	....	....	....	....	....	....	....	20	19,700		9	4,700
7	2,100	1,140	59	28,200	....	....	....	....	....	....	....	....	22	9,330		....	......
....	......	....	53	21,200	....	....	....	....	....	....	....	....	19	5,350		....	......
....	......	....	....	....	....	....	5	67	250	50	....	....	23	36,250		23	22,700
8	3,200	955	....	....	....	....	....	....	....	....	....	....	8	3,300		1	600
7	2,675	975	....	....	....	....	....	....	2,200	40	....	....	3	1,650		....	......
6	2,400	800	2	1,000	....	....	....	....	400	6	....	....	2	1,900		1	600
20	15,090	6,185	....	....	....	....	....	....	800	15	....	....	2	1,800		1	600
....	......	....	4	1,500	....	....	....	....	100	3	....	....	1	500		....	......
4	285	155	29	8,450	....	....	31	90 50	425		....	....	14	8,250		....	......
....	......	....	5	1,500	....	....	6	15 00	......		....	....	6	1,400		2	100
....	......	....	....	....	....	....	11	4	9,300		....	....	....	......		....	......
62	28,350	11,680	297	150,080	....	....	63	286 50	13,475	115	....	....	149	113,430		38	33,300

of fish caught during the year 1912.

Sturgeon.	Eels.	Perch.	Tullibee.	Catfish.	Mixed and coarse fish.	Caviare.	Sturgeon Bladders.	Carp.	Value.
lbs.	lbs.	lbs.	lbs.	lbs.	lbs.	lbs.	No.	lbs.	$ c.
....	....	85,792		153	7,972	....	....	....	38,649 92
17,875	....	130,052	150	26,060	219,125	1,549	506	184,540	248,499 69
5,881	....	220,556		86,750	247	....	700	181,745 06
5,045	....	217,893		8,080	57,879	106½	1	194,963	154,248 94
....	....	76,400		....	85,000	....	....	....	186,622 00
....	....	181,879		2,005	6,856	....	....	....	290,173 14
....	....	8,000		....	....	....	....	....	11,237 10
....	....	44,291		1,288	60,851	....	....	63,214	11,526 59
3,815	....	38,703		7,432	54,840	407½	....	104,300	59,317 67
390	....	36,892		3,582	165,445	96	....	50,045	26,157 87
....	....	6,438		7,557	43,746	....	....	214,098	19,724 63
920	....	3,425		575	8,085	90	....	....	30,625 00
11,520	....	50,445		795	61,857	319	111	57,040	63,046 36
....	....	12,276		63	13,553	36	....	125	22,978 60
6,821	....	2,154		134	9,184	529	32	....	5,079 42
52,967	....	1,110,201	150	52,967	880,592	3,430	652	899,525	1,289,121 69
$ c. 7,840 05	....	$ c. 55,510 05	$ c. 9 00	$ c. 4,237 36	$ c. 44,029 65	$ c. 3,430 00	$ c. 391 20	$ c. 17,990 50	$ c. 1,289,121 69

ONTARIO

Return of the number of fishermen, tonnage and value of tugs, vessels and boats, the
industry during

Number.	District.	Tugs or vessels.				Boats.			Gill-Nets.	
		No.	Tonnage.	Value.	Men.	No.	Value.	Men.	Yards.	Value.
				$			$			$
	Lake Ontario.									
1	Lincoln County	2	32	8,000	6	27	4,691	43	98,725	5,033
2	Wentworth County					19	3,150	25	42,200	2,110
3	Halton County					16	4,700	36	93,000	4,215
4	Peel County					3	1,100	4	12,000	1,100
5	York County					9	1,900	18	53,800	2,750
6	Ontario County					6	530	12	10,050	605
7	Durham County					1	250	2	5,000	250
8	Northumberland County					40	2,500	49	88,640	2,142
9	Prince Edward County					109	4,210	178	201,290	3,081
10	Bay of Quinte (proper)					177	8,014	276	96,800	4,930
11	Bay of Quinte (North Channel)					19	1,965	29	73,800	3,115
12	Wolfe Island and vicinity...					28	1,537	42	26,500	630
	Totals	2	32	8,000	6	455	34,547	714	728,305	31,182

Return of the kinds, quantities and values

Number.	District.	Herring, salted.	Herring, fresh.	Whitefish, salted.	Whitefish, fresh.	Trout, salted.	Trout, fresh.	Pike.	Pickerel or Dore.
	Lake Ontario.	brls.	lbs.	brls.	lbs.	brls.	lbs.	lbs.	lbs.
1	Lincoln County	....	285,400	25	42,686	....	11,504	1,222	46,016
2	Wentworth County	....	97,788	....	17,650	....	6,900	23,530	475
3	Halton County	....	70,900	....	12,100	....	21,500	500	....
4	Peel County	....	15,000	520	....	....	175,000	....	....
5	York County	....	16,800	....	21,800	....	10,865	....	....
6	Ontario County	....	4,157	....	10,304	....	1,369	632	9
7	Durham County	....	6,000	....	1,000	....	500	....	....
8	Northumberland County	26	21,013	....	12,685	....	30,500	55,265	35
9	Prince Edward County	....	....	....	140,898	....	232,149	53,537	300
10	Bay of Quinte (proper)	25	54,602	9	182,484	....	250	100,481	25,315
11	Bay of Quinte (North Channel)	....	....	....	59,966	....	77,536	1,300	2,176
12	Wolfe Island and vicinity...	....	....	1	12,400	160	27,501	23,650	900
	Totals	51	539,760	555	514,923	180	596,162	236,017	75,128
		$ c.	$ c.	$ c.	$ c.	$ c.	$ c.	$ c.	$ c.
	Values	510 00	26,988 00	2,550 00	51,492 30	1,800 00	59,516 20	18,881 36	7,512 60

FISHERIES.

quantity and value of all fishing materials and other fixtures employed in the fishing
the year 1912.

	Fishing material.														Other fixtures used in fishing.			
	Seines.			Pound nets.		Hoop nets.		Dip nets.		Night Lines.		Spears.		Freezers and Ice Houses.		Piers and Wharves.	
No.	Yards.	Value.	No.	Value.	No.	Value.	No.	Value.	No. Hooks.	Value.	No.	Value.	No.	Value.	No.	Value.	No.	Value.
		$		$		$		$		$		$		$		$		$
4	460	220					42	66					166	250	*189	900 2,560		
							4	5	200		4				16	1,400		
									100		5				2	400		
1	40	25													1	200		
															2	122	2	142
					54	1,550											1	100
					52	676			5,405	22					2	40		
2	13	8			344	5,765			5,500	158					1	400		
3	80	41			48	773			200 500	13					1 6	300 500	5	226
10	843	294			498	8,561	46	71	12,905	202	166	250			205	6,822	8	448

*166 of these are spearing houses valued at $1,660.

of fish caught during the year 1912.

Sturgeon.	Eels.	Perch.	Tullibee.	Catfish.	Mixed and coarse fish.	Caviare.	Sturgeon Bladders.	Carp.	Smoked Herring.	Value.
lbs.	lbs.	lbs.	lbs.	lbs.	lbs.	lbs.	No.	lbs.	lbs.	$ c.
	50	20,615		886	7,601			36,070		26,123 04
		2,400			550					9,643 20
	875								123,900	19,282 50
	300	1,100		500	4,000			100		21,805 00
		20		40	4,615					4,331 25
		37			3,027					1,579 81
					1,000					450 00
58	5,946	5,900	9,719	53,414	76,534					19,213 87
8,532	151,068	4,100		28,672	46,530					53,827 30
	49,333	73,078		266,783	165,888					68,415 06
	5,500	1,900		400	22,100					15,604 80
	12,900	13,835		88,210	42,155					14,332 55
8,590	225,497	122,985	9,719	887,855	373,300			36,170	123,900	$254,607 97
$ c. 1,288 50	$ c. 13,529 83	$ c. 6,149 25	$ c. 583 14	$ c. 81,028 40	$ c. 18,665 00			$ c. 723 40	$ c. 12,390 00	$ c. 254,607 97

ONTARIO

Return of the number of Fishermen, tonnage and value of tugs, vessels and boats,
fishing industry

Number.	District.	Fishing Material.								
		Tugs or vessels.				Boats.			Gill-Nets.	
		No.	Ton-nage.	Value.	Men.	No.	Value.	Men.	Yards.	Value.
	Inland Waters.			$			$			$
1	Frontenac County	......	......	....	......	58	793	85	2,170	243
2	Leeds, Lanark, Lennox and Addington	......	......	....	......	122	1,526	267	3,586	607
3	Russell, Prescott, Carleton, Renfrew and Grenville	2	......	800	12	49	574	44	1,665	78
4	Lake Simcoe	4	10	4,800	62	19	1,120	84	....	......
5	Welland County	......	......	....	......	......	....	......	....	......
	Totals	6	10	5,600	74	248	4,013	480	7,430	928

Return of the kinds, quantities and values

Number.	District.	Herring, salted.	Herring, fresh.	Whitefish, salted.	Whitefish, fresh.	Trout, salted.	Trout, fresh.	Pike.	Pickerel, or Dore.
	Inland Waters.	bris.	lbs..	bris.	lbs.	bris.	lbs.	lbs.	lbs.
1	Frontenac County	....	4,215	....	....	....	....	16,900	5
2	Leeds, Lanark, Lennox and Addington	39	6,542	....	179	....	....	13,650	100
3	Russell, Prescott, Carleton, Renfrew and Grenville	....	......	....	100	....	....	563	50
4	Lake Simcoe	....	1,448	....	2,109	7	6,361	....	......
5	Welland County	....	......	....	......	......	....	286	332
	Totals	39	12,205	....	2,388	7	6,361	31,459	487
	Values	$ c. 890 00	$ c. 610 25	....	$ c. 288 80	$ c. 70 00	$ c. 636 10	$ c. 2,516 72	$ c. 48 70

FISHERIES,

the quantity and value of all fishing materials and other fixtures employed in the
during the year 1912.

	Fishing material.														Other fixtures used in fishing.			
Seines.			Pound nets.		Hoop nets.		Dip Nets.		Night Lines.		Spears.			Freezers and Ice Houses.		Piers and Wharves.			
No.	Yards.	Value.	No.	Value.	No.	Value.	No.	Value.	No. Hooks.	Value.	No.	Value.		No.	Value.	No.	Value.		
		$		$		$		$		$		$			$		$		
....	....	....	....	....	41	960	....	....	1,900	....	....	....			....	....	....		
....	....	....	....	....	65	1,195	....	....	....	....	....	....		4	....	....	....		
7	1,200	1,050	....	....	5	100	38	38	4,000	65	....	....	60	2	50	....	....		
....	....	....	....	....	....	....	33	51	1,000	15	60	173		2	1,100	3	150		
7	1,200	1,050	....	....	111	2,245	71	89	5,900	80	60	173		5	1,150	3	150		

of fish caught during the year 1912.

Sturgeon.	Eels.	Perch.	Tullibee.	Catfish.	Mixed and coarse fish.	Caviare.	Sturgeon Bladders.	Carp.	Dog fish.	Value.
lbs.	lbs.	lbs.	lbs.	lbs.	lbs.	lbs.	No.	lbs.		$ c.
....	24,630	3,330	....	64,001	61,165	....	....	....	4,200	11,374 68
....	1,950	51	....	28,622	28,385	....	....	....	....	5,663 06
6,400	100	1,700	....	14,648	20,668	....	....	123,871	....	3,315 38
....	....	122	....	....	32,992	....	....	....	....	5,122 52
....	....	188	....	462	1,995	....	....	....	....	202 19
6,400	26,680	5,391	....	1,077 28	145,155	....	....	123,871	4,200	25,678 83
$ c. 960 00	$ c. 1,600 80	$ c. 169 55	....	$ c. 8,618 34	$ c. 7,257 75	....	....	$ c. 2,477 42	$ c. 84 00	$ c. 25,678 83

ONTARIO

Recapitulation of the number of fishermen, tonnage and value of tugs, vessels and boats, industry during

Number	District.	Fishing material.								
		Tugs or vessels.				Boats.			Gill-Nets.	
		No.	Tonnage.	Value.	Men.	No.	Value.	Men.	Yards.	Value.
				$			$			$
1	Kenora and Rainy River	3	61	2,220	8	52	12,560	112	78,750	19,615
2	Lake Superior	23	541	55,575	124	53	6,055	124	652,200	19,618
3	Lake Huron (North Channel)	60	745	90,875	193	69	6,725	83	1,150,550	449,145
4	Georgian Bay	18	248	43,300	80	124	19,085	215	1,261,950	43,195
5	Lake Huron (proper)	10	335	15,700	49	112	16,222	203	547,205	23,164
6	Lake St. Clair, etc.	12	......	2,325	15	161	14,826	205	....	....
7	Lake Erie	55	1,566	223,500	243	547	63,85	628	569,753	100,943
8	Lake Ontario	9	32	8,000	6	485	34.6 7	714	728,305	31,192
9	Inland waters	6	10	5,600	74	248	4,843	430	7,430	925
	Totals	197	3,388	449,695	792	1,651	183,080	2,812	4,996,143	675,779

Recapitulation of the kinds, quantities and values of

Number	District.	Herring, salted.	Herring, fresh.	Whitefish, salted.	Whitefish, fresh.	Trout, salted.	Trout, fresh.	Pike.	Pickerel or Dore.	Sturgeon.
		brls.	lbs.	brls.	lbs.	brls.	lbs.	lbs.	lbs.	lbs.
1	Kenora and Rainy River	....	....	....	994,428	1,000	55,643	456,994	669,311	117,925
2	Lake Superior	....	1,763,315	....	573,674	690	1,475,924	122,631	217,847	3,547
3	Lake Huron (North Channel)	276	400	2½	660,160	1,002½	1,690,708	68,516	424,556	22,915
4	Georgian Bay	1,123½	67,350	40	287,161	913½	1,027,027	34,826	58,012	978
5	Lake Huron (proper)	117	150,524	....	38,733	638½	631,235	752	187,177	48,063
6	Lake St. Clair, etc. .	....	....	....	158,443	....	....	37,539	57,917	48,513
7	Lake Erie	4,619	13,041,418	1,720	2,236,428	....	3,489	1,485,166	975,130	83,367
8	Lake Ontario	51	539,760	355	514,923	180	595,162	236,017	75,123	3,551
9	Inland waters	39	12,205	....	2,888	7	6,361	31,459	687	6,600
	Totals	6,225½	15,574,972	2,117½	5,466,842	4,431½	5,484,539	2,473,200	2,665,613	369,12
	Values	$ c. 62,255 00	$ c. 778,748 60	$ c. 21,175 00	$ c. 546,684 20	$ c. 44,315 00	$ c. 548,453 90	$ c. 197,856 00	$ c. 266,561 30	$ c. 46,384 20

FISHERIES.

the quantity and value of all fishing material and other fixtures employed in the fishing the year 1912.

												Fishing material.—*Continued.*						Other fixtures used in fishing.			
Seines.			Pound nets.		Hoop nets.		Dip nets.		Night Lines.		Spears.		Freezers and Ice Houses.		Piers and Wharves.	
No.	Yards.	Value.	No.	Value.	No.	Value.	No.	Value.	No. Hooks.	Value.	No.	Value.	No	Value.	No.	Value.
		$		$		$		$		$		$		$		$
....	....	....	28	9,000	6	1,025	....	....	....	....	....	....	15	9,250	11	2,450
....	....	....	46	9,900	....	....	....	....	....	....	....	....	20	16,700	12	12,600
....	....	....	106	35,950	....	....	....	....	....	....	....	....	9	2,900	4	1,500
....	....	....	9	3,500	12	605	....	....	....	....	....	....	19	7,500	9	3,535
5	374	315	78	19,600	1	20	8	12	....	....	....	....	24	7,665	....	....
49	5,338	2,800	12	3,580	155	7,390	86	463	6,900	1,565	....	....	9	3,550	16	2,550
62	26,850	11,630	297	150,080	....	....	65	286	13,475	115	....	....	19	113,430	38	53,300
10	543	294	....	....	493	8,564	46	71	13,905	202	166	250	205*	6,822	8	448
7	1,200	1,050	....	....	111	2,245	71	89	6,900	80	60	173	8	1,150	3	150
133	35,804	15,989	576	231,580	783	19,849	274	921	40,180	1,962	226	423	458	167,967	101	56,783

*166 of these are spearing houses valued at $1,660.

fish caught during the year 1912.

Eels	Perch.	Tullibee.	Catfish.	Mixed and coarse fish.	Caviare.	Sturgeon Bladders.	Carp.	Buffalo Fish.	Smoked Herring.	Dog Fish.	Value.
lbs.	lbs.	lbs.	lbs.	lbs.	lbs.	No.	lbs.	lbs.	lbs.	lbs.	$ c.
....	....	105,579	28,450	33,898	2,796	213	....	91,076	....	....	256,702 94
....	....	550	....	....	....	....	....	....	....	....	332,188 78
....	11,454	3,260	2,486	302,491	405	....	....	....	....	....	315,653 11
....	3,000	35,414	1,067	42,363	100	....	8,100	....	....	....	168,990 53
405	61,499	277,200	148	90,873	1,777	11	100	....	....	....	134,701 99
....	30,649	....	75	462,896	1,035	....	73,060	....	....	....	C5,731 95
225,497	1,110,201	150	52,967	380,593	3,430	652	899,525	....	....	....	1,289,121 69
26,680	122,985	9,719	387,855	373,300	....	....	36,170	....	123,900	....	254,607 97
....	3,391	....	107,723	145,155	....	....	123,871	....	....	4,200	25,678 83
252,582	1,398,179	431,947	632,095	2,330,996	9,543	876	1,140,826	91,076	123,900	4,200	2,842,877 09
$ c. 15,154 92	$ c. 69,658 95	$ c. 25,916 82	$ c. 50,567 60	$ c. 116,549 80	$ c. 9,543 00	$ c. 525 60	$ c. 22,816 52	$ c. 7,286 08	$ c. 12,390 00	$ c. 84 00	$ c. 2,842,877 09

Comparative Statement of yield for 1911-12, according to Districts.

	1911.	1912.	Increase.	Decrease.
Kenora and Rainy River District:				
Herring....................bbls....	....	....	....	....
Herring.....................lbs....	....	....	....	....
Whitefish ....bbls....	....	....	....	....
Whitefish ....lbs....	761,487	994,428	232,951	....
Trout.....................bbls....	....	1,000	1,000	....
Trout......................lbs....	92,385	55,643	....	36,742
Pike .... ''	346,275	456,994	110,719	....
Pickerel (Dore) .... ''	402,701	669,311	266,610	....
Sturgeon................. ''	73,290	117,933	44,643	....
Eels	....	....	....	....
Perch	....	....	....	....
Tullibee .... ''	128,689	105,579	....	23,110
Catfish .... ''	6,000	28,450	22,450	....
Mixed and Coarse fish .... ''	34,770	33,893	....	877
Caviare .... ''	1,792	2,796	1,004	....
Sturgeon Bladders...........No.	186	213	27	....
Buffalo Fish ....lbs.	....	91,076	91,076	....
Lake Superior:				
Herring ....bbls.	....	....	....	....
Herring....................lbs....	784,280	1,763,315	979,035	....
Whitefish ....bbls....	1,005	....	....	1,005
Whitefish ....lbs....	502,653	573,674	71,021	....
Trout ....bbls....	1,441	690	....	851
Trout......................lbs....	1,441,137	1,475,924	34,787	....
Pike .... ''	62,773	122,631	59,858	....
Pickerel (Dore) .... ''	81,569	217,847	136,278	....
Sturgeon................. ''	7,267	3,567	....	3,700
Eels	....	....	....	....
Perch	....	....	....	....
Tullibee .... ''	2,235	550	....	1,685
Catfish	....	....	....	....
Mixed and Coarse fish ''	920	....	....	920
Caviare .... ''	40	....	....	40
Sturgeon Bladders ....No.	....	....	....	....
Carp...................... lbs.	....	....	....	....
Lake Huron, North Channel:				
Herring..................bbls....	3,809	276	....	3,533
Herring ....lbs....	4,600	400	....	4,200
Whitefish ....bbls....	422	2½	....	419½
Whitefish ....lbs....	665,481	660,160	....	5,321
Trout.....................bbls....	1,270	1,002½	....	267½
Trout......................lbs....	1,618,134	1,690,708	72,574	....
Pike .... ''	67,954	68,516	562	....
Pickerel (Dore) .... ''	287,543	424,556	137,013	....
Sturgeon................. ''	18,816	22,018	3,202	....
Eels .... ''	....	....	....	....
Perch.................... ''	11,282	11,454	172	....
Tullibee.................	....	3,260	3,260	....
Catfish .... ''	13,799	2,486	....	11,313
Mixed and Coarse fish .... ''	201,886	302,491	100,605	....
Caviare .... ''	200	405	205	....
Sturgeon Bladders ....No.	....	....	....	....
Carp .... lbs.	....	....	....	....
Georgian Bay:				
Herring..................bbls....	1,828	1,123½	....	705½
Herring ....lbs....	101,148	67,350	....	33,798
Whitefish. ....bbls....	33	40	7	....
Whitefish..................lbs....	347,855	287,161	....	60,694
Trout ....bbls....	559	913½	354½	....
Trout ....lbs....	1,273,948	1,027,027	....	246,921

Comparative Statement of yield for 1911-12, according to Districts—Continued.

. —	1911.	1912.	Increase.	Decrease.
Georgian Bay—Continued :				
Pike.................................lbs....	73,356	34,326	....	39,030
Pickerel (Dore)............... "	86,528	58,012	....	28,516
Sturgeon........................ "	291	976	685	....
Eels	....	....	....	....
Perch............................ "	6,675	3,000	....	3,675
Tullibee........................	....	35,414	35,414	....
Catfish......................... "	285	1,067	782	....
Mixed.and Coarse Fish'.................	35,081	42,363	7,282	....
Caviare .... "	....	100	100	....
Sturgeon Bladders............. "	....	....	....	....
Carp.........................No....	1,000	8,100	7,100	....
Lake Huron (proper) :				
Herring....................... bbls....	226	117	....	109
Herring ....lbs....	175,810	150,524	....	25,286
Whitefish ....bbls....	1	....	....	1
Whitefish.................. ...lbs....	70,152	38,738	....	31,414
Trout`......................bbls....	743	638½	....	104½
Trout ....lbs....	767,433	631,225	....	136,208
Pike............................ "	2,027	752	....	1,275
Pickerel (Dore)................ "	175,588	187,177	11,589	....
Sturgeon....................... "	8,744	48,663	39,919	....
Eels...........................	....	405	405	....
Perch .... "	104,780	61,499	....	43,281
Tullibee....................... "	212,000	277,200	65,200	....
Catfish .... "	406	146	....	260
Mixed and coarse fish.......... "	80,256	90,373	10,117	....
Caviare........................ "	736	1,777	1,041	....
Sturgeon Bladders ....No....	54	11	....	43
Carp ....lbs....	....	100	100	....
Lake St. Clair and Detroit River :				
Herring ....bbls....	....	....	....	....
Herring ....lbs....	100	....	....	100
Whitefish ....bbls....	....	....	....	....
Whitefish ....lbs....	63,983	158,442	94,459	....
Trout ....bbls....	....	....	....	....
Trout ....lbs....	....	....	....	....
Pike........................... "	38,745	37,339	....	1,406
Pickerel (Dore)................ "	68,084	57,917	....	11,117
Sturgeon....................... "	46,985	48,818	1,833	....
Eels........................... "	....	....	....	....
Perch .... "	66,796	80,649	13,853	....
Tullibee....................... "	....	75	75	....
Catfish........................ "	39,416	51,396	11,980	....
Mixed and coarse fish.......... "	515,893	462,828	....	53,065
Caviare .... :................. "	600	1,035	435	....
Sturgeon Bladders.............No....	....	....	....	....
Carp ..... :................... lbs....	224,990	73,060	....	151,930
Lake Erie :				
Herring......................bbls....	73	4,619	4,546	....
Herring.......................lbs....	9,924,292	13,041,418	3,117,126	....
Whitefish.....................bbls....	....	1,720	1,720	....
Whitefish ....lbs....	1,139,845	2,236,428	1,097,083	....
Trout ....bbls....	....	....	....	....
Trout ....lbs....	2,799	2,489	....	310
Pike........................... "	1,099,214	1,485,166	385,952	....
Pickerel (Dore)............... "	802,067	975,180	173,113	....
Sturgeon....................... "	67,685	52,267	....	15,418
Eels........................... "	....	....	....	....

Comparative Statement of yield 1911-12, according to Districts.

	1911.	1912.	Increase.	Decrease.
Lake Erie.—Continued:				
Perch................lbs....	874,304	1,110,201	235,997	....
Tullibee.................. "	15,834	150	....	15,684
Catfish.................. "	49,540	52,267	2,817	....
Mixed and coarse fish.......... "	1,327,645	880,593	....	447,052
Caviare.................. "	3,684	3,430	....	254
Sturgeon Bladders ....No....	149	652	503	....
Carp ....lbs....	644,621	899,525	254,904	....
Lake Ontario:				
Herring....................bbls....	30	51	21	....
Herring.....................lbs....	944,694	539,760	....	404,934
Whitefish ....bbls....	16	355	339	....
Whitefish ....lbs....	582,528	514,923	....	67,605
Trout ....bbls....	....	180	180	....
Trout ....lbs....	384,567	595,162	210,595	....
Pike..................... "	347,334	236,017	....	111,317
Pickerel (Dore)............. "	98,019	75,126	....	22,893
Sturgeon.................. "	138	8,590	8,452	....
Eels..................... "	138,710	225,497	86,787	....
Perch.................... "	214,441	122,985	....	91,456
Tullibee .... "	6,100	9,719	3,619	....
Catfish .... "	411,738	387,855	....	23,883
Mixed and Coarse fish.......... "	474,177	373,300	....	100,877
Caviare .... "	10	....	....	10
Sturgeon and Bladders..........No....	....	....	....	....
Carp ....lbs....	85,500	36,170	....	49,330
Herring, Smoked .... "	....	123,900	123,900	....
Inland Waters:				
Herring...................bbls....	69	39	....	30
Herring ..../lbs....	20,104	12,205	....	7,899
Whitefish ....bbls....	....	....	....	....
Whitefish ....lbs....	25,285	2,388	....	22,897
Trout......................bbls....	....	7	7	....
Trout ....lbs....	980	6,361	5,381	....
Pike .... "	60,839	31,459	....	29,380
Pickerel (Dore) .... "	20,446	487	....	19,959
Sturgeon .... "	2,100	6,400	4,300	....
Eels...................... "	6,388	26,680	20,292	....
Perch .... "	22,801	3,391	....	19,410
Tullibee................... "	50	....	....	50
Catfish .... "	130,770	107,728	....	23,042
Mixed and Coarse fish......... "	136,294	145,155	8,861	....
Caviare .... "	....	....	....	....
Sturgeon Bladders.............No....	200	....	....	200
Carp ....lbs....	462,406	123,871	....	338,535
Dog fish .... "	....	4,200	4,200	....

Comparative Statement of the yield of the Fisheries of the Province.

	1911	1912	Increase.	Decrease.
Herring.....................bbls....	6,044	6,225½	181½	....
Herring ....lbs....	11,953,228	15,574,972	3,621,744	....
Whitefish ....bbls....	1,556	2,117½	561½	....
Whitefish ....lbs....	4,142,769	5,466,342	1,323,573	281½
Trout ....bbls....	4,713	4,481½	....	281½
Trout ....lbs....	5,569,383	5,484,539	....	84,844
Pike...................... "	2,098,517	2,473,200	374,683	....
Pickerel (Dore)............... "	2,022,495	2,665,613	643,118	....
Sturgeon..................... "	225,316	309,232	83,916	....
Eels .... "	145,196	252,582	107,386	....
Perch....................... "	1,274,079	1,393,179	119,100	....
Tullibee .... "	375,658	431,947	56,289	....
Catfish .... "	651,954	632,095	....	19,859
Mixed and Coarse fish........... "	2,806,922	2,330,996	....	475,926
Caviare..................... "	7,062	9,543	1,481	....
Sturgeon Bladders..............No.	589	876	287	....
Carp........................lbs	1,418,517	1,140,826	....	277,691
Herring, smoked............... "	....	123,900	123,900	....
Buffalo Fish.................. "	....	91,076	91,076	....
Dog Fish...................	....	4,200	4,200	....
Total Barrels	12,313	12,774½	....	....
Total Pounds	32,691,685	38,385,118	....	....
Total Increase of Barrels, 1912.......	....	....	461½	....
Total Increase of Pounds. 1912.......	....	....	5,693,433	....

Statement of the yield and value of the Fisheries of the Province for the year 1912.

Kinds of Fish.	Quantity.	Price.	Value.
		$ c.	$
Herring ....bbls....	6,225½	10 00	62,255 00
Herring ....lbs....	15,574,972	05	778,748 60
Whitefish ....bbls....	2,117½	10 00	21,175 00
Whitefish ....lbs....	5,466,342	10	546,634 20
Trout ....bbls....	4,481½	10 00	44,815 00
Trout ....lbs....	5,484,539	10	548,453 90
Pike .... "	2,473,200	08	197,856 00
Pickerel (Dore) .... "	2,665,613	10	266,561 30
Sturgeon .... "	309,232	15	46,384 80
Eels ....lbs....	252,582	06	15,154 92
Perch .... "	1,393,179	05	69,658 95
Tullibee .... "	431,947	06	25,916 82
Catfish .... "	632,095	08	50,567 60
Mixed and Coarse Fish .... "	2,330,996	05	116,549 80
Caviare .... "	9,543	1 00	9,543 00
Sturgeon Bladders ....No.	876	60	525 60
Carp ....lbs	1,140,826	02	22,816 52
Herring, smoked.................... "	123,900	10	12,390 00
Buffalo Fish...................... "	91,076	08	7,286 08
Dog Fish...........................	4,200	02	84 00
Total..			2,842,877 09

RECAPITULATION

Of the Fishing Tugs, Nets, Boats, etc., employed in the Province in the Fishing Industry.

Articles.	Value.
197 Tugs (8,888 Tons) (792 men)...	$449,695 00
1,651 boats (2,812 men)	183,080 00
4,996,143 yards Gill-net..	678,790 00
183 Seines (35,804 yds.)	15,989 00
576 Pound nets	231,580 00
783 Hoop nets...	19,849 00
274 Dip nets..	921 00
40,180 Hooks on Set Lines	1,962 00
226 Spears	423 00
458 Freezers and Ice Houses	167,967 00
101 Piers and Wharves	56,733 00
Total value of Fishing Apparatus...................................	$1,806,939 00

Value of Ontario Fisheries from 1870 to 1912, inclusive.

Years.	Value.	Years.	Value.
	$	Brought forward........	$ c. 19,397,564 00
1870.......................	264,982	1892.......................	2,042,198 00
1871.......................	193,524	1893.......................	1,694,980 00
1872.......................	267,633	1894.......................	1,659,968 00
1873.......................	293,091	1895.......................	1,584,478 00
1874.......................	446,267	1896.......................	1,605,674 00
1875.......................	458,194	1897.......................	1,289,822 00
1876.......................	437,229	1898.......................	1,433,631 00
1877.......................	438,223	1899.......................	1,477,815 00
1878.......................	348,122	1900.......................	1,333,293 00
1879...,...................	367,133	1901.......................	1,428,078 00
1880.......................	444,491	1902.......................	1,265,705 00
1881.......................	509,903	1903.......................	1,535,144 00
1882.......................	825,457	1904.......................	1,793,524 09
1883.......................	1,027,033	1905.......................	1,708,963 00
1884.......................	1,133,724	1906.......................	1,734,865 00
1885.......................	1,342,692	1907.......................	1,935,024 90
1886.......................	1,435,998	1908.......................	2,100,078 63
1887.......................	1,531,850	1909.......................	2,237,544 41
1888.......................	1,839,869	1910.......................	2,348,269 57
1889.......,..............	1,963,123	1911.......	2,419,178 21
1890.......................	2,009,637	1912.......................	2,842,877 09
1891.......:...........	1,806,389	Total	$56,850,324 81
Carried forward	$19,379,564